P9-DVU-936

DATE DUE

DE 1997			

DEMCO 38-296

Inarticulate

Longings

Inarticulate

Longings

The Ladies' Home Journal,

Gender,

and the

Promises

of Consumer Culture

by Jennifer Scanlon

ROUTLEDGE: New York and London

Riverside Community College
Library
4800 Magnolia Avenue
Riverside, California 92506
APR '97

HC 110 .C6 S27 1995

Scanlon, Jennifer, 1958-

Inarticulate longings

Published in 1995 by

Routledge
29 West 35 Street
New York, NY 10001

Published in Great Britain in 1995 by

Routledge
11 New Fetter Lane
London EC4P 4EE

Copyright © 1995 by Routledge

Printed in the United States of America

All rights reserved. No part of this book may be reprinted or reproduced or utilized in any form or by any electronic, mechanical, or other means, now known or hereafter invented, including photo-copying and recording, or in any information storage or retrieval system without permission in writing from the publishers.

Library of Congress Cataloging-in-Publication Data

Scanlon, Jennifer, 1958–
Inarticulate longings : the ladies' home journal, gender, and the promises of consumer culture/Jennifer Scanlon
p.   cm.
Includes bibliographical references
ISBN 0-415-91156-7 (hb) – ISBN 0-415-91157-5 (pb)
1. Women consumers–United States–History 2. Advertising. Magazine–United States–History.
3. Popular literature–United States–History and criticism. 4. Ladies' home journal.
I. Title.
HC110.C6S27   1995
659.13'2–dc20

*For my Mother and
Father with Love*

Contents

	Acknowledgments	ix
	Introduction	1
one	*A Profile of the* Ladies' Home Journal	11
two	*Housekeeping* The Greatest Business in the World	49
three	*Women's Paid Work* Setting and Stretching the Boundaries	79
four	*Stoves for Women, Votes for Men* The *Journal* and Women's Political Involvement	109
five	*The Amateur Rebel* Female Protagonists in *Ladies' Home Journal* Fiction	137
six	*Advertising Women* The J. Walter Thompson Company Women's Editorial Department	169
seven	*"Every Woman Is Interested in This"* Advertising in the *Ladies' Home Journal*	197
	Conclusion	229
	Notes	235
	Index	273

Acknowledgments

t is a pleasure to have the opportunity to thank the many people who helped me intellectually, professionally, and personally as I worked my way through this project. My first debt is to Sarah Elbert, my dissertation director, whose intellectual excitement for U.S. cultural history encouraged me to follow my dream and look seriously at women's popular culture. Her mark is on my work, and her friendship continues to sustain me. Alice Kessler-Harris also provided me with invaluable patterns of learning and questioning when I was a student, and she continues to offer reassurance, through her work and example, that history matters.

I am grateful, too, for the generous financial assistance I received from several sources. A Woodrow Wilson Women's Studies Research Grant and two dissertation year fellowships from Binghamton University helped me complete my dissertation, from which this book originates. SUNY Plattsburgh provided me with a Mini Grant and, in conjunction with my union, United University Professions, a travel grant and then a Dr. Nuala Drescher McGann Affirmative Action Leave. The leave provided me with funding for travel and, most importantly, time free from teaching to think, read, and write.

The staffs of the Boston Public Library, the New York Public Library, the Schlesinger Library at Radcliffe College, the University of Pennsylvania Library, and the J. Walter Thompson Company Archives at Duke University Library provided me with a great deal of assistance, searching for dusty copies of documents or checking and rechecking obscure details that didn't seem to match up. I'm especially grateful to Ellen Gartrell and Marion Hirsch at the J. Walter Thompson Archives; their enthusiasm for the materials matched my own, and that is a rare treat. Carol Hunter and Mark Hirsch provided valuable comments on parts of the manuscript, and I owe a special debt to my editor at Routledge, Cecelia Cancellaro, for her interest in the project and care with the text. For preparation of this manuscript, I am also grateful to Claudia Gorelick, Terence Dougherty, and Matthew DeBord of Routledge and Jill Benz of the *Ladies' Home Journal.*

I want to thank a few others for their support as well: Robin Prenoveau, whose attention to detail and determination to send out a clean copy of this text surpassed even my own; Rose Nadeau, for searching out copyright information and histories of companies long since out of business; and my colleagues in women's studies, who have remained enormously supportive of my work. The mark of my students is also on this book; they keep me inspired, and I am grateful to share my ideas and my days with them.

My friends and family, especially those who have sustained me during the past couple of years, know they have my enduring thanks and love. I offer special thanks to Julie Boss for her continued interest in and enthusiasm for my work, and to my nieces, Alison, Lindsay, Maura, and Kaitlin, for helping me connect women's past with our future. I'm most grateful to Michael Arthur, whose life provides me with many lessons and whose calypsos keep me smiling.

Finally, this book is dedicated to my parents, Mary Barry Scanlon and William Scanlon, with love and gratitude for the many gifts they have given me.

Introduction

To the uninitiated, a woman's magazine may seem
merely a powdery bit of fluff. No notion could
be more unreal or deceptive. That is just the
style in which the magazines express themselves,
for if the top layer seems fluffy, the base is
solid and powerful.
—Helen Woodward, *The Lady Persuaders*

This study examines women's experiences with the developing consumer culture of the early twentieth century as reflected in the most popular women's magazine of the day, the *Ladies' Home Journal*. This magazine, the first to reach a circulation of one million, transformed the whole magazine industry by creatively addressing women's household roles and opportunities outside of the home, their dependence on men, their interdependence among themselves, and their chances for independence. Its success also provided many women with job opportunities in the magazine and advertising industries, thus facilitating the entrance of middle-class women into the workplace. The target audience for the *Journal* was white, native-born, middle-class women, who lived with the uncertain legacies of the nineteenth-century women's rights movement and who tried to find a comfortable role in the rapidly changing world of the expanding middle class. The *Ladies' Home Journal* both modeled and adapted to the expectations of its readers. The manner in which it alternately and at times even simultaneously acknowledged and neglected, celebrated and decried, promoted and impeded social changes and their accompanying conflicts is fascinating to examine. The magazine offered clear and limited cultural definitions of womanhood, but it also recognized and gave voice to women's own concerns—and in doing so the *Journal* helped sow the seeds for women's later demands for autonomy and self-definition. As an element of mass or popular culture, the magazine promoted the middle-class mainstream at the same time that it exposed its many shortcomings. In this work, the *Ladies' Home Journal* is the terrain upon which to study the lives of several groups of women as they reluctantly and/or eagerly participated in the development of what has become a particularly female twentieth-century consumer culture.[1]

The *Ladies' Home Journal* was not the first popular magazine for women, and its editors and owner took some of the cues for success from the *Journal's* early nineteenth-century predecessors. Sarah Josepha Hale, editor first of the *Ladies Magazine* and then of *Godey's Lady's Book*, forms a pivotal character in the history of women's magazines. Although there were other women's magazines before hers, they had all been controlled by men; Hale brought a woman's voice to the industry. Sarah Josepha Hale was hired in 1928 to edit the *Ladies Magazine*. Her purpose, as she put it, was to "make ladies better acquainted with their duties and privileges." Hale wrote a great deal of the material herself, often instructing women about their proper spheres of activity. Her vision of womanhood was clear: women were moral beings who could influence the men around them to improve society. Woman's sphere was influence, not power. Although historians have largely moved beyond a strict private/public, female/male dichotomy in looking at real women's lives during the nineteenth century, Hale and others actively maintained this perspective and encouraged women to live in a private sphere separate from men and centered in the household. Sarah Hale's ideals clearly fit prevailing notions about domesticity and true womanhood in nineteenth-century prescriptive literature if not in life.[2]

Although the *Ladies Magazine* was a popular periodical, it experienced financial losses in the 1830s. A depression in 1834 caused its initial decline, and by 1836 the magazine no longer seemed to have much of a future. In 1837, when Louis Godey, owner of a women's magazine in Philadelphia, offered to buy out the *Ladies Magazine* but keep Sarah Josepha Hale on as editor of the consolidated publication, Hale agreed. She continued to write tales of women's duties and obligations for *Godey's Lady's Book*, her new magazine, but the magazine itself began to develop a more modern style and promote a revised definition of womanhood. Emphasizing women's fashion and consumer possibilities rather than a vision of simplicity and lack of attachment to the material world, *Godey's Lady's Book* rapidly moved away from Hale's vision but remained, nevertheless, quite popular. When Sarah Hale died in 1879, *Godey's* declined in popularity, even though it had succeeded in tapping a national audience. Only a few years later, in 1883, the *Ladies' Home Journal* would tap the same "woman's" market and then expand that market to a degree unprecedented in the history of magazines.[3] The *Journal* would accomplish this by further developing and promoting a domestic ideology that defined editors as experts, advertisers as prophets, and, most importantly, women as consumers.[4]

"If Sarah Josepha Hale was the mother of American women's magazines, then Edward Bok was their father," wrote Helen Woodward in 1926.[5] Edward Bok is the name most commonly associated with the *Ladies' Home Journal*, but the magazine's story begins not with this famous editor but with the publisher, Cyrus Curtis, and his wife, Louisa Knapp Curtis. Cyrus Curtis entered a partnership on a four-page weekly magazine called *Tribune and Farmer* in 1879. He assembled clippings about women's concerns from other sources in a column entitled "Woman and the Home." One day his wife asked him who wrote that column, and when he told her that he did, she laughed. "I don't mean to make fun of you," she told him, "but if you really knew how this sounds to a woman, you would laugh, too."[6] Louisa Knapp Curtis then took over the women's column, and before long it became the most popular section of the *Tribune and Farmer*. In December of 1883, based on the tremendous success of "Woman and the Home," Curtis launched an entire magazine dedicated to women; thus the *Ladies' Home Journal* was born, with Louisa Knapp Curtis its first editor. Cyrus Curtis had great expectations for his new publication. "We propose to make it a household necessity—so good, so pure, so true, so brave, so full, so complete," he declared, "that a young couple will no more think of going to housekeeping without it than without a cookstove."[7]

In September of 1889, with the *Ladies' Home Journal* already the best-selling magazine in the nation, Louisa Knapp Curtis decided that she could no longer combine her household and family responsibilities and her career, so she resigned as editor of the *Journal.* Cyrus Curtis hired Edward Bok, then a twenty-five-year-old writer of a syndicated column, the "Bok Page," to take her place.[8] Bok, who later married the Curtis' daughter, Mary Louise, brought the magazine to new heights in circulation and changed the nature of the magazine business in the United States. In a sense, Bok combined the visions of the two magazines edited by Sarah Josepha Hale. He believed that women were essentially domestic creatures who could best serve the nation by influencing their husbands and sons. He believed as firmly, however, in the modern order and in women's expanding role as consumers. Bok viewed his magazine as an aide to help women brave this sometimes contradictory path. The *Journal* presented an odd mixture of morality and consumerism, but the recipe worked: the *Ladies' Home Journal* truly became a household word. Known as the "monthly Bible of the American home," the *Journal's* circulation reached one million by January of 1904.[9]

This book explores the relationship between popular culture and the culture of consumption between 1910–1930. The *Ladies' Home Journal,* both a medium of popular culture and a business enterprise, promoted for its women readers traditional "woman's values" and full participation in the consumer society. Contradictions naturally followed. It was not an easy task to promote a simple life for women, while at the same time promoting the primacy of consumer goods and material desires, nor was it easy to praise women's growing independence from onerous household tasks at the same time that one pleaded with women to limit the boundaries of that independence. Yet another contradiction, which readers themselves occasionally pointed out, was that much of the editorial and advertising content of the magazine was produced by women who led lives distinctly unlike those they counseled readers to live. Finally, the notion of choice, central to the magazine's message and to the ideology of the larger consumer culture, was often illusory, as the magazine promoted fairly limited roles for women and often ignored or dismissed many of the choices real women faced.

Central to this study is the development of mass or popular culture, which delivered through many vehicles notices of what it meant to be an American. Early analyses of mass culture were hopeful: media participation was deemed a sign of increased literacy and a certain impetus to individuals' greater participation in all elements of the social system. This has not, however, been the case. By its very nature, mass culture has often discouraged rather than encouraged democratic participation. In the case of mainstream magazines, for example, the need for continuity from issue to issue demands a formulaic view of the world. The backdrop for this formula, the ideology of dominant social groups, is a given and, hence, rarely questioned. In many forms of popular culture, the desire for a "mass" appeal negates much discussion of issues that fall outside of the mainstream. The mass appeal also leaves out significant numbers of people, since mass is often associated with race, the white race, and with class, the middle class. For example, literacy gains were enormous in the population at large at the turn of the century, but they were most significant in the black population, which went from an almost 80 percent illiteracy rate to an almost 80 percent literacy rate.[10] Nevertheless, African-Americans, regardless of their literacy or purchasing power, failed to be considered a target market by the consumer culture that produced the *Ladies' Home Journal* and other popular magazines. An enterprising young man took out a classified advertisement in *Printer's Ink*, the advertising journal, in 1917, in which he called the "ten million Negro-Americans" an "undeveloped volume" for advertising interests. Apparently no one took up his offer, since it was not until 1942 that the first popular periodical for blacks, *Negro Digest*, was founded, and it was not until 1970 that the first mass magazine for black women, *Essence*, reached the newsstands.[11]

In addition to carving out a limited definition of a mass audience, magazines also provide a fairly predictable emotional formula: a balance between the fostering of anxiety that draws readers to seek out advice and the offering of positive messages that encourage them to return the following month. The resulting formula, which worked so well for the *Ladies' Home Journal*, ultimately encouraged inaction rather than action, conformity rather than individual expression, guided rather than self-generated change.[12] In an era in which many different groups of women experimented with definitions of democracy that would include rather than exclude them, the *Journal* suggested that democracy for women meant little more than the choice between one brand of soap and another, one flavor of soup and another.

At the dawn of the twentieth century, women in the United States had no few lifestyles; their varied roles were determined in part by region, race, age, and ethnicity. But by 1930, women's magazines and the consumer culture they offered related the story of a common woman, the "average" woman, the "American" woman. That image obscured the many differences among women and offered instead a promise: if you did not know your neighbor, as people moved from towns to cities and as definitions of community changed, you could tell a lot about her by the brand names she chose.[13] And, in fact, as women's magazines bridged some of the gaps of region and age, if not race and ethnicity, and as the middle class grew, women's lives increasingly became defined by spending power and habits. The *Ladies' Home Journal* played a significant role in that cultural transformation. This work examines who such definitions of womanhood included, who they left out, and how women both embraced and struggled with the limited definitions of behavior and life the consumer culture offered.

The emergence, tremendous success, and lasting influence of magazines like the *Ladies' Home Journal* and the many magazines of this genre which followed reveals a great deal about the gender issues historians have identified as most significant during the early twentieth century. In a time of tremendous actual and potential societal changes, when middle-class white women faced new opportunities and new challenges in education, in the workforce, and, due to changing technology, in their households, this magazine specifically encouraged them to read rather than act, to conform to middle-class mores rather than seek out new and possibly more revolutionary alternatives. Ironically, the consumer definition of womanhood became dominant at the same time that other essentialist definitions met with conscious and resolute challenges. For example, throughout the nineteenth century, the largest groups of women's rights advocates spoke not of "women's" rights but of "woman's" rights. Secure in their own identity as white, native born, and middle-class, these women included in their definition of womanhood only those who looked and acted like them. But by the early twentieth century, several groups of feminists spoke of "women's" rights, recognizing not only the diversity of women but also that through their diversity women had some common goals. They made some political progress, operating from this standpoint, as diverse groups, initially organized on the basis of social class, race, or occupation, worked together to achieve women's expanded political participation in general and suffrage in particular.[14] Like the Progressive movement they were a part of, however, divisions of race, class, and ethnicity proved powerful, and few diverse organizations survived into the 1920s.[15]

Internal differences divided groups of women, as did the larger culture, of which women's magazines were just one part. Political in a largely nonpartisan sense, the *Ladies' Home Journal* and other magazines obscured fundamental differences among women in every issue, creating in the consuming woman an amalgam defined and limited by race, class, and ethnicity but promoted now as "average." This "average" woman had certain characteristics: she was, for the most part, married, living what might be called a "his" and "hers" marriage divided by strict gender definitions of work, nurturing, and communication. She was white and native born. A middle-class woman, she resigned her job or career at marriage and preferred spending money to producing goods. Truly modern, she purchased the latest appliances, served her family canned foods, participated in leisure activities. Finally, although she occasionally griped about her husband's lack of attention or her children's selfishness, the "average" woman felt enormous satisfaction with her life.

This *Ladies' Home Journal* prototype increasingly came to define womanhood for the early twentieth century and beyond and for the middle class and beyond. Her limitations would form the composite of women's possibilities, and her activities would shape the vocabulary of gender. Of course, the *Ladies' Home Journal* woman left out as many women as she included. She could not explain the very real gender/generational conflicts faced by older and younger women of the day. She could not explain the women who never married, those who spent their lives with other women, or the African-American, immigrant, or working-class white women whose lives were still defined by work rather than by spending. She did not include the women who found paid work rewarding or those who sought to broaden their political sphere by taking on local, state, or national governments. The composite woman failed all these women by leaving them out of the discussion. Interestingly enough, however, this "average" woman also failed the women who most closely resembled her, since, as this study reveals, even women who most closely fit the bill ultimately failed to have their needs met by the magazine or the consumer culture it promoted.

The *Ladies' Home Journal*'s domestic ideology essentially urged its readership to expand their role as consumers rather than producers, to accept the corporate capitalist model and their home-based role in it. It did this by presenting fragments of opinion—in this case fiction, advertisements, and editorial matter—and then organizing those fragments into a whole which could be called the "consensus" view. These stories, editorial pieces, and advertisements, although seemingly fragmentary and perhaps unrelated, actually worked together to provide this larger, dominant picture. And by offering several elements and distinct points of view, the magazine promoted the idea that there were many choices for women to make, but that the average woman—the middle-class woman with aspirations—was represented by the consensus view. In this way the magazine supported the notion that women benefitted by the nation's philosophy of bourgeois individualism; they too had free choice. In this sense, the *Journal* offered images of what readers could be if they wished to conform, what they would reject if they did not. In retrospect, however, the women readers' choices appear clearly delineated rather than open ended, as the *Journal* essentially encouraged women to internalize norms rather than explore alternatives while they made sense of their changing world.[16]

The format and form of the magazine play a role in this as well. It is in part because magazines are composed of many elements that they correspond so well to women's lives. The readers of the *Journal*, privileged though they were in considerable ways, were not for the most part wealthy women of leisure. Household and family responsibilities meant that they did not have long periods of time during which they could read. Magazines met the challenge of addressing these women's reality by offering them "a little of this and a little of that." They could read a short story while the floors dried, glance through the advertisements while supper was cooking, read a column of advice before bed.[17] And the very form of magazines follows a cardinal rule of the consumer culture: they are disposable, replaced each month by a fresh set of images. The form, format, and formula obviously worked well for the *Ladies' Home Journal*, which remained the top-selling women's magazine through the 1950s.[18]

This work examines the *Ladies' Home Journal* both as an artifact and as an industry. Then, focusing on the editorial advice, fiction, and advertising, it weaves together the seemingly disparate messages provided in different areas of the magazine. The chapters on advice address both the editorial matter and the editorial writers and explore the ways in which the advice, replete with contradictions, reflects the ambivalence of advice givers, readers, and the culture at large when faced with real changes in women's lives. The *Journal* offered women an encouraging if fairly limited model for change in the three areas under discussion here: housekeeping, paid work, and political participation. Ultimately, the magazine failed to acknowledge women's loss of economic power as their productive functions continued the already well-established trend of leaving the household, and as their personal needs subsequently changed. The tension between the editorial writers, their work, and their audience is especially telling in this regard. Advertising is covered in detail in two later chapters, but a brief discussion of advertising also accompanies each examination of editorial matter. Tensions between editorial matter and advertising, two mutually dependent but often conflicting elements of any magazine's message, play out clearly in the pages of the *Ladies' Home Journal*.

This study also examines several pieces of fiction in the *Journal*, reading them "against the grain" to examine the ways in which the fiction both supported and undermined traditional notions of womanhood, femininity, and domesticity.[19] An important and popular element of the magazine, the fiction presented stories of love and of conflict, of reaching for perfection and settling for mediocrity. While it often hearkens back to nineteenth-century roles for women, the fiction also points out the limits of such a retreat. It recognizes women's sexuality, providing readers the opportunity to daydream or fantasize about the possibilities for intimacy they might encounter in their lives. The discussion here focuses on the ways in which the fiction both mystifies and mourns some of the realities of married life: the subordination of women's interests and ideals to those of their families, inequitable distributions of work and power in the household, and the loss of intimacy and sensuality that results from the demands of other marital responsibilities.

The final component of the magazine under discussion here, and perhaps, in the end, the most significant influence on women's lives, is the advertising. It was not enough that women bought the *Ladies' Home Journal*; to keep the magazine alive they had to be persuaded to buy the products advertised in its pages. In the early twentieth century the magazine and advertising industries grew in conjunction. While magazines depended on advertisers to support their efforts financially, advertisers relied on magazines to tap into a growing national audience. Advertisements competed with and, in fact, often surpassed the editorial matter in making a connection with the reading audience. This work explores the tensions between the advertising and editorial matter in the pages of the *Journal*, in the work lives of the women who wrote advertisements to encourage other women to consume, and in the lives of women consumers, who simultaneously struggled against essentialist definitions of womanhood and embraced the goods and the promises of the consumer culture.

This work examines women's history by looking at the gendered nature of popular culture and consumer culture in the early twentieth century. The women's magazine was and still is an important cultural medium for female readers. Many of the magazines which started or which gained large readerships during the early years of the century, including the *Ladies' Home Journal*, still circulate widely today, and although they have changed both in appearance and in content from the earliest volumes, many of the policies set in the 1910s and the 1920s remain in effect. Reader interests compete with advertising interests; publishers seek a workable and profitable balance between the two. By exploring these early years, this work raises important questions about gender and popular and consumer culture. It provides a glimpse of what has been called women's culture while it makes clear that women's culture does not exist in isolation. The research bridges several areas of feminist thought and brings an interdisciplinary focus to the study of women's cultural history in the early twentieth century. In this work, then, the *Ladies' Home Journal* serves as a vital tool for the study of a transition in the lives of middle-class women in the United States. And while race, class, and ethnic distinctions amongst *Journal* readers must continually be considered for this time period, the "life" of the magazine has implications for far greater numbers of American women than those the magazine targeted, since purveyors of popular culture continually responded less to and imposed more on new groups of women as they entered the American female consumer culture of the twentieth century.

When Lois Ardery of the J. Walter Thompson advertising agency wrote an article in 1924 entitled "Inarticulate Longings," she argued that the modern woman "wants it but she doesn't know it—yet!"[20] Ardery was referring to women and consumer goods—women had inarticulate longings, longings which could be met through consumerism. She was correct in identifying women's inarticulate longings, which did become voiced in this period, but they were not all met by purchasing. Women's inarticulate longings for personal autonomy, economic independence, intimacy, sensuality, self-worth, and social recognition were acknowledged and voiced in the *Ladies' Home Journal.* They could not be met or controlled, however, by the magazine, by promises of bourgeois individualism, or by the culture of consumption. Unmet, they brewed beneath the surface and formed perhaps what Helen Woodward meant when she spoke of the powerful base of the women's magazine. This work attempts to give voice to some of those inarticulate longings and analyze the degree to which women's needs were or were not met in the *Ladies' Home Journal* or in the consumer culture which the magazine so successfully promoted.

people moved from towns to cities and as definitions of community changed, you could tell a lot about her by the brand names she chose.[13] And, in fact, as women's magazines bridged some of the gaps of region and age, if not race and ethnicity, and as the middle class grew, women's lives increasingly became defined by spending power and habits. The *Ladies' Home Journal* played a significant role in that cultural transformation. This work examines who such definitions of womanhood included, who they left out, and how women both embraced and struggled with the limited definitions of behavior and life the consumer culture offered.

The emergence, tremendous success, and lasting influence of magazines like the *Ladies' Home Journal* and the many magazines of this genre which followed reveals a great deal about the gender issues historians have identified as most significant during the early twentieth century. In a time of tremendous actual and potential societal changes, when middle-class white women faced new opportunities and new challenges in education, in the workforce, and, due to changing technology, in their households, this magazine specifically encouraged them to read rather than act, to conform to middle-class mores rather than seek out new and possibly more revolutionary alternatives. Ironically, the consumer definition of womanhood became dominant at the same time that other essentialist definitions met with conscious and resolute challenges. For example, throughout the nineteenth century, the largest groups of women's rights advocates spoke not of "women's" rights but of "woman's" rights. Secure in their own identity as white, native born, and middle-class, these women included in their definition of womanhood only those who looked and acted like them. But by the early twentieth century, several groups of feminists spoke of "women's" rights, recognizing not only the diversity of women but also that through their diversity women had some common goals. They made some political progress, operating from this standpoint, as diverse groups, initially organized on the basis of social class, race, or occupation, worked together to achieve women's expanded political participation in general and suffrage in particular.[14] Like the Progressive movement they were a part of, however, divisions of race, class, and ethnicity proved powerful, and few diverse organizations survived into the 1920s.[15]

Internal differences divided groups of women, as did the larger culture, of which women's magazines were just one part. Political in a largely nonpartisan sense, the *Ladies' Home Journal* and other magazines obscured fundamental differences among women in every issue, creating in the case. By its very nature, mass culture has often discouraged rather than encouraged democratic participation. In the case of mainstream magazines, for example, the need for continuity from issue to issue demands a formulaic view of the world. The backdrop for this formula, the ideology of dominant social groups, is a given and, hence, rarely questioned. In many forms of popular culture, the desire for a "mass" appeal negates much discussion of issues that fall outside of the mainstream. The mass appeal also leaves out significant numbers of people, since mass is often associated with race, the white race, and with class, the middle class. For example, literacy gains were enormous in the population at large at the turn of the century, but they were most significant in the black population, which went from an almost 80 percent illiteracy rate to an almost 80 percent literacy rate.[10] Nevertheless, African-Americans, regardless of their literacy or purchasing power, failed to be considered a target market by the consumer culture that produced the *Ladies' Home Journal* and other popular magazines. An enterprising young man took out a classified advertisement in *Printer's Ink*, the advertising journal, in 1917, in which he called the "ten million Negro-Americans" an "undeveloped volume" for advertising interests. Apparently no one took up his offer, since it was not until 1942 that the first popular periodical for blacks, *Negro Digest*, was founded, and it was not until 1970 that the first mass magazine for black women, *Essence*, reached the newsstands.[11]

In addition to carving out a limited definition of a mass audience, magazines also provide a fairly predictable emotional formula: a balance between the fostering of anxiety that draws readers to seek out advice and the offering of positive messages that encourage them to return the following month. The resulting formula, which worked so well for the *Ladies' Home Journal*, ultimately encouraged inaction rather than action, conformity rather than individual expression, guided rather than self-generated change.[12] In an era in which many different groups of women experimented with definitions of democracy that would include rather than exclude them, the *Journal* suggested that democracy for women meant little more than the choice between one brand of soap and another, one flavor of soup and another.

At the dawn of the twentieth century, women in the United States had no few lifestyles; their varied roles were determined in part by region, race, age, and ethnicity. But by 1930, women's magazines and the consumer culture they offered related the story of a common woman, the "average" woman, the "American" woman. That image obscured the many differences among women and offered instead a promise: if you did not know your neighbor, as

In September of 1889, with the *Ladies' Home Journal* already the best-selling magazine in the nation, Louisa Knapp Curtis decided that she could no longer combine her household and family responsibilities and her career, so she resigned as editor of the *Journal.* Cyrus Curtis hired Edward Bok, then a twenty-five-year-old writer of a syndicated column, the "Bok Page," to take her place.[8] Bok, who later married the Curtis' daughter, Mary Louise, brought the magazine to new heights in circulation and changed the nature of the magazine business in the United States. In a sense, Bok combined the visions of the two magazines edited by Sarah Josepha Hale. He believed that women were essentially domestic creatures who could best serve the nation by influencing their husbands and sons. He believed as firmly, however, in the modern order and in women's expanding role as consumers. Bok viewed his magazine as an aide to help women brave this sometimes contradictory path. The *Journal* presented an odd mixture of morality and consumerism, but the recipe worked: the *Ladies' Home Journal* truly became a household word. Known as the "monthly Bible of the American home," the *Journal*'s circulation reached one million by January of 1904.[9]

This book explores the relationship between popular culture and the culture of consumption between 1910–1930. The *Ladies' Home Journal,* both a medium of popular culture and a business enterprise, promoted for its women readers traditional "woman's values" and full participation in the consumer society. Contradictions naturally followed. It was not an easy task to promote a simple life for women, while at the same time promoting the primacy of consumer goods and material desires, nor was it easy to praise women's growing independence from onerous household tasks at the same time that one pleaded with women to limit the boundaries of that independence. Yet another contradiction, which readers themselves occasionally pointed out, was that much of the editorial and advertising content of the magazine was produced by women who led lives distinctly unlike those they counseled readers to live. Finally, the notion of choice, central to the magazine's message and to the ideology of the larger consumer culture, was often illusory, as the magazine promoted fairly limited roles for women and often ignored or dismissed many of the choices real women faced.

Central to this study is the development of mass or popular culture, which delivered through many vehicles notices of what it meant to be an American. Early analyses of mass culture were hopeful: media participation was deemed a sign of increased literacy and a certain impetus to individuals' greater participation in all elements of the social system. This has not, however, been the financial losses in the 1830s. A depression in 1834 caused its initial decline, and by 1836 the magazine no longer seemed to have much of a future. In 1837, when Louis Godey, owner of a women's magazine in Philadelphia, offered to buy out the *Ladies Magazine* but keep Sarah Josepha Hale on as editor of the consolidated publication, Hale agreed. She continued to write tales of women's duties and obligations for *Godey's Lady's Book*, her new magazine, but the magazine itself began to develop a more modern style and promote a revised definition of womanhood. Emphasizing women's fashion and consumer possibilities rather than a vision of simplicity and lack of attachment to the material world, *Godey's Lady's Book* rapidly moved away from Hale's vision but remained, nevertheless, quite popular. When Sarah Hale died in 1879, *Godey's* declined in popularity, even though it had succeeded in tapping a national audience. Only a few years later, in 1883, the *Ladies' Home Journal* would tap the same "woman's" market and then expand that market to a degree unprecedented in the history of magazines.[3] The *Journal* would accomplish this by further developing and promoting a domestic ideology that defined editors as experts, advertisers as prophets, and, most importantly, women as consumers.[4]

"If Sarah Josepha Hale was the mother of American women's magazines, then Edward Bok was their father," wrote Helen Woodward in 1926.[5] Edward Bok is the name most commonly associated with the *Ladies' Home Journal*, but the magazine's story begins not with this famous editor but with the publisher, Cyrus Curtis, and his wife, Louisa Knapp Curtis. Cyrus Curtis entered a partnership on a four-page weekly magazine called *Tribune and Farmer* in 1879. He assembled clippings about women's concerns from other sources in a column entitled "Woman and the Home." One day his wife asked him who wrote that column, and when he told her that he did, she laughed. "I don't mean to make fun of you," she told him, "but if you really knew how this sounds to a woman, you would laugh, too."[6] Louisa Knapp Curtis then took over the women's column, and before long it became the most popular section of the *Tribune and Farmer*. In December of 1883, based on the tremendous success of "Woman and the Home," Curtis launched an entire magazine dedicated to women; thus the *Ladies' Home Journal* was born, with Louisa Knapp Curtis its first editor. Cyrus Curtis had great expectations for his new publication. "We propose to make it a household necessity—so good, so pure, so true, so brave, so full, so complete," he declared, "that a young couple will no more think of going to housekeeping without it than without a cookstove."[7]

women with job opportunities in the magazine and advertising industries, thus facilitating the entrance of middle-class women into the workplace. The target audience for the *Journal* was white, native-born, middle-class women, who lived with the uncertain legacies of the nineteenth-century women's rights movement and who tried to find a comfortable role in the rapidly changing world of the expanding middle class. The *Ladies' Home Journal* both modeled and adapted to the expectations of its readers. The manner in which it alternately and at times even simultaneously acknowledged and neglected, celebrated and decried, promoted and impeded social changes and their accompanying conflicts is fascinating to examine. The magazine offered clear and limited cultural definitions of womanhood, but it also recognized and gave voice to women's own concerns—and in doing so the *Journal* helped sow the seeds for women's later demands for autonomy and self-definition. As an element of mass or popular culture, the magazine promoted the middle-class mainstream at the same time that it exposed its many shortcomings. In this work, the *Ladies' Home Journal* is the terrain upon which to study the lives of several groups of women as they reluctantly and/or eagerly participated in the development of what has become a particularly female twentieth-century consumer culture.[1]

The *Ladies' Home Journal* was not the first popular magazine for women, and its editors and owner took some of the cues for success from the *Journal*'s early nineteenth-century predecessors. Sarah Josepha Hale, editor first of the *Ladies Magazine* and then of *Godey's Lady's Book*, forms a pivotal character in the history of women's magazines. Although there were other women's magazines before hers, they had all been controlled by men; Hale brought a woman's voice to the industry. Sarah Josepha Hale was hired in 1928 to edit the *Ladies Magazine*. Her purpose, as she put it, was to "make ladies better acquainted with their duties and privileges." Hale wrote a great deal of the material herself, often instructing women about their proper spheres of activity. Her vision of womanhood was clear: women were moral beings who could influence the men around them to improve society. Woman's sphere was influence, not power. Although historians have largely moved beyond a strict private/public, female/male dichotomy in looking at real women's lives during the nineteenth century, Hale and others actively maintained this perspective and encouraged women to live in a private sphere separate from men and centered in the household. Sarah Hale's ideals clearly fit prevailing notions about domesticity and true womanhood in nineteenth-century prescriptive literature if not in life.[2]

Although the *Ladies Magazine* was a popular periodical, it experienced

Introduction

> To the uninitiated, a woman's magazine may seem
> merely a powdery bit of fluff. No notion could
> be more unreal or deceptive. That is just the
> style in which the magazines express themselves,
> for if the top layer seems fluffy, the base is
> solid and powerful.
> —Helen Woodward, *The Lady Persuaders*

This study examines women's experiences with the developing consumer culture of the early twentieth century as reflected in the most popular women's magazine of the day, the *Ladies' Home Journal.* This magazine, the first to reach a circulation of one million, transformed the whole magazine industry by creatively addressing women's household roles and opportunities outside of the home, their dependence on men, their interdependence among themselves, and their chances for independence. Its success also provided many funding for travel and, most importantly, time free from teaching to think, read, and write.

The staffs of the Boston Public Library, the New York Public Library, the Schlesinger Library at Radcliffe College, the University of Pennsylvania Library, and the J. Walter Thompson Company Archives at Duke University Library provided me with a great deal of assistance, searching for dusty copies of documents or checking and rechecking obscure details that didn't seem to match up. I'm especially grateful to Ellen Gartrell and Marion Hirsch at the J. Walter Thompson Archives; their enthusiasm for the materials matched my own, and that is a rare treat. Carol Hunter and Mark Hirsch provided valuable comments on parts of the manuscript, and I owe a special debt to my editor at Routledge, Cecelia Cancellaro, for her interest in the project and care with the text. For preparation of this manuscript, I am also grateful to Claudia Gorelick, Terence Dougherty, and Matthew DeBord of Routledge and Jill Benz of the *Ladies' Home Journal.*

I want to thank a few others for their support as well: Robin Prenoveau, whose attention to detail and determination to send out a clean copy of this text surpassed even my own; Rose Nadeau, for searching out copyright information and histories of companies long since out of business; and my colleagues in women's studies, who have remained enormously supportive of my work. The mark of my students is also on this book; they keep me inspired, and I am grateful to share my ideas and my days with them.

My friends and family, especially those who have sustained me during the past couple of years, know they have my enduring thanks and love. I offer special thanks to Julie Boss for her continued interest in and enthusiasm for my work, and to my nieces, Alison, Lindsay, Maura, and Kaitlin, for helping me connect women's past with our future. I'm most grateful to Michael Arthur, whose life provides me with many lessons and whose calypsos keep me smiling.

Finally, this book is dedicated to my parents, Mary Barry Scanlon and William Scanlon, with love and gratitude for the many gifts they have given me.

Acknowledgments

*I*t is a pleasure to have the opportunity to thank the many people who helped me intellectually, professionally, and personally as I worked my way through this project. My first debt is to Sarah Elbert, my dissertation director, whose intellectual excitement for U.S. cultural history encouraged me to follow my dream and look seriously at women's popular culture. Her mark is on my work, and her friendship continues to sustain me. Alice Kessler-Harris also provided me with invaluable patterns of learning and questioning when I was a student, and she continues to offer reassurance, through her work and example, that history matters.

I am grateful, too, for the generous financial assistance I received from several sources. A Woodrow Wilson Women's Studies Research Grant and two dissertation year fellowships from Binghamton University helped me complete my dissertation, from which this book originates. SUNY Plattsburgh provided me with a Mini Grant and, in conjunction with my union, United University Professions, a travel grant and then a Dr. Nuala Drescher McGann Affirmative Action Leave. The leave provided me with

Contents

	Acknowledgments	ix
	Introduction	1
one	*A Profile of the* Ladies' Home Journal	11
two	*Housekeeping* The Greatest Business in the World	49
three	*Women's Paid Work* Setting and Stretching the Boundaries	79
four	*Stoves for Women, Votes for Men* The *Journal* and Women's Political Involvement	109
five	*The Amateur Rebel* Female Protagonists in *Ladies' Home Journal* Fiction	137
six	*Advertising Women* The J. Walter Thompson Company Women's Editorial Department	169
seven	*"Every Woman Is Interested in This"* Advertising in the *Ladies' Home Journal*	197
	Conclusion	229
	Notes	235
	Index	273

*For my Mother and
Father with Love*

HC 110 .C6 S27 1995

Scanlon, Jennifer, 1958-

Inarticulate longings

Published in 1995 by

Routledge
29 West 35 Street
New York, NY 10001

Published in Great Britain in 1995 by

Routledge
11 New Fetter Lane
London EC4P 4EE

Copyright © 1995 by Routledge

Printed in the United States of America

All rights reserved. No part of this book may be reprinted or reproduced or utilized in any form or by any electronic, mechanical, or other means, now known or hereafter invented, including photo-copying and recording, or in any information storage or retrieval system without permission in writing from the publishers.

Library of Congress Cataloging-in-Publication Data

Scanlon, Jennifer, 1958–
Inarticulate longings : the ladies' home journal, gender, and the promises of consumer culture/Jennifer Scanlon
p.   cm.
Includes bibliographical references
ISBN 0-415-91156-7 (hb) – ISBN 0-415-91157-5 (pb)
1. Women consumers–United States–History 2. Advertising. Magazine–United States–History.
3. Popular literature–United States–History and criticism. 4. Ladies' home journal.
I. Title.
HC110.C6S27   1995
659.13'2–dc20

K

Inarticulate

Longings

The Ladies' Home Journal,

Gender,

and the

Promises

of Consumer Culture

by Jennifer Scanlon

ROUTLEDGE: New York and London

Riverside Community College
Library
APR '97   4800 Magnolia Avenue
Riverside, California 92506

Inarticulate Longings

P9-DVU-936

DATE DUE

DE 1997			

DEMCO 38-296

A *Profile* of the Ladies' Home Journal

$\mathcal{T}$ he *Ladies' Home Journal* emerged in the late nineteenth century neither as a unique cultural phenomenon nor as the blind successor to *Godey's Lady's Book.* The *Journal* fit into a context in which women were targeted as readers of uniquely "female" information. During the 1890s, for example, women's columns, discussing fashions and mores, blossomed in newspapers throughout the country. Syndication of such materials, also occurring in the last decade of the nineteenth century, assured their rapid and widespread distribution. What has been called the "golden age" of magazines occurred at the same time. Capitalizing on the tremendous success of women's pages, publishers expanded the female world of several columns or a few pages to whole publications complete with illustrations and advertisements. The young Edward Bok, in fact, had attracted the attention of publisher Cyrus Curtis because of the enormous success of his syndicated column, the "Bok Page."[1] Those who could afford to gathered information from these specialized women's publications, information that would help them negotiate their way in their families and in the larger world outside their homes. In article after article they learned how to manage a household, consume goods in a thrifty and modern manner, survive run-ins with men and romance. They received lessons in civics and democracy and in using their femaleness to their advantage. The women's magazine, far more than the daily newspaper, provided all of this information in an inviting, aesthetically pleasing format.

Magazines entered their heyday in part because of very real and noticeable social changes. The middle class expanded rapidly in the late nineteenth and early twentieth centuries, and with increased income came increased leisure time and an expanded range of interests among people. Between 1910 and 1929, the average purchasing power of Americans rose 40 percent.[2] Now the middle class could join the wealthy in purchasing more news and entertainment. The spread of electricity, which occurred rapidly, helped further the process of reading as a leisure activity in a time when minimal literacy was as high as 94 percent for the total population. In addition, the U.S. Post Office's introduction of rural free delivery in 1898 made it possible for almost all women to receive these messages simultaneously and hence to consider themselves part of a national culture. Magazines directed at the middle class promoted mild political and social reforms, catering to an important characteristic of this group: they wanted a better world, but they did not want radical social changes, especially when they themselves were clearly the economic beneficiaries of the status quo.[3] Finally, the consumer culture the magazines embodied provided people, particularly women, with a way to spend both their leisure time and their money.

The social climate was right for the emergence and growth of middle-class women's magazines. Low in price and lavish in their use of drawings and photographs, magazines had a visual as well as thematic appeal. In the time period under discussion here, especially during the second half of the teens decade, magazines made their greatest advances with the use of color. Providing a visual experience, magazines created an audience of spectators and, by extension, consumers. With an attractive format, intriguing advertisements, and compelling editorials, they promoted a world in which both pleasure and leisure were linked to consumer pursuits.[4] The home was considered the "natural" consumer unit, the housewife the "natural" consumer.[5] Of course, there was little that was actually natural about this process. In surveying the development of retail stores from 1880–1920, William Leach found that "what was remarkable about the nation's commercial growth was that, almost uniformly, it far outpaced the needs of the population." Desire, he argued, was pumped into the American discourse at all levels.[6] One way to overcome the problem of overproduction, of course, was to encourage consumption, or as advertising historian Roland Marchand puts it, educate people in "stylistic obsolescence."[7] Grocery stores, department stores, mass magazines, Sears and Montgomery Ward catalogs, and the advertising industry helped transform the society, as Jackson Lears notes, from an entrepreneurial, production-oriented economy, dependent upon self-control and thrift, to a bureaucratic and consumer economy, dependent upon more spend-free attitudes.[8] Women's magazines, an important component of this emerging social landscape, helped naturalize women's link to the marketplace through consumption.

The *Ladies' Home Journal* emerged as one of many magazines entering and framing this burgeoning market, and like the others it had to decide on a specific audience–the more specific the target audience, the more successful the magazine. The *Journal,* while clearly targeted toward white, native-born women and, more narrowly, toward women with discretionary income to support the magazine's advertisers, was initially somewhat unclear about the real economic status of its intended audience. Owner Cyrus Curtis insisted at the start that the *Journal* would appeal to and be directed toward a high-class audience. In 1893, he sent a prospectus of one issue's contents to all of the people listed in the *Blue Book,* or social register, in San Francisco, Boston, and Milwaukee.[9] During the same year, in a letter written to an expensive department store in Paris, Bon Marché, Curtis claimed that his readers were in fact potential Bon Marché customers; none, he said, were tuberculous or epileptic, and none were "poor" people.[10] When the publishing world's journal, *Printer's Ink,* classified the readers of the *Ladies' Home Journal* with those of *Farm and Journal,* Curtis wrote indignant letters of protest. He repeatedly denied the rural, hence working class, label that others imposed on his magazine. *Journal* readers were cosmopolitan rather than rural, he claimed; they were more like readers of *The Atlantic* or *Scribner's* than *Farm and Journal.*

Acknowledging that the *Journal* originated from a farm magazine, Curtis nevertheless maintained that it had moved sufficiently far from its rural roots to claim a place in the mainstream of United States culture, which was quickly becoming urban.[11]

The majority of *Ladies' Home Journal* readers did, in fact, live in the suburbs of large cities by the middle of the 1890s. While Curtis argued that this fact proved that his audience was composed of professionals, of "respectable, church attending people," Edward Bok was less certain that region dictated social class. An editor of *The Atlantic* later recalled a discussion he and Bok had when they discovered their publications had the same number of subscribers on Boston's fashionable Beacon Street. As Ellery Sedgwick remembered it, Bok was careful to distinguish their audiences: "'But there is a difference,' he remarked. 'You see, Sedgwick, you go in at the front door, and I at the back. I know my place.'"[12] Bok jokingly underestimated the class status of his audience, but he also took pride in addressing middle-class rather than wealthy women.

It was not until Cyrus Curtis bought the *Saturday Evening Post* in 1897 that he fully accepted the middle-class direction of the *Ladies' Home Journal*. Apparently he decided rather quickly that the *Post* would be the more upscale magazine. The *Journal*, he declared, "will be in every sense a popular home magazine. . . . It will appeal to the income of the many rather than the few."[13] In saying this Curtis essentially acknowledged a process that was already underway, and the *Ladies' Home Journal* became solidly identified as a "handbook for the middle class."[14] At an advertising conference within the Curtis company in 1915, the target audience for the *Journal* was described in terms of its income. The magazine would reach middle-class woman, those from families whose incomes were between $1200 and $2500 per year. More wealthy women, those from upper middle-class and wealthy families with incomes between $3000 and $5000 per year, would only be "supplementary" customers.[15] Apparently women with incomes lower than $1200, who could sustain neither the magazine nor its advertisers, would not be sought after as readers.

After selecting this audience, the magazine had to further secure its desired group of readers. By 1900, the *Ladies' Home Journal* was the most widely advertised magazine in the nation.[16] By advertising the *Journal* in many other publications, Curtis reached potential advertisers and readers alike. To increase circulation more directly, the *Journal* hired subscription agents to market the magazine regionally. In cities all over the country boys and young men acted as subscription agents, enticing readers to make the commitment to a year's subscription. By 1901, these agents numbered 30,000.[17] Curtis developed his own strategies for attracting key advertisers to his magazine. He solicited advertisements that generally matched the kinds of articles in the *Journal* and became personally involved in their presentation. Curtis himself spent a good deal of time clipping ads from other sources, editing them, and mailing them to the advertising agencies with suggestions about how they would work most effectively in the *Ladies' Home Journal*. The art department at the *Journal* was considered the best in the nation by the early 1900s, and in 1911, Curtis started the Marketing Research Division to study the publishing and advertising industries and to canvas potential markets.[18] While these activities eventually became an integral part of publishing, Curtis was at the forefront of change.

By 1910, when this examination of the *Journal*'s contents officially begins, the magazine-as-industry was successful enough to begin construction on an enormous, modern building in Independence Square in the heart of Philadelphia, a city with a long history of magazine publishing. By 1800 over one hundred magazines had been founded there, and although many of those were short-lived enterprises, Philadelphia was undoubtedly an exciting place for the *Ladies' Home Journal*.[19] The Curtis building, placed in the center of the city's activities, was a stately structure complete with a 160-foot long recreation room with glass windows, an open promenade, a dance floor with a piano, a room with baths, a clothes washing and drying room, and umbrella rentals and Saturday sewing classes. The Curtis Company promoted an image of middle-class respectability at all levels, even inviting *Ladies' Home Journal* readers to visit this new building which, for many readers and certainly most if not all of the women workers, had more amenities than they enjoyed at home.[20]

The *Ladies' Home Journal* of the early twentieth century was both an important purveyor of twentieth-century culture and an enormously successful business enterprise. It succeeded on both counts by recognizing, promoting, and manipulating gender differences in the society. The women's magazine has much in common with the department store, which also flourished during this period. A process Susan Porter Benson described for department stores holds true for the women's magazine business as well; magazines made money by addressing the fact that there was still something, especially for the middle class, called women's space, a place where women could be catered to because of who they were, the social roles they played, and the values they shared. Like the department stores that invited women in to look, dream, and purchase, magazines invited women to claim some printed material as their own—and to use it also to look, dream, and decide on purchases. Like department stores, women's magazines made deliberate choices about how they handled race and class as well as gender. African-American and immigrant women found their way into the pages of the *Journal* in one of two ways: as the subject of jokes or as domestic help featured in advertisements or editorial discussions; otherwise, they were ignored. Such definitions of "women" in popular magazines surely helped shape the nation's definitions of womanhood for the twentieth century. It is crucial to note that definition and understand who it excludes as well as includes, and for what reasons.[21]

While the department store appears on the surface to be a more sales-oriented medium of culture, and the magazine a more service-oriented medium, the distinctions are not so clearly drawn. The department store aimed to break down women's resistance to spending money and integrate them more fully into their role as consumers; women's magazines did the same. Using some of the same tools—addressing women's sense of themselves as able mothers, attractive women, and competent housekeepers—magazines and department stores urged women to buy the goods that would help them achieve their aims in a more efficient if not more exciting manner. The successful department store and the successful women's magazine had to indulge customers and manipulate them at the same time. The *Journal* did this well, all in the interest of attracting both loyal advertisers and loyal readers.

Susan Porter Benson's insights about the give-and-take relationship between customers and department stores also applies to the *Ladies' Home Journal* and its readers. Like the department store, the *Journal* did not function simply as an agent of capitalism working to disarm and retrain unwitting women. Department store shoppers may have relished the store displays and the invitations to consume, but they were hardly automatons. And readers, like shoppers, responded to the magazine's consumer exhortations in a variety of ways, choosing what worked for them and manipulating the system as it attempted to manipulate them. There was a good deal of give-and-take in the *Journal* as women readers exercised their choices and let the magazine know their likes and dislikes. The *Journal* as business, however, effectively balanced that give-and-take as it consciously addressed women, celebrated their differences from men, acknowledged their difficulties as well as their joys, and offered them somewhat satisfying, if ultimately unsatisfactory, roles to play in the twentieth-century world.[22]

What follows is a profile and comparison of two issues of the *Ladies' Home Journal*, one from March of 1914, the other from August of 1924. This summary gives today's reader an idea of what the *Journal* reader got when she received her issue in the mail, bought it at the newsstand, or borrowed it from a friend. There was a certain formula to the magazine, one which readers probably came to expect and rely on. But although the mixture of editorial matter, fiction, and advertisements was a fairly consistent one, there were some important changes over time. Gradual, seemingly subtle changes such as the appeal to specific age groups, location of advertisements, or degree of editorial presence actually represent more significant changes in the magazine's direction and purpose. The most significant change during the two decades is that the magazine's definition of service increasingly focused on the training of skilled but ready consumers. The "home" in the magazine's title was increasingly defined as a site of consumption, with a woman consumer front and center.

The *Ladies' Home Journal* for March 1914 is a 104-page text, printed primarily in black and white, but with a color cover, several color ads, and some color features as well, principally fashion articles. The cover drawing, the magazine's own most important advertisement, is romantic with its use of pastels and features a woman playing piano and a man leaning over the piano watching her play. She is dressed in a long, pink chiffon gown, he in a dinner jacket and white shirt and tie. The picture promises romance, and one wonders if this illustration provides any indication of what the magazine holds between its covers.[23]

Following a full-page advertisement for Fairy Soap on the inside cover, the Editor's "Personal Page" is page one. As is characteristic of Edward Bok's tenure at the *Journal*, which lasted through 1919, the editorial presence is immediate and strong. On the Editor's "Personal Page" and then several pages later on the editorial page Bok expresses his personal opinion, which quickly becomes the voice of the magazine. Because Bok editorializes often but never signs his name to any of his comments, his words read like the opinion of the magazine rather than of an individual. This personal page contains brief replies to or comments about letters Bok had received from readers. One reader complained that Bok catered to Jews and another that he catered to Catholics, a third reader suggested that he invite Jane Addams to write for the *Journal*, and a pro-suffrage reader argued that Bok should endorse woman suffrage. Bok's brief responses put the readers in their place: he has also been called a Jew-hater and a Catholic-hater, and he accepts living with reader dissatisfaction. Bok provides no real response about suffrage but tells the Jane Addams fan to read more carefully: Jane Addams had written in every issue during the previous year. The layout of this "Personal Page" is interesting as well. Bok's paragraphs of response frame three photographs in the middle of the page. The photos show the *Ladies' Home Journal* displayed in cities around the world: Panama, Tokyo, Berlin. With the looming but seemingly generic voice of the editor surrounding these photos, the reader gets the sense that the voice of the editor as well as the voice of the magazine is prominent across the globe. In fact, by 1914 the magazine could be found in many places outside the United States, including Alaska, Cuba, Puerto Rico, Mexico, and the Hawaiian and Philippine Islands.[24]

These snippets from the editor are intriguing because they provide today's readers with some context and introduce us to the dialogue established between this editor and his readers. They also reveal something of the world outside the *Journal* as well as the magazine's relationship to that world. Complaints about Jews and Catholics mirror the nativist sentiment that gained favor in the United States as national demographics changed. In 1900, 80 percent of all New Yorkers and one-third of all Americans were immigrants or the children of immigrants.[25] The influx of white immigrants from Europe and black migrants from the South threatened the already somewhat insecure white middle class, which believed that it formed the solid basis upon which the society rested. Although Bok dismissed the accusations that he favored or hated both Jews and Catholics, the magazine, like other elements of popular culture, promoted a narrow definition of the true American, who was often both Protestant and native-born.

Turn-of-the-century magazines, popular theater, and World's Fairs, as cultural historians have documented, educated people to exercise prejudices against difference in general, and against racial, ethnic, and religious difference in particular. Catholicism, still significantly feared and misunderstood, found itself next to Judaism on the hierarchy of religious hatred. Race and ethnicity often also formed the basis of social attacks in a changing business world. Local grocers in the South, threatened economically by the inroads made by Sears and Montgomery Ward through their "wish book" catalogs, started rumors that both men were African-American. Sears published photos of himself in response; Ward offered a cash reward for information leading to the source of the rumor.[26] Business success, inside and outside of the *Ladies' Home Journal*, depended in part on the image, if not the stamp, of proper pedigree.

The argument about Jane Addams is indicative of the magazine's

THE LADIES' HOME JOURNAL
INCORPORATING THE HOME JOURNAL
Registered in the United States Patent Office

PUBLISHED ON THE TWENTIETH OF EACH
MONTH PRECEDING DATE OF ISSUE BY

THE CURTIS PUB-
LISHING COMPANY
INDEPENDENCE SQUARE
PHILADELPHIA, PENNSYLVANIA

CYRUS H·K·CURTIS
PRESIDENT
EDWARD W·BOK
VICE-PRESIDENT AND EDITOR
C·H·LUDINGTON
SECRETARY AND TREASURER

EDITED BY EDWARD W·BOK
KARL EDWIN HARRIMAN, MANAGING EDITOR

Copyright, 1914 (Trade-mark registered) by The Curtis Publishing Company, in the United States and
Great Britain. Entered at Stationers' Hall, London, England. All rights reserved. Entered as second-class
matter May 6, 1911, at the Post Office at Philadelphia, Pennsylvania, under the Act of March 3, 1879.

A Special Word to Subscribers

WHEN you receive notice that your subscription has
expired renew it at once, using the blank inclosed
in your final copy. Please sign your name exactly as it
appears on your present address label. Sometimes a
subscriber who has already renewed may receive this
blank. We begin to pack in mail-bags two weeks or
more before mailing, and the renewal may have reached
us after the copy containing the blank has been packed.
In requesting a change of address please give us four
weeks' notice.

Should your subscription expire with this issue of
THE JOURNAL your renewal must reach us before the
sixth of April to avoid missing the next issue. We cannot begin subscriptions with back numbers. Subscribers should always use Postal or Express money orders in
remitting. All Rural Free Delivery carriers can supply
Postal money orders.

The Price of The Journal

PUBLISHED once a month. By subscription: One
Dollar and Fifty Cents a year, postage free in the
United States, Alaska, Cuba, Porto Rico, Mexico, and the
Hawaiian and Philippine Islands. Single copies: 15 cents
each. In Canada, $2 a year, except in Toronto, where
the price is $1.50 a year. Single copies in Eastern Canada:
15 cents each; west of Ontario, 20 cents each.
To Foreign Countries in the International Postal Union
other than those named above: Subscription, postpaid,
per year, 11 shillings, 3 pence, payable by International
money order ($2.85 in American money). Single copies:
1 shilling net each (25 cents in American money).

Our Advertising Branch Offices
[For advertising business only. Subscriptions not received.]
NEW YORK: Madison Avenue and 23d Street
BOSTON: Merchants' National Bank Building
CHICAGO: Home Insurance Building
SAN FRANCISCO: First National Bank Building
LONDON: 6, Henrietta Street, Covent Garden, W.C.

The Editor's Personal Page

ROSES AND EGGS

"ABUSE," says Emerson, "is a pledge that you
are felt." In THE JOURNAL, then, felt in some
quarters? For witnesseth:

Do you know that your magazine is getting worse
and worse?

We did not know it, we confess. Nor can the
knowledge be very general, unless the public buys
the magazine to find out that it is getting "worse and
worse," for the last figures given us show an increased
sale of twenty thousand over the previous issue.

This friend is very much exercised over a racial
emphasis on our part that he sees so clearly and we
so dimly:

That's right; go on baiting the Jew, and get his
subscription. But remember this: for every Jew you
get you will lose two Gentiles.

How interesting! And written from a church
parsonage too! So progresses true Christianity!

This lady waxeth sarcastic:

It must be gratifying to you that the greater
emphasis you place on American fashions the
more generally are Paris fashions worn by American
women.

And likewise gratifying is it that the imports from
Paris decreased last year over ten millions of francs.
So much depends upon the angle of gratification.

We are "profound" to this reader:

I understand that in your profound editorial wisdom you have decreed you will not editorially use the
word "die," as "we die." Why?

Well, do we?

Here we are certainly asked to do something:

I was looking over your magazines for 1871 last
evening and they were infinitely better then, although
not so pretentious as your present numbers. Why
not go back and get the spirit of 1871 into your
present work?

How can we, dear lady, when the first number of
THE LADIES' HOME JOURNAL was not published
until twelve years after the "magazines of 1871"
that you read "last evening?"

Mixed not so much in his statement as in his fact is
this reader—a man:

For absolute gall your writings are the limit!
Take the article I refer to: it shows youth and inexperience in every line.

Fine! "Youth" the author will admit, I am sure,
but will he concede "inexperience"? For at seventy-
nine one usually has had some experience. And the
world generally concedes this fact in the case of
Lyman Abbott, who wrote the article that "shows
youth and inexperience in every line."

Here is where we are punished because:

There is no excuse whatever for your publication
of the new story by ———, whom I consider
the most immoral writer of fiction today, particularly for young girls. Hence I will not renew my
subscription.

And yet THE JOURNAL has never published a story
by the writer in question!

Curious how two persons can see the same way:

Grossly immoral I call the story "Her Soul's Revolt," and, as a father of three young daughters, I
protest and cancel my subscription.

Another sin of omission are we punished for, since
the story in question was not in THE JOURNAL at all,
but in another magazine!

A man seeks to widen our horizon:

Have you, in your limited observation, ever heard
of a woman named Jane Addams? And don't you
think it might be a great stroke to ask her (she lives
in Chicago) to write something for your magazine?
You might get a little strength in its pages in this
way.

That is what we thought, and that is why Miss
Addams wrote for the very first issue of THE JOURNAL last
year, and has, all told, contributed more than
twenty-five articles to the magazine.

THE LADIES' HOME JOURNAL in Panama. Here is a JOURNAL
Circulator Being Welcomed on His Monthly Visit to a Typical
Settlement Down in the "Big Ditch" Country

In Tokio Schools the Children are Given Their First Lessons in
the Method of Western Life, and Their First Glimpses of the
Pictorial Side of That Life, Through THE LADIES' HOME JOURNAL.

Possibly the Presence of Men Like These Selling THE JOURNAL
Will Not be New to Most City Dwellers, Only the Picture is Not
of a Scene in an American City, but in Berlin

WITH NOT A ROSE

We expected reproofs from some women for having
published Mrs. Heath's article, "Are Wives Wasting
Their Husbands' Money?" Our expectations have
been realized. But we didn't expect this convincing
argument for the defense:

If women had the vote no butcher would dare keep
back the trimmings. But with her hands tied what
can woman do?

For one thing, she might ask the butcher for the
trimmings.

Here we are taught grammar:

Don't you know that a corroborative can never be
an adjective?

Really?

And now we are charged with being accessory
before the fact in a possible attack:

Do you, then, approve of the rough handling of
those returning American women whose hats are
snatched from their heads by the New York customs
inspectors if the hats happen to be trimmed with
nigrets or paradise plumes? Probably the women
were unaware of the passage of the law forbidding
the importation of the feathers.

We've no supported evidence that any hats have
been "snatched" from heads. We do approve of the
law, however, and we state a fundamental in justice
when we quote: "Ignorance of the law excuses no
one."

This is very ungallant from a man:

Do you really think any one believes a real widow
wrote that amazing article in your February issue,
"Why I Have Not Remarried—Yet"? It has the
half-mark of "man made" all over it.

We wonder what the author will say when she gets
that letter—she being a most feminine person—for
fifteen years a widow, and with a son in Princeton.

Take your choice:

As a Protestant woman I express my faith when
I "protest" most emphatically against the Catholic
articles you have published by Cardinal Gibbons and
others. [Who are the others?]

Then this:

You may or may not be interested to learn that at
least one Catholic woman means not to re-subscribe
to THE JOURNAL when her year is up, due to the
articles by Lyman Abbott which you are publishing.

This is neither a rose nor an egg from an Iowa
woman:

I have written you two letters protesting that my
JOURNAL always reaches me with pages missing.
Forgive me. I have discovered that my husband,
who gets all the mail at our post office, runs through
the magazine and tears out pages he thinks I
shouldn't read. A neighbor saw him do it and told
me. I charged him and he confessed. He said he
thought the articles he tore out would have made
me restless! Now we're happy again.

Oh, the duplicity of man!

And here is just a general objection and a most apt
suggestion:

I am tired of THE LADIES' HOME JOURNAL. Why
don't you publish a magazine like ———? A
most excellent periodical about as closely related in
scope and purpose to THE JOURNAL as—we can't
think of a comparison sufficiently long-drawn.]

Besides, dear lady, that is their job; ours is publishing THE LADIES' HOME JOURNAL. And if you
still feel the need of another magazine "like" the
one you mention, why not buy two copies of it?
There's a solution to your problem.

This Month's Harrison Fisher Cover

HARRISON FISHER'S covers are always most
pleasing—none more so than the one used for
this issue of THE LADIES' HOME JOURNAL. As Mr.
Fisher's work is so popular, and so much sought after
by girls, we have had this month's cover printed as
a poster, which can be had for ten cents, post-free, or
three copies for twenty-five cents. It is just like the
original—in full color—but without any advertisement on the back.

In 1914, the editor of the *Journal* reassured his European-American readers that the magazine provided "other" women, men, and children across the globe with lessons "in the
Method of Western Life."

ambivalence in addressing women's expanding public sphere. Bok, who could hardly ignore the famous settlement house worker's presence in the national arena, invited her to write for the *Journal*. Since he never highlighted her work the way he did that of others, however, one reader at least missed her contributions. A household magazine, the *Ladies' Home Journal* stumbled over definitions of womanhood that took women out of that domestic sphere. Women's clubs, for example, whose memberships grew steadily in the nineteenth century and "soared" in the twentieth, found only a lukewarm reception in the pages of the *Journal*. When writers did discuss women's clubs, they took great pains to describe the clubs' maternal nature.[27] In this same era, Jane Addams and scores of other women discovered what feminists of a later generation would put in words: the personal is political. As Nancy Dye explains, they realized that "the home and the community were inextricably bound together, and those concerns once defined as the private responsibility of individual housewives and mothers were in actuality public and political."[28] The *Ladies' Home Journal*, though, dependent as it was upon the notion and the practice of divided spheres, would attempt to mystify these connections and maintain public/private, power/influence distinctions.

The presence of Editor Bok, once established in the beginning of the magazine, does not disappear. Four pages later, on pages five and six, one finds the editorial pages. Here again, the editor addresses many issues in brief, and although some of the discussions come from readers' letters, others are simply items the editor wants to raise. And again, he does not always provide answers or solutions. The first piece concerns the more than eight million unmarried men over age twenty in the United States. Seven million of them, Bok alerts us, fall between the ages of twenty and forty-four, "in other words, on the sunnyside of confirmed bachelorhood." Even more women, nine million, remain unmarried. The reasons for this situation are unclear, Bok argues, but it brings profound results: a declining birth rate, an increase in personal extravagance, and an increase in immorality and vice. While Bok provides no specific solution, one can infer that he places the burden for finding a solution with his readers, namely women.[29] Perhaps men remain unmarried because women are not doing all that they can to allure and then secure them. Perhaps this magazine can help. This discussion is as interesting for what it does not, as what it does, say. The declining birth rate Bok fears, one imagines, is that of the native-born white population, not that of the immigrant or African-American populations. Bok may be echoing the nativist sentiment he seemed to disregard several pages earlier.

The other brief editorials in this month's collection do contain specific advice: give stepmothers a chance to succeed at their roles; be aware of merchandising tricks; resist Parisian fashions; avoid the common drinking cup and common towel in public rest areas; do away with fireworks. Finally, Bok admonishes, if women want their husbands to notice them, they must notice their husbands. The voice of the editor comes across as a powerful one from the outset, guiding reader actions with absolute conviction. Bok, ready to fight for a better world, expects his readers to engage in each battle with him.[30]

This issue of the *Journal* contains many other features. Although they are scattered throughout the issue rather than grouped, a thematic rather than chronological discussion makes more sense here. Articles occasionally target children, for example. "Flossie Fisher's Funnies" is a comic strip for children and a regular offering of the *Ladies' Home Journal,* while "Self-Made Pictures for the Children's Rooms," a one-time feature, provides pictures of the White House for children to cut and paste. A few articles on medical issues are scattered through the magazine as well: how to deal with warts and moles, how to dress a baby in winter, how a young mother can handle her children's medical problems. The issue contains many articles on food, most of which provide recipes or, as does "My Best Recipe," solicit and then pay readers for the best recipes received. Other articles help women find ways to save money: in "The Housewife Who Wants to Economize," a woman who knows thirty-eight ways to use ham counsels her readers to buy a whole ham and use it again and again in different ways. In "Unique School Parties Where Eats Are the Thing," a writer describes how foods can mirror the academic activities of children in school; they can prepare a botanical banquet, a greek symposium, or a scientific revel. Some of the food columns are regular monthly features, while others, like the school party recipes, are one-of-a-kind articles.[31]

Articles about household advice abound in the March 1914 *Ladies' Home Journal.* In "The Old Back-Yard Fence," Frances Duncan provides readers with advice and illustrations about fence repair and decoration. In "How You Can Furnish a Five-Room Apartment for $300," the writer argues that good taste does not have to be costly and that a careful shopper can furnish her apartment both inexpensively and tastefully. This article is somewhat unique because of its use of color in the drawings of various rooms of an apartment. In addition to the color drawings, though, the article provides something fairly typical of the *Journal*: it includes lists of prices of the new items, including everything from the overstuffed chair for $12.50 to the newspaper basket for $2.25. One of the most interesting articles about the household, a regular monthly feature, is "What Other Women Have Found Out About Economy in the Kitchen." The editor of this column paid readers "a crisp dollar bill" for their helpful hints, and in this issue women counsel fellow readers to put dishes in the sink to soak so they won't harden, use bread crusts to grease pans, note the cost of recipes on the recipe cards, and dip the knife in boiling water each time they cut a slice of butter. The *Journal* truly acts as a forum here, providing an arena for women to share the things, however trivial they might appear now, that actually worked for them in their kitchens and homes. This month's issue includes twenty-four reader hints.[32]

Fashion-related articles constitute another regular feature of the March 1914 edition of the *Journal*. In general, fashion articles in the *Journal* are more aesthetically pleasing than are many of the other types of articles, for they display drawings not only of beautiful clothing but of attractive women models as well, and most of this in color. From "What I See on Fifth Avenue" to "May I Trim Your Hat," the displays are elegant, the space attributed to the drawings is generous, and the many accessories featured provide even further incentive to try new ideas. Fashion writers make promises to women of all ages, displaying special patterns for young girls, young women, and the elderly, as well as special designs for spring, for church, for parties. Since most women still made rather than purchased their own clothing, the fashions displayed here do not offer ready-to-wear clothes available in department stores or even through the mail. Instead, they offer *Ladies' Home Journal* designs with patterns available exclusively from the *Journal*. Small black and white drawings accompany the larger ones and illustrate the make-up of the patterns. The *Journal* also offers patterns for all the accessories as well, from hats to bags to vests to undergarments. This fashion component of the magazine, which begins in the middle of the issue and becomes more pronounced towards the end, not only entices readers with its inviting drawings and styles but also provides increased revenue for the fashion business of the Curtis Company. Although the magazine increasingly promoted women's buying of goods rather than their continued preparation at home, fashion remained an exception to this rule. Although it occasionally contained advertisements for other clothing designs or for pattern manufacturers, the *Journal* primarily featured, highlighted with color, its own designs. One wonders now if Edward Bok's strong dislike for Parisian fashions, which he and others often proclaimed in the pages of the *Journal*, had something to do with the fact that some Parisian fashions were ready-to-wear or at least sold elsewhere, while the "American" fashions in the magazine were *Ladies' Home Journal* exclusives.[33]

The *Journal* of the 1910s often focused on women's ability to earn or control money, and the March 1914 issue contains two such articles. "What Can I Do? How Can I Make Money and Stay at Home?" was a regular feature of the magazine during the teens decade. Again, this article provides readers' ideas: one buys baskets in Chinatown and then dyes, decorates, and sells them; a second does shopping for her neighbors; another sews ironing board covers. These endeavors, neither formalized nor marketed, could hardly provide particularly steady or lucrative employment. Married women readers of the *Journal* were expected to earn money only at home and only to supplement their husbands' incomes, not to foster their own independence, economic or otherwise.[34] The kind of work the *Journal* chose to promote is again evident in a second article, "What 35,000 Girls Have Told Me," by the manager of the *Ladies' Home Journal*'s Girls' Club, "who is herself a girl." Club members worked, essentially, as subscription agents, although unlike the young male agents mentioned earlier, these girls and women did not stand on street corners or travel through city neighborhoods soliciting magazine subscriptions. Instead, they worked through a female network, encouraging family members, friends, and the friends of friends to try the *Journal.* In this way they earned not salaries but gifts, money, prizes, and scholarships set up by the magazine. The manager of the club continually stated that the only requirement to join was "a desire to earn money," yet, the many discussions of the club indicate that no significant money earning was taking place, at least not on a regular basis. Women had the capacity to earn money, the *Journal* acknowledged, but they were advised to do so only in non-structured and hence non-threatening ways. Nevertheless, the writer acknowledged that she had received 144,000 inquiries about the club, an indication that the readers' needs to earn money could not be met by the magazine's meager suggestions for employment.[35]

This issue of the *Journal* acknowledged class differences among young working women in an unspoken way. Middle-class unmarried women could work as subscription agents, as participants in the "Girls' Club," but they would not be identified as workers, merely as club members. Working class women, on the other hand, actually worked, as Una Nixson Hopkins's article, "The New Girls' Camp," illustrates. Hopkins provided a photo essay of a YWCA camp for young working girls. The unstated assumption in the article is that the readers of the *Journal* have more in common with the YWCA social workers than with the young working women attending the camp.[36] Although the magazine acknowledged that young women lacked money, it took great care in identifying its readers with certain types of employment.

Articles that offered women more personal advice formed another important component of the magazine's offerings. While these articles covered many aspects of life and sometimes overlapped with advice about the household or about money, these articles can also be looked at in terms of addressing "family" issues. In "Girls' 'Affairs,'" a regular feature, a writer responds to a girl's query about proper dating etiquette with men. Many of the girl's acquaintances "familiarities" with men, familiarities she thought were reserved for the man one planned to marry. The writer cautions her to be more discreet than her friends but, interestingly enough, does not challenge the idea that certain unspecified behaviors are acceptable if the man is a prospective husband and not merely a suitor. This letter exemplifies how the youth culture often identified with the 1920s occasionally found mention even in the *Ladies' Home Journal* during its teen years. In the culture at large, young women and men, more openly than at any time previous, debated what they wanted in a mate: sensuality or stability. And while they may have spoken more euphemistically about sexuality in the *Journal* than elsewhere, *Journal* readers did express a great deal of concern about men's advances and their own desires to accept or reject them.[37]

Many of the advice writers provided etiquette lessons about men or about social issues, reminding readers of values supposedly already shared by the readership, but that nonetheless warranted repeating. In "The Ideas of a Plain Country Woman," a regular feature discussed in detail in a later chapter, the practical writer reminded readers continuously of the values that formed the basis, as she saw it, of the society. This month she warns her readers not to "idiotically aspire" to "the regime of the bourgeoisie," which is to languor away; instead they can find ways to be useful in the world. Another article, written by a mother-in-law, reminds her sisters how they need to act with their own daughters-in-law. Perhaps they forget and spend too much time at their sons' houses, or they provide unsolicited advice. This article serves as a patient yet stern reminder that rules must be followed.[38]

Some of the advice articles discuss larger social problems as well. "A Man Who is Casting Out Divorce: How Kansas City Has Tried to Solve the Problem," features a divorce "proctor," W. W. Wright, hired by the city to curb the number of divorces granted. In one year, the article contends, he reduced the divorce rate in Kansas City by nearly 40 percent. This article speaks to an increasingly common national occurrence; in 1914 the divorce rate reached 100,000 per year, and by 1925 it reached 205,000.[39] Wright's conclusion about this development was that people divorced for trivial reasons and should not have been allowed legally to separate so easily. The usual divorce, he argues, is "nothing more or less than a crime." The experience of one couple featured in the article is worth repeating here. This couple came in led by the wife, who was seeking the divorce. Wright saw a problem immediately, as the man was dressed rather shabbily while the woman was in "tawdry finery"—more fashionably dressed, but within her obviously limited means. The husband revealed that he was quite happy with his wife; he did not want the divorce and, in fact, could not understand why his wife wanted to end the marriage. When the woman spoke she revealed the source of her suffering: she was embarrassed by her husband's shabbiness, tired of the poverty they shared, and desirous of a better life. The proctor analyzed the situation and concluded that no divorce was necessary in this case. The woman had to straighten out and accept the fact that her husband was doing the best he could. Wright's final advice directed them to a much stronger commitment, for good or bad: they were to buy a house on the installment plan and start having children who, the author tells us, "bind married folks together."[40]

While this article is unique in this issue, it typifies an approach commonly taken in the *Ladies' Home Journal.* When marital woes were revealed, women were most often expected to find ways to make the marriage work, to change themselves somehow so that the marital partners could be both satisfied and satisfying. The advice given here promotes a more difficult economic situation for the couple. Had he encouraged the wife to get a job, the proctor might have helped solve her unhappiness as well as their economically unstable situation. One can conclude from the advice provided, however, that the woman's employment would pose a greater threat to the stability of the marriage than does her very real emotional discontent. Perhaps that is true, as an isolated and discontented woman may be less likely to make a change than would a somewhat more independent working woman. Elaine Tyler May, in a study of Los Angeles divorce records from 1920, found that women's jobs provided a frequent source of conflict in marriage and that work was a more common experience among women who divorced than among women as a whole.[41] The criticism of the woman's materialism provides another irony, since she largely followed the dictates of the magazine in wanting to wear even "tawdry" finery and in desiring a "better" life.

Regardless of the circumstances or the ironies of real life, in the *Journal,* at least, women held the responsibility for making things work—and making things work in traditional ways.

Even when advice articles did find fault with male behavior, as they occasionally did, there were no strict admonishments to the men as there were to the women. An article entitled "The Tired Business Man at the Theater" describes the likes, dislikes, and behavior of men at the theater. "Your tired business man wants facts, not fairies," Annie Russell tells us, referring to men's apparently genetic dislike of *A Midsummer Night's Dream.* The T.B.M., as she calls him, thinks all week and must be entertained, never challenged, when he is away from work. "To be candid," she writes, "the T.B.M. is mentally lazy." Apparently women who wanted to go to the theater had to accept this situation. They had to choose their plays to fit male expectations. "If one of the characters in the play should be a woman doctor, she must be caricatured," Russell argues. "A real, normal professional woman with charm of appearance and manner wouldn't be the real thing to him. Jews, Irishmen, suffragettes, professors, poets—all must represent old, stage-worn traditional types."[42] Apparently men could be counted on to leave their brains at the office. What, then, did they expect of the women they came home to? Most likely, this article suggests, they wanted little more than stereotypical, non-thinking females to cater to their non-thinking selves. The type of entertainment this T.B.M desired was readily available in the early twentieth century, when popular theater productions, which excluded people of color from the audience but exaggerated racial differences on stage, also relied heavily on ethnic and gender stereotypes.[43] Middle- and even working-class people spent more and more money on leisure pursuits in the 1910s and 1920s, but those outlets offered them little exposure to a broadly defined notion of America.[44]

The *Journal* was rich with information and advice of all kinds. As a forum it encouraged debate and reader response to many issues, including men, romance, family life, even religion.[45] For the most part, however, the magazine leaned toward advocating changes and promoting a way of life that was overwhelmingly middle class and decidedly conservative. This comes across obviously in the advertisements, with their visual appeal, but it is no less present in the editorial matter or fiction. Those outside the middle-class culture, including immigrants and African-Americans, are repeatedly depicted either as stereotypes or as individuals worthy of respect because of the ways in which they are the exceptions that prove the rule about people of their race or nationality. In the March 1914 edition, the first joke on the joke page makes fun of the "colored" way of talking, which seemingly also indicates an ignorant way of thinking.[46] In an article entitled "My Experiences with my Servants," Dorothea Pearson Greene relates the story of Katie Quinn, the Irish servant girl who came to work for her when Greene had been married for a year and a half and had a six-week-old baby daughter. A black-and-white drawing of a haggard looking young woman with a broom in one hand and a bucket in the other accompanies the article. Greene describes this young Katie as a good servant who performed her work well, went out only in the company of a woman friend, and came in early at night. One night the couple went out and left Katie with their daughter; when they returned they found her kneeling at the crib. "She had the Celtic genius for motherhood," Greene relates. Once they discovered that Katie had inherent tendencies toward childcare, they assigned her that task, and the baby grew more attached to Katie than to her own mother. This apparently caused no problems, although Katie did have one shortcoming: "Like many Irish peasant women Katie was long on love but short on discipline."

Eventually Katie became engaged but refused to marry and leave the family as long as Dorothea was ill. When the loyal Katie did finally marry, she had two babies herself, then became widowed when her husband was killed by a train. The Greenes decided to offer Katie a job again. They did this anticipating problems, as the two families of children would grow up together but be of different classes, and because Katie, although loyal, did have her faults. When Katie remarried and moved away the families lost touch. But nine years later Dorothea read in the newspaper that Katie's son had received a scholarship to prep school and remarked that her family "felt that Katie's boy had reflected credit on the family in winning that scholarship." One wonders what Katie's perspective would have been. Perhaps the Greenes fulfilled her stereotypes as well: a mother who didn't care for her own children, people who were short on love but long on discipline.[47]

Some of the fiction in the March 1914 issue of the *Ladies' Home Journal* explored class differences even more explicitly. "You and Me: A Story of Love that Moves Mountains" describes the lives of Molly and Lot, two immigrants. In this case the *Journal* functions as an advocate, declaring that there are ways to alleviate the stress of workplace struggles without resorting to violence or radical change. Molly and Lot both work in the Graves Garment Company, where they and their coworkers are seemingly all young and healthy, "fine and robust Swedes and Norwegians, ruddy Germans, and tall Americans."[48] Although Molly and Lot plan to marry and purchase a home, they find their daydreams overshadowed by workplace problems about which they cannot agree. The workers at Graves have asked for a ten-cent pay raise, which would bring their pay from eighty to ninety cents per day. When the owner complains of hard times and refuses the request, the workers plan to strike. Although Molly vocally supports the strike, the skeptical Lot remains silent at shop meetings. When they talk alone, Lot tells Molly that he wants to find another way to solve the conflict. The boss, he argues, probably does not realize he is cheating the workers. Molly reluctantly agrees to try Lot's plan to educate Mr. Graves about the workers' lives.

The following morning Lot convinces the other workers to try his idea out before they strike. They all walk to the boss' house on the birthday of his son, singing the birthday song. The son, these workers' contemporary but certainly not their peer, comes outside with his fiancé, and the boss trails behind. When the eighty workers finish singing, Lot explains their grievances in terms of how the lack of money affects them personally. Many of them want to marry but cannot without the additional income. The young Mr. Graves and his bride-to-be, obviously quite moved, declare that they will use their $10,000 wedding gift from the elder Mr. Graves to pay the workers the extra rate until things improve financially at the factory and the owner can handle the wage increase on his own. The workers leave but meet again to discuss the offer, which the young Mr. Graves has put in writing. Following Lot's lead, they unanimously vote not to take the money offered, and their return letter proves that these working-class women and men can act even more genteel than the wealthy Graves: "We, the undersigned, wish to express our deep gratitude to Mr. Lawrence Graves and his lady for what they have done. But we, the undersigned, don't feel we can take it of you, and we would rather wait a while longer and see if business don't improve."[49] When the boss receives this letter, even he breaks down and gives in. "Have your own way. Make dooks and duchesses out of 'em!" he argues. "But I'll be hanged if I understand this new generation."[50] The *Journal* wanted its readers to be part of a "new generation" of people who understood and accepted basic class differences but nevertheless looked for and found common ground.

In this and other articles, the *Journal* skirted the real issues that promised to alter the nation. Immigrants like Molly and Lot found their civil rights and their job opportunities threatened as the xenophobia of the teens brought on immigration restrictions in the twenties. Employers promised but rarely provided the new welfare capitalism like that described in Molly and Lot's story. Immigrants and African-Americans continued to meet barriers to full and adequate employment. Although the black population of the Northeast almost doubled between 1900 and 1920, few African-Americans found gainful employment. New job opportunities favored white, native-born citizens, and while women in that group entered white-collar jobs in growing numbers, black women found employment primarily in domestic service, where they replaced the white women workers. Class issues, mystified here in the *Journal*, continued to plague the majority of the nation's residents.[51]

The *Journal* promoted the notion that individuals could rise above both their own circumstances and the lures of a changing world. As a consequence, it often promised simple solutions to complex social problems. "My Pretty Young Daughter: A Young Girl's Dreams at 19 and How I Met Them: By Her Mother" is the story of Rusty, a nineteen-year-old who, once she gets hold of a best-selling novel, can do little else but read it. She barely leaves her bedroom although it is stifling hot. Rusty reluctantly joins the family to eat, only to run off to her book when she finishes supper. When her brothers ask her about her behavior Rusty tells them she is absorbed in a bestseller but only reluctantly admits that it is the same book banned at the local library. Rusty's mother says little but wonders about her daughter's choice. A friend and well-respected world traveler joins the family for supper the following night, and the subject of books comes up. The traveler lists the books he carries with him on his journeys: a bible, a biography, a history, a book of essays and one of verse, a book about photography, and a novel. When one of the brothers coyly asks if he had heard of Rusty's bestseller, the traveler laughs. Yes, he recalls, one of his shipmates had it and told him the plot as he went along. Once he had finished reading it, the man threw the book overboard, "But—it didn't make much of a splash." Convinced, Rusty buries the bestseller in the yard the next day.[52]

Although the reader never discovers the exact content of Rusty's bestseller, we do learn that, regardless of artistic merit, it makes for compelling reading. Rusty apparently found herself absorbed in a heavy dose of romance. It is interesting that this piece is included in an issue of the magazine for which the cover painting suggests the same kind of romance Rusty's story seems to warn against. The *Journal* even recognized the popularity of this artist's magazine covers, "none more so than the one used for this issue," and sold it as a poster.[53] While the *Journal* was perhaps never as blatant on the subject of romance as were best selling novels, the appeal to the sexual imagination of young women formed an aspect of the magazine that permeated not only the fiction but also the advertisements, and, occasionally, the advice. Rusty's story characterizes the magazine's tendency to promote a mixed message about women's sexual behavior.

Confusion about sexuality in the 1910s was not limited to the *Journal*, in particular, or even women's magazines in general. Sigmund Freud lectured in the United States in 1909, and by 1920 two hundred books had been published on his theories.[54] Scientific researchers as well as the popular press began to document the sexual practices of Americans young and old, and the young, as far as they could tell, represented the vanguard. Contemporary historian Frederick Lewis Allen observed that no mothers "had any idea how casually their daughters were accustomed to being kissed."[55] High school and college administrators joined parents in an attempt to swell the tide of young women's sexual activity, often presenting a double standard of women's and men's behavior. "While the emanations from the 'revolution in manners and morals' were clearly rocking the high school," writes Dorothy Brown, "it was equally clear that high school girls more than boys had the major responsibility for upholding propriety and safeguarding tradition."[56] In having difficulty determining safe or morally upstanding explorations of romance and sexuality, Rusty, like the young woman who sought advice about "familiarities" with men, was not alone.[57]

Advertisements, an important aspect of the *Journal* fiscally, also formed an important visual component of the magazine. In this particular issue, characteristic of the magazine's layout in the 1910s, the first quarter of the magazine contains few advertisements: the first 23 pages contain only two ads. The advertisements which appear in the early pages of issues of the *Journal* are generally either full-page ads or one-column, quarter-page ads. Visually exciting and often more technically advanced than the rest of the material in the magazine, these ads are appealing but not overwhelming in number. By the middle of the magazine, the advertisements become more numerous; two-to-a-page, one-column ads generally surround and frame the text. The end of the magazine contains significantly more advertisements per column and per page. In all, the 104-page issue contains 235 advertisements, with the vast majority placed in the back half of the magazine. Visually, advertisements form a more integral part of the magazine the further back one goes. This is satisfying for the reader, for the text on the earlier pages is more likely to have drawings that accompany it than is the later text, which is often simply the endings of articles and stories begun earlier on. Advertisements provide the visuals for the latter part of the magazine. Edward Bok was instrumental in making this policy of "tailing" fiction into advertising an industry standard.[58]

Already, by 1914, most of the large advertisements and a majority of the one-column ads promoted national brands, including Ivory Soap, Crisco, Jello, Grape Nuts, Welch's, Nestle, Kodak, Campbell's, Quaker Oats, and Kellogg's. Other products, such as Woodbury's, Pompeiaan, or Old Dutch, have lost the national reputation they once had. The advertisements consciously used the fact that they were national brands to signify quality and consistency, as does the Post Toasties message, "Anywhere in America."[59] Many of the smaller advertisements and virtually all of the one-inch column ads promoted more local products, including flower seeds, ostrich plumes for dusting, short story writing lessons, dress patterns, massage creams, and wedding announcements. Historian Susan Strasser, in her study of the development of the American mass market, found that by the early 1920s Americans were requesting brand names from their grocers. The rapid ascendancy of national advertising in the *Journal* certainly provided part of the consumer education and manipulation behind that development.[60]

The advertisements reveal the kind of reader the *Ladies' Home Journal* hoped to secure. Most assume that the purchaser is a mother who stays at home with her children. Perhaps she has a servant to help her occasionally with her household chores, but this reader is neither wealthy nor working-class. In a Wizard mop advertisement with the headline "Happy Housecleaning," a smiling woman sweeps her floor while her daughter dusts the piano in the background and her two younger children play on the floor in the foreground. A Quaker Oats ad, typical of food advertisements, features a recipe for the mother who is busy but who wants, nevertheless, to feed her children well. The only advertisement in this issue featuring a domestic worker shows her helping rather than replacing the woman as she serves Welch's grape juice at a child's birthday party.[61] The woman reader is assumed to be at home and have some discretionary income or, at least, be in training for the day when she will have a home and discretionary income. A Campbell's soup advertisement portrays a woman sitting in her automobile. The grocer comes out to take her order and she reminds him not to forget the Campbell's soup. Few readers of the *Journal,* few women at all, in fact, would have called the grocer to their car to take an order. And, arguably, few women who could have afforded such a luxury would have purchased pre-made soups: they would have had their servants prepare soups at home. This advertisement demonstrates the very real appeal that wealth could have for readers at any income level. Another ad that urges women to consume in line with or above their incomes is a full-page, color advertisement for Pompeiaan massage cream. "Shun cheaply made imitations," the ad cautions.[62]

Along with an assumption that women had real or hoped for discretionary income, the advertisements in the March 1914 *Ladies' Home Journal* reveal other popular tactics used by advertisers. Whether the appeal was to status, beauty, economy, motherhood, or any number of other issues, the advertisements recognized women's roles in the society and promised to make those roles more equitable, exciting, romantic, fulfilling. In short, the advertisements promised to meet women's inarticulate longings. The Welch's grape juice ad mentioned earlier appealed to status: women who could afford servants bought Welch's. A Woodbury's facial soap advertisement appealed to women's sense of beauty: with Woodbury's they could counteract all the negative effects of the environment on their skin. This Woodbury's advertisement includes an appeal that has long been associated with the later ads of the 1920s decade—avoiding the evils of bacteria and germs: "It is no exaggeration to describe the streets as slums from the bacterial point of view. Bacteria exist everywhere. They are carried into the pores of your skin with every particle of dust, soot and grime. They become active and produce their evil effects the moment the resistive powers of your skin are weakened."[63]

Woodbury's Soap could help keep bacteria away and preserve women's beauty. The struggle for beauty, however, was an ongoing one, and even as early as the 1910s, women could not afford to slip up. New cosmetic products found their way to the market, and each promised enhanced beauty, sustained youth, and the undying attentions of men. And dangers in the air threatened not only women but also their babies and, hence, women's abilities to serve as good mothers. A Nestle formula advertisement tells how it is "dangerous business" to be a baby. The text illustrates the double appeal to cleanliness and proper motherhood: "Dangerous indeed when we see the tiny bodies menaced by dirty dairies, by sick cows, by ignorance, by disease; and dangerous indeed when we know that one baby out of six last year died."[64] In an era in which infant mortality loomed high, advertisers targeted women rather than milk producers, the national government, or the medical establishment as the responsible parties. Standards of womanhood rose as products proliferated. At the turn of the century women felt that they provided adequate care for their children if they kept them fed, clean, and dry. Over the course of the next thirty years, however, standards rose and women found that they had to be more attentive than ever—all the while maintaining youthful standards of beauty for themselves. Motherhood was

Happy Housecleaning!

This year, housecleaning loses all its old-time drudgery and discomfort. Three things make it all easier and happier:

The **Wizard Triangle Mop**—the mop that "gets-in-the-corners"—brings every out-of-the-way place within easy reach.

Wizard Polish gives an added newness to furniture and woodwork in half the time required by old-fashioned methods.

And while the work is being done, the children are enjoying themselves with the wonderful "Wizzikin" Theatre which delights them for hours at a time.

Read on and learn of this three-fold efficiency and comfort.

WIZARD
Triangle Polish Mop
The Mop that "Gets-in-the-Corners"

Reaches everywhere—to nearby corners, corners under beds and tables, to tops of doors and high moldings. Reaches and beautifies all in one short, easy sweep. Fine for polished floors as well as for oilcloth and linoleums.

Has a "Human Elbow"

Handle now made with a "human elbow" which sets mop at any desired angle instantly for any cleaning need. Mop comes already treated. Does not make floors oily and slippery. The 11,154 mop ends pick up all dust and restore the original finish to floors and woodwork as you go along.

Price $1.50

Sold by over fifty thousand dealers. If unable to get one, send us $1.50 and we will see that you are immediately supplied. Also obtainable in chemically treated form, especially adapted for use on wax floors.

Has a 54 inch Adjustable Handle.

WIZARD POLISH
"More Than a Furniture Polish"

Removes dust, finger marks, blemishes and scratches. Makes everything bright and new as you dust with it. No shaking. No special directions. No objectionable varnish odor.

Secret Oriental Oil

This scientific ingredient for which we send eleven thousand miles gives that hard, dry, lustrous finish you like to see on your furniture.

It is this ingredient that makes WIZARD POLISH a varnish food—that keeps finest finishes from cracking and checking.

It is this that keeps your good furniture at its best all the time, without fear that some day the dainty finish will be marred by some harsh polish made only for *temporary* beauty.

Many sizes. 25c up. Read the WIZZIKIN Theatre offer and learn of the prize that any bottle brings you.

WIZZIKIN THEATRE
2 Acts   8 Characters
Transformation Scene

Read How To Get It

This real working model of a real theatre will make a big hit with the children. Size 9 x 12 in.

It has two fine acts and one grand transformation scene. The eight characters are Miss Busybee, her mother and brother, and a band of five WIZZIKIN fairies from the moon. Theatre beautifully lithographed in 8 colors.

Wonderful Tricks

The Wizzikins do many wonderful tricks. Their antics will delight the children for hours at a time.

Send us the coupon found in any carton of Wizard Polish, and the small sum it calls for in stamps or silver, and the theatre and a fine 20-page book of Wizzikin verses go to you without further cost. Unless you send the coupon you must send $1. The theatre cannot be bought for less anywhere.

Do it now. Get the WIZARD POLISH today. If you can't get it, write us. Price of mop and polish the same in Canada as in the United States.

WIZARD PRODUCTS COMPANY, Inc., 1475 West 37th St., CHICAGO, ILL.

The happy housekeeper, as much an ideal promoted by advertisers as she was a natural development in the rising middle class, used aids like this mop with a "human elbow" to help her complete her housework. (*Ladies' Home Journal*, March 1914, p. 59) no mean feat, increasingly dependent as it was on correct consumer behavior.

Other advertisements addressed overworked women or appealed to their need to economize in the home. From Hormel hams to Wizard mops, advertisers promised women an easier time of things at home. To attract and ideally secure customers, the vast majority of the advertisements in the March 1914 *Ladies' Home Journal* offered free or cheap trial offers. Readers simply clipped the corner coupon, filled it in, and sent it with six, eight, or ten cents worth of stamps or coins to receive the sample. At times advertisers offered more: the Wizard mop ad mentioned above offered a toy theater for a dollar or free with a coupon from a Wizard product. Young children could use the theater to assist the main character, Miss Busybee, with her home-making responsibilities.[65]

Virtually all of the women depicted in these advertisements are white, fair-skinned and fair-haired, young, and lovely. The only example of African-Americans used in ads in this issue is for Gold Dust Twins, a well-known example of stereotypes in advertising. "Let the Gold Dust Twins do your work," the ad declares, as the literally black naked babies appear overjoyed to do any housework available.[66] When advertisements in this month's *Journal* feature domestic servants, their dress is the only feature that distinguishes them from their employers; even they are white and appear healthy, young, and middle class. When *Journal* advertisements in the 1910s and 1920s occasionally featured black women as domestic servants, their exaggerated features, physical distance, and averted look reflected cultural stereotypes. As a result of these depictions, the white women in the drawings and, arguably, the white women readers, found definition as much by not being black as by being young and middle class. The advertisements in this issue of the *Journal*, along with the advice and the fiction, depicted a comfortable, sensible, middle-class life, the world of women who were members of this class or aspired to it. They favored reforms based on common sense, bought products to help them live a clean, genteel life, and made life choices that mirrored the choices of their mothers perhaps even more closely than they would have liked to admit.

In an era in which Anglo-Americans freely promoted racial and ethnic stereotypes, advertising followed suit. Popular leisure time activities of the day included minstrel shows that demeaned African-Americans and vaudeville shows built on ethnic stereotypes. A 1911 *Journal* comic strip for children was titled "The Snowmen and the Pickaninnies." An article about eugenics warned of bad blood invading the nation, described the good blood of Pennsylvania, where followers of William Penn lived, and argued the necessity to weed out those who could not trace good blood through the generations.[67] During the first six months of 1918, blacks were featured on the jokes page in four of the six issues. A Cream of Wheat advertisement in 1921, featured on the inside cover of the magazine, showed a gray-haired African-American man pulling a boy along in a cart. "Giddyap," the boy yelled as he struck a whip to the old man.[68]

The *Ladies' Home Journal* of the early twentieth century was said to reach "an ideal type of home."[69] Although the ideal was based on purchasing power, dollars alone did not provide one with membership in the group. Race and ethnicity figured as prominently as income in determining who was included and who was left out. "Bridget" and "Dinah," names used most frequently in the *Journal* to depict Irish immigrant and African-American women respectively, had no place in the magazine's definition of womanhood. For the first three decades of the century and, arguably, far beyond, as the *Journal* limited its scope to native-born Anglo-Americans, it participated in what scholars in a variety of disciplines are calling the social construction of whiteness.[70] In a changing and volatile world, the whiteness offered by the *Ladies' Home Journal* and other popular magazines may have been as therapeutic to readers as were the individual advertisements the magazines housed.

It would be unlikely that, in such a climate of racism and ethnocentrism, a popular women's magazine interested primarily in women's consumer abilities would address injustices against particular groups of Americans. Nevertheless, the way in which the magazine overwhelmingly presented domestic help as white is telling. African-American women migrated north in tremendous numbers during this time period. They had no choice but to fill the jobs that white women left for pink-collar or industrial jobs, and those remaining jobs were, most often, in domestic service. Between 1900 and 1930, the number of white native-born domestics fell by 40 percent; at the same time, the number of black domestics rose by 43 percent.[71] These numbers are not reflected either in the advertising or the editorial matter of the *Journal.* Roland Marchand, in a study of advertising during this period, found that white women outnumbered black women as maids by more than ten to one.[72] The only *Journal* articles indicating that white women and black women had any contact during this twenty-year period were "12 Presents for Stout Colored Women," which repeated the stereotypes of the Mammy so

Images of white domestic servants mirrored closely the images of their employers; these domestic servants were consumers-in-waiting. In this ad, the two women smile as they share an activity. (*Ladies' Home Journal*, February 1918, p. 80)

HOW TO MAKE EVEN ORDINARY COTTON GOODS
LOOK AND FEEL LIKE LINEN

THE new and easy method of making all wash garments and household fabrics look and feel like linen is simply to starch with Linit, the remarkable new starch.

Linit is entirely different from any starch you have ever used. When ready for use, your Linit mixture is thin and free running like water. When you dip your fabrics into this Linit mixture, Linit instantly penetrates every thread. This fastens back into place all loosening bits of thread fibre and lint. Each thread strengthens with Linit and the life of your garments is thereby prolonged. You'll notice, too, that your ironing is much easier

Linit restores to all fabrics that soft, cool, pliable finish you admire in new goods at the store.

Once you starch with Linit, you will never go back to old-fashioned starches.

IMPORTANT NOTICE

Every effort is being made to supply grocers our only distributors, throughout the country. If your grocer cannot supply you with LINIT, send in this coupon and we will send you by return mail prepaid, the amount of LINIT you desire.

CORN PRODUCTS REFINING CO.
DEPT 12, ARGO, ILLINOIS

Enclosed is _____ ¢ for which please send me _____ full size 10¢ packages of Linit. [Enclose 10¢ for each package Linit desired]

NAME

ADDRESS

TOWN

GROCER'S NAME

Images of African-American domestic servants contrasted greatly with images of their employers; black women were not depicted as potential consumers. In this ad, the black servant smiles, yet she is literally blocked out of the space occupied by the two white women. (*Ladies' Home Journal*, September 1924, p. 107) prevalent in the culture during this time, and a cartoon in which a white woman's wishes come true and "Mammy" takes a cut in pay and agrees to stay for life—a not-so-subtle allusion to slavery.[73]

The advertisements and editorial pieces depicting the lives of domestic workers offered not only a "whitened" picture but also a distorted picture of the work involved. Most women who had a choice stayed away from domestic work because of the difficulty of the work and the loss of control over one's personal life it entailed. The physical comfort of domestic workers was an afterthought for most employers; Dorothy and Carl Schneider report that live-in domestics slept "on ironing boards propped over bathtubs, on mattresses laid over basement washtubs, on pallets spread on dining-room tables."[74] The fear of and experience of sexual harassment also caused many women to prefer factory jobs to domestic work: "The dark satanic mills did not look nearly so dark or so satanic," writes historian Ruth Schwartz Cowan, "to young women who knew what it was like to work in some of America's dark satanic kitchens."[75] The *Journal* glorified "homemaking" for two classes of women: those who purchased the magazine and those employed in the readers' kitchens and homes.

In the *Journal*, as in the culture, some things changed enormously in the course of a decade while others changed little if at all. On first glance, the *Ladies' Home Journal* of 1924 looks more similar to than different from the *Journal* of 1914. Service remained the key, and women's roles as family members, homemakers, and consumers received a great deal of attention. The reader of 1924, however, did encounter a different magazine than had her counterpart ten years earlier, as the definition of "service" had changed significantly. Although the *Journal* of 1924 continued to provide its readers with a combination of editorial matter, fiction, and advertisements, both the mixture of those elements and the larger message changed significantly in the course of ten years, influencing the directions of middle-class women's lives and the culture's definition of womanhood in lasting ways.

The cover of the August 1924 edition points to two changes in the business end of the *Ladies' Home Journal* between the teen years and the twenties. The color drawing features two Chinese children sitting on a couch watching a bird in a cage. The vibrant colors of the children's clothing and the setting would not have been possible in the teen years. Advancements in color printing in the 1920s allowed significant improvements in the appearance of the *Journal*, particularly with the advertisements but with the covers and editorial matter as well. New colors and printing techniques provided a more true-to-life depiction of people, objects, colors, and textures. The magazine had also taken on even more of a global market. In addition to the cities and countries mentioned in 1914, the 1924 *Journal* had expanded further, reaching almost every continent. The magazine was now shipped out not only from Philadelphia but from twelve other cities as well. While the majority of the features in the *Journal* of the twenties continued to reflect primarily the experience of women in the United States, women from other nations occasionally found their way into the magazine, and the marketing agenda of this clearly multinational enterprise became increasingly evident and celebrated.[76] This development mirrored changes in the advertising industry, which made tremendous headway during the 1920s into Europe and Latin America, translating both advertising copy and American equations of the gendered nature of consumption into other languages and other contexts.[77]

The August 1924 *Journal* reveals a significant format change from the earlier decade. The editorial presence, clear and strong in the opening pages of the March 1914 edition, has become less so by 1924. The editor no longer claims a "personal page," and the editorial page does not appear until page twenty. Part of this may be attributed to personal style, as Bok had retired in 1919 and been replaced by Barton Currie, who commanded less of

This advertisement promised that mothers "of almost every race" fed their children Quaker, yet the drawings that accompanied the text feature children of various ethnicities but only one race. (*Ladies' Home Journal,* March 1913, p. 69)

a presence in the magazine. Nevertheless, it is significant that the reader first encounters, rather than the masthead and an editorial presence, advertising. Not only the inside cover, but pages one and two contain, in fact, full-page advertisements. Even the table of contents, which had almost always come early in the issue and which reflected editorial directives, has been moved to the back of the magazine, as has the jokes page. These changes indicate the continued and growing importance of advertising to the magazine's business. They also suggest, however, the degree to which advertising could become an editor's cultural program. The editor's job was to steer women in their proper direction, and that direction increasingly came to be dictated by advertisers, whose visually appealing and ideologically sophisticated messages had become the opening and, arguably, the central message of the *Ladies' Home Journal.*

All of this is not to say that the editorial presence in the *Journal* was completely subsumed by advertising. The editorial comes as late as page twenty, but when it comes it is forceful. Barton Currie presents one long rather than many short editorials. This one, "The Filth Uplifters," argues that women need to clean up their communities, which have been overrun by filth, in this case filthy magazines read by minors. The editorial suggests that women do have a social role to perform other than motherhood and other than a consumer role, but again, they are to act in the name of motherhood and for the youth of the nation. Following the editorial page, "The Rising Tide of Voters" highlights the efforts of the League of Women Voters and encourages women to register to vote and to become politically involved in their communities. It discusses the failure of women to change things radically in their first national election and counsels them to focus instead on grassroots work. The article makes a clear argument that politics is, on all levels, women's work.[78] There seems to be a more marked awareness in 1924 than in 1914 that women desired and excelled in activities that took them away from the home or the grocery store. Since women had won the vote four years earlier, these positive comments cannot simply be attributed to an immediate post-suffrage enthusiasm for women's political opportunities. Instead, they indicate a partial editorial acceptance of changes that had been taking place in women's consciousness and in their lives. Of course, this homemaking magazine features few articles of this type in any issue in the 1920s, continuing to focus primarily on women's roles in the home.

Another article in this issue furthers the notion that political action could complement rather than threaten women's roles at home. "The Technic of

Being a Club Woman," by Alice Ames Winter, explains, defends, and encourages participation in women's clubs. She states that women's clubs provide a place for women to go to "get things done," not simply to gossip and model new fashions. But like writers ten years earlier, Ames provides a careful context for her discussion of women's broader sphere: club work, she argues, reflects home-based values and forms "one more expression of that mother instinct."[79] While the *Journal* of 1924 appears at first glance to be more supportive of women's political work in terms of the number of articles addressing women's political participation, it continues to emphasize those political activities that complement women's traditional roles as wives and mothers. In this way it offers no radical departure from the *Journal* of 1914; women could have other interests as long as their homes and families came first. In the early twentieth-century debate over women's essential difference from or similarity to men, the *Journal* clearly favored women's innate differences from men and their natural ties to the home.[80]

An important change in the *Journal*'s editorial matter by 1924 is the new emphasis placed on young women. The college girl becomes an important subject and target audience of the *Journal* of the 1920s. This is no surprise, as the numbers of women attending college increased dramatically in the early twentieth century. In 1900, 85,000 women attended college; in 1920, the figure was 283,000, and in 1930, 481,000. These women represented only 10 percent of all American women ages 18 to 21 in 1930, but by the early 1920s they represented an increasing segment of the *Journal*'s reading public.[81] Although the *Journal* only indirectly singled out college women as consumers in the pages of the magazine, it may well have pointed out their purchasing power to potential advertisers.[82]

The August 1924 edition of the *Journal* contains five articles addressing the college girl and her mother, including "A Hat From Paris for Every College Girl," and "Lingerie for the College Girl and Her Admiring Younger Sister." One of these articles recognizes a generational change that some feminists of the day might have lamented: the college girl of 1924 demonstrated a greater interest in fashion than did her "maiden aunts" who went to the seven sisters colleges "back in the days when a 'college woman' was by tradition either neatly masculine or carelessly eccentric in her costumes." College girls, we learn, are everywhere in the nation in 1924, not just in New England. One article provides a chart of four groups and kinds of colleges, from the Far West to the South, and features the fashions most popular in each region and at each kind of college.[83] These articles point to generational differences among educated women of the late nineteenth and early twentieth centuries. The older women, those whom Carroll Smith-Rosenberg calls the first generation of New Women, were viewed by the second generation as frumpy, even sexually repressed, women. Rather than receiving acknowledgment for their valuable accomplishments, these women found themselves labeled the enemy of the younger generation.[84] The consumer culture provided one of the important divisions among these women, as the younger women more clearly felt and responded to its pull.

A *Harper's* article in 1927, for example, outlined the feminists' "new style" and "old style." Old-style feminists cared less for fashions and opted for career rather than family. The new-style feminist wanted it all; she was a "pal" to men, a "good dresser," and decidedly committed to career, marriage, and children.[85] In other contexts, younger feminists berated not only the lack of fashion sense but the ethics of the older generation. One college woman, summing up the new philosophy, argued, "We're not going to suffer over how the other half lives." They organized not for social causes but for personal freedom. A celebrated victory among Wellesley students, for example, was the right to attend movies unchaperoned and go for automobile rides on Sundays and early in the evenings.[86] The discussions and deliberations about such generational differences was more toned down in the *Journal* than elsewhere, but the younger, more fashion conscious women in the magazine made an interesting connection between freedom and consumer choices.

Although the *Journal* of 1924 recognizes women's increased access to education, it is less sensitive to their economic needs than was the *Journal* of 1914. While true that twice as many small advertisements promote ways for women to earn money through nursing, decorating candlesticks, knitting, dressmaking, or running a tea room, fewer editorial pieces acknowledge that women are economically needy. In March of 1914, for example, nine articles addressed women's need to economize or to earn money. These ranged from "For the Housewife Who Wants to Economize" to "The Economical Dress With the Smart Touch." In August of 1924, however, one fashion article plus the three Curtis Company advertisements soliciting part-time women workers constitute the extent of the magazine's acknowledgment of women's economic concerns. In ten years the *Ladies' Home Journal* has become no more attentive and, in fact, arguably less attentive to the economic realities of women's lives.[87] The composite middle-class woman, defined more and more by spending rather than by earning, has become even more central to the magazine's definition of its readership.

The *Journal* of 1924 is less attentive to women's lives in other ways as well. With forty additional pages, the magazine has fewer advice or informational columns than did the 1914 issue. There are no articles about furnishing, cleaning, or maintaining the home. The first of six articles about food, "We Like to Stuff Our Vegetables," comes as late as page 96. "Ask the Ladies' Home Journal," the listing of advice givers and their topics, which had been a popular and free feature of the magazine in the teens decade, has been replaced by a much shorter list, each requiring a fee of between five and fifty cents.[88] The notion of service in the *Journal* has changed in a fundamental way; the 1924 issue increasingly depends upon the advertisements rather than its paid writers to provide readers with the advice they need to negotiate a continually changing world. This is the most substantial and far-reaching change in the *Ladies' Home Journal* in these two decades. Interestingly enough, it is not in number that the advertisements become a more significant part of this magazine; there were nearly twice as many ads in the 1914 issue as in the 1924 issue. The important changes regarding the advertisements instead involve quality, size, position, and message. Full-color, full-page advertisements predominate, as all ads make their way from the back of the magazine to the front. Just as the layout of department stores became standardized, with bargains in the basement, furniture on the top floor, and women's items in central locations, the *Journal* became standardized, with the editorial and the advice columns moving further to the back and advertisements moving further to the front. By 1924, advertisements had begun to monopolize the service role of the magazine.[89]

In the teens decade, it was not unusual for an editor to comment on or include pieces of readers' letters. The March 1914 issue contained "What Other Women Have Found Out About Economy in the Kitchen." In the 1924 issue, however, it is the Lever Brothers advertisement for Lux soap that fulfills that role. Mrs. Margaret Lewis, from the laundering department at Lever Brothers, includes quotes from readers' letters from Brooklyn and from Springfield, Massachusetts. Her signature accompanies the ad, much as editorial writers' signatures had regularly accompanied their advice columns.[90] In another instance, a Cavalier Furniture ad tells women how they can furnish their homes on a fixed budget, much as the advice writer had counseled readers how to furnish a home for $300 in the March 1914 edition, and an Armstrong Linoleum advertisement features Mrs. Wright, former president of the Interior Decorator's League of New York. In the ad, rather than in an advice column, Mrs. Wright provides advice about how to use, decorate with,

September, 1925 · *The Ladies'* HOME JOURNAL

JUNIOR PROM NIGHT AT COLLEGE
We interviewed nearly two thousand girls at Smith, Bryn Mawr, Wellesley, and Barnard on the kind of soap they use for the care of the skin. Their answers brought out the fact that Woodbury's enjoys more than double the popularity of any other soap among these young college girls.

Four Hundred & Fifteen Girls at WELLESLEY and BARNARD
tell why they are using this soap for their skin

This Treatment will keep a sensitive skin smooth and soft —

She is one of the most charming things America has produced—the American college girl.

No other country has a type that at all compares with her. Eager, fearless, inquisitive—naïve, and at the same time self-possessed—joyously alive in mind, nerve, body—she has the flavor of America itself, a fresher, keener flavor than one finds in older countries.

HOW does the American college girl take care of that smooth, clear skin of hers? What soap does she use? Why does she choose it? What qualities about it especially appeal to her?

To get their own individual answers to these questions, we conducted an investigation among nearly two thousand college girls at Wellesley, Barnard, Smith, and Bryn Mawr.

Nearly two thousand college girls answer our questions

Of 804 girls at Wellesley and Barnard, more than half were Woodbury users. The rest showed a wide scattering of selection over 51 different brands of soap.

At Smith and Bryn Mawr, out of 927 girls, 520 said they were using Woodbury's Facial Soap. Four hundred and seven girls used other brands of soap, their choice ranging over 56 different kinds.

Why is it that among these nearly two thousand college girls at Smith, Bryn Mawr, Wellesley, and Barnard Woodbury's enjoys more than double the popularity of any other soap?

Their answers, in their own words

The girls themselves answer the question—

"The only soap that doesn't irritate my skin."

"Seems to agree with my skin better than other soaps do."

"Keeps my skin in better condition than any other soap I have used."

"After trying other soaps, Woodbury's seemed to be the only one that helped me. Other soaps irritated my skin."

These were characteristic comments, repeated in varying language, over and over again.

Six hundred and forty-four girls spoke of the purity of Woodbury's Facial Soap, or its soothing non-irritating effect on their skin.

Many girls told at length how Woodbury's had helped them to overcome undesirable skin conditions and to gain a clear, flawless complexion.

Thirteen girls said they were using Woodbury's at the recommendation of their physician.

Dip a soft washcloth in warm water and hold it to face. Do this several times. Then make a light warm water lather of Woodbury's Facial Soap and dip your cloth in it until the cloth is "fluffy" with the white lather. Rub this lathered cloth gently over your skin until the pores are thoroughly cleansed. Rinse the face lightly with clear cool water and dry carefully.

Why Woodbury's is unique in its effect on the skin

A skin specialist worked out the formula by which Woodbury's is made. This formula not only calls for absolutely pure ingredients. It also demands greater refinement in the manufacturing process than is commercially possible with ordinary toilet soap. In merely handling a cake of Woodbury's one notices this extreme fineness.

Around each cake of Woodbury's Facial Soap is wrapped a booklet containing special cleansing treatments for overcoming common skin defects. Get a cake of Woodbury's today, and begin tonight, the treatment your skin needs!

A 25c cake of Woodbury's lasts a month or six weeks.

FREE—A guest size set, containing the new, large-size trial cake of Woodbury's Facial Soap, and samples of Woodbury's Facial Cream and Facial Powder.

THE ANDREW JERGENS CO.,
101 Spring Grove Ave., Cincinnati, Ohio

Please send me FREE
The new large-size trial cake of Woodbury's Facial Soap, samples of Woodbury's Facial Cream and Facial Powder, and the treatment booklet, "A Skin You Love to Touch."

If you live in Canada, address The Andrew Jergens Co., Limited, 109 Sherbrooke St., Perth, Ont. English Agents: Quelch & Gambles, Ltd., Blackfriars Road, London, S. E. 1.

Name.....................

Street.....................

City..................... State.....................

Cut out the coupon and send it today!

College girls became a new target market as well as an important symbol for advertisers in the 1920s. (*Ladies' Home Journal*, September 1925, p. 35)

complement, clean, and wax a linoleum floor—an Armstrong linoleum floor. Sunkist Lemons provides seven recipes for salad dressings, just as a columnist had provided thirty-eight ways to use ham a decade earlier, and a Swan's Down Cake Flour ad provides instructions on baking a cake. Other advertisements provide information services: an Odorono deodorant ad tells what makes a flapper a flapper, and a Cutex ad provides step-by-step instructions for a manicure. Finally, articles about how to save time and energy in the kitchen have been replaced by ads as well: Beech Nut canned foods and Hoover electric vacuums describe the ways in which their expertise will aid the housewife. Health columns have been replaced by advertisements for products, like Post Bran Flakes, which includes a mother's note about the product, or Johnson & Johnson Baby Powder, which relates how wise mothers follow the lead of physicians and nurses in purchasing this brand. Although the advertisers by no means completely take over the role of the advice giver, in one decade they have made significant inroads in defining themselves as the experts.[91]

This process developed most completely with what had been an enormously important element of the magazine: recipes. In the teen years, advertisers caught on to the idea of advertising food products near recipes that required those products. Such a practice, according to the authors of an early text on advertising, meant "obviously approaching the maximum of suggestion." Highlighting labor saving devices in women's magazines, they continued, "comes very close to the acme of periodical media efficiency."[92] By the late twenties, the *Journal* had not only mastered such page engineering but had gone a great deal further. Loring Schuler, the editor of the *Journal* following Barton Currie, gave an uncharacteristically revealing talk at the J. Walter Thompson Advertising Agency. The *Journal* used to see itself primarily as a service vehicle, he stated. However, with the advent of modern advertising, they had to take a different approach. One example of this was with recipes. At one time, the *Journal* published many recipes, but they ended this practice. "When we continue to run any vast number of recipes," he explained, "we are simply putting ourselves into direct competition with our own advertisers which, I think, is very bad business."[93] The August 1924 issue offers none of that bad business. The few food related articles complement, rather than compete with, advertisements. One such article, "Let a Salad Make the Meal," is followed ten pages later by a Kraft cheese advertisement, entitled "Speaking of Salads." As Ellen McCracken has described for women's magazines of the 1980s, the advertisements appear as natural extensions of the editorial matter rather than interruptions to it. As early as the 1920s, advertisers provided a "service" to magazine readers, and the service of the *Ladies' Home Journal* began to evolve and revolve around the needs and directives of advertising.[94]

The scope of the advertisements was not limited, however, to topics for which there had been or continued to be editorial advice available. One development in advertising content, which most likely represented a strong economy as well as a growing cultural role for women, was an increased emphasis on home decorating. Wallpapers and linoleum featured prominently in advertisements in the 1924 issue.[95] Ads also increasingly featured convenience foods, particularly canned foods such as Beech Nut canned spaghetti or Campbell's soups. The international scope of the magazine was emphasized in these ads, which showed pineapples in Hawaii or, in a double-page advertisement, Lux soap around the world. Leisure activities also received more attention in 1924 than they had in 1914. A full-page ad for Paramount Pictures, an often-encountered ad in the *Journal* of the 1920s, lists forty new films and many famous actors, including Gloria Swanson and Rudolph Valentino.[96] Not surprisingly, automobile advertisements figured more prominently in this issue as well. This change reflects not only the increased importance of automobiles in U.S. society but also the increased attention to a new target market for those automobiles: women. The first woman to secure a driver's license in the United States did so in 1911. By 1914, Ford had produced half a million cars, and manufacturers recognized that women both influenced and made automobile purchasing decisions.[97] They also recognized women's inarticulate longings for independence and status and quickly figured the American automobile as a symbol of the fulfillment of such longings.[98] Women, in fact, consciously used the automobile as a symbol of their increasingly public role in the late teens and twenties. As early as 1913, Olive Schultz operated the first woman-owned taxi service, a sort of shuttle service for suffragists and other women; in 1914, a group of suffragists led by activist Crystal Eastman promoted the hiring of women as automobile salespersons; and in 1915, expert mechanic Wilma Russey became the first woman to make a living driving a taxi in New York City.[99] Thus, the symbolism of the automobile was not only imposed on women in women's magazines; women also deliberately used it themselves to define womanhood as more free and more mobile.

Finally, advertisements that appealed to the growing youth market were far more prominent in 1924 than they had been in 1914. An Odorono deodorant advertisement describes interview results with two hundred flappers, an emergent youth subculture. A full-page color ad for a hairnet, entitled "A Hint to the Bobbed," obviously appeals to the younger woman rather than the housewife and mother.[100] One aspect of these ads remains a constant over time, however: the appeal to status and the assurance of middle-class respectability through proper consumption. The women featured in the ads still appear fairly young, and all but one domestic servant, featured in a small soap ad, are white and seemingly middle class, and conform to traditional standards of beauty. Advertisers deliberately tried to associate their products with the up-and-coming, if not the privileged. A Beech Nut advertisement goes so far as to describe the canning factory in such a way as not to offend the middle-class sensibilities of the *Journal* readers: ". . . a pleasant sight and always open to visitors during working hours. The little valley town swept by pure air from the foothills of the Adirondack mountains—the glowing sunlight flooding the white workrooms—and above everything else the vigorous native-born Beech Nut workers—it is a picture to carry away and remember."[101]

The fiction in the August 1924 edition of the *Journal*, like the editorial matter, did not differ radically from that found in the 1914 issue. More than one story documented the female world of sacrifice and love. Romance, that vexed issue for Edward Bok, comes up again in several stories, one of which tells of a young couple who discovers that their ancestors had been lovers; they too fall in love through their correspondence. Another, "Miss Miggs of Monte Carlo," hints more strongly at sensuality. Miss Miggs, a forty-something-year-old spinster, decides to go to Monte Carlo on a vacation. "Things could happen," her friends warn her. Miss Miggs lets on, however, that she wants things to happen! The relatively independent Miss Miggs does have a series of adventures with men on her travels, although the author hints at rather than discusses the amorous nature of the relationships. Fictional pieces emphasize middle-class values as well: one explores the shallow values of the wealthy and the solid values of the middle class. Stories celebrate the female world but also intimate that that women's world is enormously enhanced by the presence and attentions of men.[102] On the surface this fiction appears to emphasize only the middle-class values typical of the rest of the *Journal*. A closer reading, however, which occurs in a later chapter, explores how the *Journal*'s fiction also reveals some of the shortcomings of the middle-class agenda.

The most significant changes from the 1914 issue to the 1924 issue have to do with the placement and importance of the advertisements. Advertisers lured women into the world of consumption, and the *Journal* facilitated this cultural process. It did so by providing not simply a series of advertisements but instead an appealing combination of advertisements, advice, and fiction—a winning combination of features that worked together both to further promote consumer roles for women in the modern world and to ensure that women's ability to consume, rather than any other similarities or differences

TOURING

$495

f.o.b Toledo

Women Do Value
Mechanical Excellence

Women everywhere favor Overland because women everywhere have a sharp eye, a good ear and an unerring sixth sense in matters of value. In these modern days, the daughters of Eve are as car-knowing as the sons of Adam!

With true feminine insight, women see greater safety in the Overland touring car's *all-steel* body —and appreciate the enduring beauty of its baked-enamel finish. In all phases and features of Overland engineering, women see the certainty of greater reliability—therefore, *greater pleasure and less worry.*

Women thrill to the power of the big Overland engine as keenly as any man—and enjoy the cradled sensation of comfort yielded by Overland's *patented* Triplex Springs—and have absolute confidence in the steadfast sturdiness of

the big Overland axles—(tough Mo-lyb-den-um shafts fortified by Timken and New Departure bearings). *All's well on any road!*

Then there are the many easy-driving conveniences—the dependable Auto-Lite starting and lighting system—the enclosed disc-type clutch— the handiness of brake and gear shift levers—the easy-parking wheelbase.

Finally, all the Overland economies—in upkeep, gasoline, oil, tires, everything—appeal to a woman's inborn desire to save. When you total up the benefits and superiorities of Overland it is clear as crystal why owners call Overland the most automobile in the world for the money.

As a personal car for everyday use and pleasure, Overland has won its way into a warm corner in the hearts of American women.

Other Overland Models: Chassis $391, Roadster $495, Coupe-Sedan $595, Business Coupe $650, Blue Bird $725, Sedan $795, Speed Commercial Car $623; all prices f.o. b. Toledo. *We reserve the right to change specifications or prices without notice.*

WILLYS-OVERLAND, INC., TOLEDO, OHIO · WILLYS-OVERLAND SALES CO. LTD., TORONTO, CANADA

Automobile advertisers recognized women's longings for autonomy and social identity and promised the "daughters of Eve" that equality with the "sons of Adam" could be measured, perhaps, on the open road. (*Ladies' Home Journal*, August 1924, p. 45)

---

among women, would define their lives. And as the years passed and other groups of women entered the consumer culture, they too would find themselves defined along these same lines and by these same limits established early in the century. The following three chapters explore in detail the first ingredient in the *Journal*'s recipe for defining womanhood: advice.

48

two

Housekeeping

*The Greatest Business
in the World*

$\mathcal{T}$he editorial matter in the *Ladies' Home Journal* during the 1910s and 1920s urged women to accept modern roles and responsibilities while they held on to the traditional feminine qualities that were supposedly innate and timeless. Women's roles in their homes and communities, their entrance into the worlds of fashion and beauty, their relationships with husbands and children, their attempts at upward mobility—all of these topics were within the realm of the *Ladies' Home Journal* editorial departments. The *Journal* continually reinforced the appeal of this feast of subject matter by consciously including women readers in its preparation: the magazine solicited, received, and responded to hundreds of thousands of letters from readers.[1]

When the editorial matter addressed women's responsibilities at home, the *Journal* as forum followed the lead of its readers by providing them with what they asked for: money-saving recipes, household cleaning tips, pep talks about the importance of housework, decorating ideas. The *Journal* as advocate, however, regardless of changing demographics or the changing interests and needs of its readers, consistently promoted housekeeping as women's only true work. Although the word "house" was only inadvertently added to the title of the *Ladies' Journal* in its first printing, the connection between women and the home quickly became the primary focus of the editorial content and of the magazine as a whole.[2]

Edward Bok knew enough about running a women's magazine to allow his readers to help frame the discussion of housekeeping. When he took over the editorship of the *Journal* in 1889, Bok originated a column called "Side Talks with Girls," which he began under the female pseudonym of Ruth Ashmore. This column received 158,000 letters in 16 years and revealed the possibilities for intimate magazine-reader relationships.[3] Following his own lead, Bok directed department editors to continue cultivating such relationships with readers in columns concerning the home, fashion, beauty, babies, children, relationships, cooking, sewing, and decorating. Bok hired someone to write a thematic column for a year or so. After this period, following his general policy, Bok discontinued the column but placed the heading in a service listing so that readers who were still interested in a particular theme could write in for further advice.[4] In this way Bok closely monitored the popularity of the various sections of the *Journal.* He encouraged readers to write in by promising a personal response to every letter.[5]

In the early days, Bok himself stayed home one to two days each week to read letters.[6] He evaluated reader reactions to columns and was able to change the focus or subject accordingly. He also monitored *Journal* writers who responded to readers' letters by sending them random letters under assumed names every six months or so to check on the content and reliability of their responses. In a letter to Christine Frederick, a consulting household editor who, in 1914, received fifteen dollars for every hundred letters she answered, Bok admitted to a clandestine letter and praised her handling of it: "It is satisfactory, it is courteous, and one felt that you had a personal interest in the correspondent. This is exactly the one which I like to get into our correspondence, and I thank you for being so careful with the correspondence."[7] Close monitoring was Bok's style, and it paid off in ever-increasing subscriptions and loyal advertisers.[8] Since he kept abreast of reader opinion, Bok could always offer something "new" and "improved" yet familiar.[9] Sometimes one column would be followed by another which was actually quite similar in content; perhaps, though, it had a different title or a slightly new twist. Television watchers today may be almost immune to the "new" dishwashing liquid which has replaced the "improved" product, but the readers of the *Journal* were far less inundated with such ploys.

Statistics point to the success of Bok's strategy. In the last four months of 1911, the *Journal* received 59,000 letters. The last four months of 1912 witnessed 97,000 letters.[10] It was a grand undertaking to deal with so much correspondence, to provide even brief responses, but Bok considered it essential to the success of the magazine. He acknowledged reader opinions in his editorials and was at times persuaded by reader responses to change his own opinion. When women readers continually requested information about government and its institutions, for example, Bok responded by providing articles in support of women's civic education. In the case of suffrage, however, nothing would convince Bok to side with his most vocal, pro-suffrage readers.[11] Barton Currie and Loring Schuler, Bok's successors in the 1920s, relied less on readers' letters for direction, although they may, in the end, have been less didactic with their own cultural agendas than was Edward Bok. It is difficult to assess the degree to which women readers actually followed the advice provided in the *Journal* during the 1910s or the 1920s, but they clearly enjoyed reading it. Bok once claimed that his magazine constituted the world's "largest possible pulpit." Increasing circulation and tremendous reader response attest to the size of this enterprise, and if the magazine was not the bible Bok claimed it to be, it certainly constituted an important document of the rising middle class.[12]

The *Journal* was not, however, simply an interchange of opinions and ideas between editors and their readers. Bok attempted to have a consistent philosophy run through every issue of the magazine. This philosophy, referred to in short as "simple living," reflected the editor's own ideal for living in the modern world.[13] It was a moral vision he hoped his readers would share. A thread of this philosophy ran through the magazine during the teens and through the twenties, even after Bok's tenure as editor had ended; it became a part of the very definition of the *Ladies' Home Journal* for decades. By simple living Bok meant an emphasis on buying simple fashions, furnishing and living in small homes, and maintaining uncomplicated relationships in the home and community.[14] The definition included a woman at home to supervise such a lifestyle. Living the simple life, women could hold on to what was good from the past as they moved their families into the future.

The simple life was in many ways a mythical life, increasingly so as the world outside the magazine and the magazine's very relation to that world became more complex and tension-filled. For example, although it advocated a simple life, every year Bok's magazine felt the stronger push from advertisers to present more ads and the urging from the growing struggles of women attempting to define and redefine their own roles. These years witnessed great changes in women's experiences, as three events of 1921 illustrate. In the same year that the Miss America pageant was inaugurated in Atlantic City, Kotex sanitary napkins were first advertised, and the Sheppard-Towner Act, providing federal funding for prenatal and infant care, passed into law.[15] While some women took greater control of their own bodies, others celebrated the objectification of their bodies. The job of a woman's magazine in such a period of change was not an easy one. While the *Ladies' Home Journal* chose its constituency deliberately and appealed most to the middle-class woman who wanted to broaden rather than negate her household and family roles, the terms of the debate, even for those women, changed constantly.

While the reader of 1912 may have been shocked into a realization of the evils of fashion while reading a "Plain Country Woman" article, for example, she had only to turn to the next page to be enticed in the opposite direction by an article entitled "What I See in New York," which outlined the latest city styles.[16] On first glance, it seems as though simple moral living and the consumer culture of the early twentieth century were contradictory or at least incompatible ideals. In fact, though, for many readers and for the *Journal* they were not. A woman could certainly try to retain the simple family values advocated on one page and still want to dress her daughter in the most up-to-date attire consistent with her age and social group. Bok and his women readers, in mixing the old and the new, acted not as hypocrites in, but rather negotiators of, a changing culture. According to Bok and other writers, and, arguably, according to many of his readers as well, desires for the old and the new, desires to live the simple life and to purchase new inventions, were far from mutually exclusive. The simple life could perhaps be more easily attained by the woman living in a bungalow, but the middle-class reader could almost as readily attain it using modern methods, especially the skills of the wise consumer. Modern conveniences such as irons and vacuum cleaners could help rather than hinder the process by simplifying women's work in the home. Furthermore, the simple life philosophy was dependent, as Bok himself put it, neither "upon condition nor station in life." [17] Instead, it depended on one's state of mind. This argument for modernity accompanied by right mindedness is best exemplified in the following statement by Bok: "Make home happy; hold loved ones first in your heart; leave off fussing over fashionable ways of living; be natural, and you will be living the simple life though you ride in a motorcar, clean home by electricity, entertain at the country club, and have every convenience known to man. The quality of the individual is what determines the simple life, never his surroundings." [18]

Bok may have appealed as much to his readers' dreams here as he did to their reality. As the Lynds found in their ground-breaking study of "Middletown," or Muncie, Indiana, in this same time period, individual women experienced very different economic possibilities, even within social classes and within neighborhoods. On the same block one found women using a broom in one household, a carpet sweeper in a second, and a vacuum cleaner in a third. For cleaning clothes, one woman used a scrubboard, a second an electric washer, a third hired help, and a fourth a laundry service. [19] The *Journal* had few readers with "every convenience known to man," but the implication was clear; one could aspire to having or actually have money and still live a morally upstanding life. Bok's agenda fit in squarely with turn-of-the-century views of simple living based on the writings of Emerson, Thoreau, and Charles Wagner, a French Protestant clergyman whose book, *The Simple Life*, provided Bok and other middle-class reformers with a golden mean on reform. The simple life philosophy, as David Shi puts it, reassured Bok and other middle class Americans that "leading a simple life required a spiritual revitalization, not a social revolution." [20] Readers of the *Ladies' Home Journal* found reassurance that the new social order, which increasingly favored the white middle-class, was not only beneficial to them but also moral, upstanding, and fair to all.

Material pleasures held a subordinate position to spiritual happiness, but simplicity in this philosophy was decidedly as much a state of mind as it was a state of the pocketbook. One could argue that this approach in the magazine simply represents one of Bok's attempts at market segmentation: he introduced various versions of simplicity and consumerism to appeal to the financial realities of his many different readers. This was the case, at least in part, as the *Journal* did want a large audience and the editor was aware of his potential markets. The most persuasive argument, however, is that the different themes simply formed different sides of the same coin. Simplicity encouraged both morality and consumerism, both nostalgia for the values of the nineteenth-century world and an eagerness to purchase the wonders of the twentieth. The simple life philosophy of the *Ladies' Home Journal* provided comfort in an simultaneously more comfortable and more discomforting world.[21]

This twentieth-century world, with its emphasis on business and manufacturing, on paid work and skilled work, provided women who worked at home with little guaranteed social status. Housekeeping remained, after all was said and done, both unpaid and unskilled work. Technological changes outside the home could have had a far more revolutionary impact on women's work than they actually had. As women acquired electrical appliances for the home and pursued new opportunities for education and work outside the home, homemaking could have become a part-time job, a hobby, a pastime. Middle-class women bore fewer children and pursued further education than they had in earlier generations. Married women's labor force participation increased markedly from 1900 to 1930. Many signs pointed to greater freedom of choice among women and fewer reasons to be tied to the household.

Some women, taking this lead, advocated for kitchenless homes, daycare centers, and increased professional and educational opportunities for women. "The private kitchen must go the way of the spinning wheel, of which it is the contemporary," argued writer Zona Gale.[22] Charlotte Perkins Gilman promoted the development of neighborhood commercial kitchens, where women could pick up hot meals at supper time. A housekeeping bureau, Gilman argued further, would send trained domestics to clean those kitchenless homes, freeing women further from household responsibilities.[23] Gilman argued that a true sign of social progress would be "making a legitimate human business of housework; having it done by experts instead of by amateurs; making it a particularly social industry instead of a general feminine function . . . is good business. It is one of the greatest business opportunities the world has ever known."[24] A Charlotte Perkins Gilman novel, *Diantha*, published in 1912, featured an enterprising heroine who started a hot meal delivery service, linking the automobile to her individual and other women's collective independence.[25]

Groups of women did experiment with alternative housekeeping arrangements throughout the early twentieth century, inside and outside of the *Ladies' Home Journal.* Apartment hotels delivered hot meals to individual rooms twice a day. The National Home Economics Association carried in its platform community kitchens for poor districts. Utopian novels, such as Edward Bellamy's *Looking Backward,* promoted cooperative kitchens, and Bellamy Clubs sprung up to put those ideas into practice. Some women chose communal living: the Jane Clubs, named after Jane Addams, offered cooperative boardinghouses and cooperative laundries to women workers. A group in Carthage, Missouri, started a cooperative kitchen when an ex-senator challenged the local suffrage group to find a way to help his wife and other women retain the strength and energy they lost in cooking. In response to the challenge, sixty people rented a house, hired a manager and cooks, and received their family meals from the Carthage kitchen for four years.[26]

Certain "women's" jobs were brought outside of the home temporarily or permanently in the early twentieth century. Sewing and care of the sick, for example, left the home permanently once ready-made clothing manufacturers and hospitals grew more available. Laundry work left temporarily, with commercial laundries reaching a heyday in the 1920s. Commercial laundries provided an enormous service, since, previously, women had to boil clothes in a tub on top of the kitchen stove, wash them with a washboard, rinse, wring, and hang them to dry. The whole operation used about 50 gallons of water, all of which women carried into the house. Commercial laundries offered some women jobs and offered many other women a lessened household burden. As Ruth Schwartz Cowan illustrates, however, electric washing machines killed the commercial laundry business. "The decline of the commercial laundry," she writes, "is, in fact, one of the few instances we have of a household function appearing to be well on its way to departing from the home—only to return."[27]

New developments in technology found an intermittent and erratic application in the household, and the failure to commercialize more of women's tasks led to long hours of housework for many future generations of women. Historians have debated the reasons why more of women's work did not leave the home during these years of experimentation and debate. Manufacturers wanted to sell, and certainly selling individual women refrigerators and washing machines generated more profit than would selling them only to commercial enterprises. In addition, women's work incurred no cost, so manufacturers found little incentive in making products work more efficiently. Some argue that within the household men preferred the individual attention of their wives to the impersonal nature of commercial enterprises. Others posit that Americans, in general, prefer to measure family autonomy by having women's work stay in individual homes. Certainly, had women's time been more valued, more of their work would have left the home. Juliet Schor, in her study of "the overworked American," argues just that: "Had housewives' time been at a premium, our homes would look very different. For starters, they'd probably be much smaller. And they'd be easier to clean." Similarly, Cowan argues that twentieth-century household technologies developed with nineteenth-century assumptions about separate gendered spheres; as a result the technologies themselves helped to promote separate and unequal household tasks for women and men.[28]

Women received more encouragement to stay at home than they did to abandon housework or turn it over to commercial enterprises, and for the most part women maintained their household responsibilities. Even the *Ladies' Home Journal* explored issues of cooperative housekeeping in advice articles, but enthusiasm about the movement was even shorter lived in the *Ladies' Home Journal* than elsewhere.[29] Rather than becoming a part-time job during this period, housekeeping became more of a full-time job than ever before, as standards of cleanliness, requirements of parenting, especially mothering, and expectations of meal variety increased. It was this role for women that the *Journal*, with its simple life philosophy, was best able to promote. Women's magazines, in fact, were one of the few places where both women's household responsibilities and their economic roles as consumers were discussed and applauded, although the *Journal* both underestimated and discouraged the political nature of women's tasks. The *Journal*'s simple life philosophy promoted women's household and purchasing roles as an aspect of women's choice rather than as socially mandated experiences, as a way to increase family harmony rather than put undue burden on any one family member, and as an example of women's emancipation rather than an obstacle to it.[30]

The voices of the 1910s and 1920s may have simultaneously looked ahead and behind, but they reflected some real changes taking place in U.S. society and in individual women's lives. Electric service spread nationwide and the price of current dropped. In 1912, 16 percent of the nation's dwelling units had electricity, and a kilowatt cost about 9 cents. In 1920, 35 percent had electricity, for which they paid 7 1/2 cents per kilowatt. By 1930, the 60 percent who had electricity paid only 6 cents per kilowatt. At the same time, however, people increasingly spent more money on electricity as they installed more lights and purchased new electrical appliances. The annual use per customer doubled, in fact, between 1912 and 1930.[31] By 1934, a home-maker with the appropriate purchasing power could buy even the most highly specialized electrical appliances, including waffle irons, chafing dishes, coffee makers, egg cookers, corn poppers, doughnut makers, wiener cookers, and baby bottle warmers.[32] Ironically, studies of housework reveal that labor- and time-saving appliances actually increased rather than decreased the amount of time women spent cooking and cleaning.[33]

The major thrust of the advice put forth in the *Ladies' Home Journal* related to such household purchasing decisions. The magazine continually acknowledged, praised, defended, and tried to professionalize the woman's role in the household. A reader could wind her way through the magazine's many paths to household success and find one that could work for her, regardless of her ability to procure helping hands, human or electrical. The *Journal* succeeded in providing examples of efficient housekeeping to readers of many means. The magazine continually held out the promise, though, that new products meant more leisure time for women. By promoting its simple life doctrine, the magazine was able to bridge the roles that women held as producers and consumers during these years.

The middle-class housewife was the main target of both the advertising and the editorial matter, but the young, single working woman, or "girl," also found her way into the discussion. A number of these women could afford to pay for the companionship of the magazine, or perhaps some of them shared copies. The *Journal* acknowledged the difficulties experienced by these working women and offered household hints designed to lighten their loads in their varied living situations. Writers described the limitations implicit in boardinghouse life in various "true-life" stories and advice columns. The healthy alternative, for the woman who could afford it, was a room of one's own. Mae McGuire Telford's column, "For the Girl Who Lives Alone," provides an example of this approach.[34] Telford and others acknowledged the difficulties in living alone: one had to do all the cleaning, the shopping, the cooking. One had to create a home out of very small quarters—a kitchen in a closet, an eating area in the bedroom. Dangers loomed for the woman who could not handle the responsibilities; if she did not take care in preparing her food, for example, she might become ill. Although the writers and the young women themselves who wrote in acknowledged these difficulties, most viewed the independence as a positive thing. After a difficult day at work, they wrote, they found a bit of privacy essential. To top it off, many advice writers argued, the experience of cooking and cleaning provided the unmarried "girl" with the skills she would need later on as a married woman. This independence, they reminded readers, was meant to be a temporary experience, a prelude to marriage.[35] Shared housing provided another alternative for the unmarried working woman. "When Girls Live in Groups," a 1918 article, advocated such an arrangement, again in the name of economy and creating a home environment.[36] By providing a case study, the article illustrated that women could live together as a family and save. This writer placed her emphasis not on the immorality of life at the boardinghouse but rather on the lack of a home environment, the lack of opportunity for women to take on the woman's inherent role of caring for a home. Obviously the writers and editors wanted to encourage women to experience this solid training for the future roles of wife and mother. But the *Journal* writers failed to acknowledge that such arrangements were beyond the realm of possibility, if not the interest, of most single working women. A majority of the published letters of working women solicited information about how to handle men and relationships rather than how to handle household duties. It appears that the advice reflected what the writers wished for this small group of readers rather than attention to the needs or wants of the women themselves.[37]

A far greater proportion of household advice addressed the young married woman in her first home. One column, entitled "Little House Problems," provided advice on how to furnish and maintain small homes. The suggestions in this regular column often pertained to any house, large or small. In a July 1911 column, for example, the writer focused on removing specks from a brass bed, cleaning a stained rug, and refinishing furniture.[38] Although the article's title implies that the problems were particular to the small house, the contents reflect the real intention of the writer: to make the woman who lived in a small house feel good about her home and her ability to work well in a small space. Some of these columns did pertain specifically to the small house; in a January 1911 article, for example, the columnist argued that people who lived in small houses should not have a formal parlor but should instead use that room for a family living room.[39] Another column offered advice about methods of heating small homes.[40] While the *Journal* argued both the feasibility and at times even the moral superiority of living in a small house, the magazine was hardly consistent in addressing the needs of the small-house family. One issue in 1914, for example, included four articles about designing or building homes.[41] One, entitled "The Six Room Bungalow," showed the readers four small year-round homes. The remaining three articles, however, featured far larger and grander homes. The title of one article, "A Country Home With Three Sleeping Porches," illustrates that although the emphasis was supposed to be on "simple living," the term was applied in a broadly defined manner.

Other articles offered advice about managing the home without the assistance of servants. Editorials, regular monthly columns, and random, one-time columns discussed the "servant problem" throughout the teens and twenties. A monthly column beginning in September 1911 opened by addressing this very problem.[42] The topic for the month was "Back to the Kitchen: But How?" and the columnist warned women readers that they had to face up to the servant problem. Factory work could provide women better pay, better working hours, and perhaps most importantly, more personal independence than could domestic work. The writer was sympathetic to working women's concerns about their personal lives and their chances to meet men, which greatly diminished when they performed domestic service. She was less sympathetic with the women at home who refused to accept and adapt to these changes. Women had two choices. They could, on the one hand, professionalize the chore and make domestic service a job which could compete with factory work in terms of employee benefits and hence employee satisfaction. If middle-class women accomplished this, working-class women would return to domestic jobs. On the other hand, women could accept the march of domestic workers from the home to the factory and take on the abandoned jobs themselves. They could learn the household skills themselves and hence render domestic service unnecessary.

This writer and many subsequent columnists and editors found this latter alternative most appealing. A wartime article entitled "I'm Glad My Servant Left" illustrates the trend.[43] Written by a woman who lost a domestic worker to a munitions factory, the article provides a picture of a household only now run efficiently and effectively. The loss of the maid provided the woman the impetus to learn the skills of household efficiency, which she applied with amazing success. Others argued not only that servants were hard to come by or less efficient than the resident women but that they were also, in fact, harmful rather than helpful. "More good and expensive food has been slaughtered in the American kitchen than the mind of man can compute," argued the Country Contributor in 1914. The simple life agenda would professionalize housekeeping, provide homemakers with some social status, and eliminate the need to bring strangers into the home.[44] Although *Journal* writers made no specific statements to this effect, one wonders about the degree to which the fear of strangers coincided with the influx of African-American women into domestic service.

Few articles addressed the concerns of women wealthy enough to maintain servants, but even these lent further responsibilities to the woman at home, who had to oversee the efforts and accomplishments of her employee or employees, provide direction and instruction, and consistently attempt to professionalize the entire housekeeping process. An idea introduced in the late teen years sought to create eight-hour assistants rather than domestic workers. These employees would work the business-like schedule of an eight-hour day rather than the often erratic and far longer day of the domestic worker. In addition, the eight-hour assistant would follow a weekly schedule that included rest periods and alternating periods of standing and sitting work. The plan necessitated not only the availability of women to work as eight-hour assistants but also a person to plan the schedule and manage the entire process; essentially, the assistant needed a person to assist. That person, the manager, was the woman at home.[45]

The *Ladies' Home Journal* appears to have been a mishmash of professional advice and helpful hints from various points of view, directed at a variety of audiences, and indeed it was. A long-running column entitled "What Other Women Have Found Out" published readers' suggestions. One woman told how she wore automobile goggles while peeling onions to avoid the stinging in her eyes.[46] In another column, "Pretty Girl Questions," a woman wrote that to avoid inhaling dust while sweeping, she made a mask from a sponge and tied it, dampened, across the nose and mouth.[47] The image of women working around the house clad in automobile goggles and sponge masks is a comical one, but it illustrates that a good percentage of the household advice offered was not professional or "expert," but simply practices that individual women incorporated into their apparently less than regimented daily routines. In the end, of course, these suggestions may have been at least as valuable as those offered by the so-called experts; the suggestions provided a sense of camaraderie among *Journal* readers eager to share their expertise in a culture that devalued their daily contributions. The subtle transformation of this service component from one dominated by readers and editors to one dominated by advertisers helped reshape both the cultural definitions of advice and the cultural definitions of information worthy of inclusion in an advice column. The end result, for readers, was greater distance from each other and, arguably, less, rather than greater, validation of their particular social circumstances. The *Journal* encouraged and mystified this development in order to sell washing machines and vacuum cleaners and itself, "the women's magazine." It did this by addressing the many facets of the household worker's tasks, the professional and the unsophisticated, the modern and the antiquated, the occasional and the mundane.

Although the *Journal* celebrated readers' ideas by printing scores of them and by rewarding contributors with small amounts of cash, doing this mostly during the teens decade, the magazine also consistently attempted to make the household more systematic, more appealing to the women who wanted to use their education and intellect as well as their rolling pins. The magazine accomplished this by hiring "expert" advice givers to write columns about the more professional or scientific side of housekeeping. Such columns increasingly took precedence, but the *Journal* never completely eliminated its household hints columns either, in all likelihood because the editors wanted to maintain a close connection with the readers by acknowledging their ideas, but also, perhaps, because the readers never fully relinquished their less professional household activities in their own movements toward professionalization.

Writers often introduced attempts to upgrade the job of housekeeping with laments over women's unbusinesslike household practices. Mrs. Julian Heath, president of the Housewives' League, argued this in a 1913 article entitled "How Housewives Make Money." "In point of fact," she stated, "my expertise leads me to believe that if one-half the men conducted their commercial business as carelessly as the majority of women conduct their business of housekeeping, the country's bankruptcy courts would be running day and night."[48] Heath faulted women primarily for their lack of economy in the purchasing of food: don't throw away meat trimmings, and be sure to eat food currently in season, she argued. The analogy of business failure and housekeeping failure, an old one by this time, remained popular in the *Journal.* At various times throughout these two decades, advice givers faulted housewives for their shortcomings concerning the buying of food, cooking, and cleaning. Although the issues changed from wasting scraps of meat to wasting steps across the kitchen floor, two things remained fairly constant: the comparison between men's dealings in the business world and women's necessarily businesslike dealings in the household, and the increasing degree to which modern methods relied on modern products.

The foremost spokesperson for the professionalization of housekeeping through more scientific approaches was Christine Frederick, longtime contributor and consulting household editor for the *Ladies' Home Journal,* popular lecturer on the Chautauqua Circuit, author of books on housekeeping and consumerism, director of the Applecroft Home Experiment Station, housekeeper, and mother of four. She was born in Boston on February 6, 1883, to Mimi (Scott) and William R. Campbell, who separated soon after her birth. Eleven years later her mother married again, to a lawyer, Wyatt

McGaffey, who adopted Christine. During her early childhood Christine lived both with her parents and, for ten years, with an aunt in Leningrad. She later attended Northwestern University and graduated in 1906. During college, Christine always held jobs to help support herself; her unpublished autobiography mentions stints tutoring other students and working as a maid at different houses on the regular maid's day off.[49]

In 1907, Christine McGaffey married Justus George Frederick, an advertising executive and one-time editor of *Printer's Ink*. The suffrage movement also attracted Christine Frederick's attention, and she participated in suffrage marches and supported various women's causes. In 1912, in response to the discrimination women faced in the advertising profession and in professional advertising organizations, Frederick and her husband founded the League of Advertising Women, later called Advertising Women of New York.[50] She also lectured extensively on women and household responsibility. Perhaps from the suffragists, Christine Frederick learned the effectiveness of militant action, which she would use to gain men's attention as she worked the lecture circuit. Her characteristic lecturing technique was to wear a formal black lace dress and begin demurely, only to drop down on her hands and knees with a bucket and cry out to the men, "Does your wife really have to work this way?"[51] As her daughter later put it when discussing her mother's suffrage activities, Christine Frederick's real calling was to challenge women's position in the home: "Mother's street militancy was short-lived," she recalled. "She was more attracted to liberating women from the inefficiency of the household."[52] Although she supported suffrage, Frederick was committed to liberating women only from the inefficiency of the household, not from the household altogether.

Frederick experienced the inefficiency of the household firsthand as a housekeeper and as a mother of small children. She wanted to do it all: care for her children, do her own housework, and have free time to pursue her own interests. In time, though, she became quite dragged out. "Indeed, I was often without much energy to 'dress up' in the evening," she recalled, "and when my husband came home, I was generally too spiritless to enjoy listening to his story of the day's work."[53] Frederick became so depressed at times that she wished she were once again single and a teacher. Something had to change. Finally, her husband began to come home and tell her stories of this wonderful business principle, scientific management. Based on the work of mechanical engineer Frederick Winslow Taylor, scientific management posited that industrial practices could be rendered more exact and hence more profitable. Taylor's followers "humanized" scientific management and brought it to public attention around 1910. Christine Frederick's husband, one of Taylor's many supporters, felt such excitement about these principles that for a time he barely spoke of anything else.[54]

The fever caught Christine as well, and she recruited her husband and his "efficiency engineer" friends to explain scientific management to her. Frederick then visited several factories to see these practices in action. In one foundry, where workers had previously used small and non-standardized shovels to work the coal, old shovels had been replaced with larger and more efficient models. Frederick, impressed and enthused, imagined incorporating the principles of Taylorism into the tasks of the housekeeper, thus reducing the stress and the distress she and others experienced. She believed that Taylor's philosophy of "the one best way" could apply equally to the household.[55] The aspect of scientific management which caught Christine Frederick's attention most thoroughly was standardized operations.[56] The best performance could be achieved when workers worked at the right height and with the right tools, under the best conditions of light, ventilation, and comfort, and with the least possible waste of energy and time. Women's work, she believed, could be made vastly more efficient if they did not have to use outmoded tools and outdated methods. The "new housekeeping" philosophy, as Frederick called it, resulted when she applied scientific management principles to her own home and her own work, housekeeping.

Frederick had an opportunity to think these ideas through and try them out on other women in the pages of the *Ladies' Home Journal,* where she served as Contributing Household Editor from 1912 to 1919.[57] She later compiled the *Journal* articles into a book entitled *The New Housekeeping: Efficiency Studies in Home Management,* published in 1913. Frederick dedicated her second book, *Household Engineering,* to Edward Bok, "to whose encouragement and progressive leadership in reaching the mass of American homemakers with the gospel of efficiency I owe much inspiration."[58] The *Journal* series, each titled "The New Housekeeping," first introduced readers to Christine Frederick and to the challenges she posited. In one month, Frederick later recalled, she received 1600 letters in response to the new housekeeping articles.[59] Readers, as startled by the idea as Frederick was, wrote unprecedented numbers of letters to the *Journal* requesting further information. Frederick received one letter from a woman with a family of ten. She had to carry in all the water the family used and desperately wanted information about how to do this more efficiently. Another writer, married three years, could not grasp the idea of "managing" her home. In an era in which the specifics of women's household responsibilities met largely with disinterest if not disdain, Frederick's promises of professionalism and systematized, easier-to-handle households struck a chord among the magazine's readers.

At a 1913 conference of the Curtis Company advertising department, Bok was asked if he would continue to promote scientific management in the home. His answer attests both to his enthusiasm for these new methods and his participation in the general cultural disregard for women's work. Would he push it? "Just as far as the freight will carry it. You know we have Mrs. Frederick at the head of that. At first when we put that in the general category, I think we got 3 or 4 letters a month. Then we had her articles, and now the letters have been steadily increasing all the time. Of course that is at the back of this whole problem. If the American woman had been onto her job we would not have had all these problems."[60]

Three years later, in 1916, Bok, now fully involved in the campaign to professionalize housekeeping, provided a succinct account of the philosophy: "We are beginning to understand that, as men are revolutionizing business methods with greater efficiency, so the housewife by introducing more system in her work, is finding the simplifying results of efficiency entering the home. No; housekeeping is no longer drudgery. Women are beginning to see in it a science: a vital factor in life; an act that calls for the highest intelligence; a business as big as the affairs of men. It is the women who hang on to the old methods of housekeeping that find it drudgery."[61] The following month's issue provided a personal account which mirrored Bok's argument. A woman told of her panic when her cook became ill just when she had a big dinner party scheduled. When she shared her fear with a friend, the woman was surprised to hear her friend suggest not that she cancel the party or find another cook, but that she prepare the meal herself. This friend, undaunted by the task, helped the woman simplify the menu so that the shopping, food preparation, cooking, and serving were systematized. "Housekeeping is the greatest business in the world," concluded the woman, who had learned to approach her tasks in a businesslike manner.[62] When done right, housekeeping in the *Journal* not only equalled men's work; it seemingly surpassed it in significance to the world. The columnists appeared to feel confident that women would welcome any chance to make their work more scientific and thus more respectable. Women's time, they argued, had to be spent in an efficient manner. "What's the Value of Your Time?" demanded one article.[63] Which was a better use of a woman's time, asked the author, buying jam or making jam, hemming diapers or paying to have them hemmed? The conclusions increasingly stressed the consumption rather than the production of goods and services, with the businesslike woman always on hand to scrutinize the quality of what she purchased.[64] Of course, as demonstrated earlier, the *Journal* only presented certain household tasks as dispensable. Gendered notions of family dictated that other female tasks remained in the woman's realm, and that deliberation rarely found a forum in the magazine.

Advocates of the new housekeeping felt confident that women would eagerly embrace this new professional definition; it was men's reactions they feared. In "I Had a Talk With My Husband," an anonymous writer told her "true" story: she received an allowance from her husband but felt that a more systematic approach to her housekeeping was needed. "Do you wish to put loving service on a weekly salary?" asked her husband. Her response was logical and professional, thus convincing: goods entered the house but her work made them valuable. The wheat and vegetables entered in a rough form, but with her attention they became a meal. When her husband reexamined the situation, he had to agree with his wife's premise: her business was her housekeeping, and her housekeeping was her business.[65] This story is revealing on several counts. Scientific housekeeping promised women more control over the household finances, acknowledged the complexities of women's work in the home, and validated women's work. In an article on home canning, Christine Frederick wrote that a woman should can goods "not because you love your family but because it is good business to do so."[66]

Although many historians have argued the limits of scientific management in the industrial setting, there is no doubt that the idea if not the actual practice of scientific housekeeping had a tremendous appeal in the 1910s and 1920s.[67] Women as well as men found it difficult to attribute to housework much real value. Frederick's philosophy addressed her own and other women's intellectual and emotional as well as physical needs. "For once I found a use for some of the college training I had despaired of ever putting into practice," Frederick wrote.[68] The "new" housekeeping suggested a change in women's roles, and the modern middle-class woman embraced a redefinition which seemed to recognize her education and radically transform her roles and responsibilities while it allowed her, essentially, to retain her position in the household. The evidence suggests that for Frederick and for many readers of the *Ladies' Home Journal*, this was the most inviting alternative to the lives they currently led; the choice of staying at home and being considered a "professional" may have been an appealing option for those who wanted to use their intellects but who had neither the impetus nor the financial and emotional support of husbands required to make other kinds of changes. For others, the new technology Frederick described may have simply seemed the only way out of extremely difficult, physically demanding, never ending, gendered work.[69]

The "new housekeeping" articles in the *Ladies' Home Journal* introduced Christine Frederick's ideas in fairly brief monthly installments. The first of these promoted one of the two principles for which Frederick was most famous: standardized heights of kitchen equipment. Kitchen sinks, tables, and ironing boards were constructed with little thought given to anatomy, and women found themselves stooped over as they worked. Frederick studied the problem and suggested a scientific remedy: if individual women were to use these items, they had to be installed or built for those particular women. Frederick calculated the exact measurements appropriate for women of different heights and published charts to direct women in their own kitchen renovations. She encouraged them to demand standardized products from manufacturers when planning a kitchen, or to organize a remodeling of the kitchens they already had by soliciting help from knowledgeable carpenters. Once women had kitchens that fit their anatomies, they would more readily handle the other items on the new housekeeping agenda.[70] Such rigid construction details would also ensure, of course, that the individual woman would be the only family member anatomically suited to perform those domestic responsibilities.

In the months that followed, Christine Frederick introduced other elements of scientific management applied to the household. In October of 1912, she discussed scheduling.[71] Women could run more efficient households if they kept weekly and hourly schedules of chores. A baby's bath, for example, took fifteen minutes; mixing a layer cake required ten minutes. Baking muffins required six minutes, she calculated, but biscuits required eight. The responsibilities of the household manager began to increase subtly here as her efficiency supposedly increased. No mention was made of the time required to keep all these records or the energy needed to store and update them; the issue instead was how much time could be saved by applying the principles. The following month's installment increased the record-keeping from knowing simply how long tasks took to recording in detail all family purchases, family clothing sizes, and the location of each item in storage. "I decided that if my husband and other men used modern filing systems and cards in their offices I could do the same to keep my house in order," reasoned Frederick.[72]

In July of 1913, Christine Frederick introduced the second idea which brought her fame: saving steps in the kitchen. The housewife, in her seemingly endless treks across the kitchen, between the cabinets and sink and pantry and table, wasted a considerable number of steps and needlessly wore herself out. Scientific management advocated saving steps across the factory floor; Christine Frederick advocated saving steps in the home factory, the kitchen. In this introductory article she divided the kitchen tasks into two activities: preparing for a meal and cleaning up after the meal. For each group of tasks, which contained several secondary activities, she drew a map of the kitchen and led the woman reader through the activities. Limit your crossing and recrossing, she urged readers. In subsequent articles on this same theme, Frederick provided numerical calculations of actual steps wasted or saved in various approaches to kitchen work.[73]

The *Ladies' Home Journal* readers received further information from Frederick, and then from her many followers, in a number of articles through the 1910s and 1920s. Each article addressed one of the housewife's responsibilities in cooking, cleaning, or home management. Frederick felt that women had unlimited potential in the home, for it was the one arena of business not yet regulated. Women could change all of that, assert themselves as management professionals in the process, and prove their worth to themselves and to the world at large. Such a movement toward professionalization appeared limitless but was in fact severely limited in one significant way in the *Journal* and in Frederick's larger sphere of influence. In keeping with the individual and household focus of the *Journal*, women's power ended at the kitchen door. In other words, scientific housekeeping assuredly bolstered the reputation of women's jobs, but it just as surely established the boundaries of women's work experiences within the four walls of the household and within the realm of unpaid work. Christine Frederick alone could not attribute to unpaid work any lasting degree of social value. And when cooperative cooking and laundry efforts failed, women found themselves further entrenched in a household institution that required their full efforts and full-time presence. Finally, although she argued that women consumers had enormous economic power, Frederick urged them to exercise that power individually rather than collectively. Hers was an impressive, if ultimately unworkable, attempt to make women's work count.

Christine Frederick's life and work point to the limits of the *Journal*'s simple life philosophy in general and its scientific housekeeping in particular. Like many women of her day, Frederick earned a living and an impressive professional reputation by promising other women that housekeeping was the greatest business in the world. As a mother, she found a unique way to care for her children, use her college training, and earn money, ultimately sacrificing none of her conflicting interests. Few *Journal* readers could claim the same; fewer still who followed Frederick's prescriptions. Christine Frederick was a self-described feminist, but because she promised something she could not deliver, namely social status for unpaid household work, her ideas appear reactionary and self-serving in retrospect. Her "new housekeeping," however, was a sincere attempt to make the most of the work that almost all of her contemporaries, regardless of their educational backgrounds or occupational aspirations, shared. Few women of Frederick's day escaped the demands of household work.

Christine Frederick rarely mentioned women working for pay, but when she did she drew the focus back to the home. "It is just as stimulating to bake a sponge cake on a six-minute schedule as it is to monotonously address envelopes for three hours in a downtown office," Frederick argued, making a valid point but ignoring the realities of many women's work and family lives.[74] She did discuss men's roles in the household in *Household Engineering,* but did not suggest they become involved in the affairs of the domestic realm. Since men worked all day, their wives could not expect any help from them. They were best to use the home primarily as a place to recuperate and prepare themselves for a "better economic position." Frederick provided a case study to illustrate her point: in one household the wife expected her husband to help with the household activities. He complied and subsequently proved a puzzlement to the neighbors because he never seemed to "get on" the way people had expected. Men could help in other ways, Frederick declared. They could be satisfied with the work their wives performed and learn to have simple standards and appreciate simple foods. Those husbands who worked in the business world could provide suggestions about household finance or budgeting, and all men, if they were handy, could help put up shelves or pictures "occasionally." There were men, admitted Frederick, who actually liked to cook or help out "*once in a while,*" but her emphasis implied that even those men could easily be pushed over the limits of reasonable expectations.[75] Frederick, like many of her readers, had low expectations of men as far as household work was concerned, and professionalizing housework was a response to this.

Christine Frederick served as the *Ladies' Home Journal*'s answer to the many transformations taking place in the household. She argued that her plans for scientific housekeeping would help women achieve further control of their lives, gain more respect from the complementary male world of business, and contribute to a more healthy society. In the process of advocating for these lofty goals, however, Frederick herself found professional success in the business end of the consumer culture, and her ties to manufacturers further complicate the notion that she was a disinterested observer aiming to improve the lives of women housekeepers. Her business dealings also suggest the degree to which, even by the early twentieth century, the interests of advertisers won out over the interests of readers of women's magazines.

Christine Frederick's work at the *Ladies' Home Journal* mirrored changes that occurred in all magazines, most especially in women's magazines, as the magazine and advertising industries grew to be increasingly mutually dependent. Of course, she alone is not responsible for the fact that women's magazines quickly became "women's advertising magazines,"[76] but changes in her career point to the ways in which advertising subtly and not so subtly became the lifeblood and organizing pattern of these publications. In letters to *Journal* readers, Frederick moved from advocating that women use new technology in their homes to advocating for the use of specific products. At the *Journal* and at Applecroft, her home experiment station, she evaluated products and specifically endorsed those that she found superior or that she was paid to endorse. This "hidden agenda" of women's magazines, which haunts readers today, with ads for cosmetics placed around editorials about the importance of skin care, has its roots with Christine Frederick and her contemporaries.[77]

The first available evidence of an ethically questionable behind-the-scenes relationship between this advice writer, the *Ladies' Home Journal*, and manufacturers occurred in 1915. A letter from managing editor Karl Harriman to Christine Frederick describes a meeting between Harriman and Mr. Sexton from the Whirlpool company. The letter contains literature about the Whirlpool dishwasher and the following proposition: "Don't you think it might be a good idea to mention the Whirlpool washer, among others, in reply to such queries as come to you as a result of your Dishwashing page in our October issue? Mr. Sexton says that he will be very glad to demonstrate the efficacy of the machine to you or give you any further information regarding it which you may desire."[78] This letter suggests that in addition to contracting with advertising agencies over specific advertisements, the *Journal* made less formal arrangements with manufacturers to promote their products. The job of the advice-giver consequently became the marketing of specific products rather than of general ideas. In 1919, Frederick received a letter from the *Journal* describing a letter they had received from the California Packing Company. Complaining that Christine Frederick had discouraged the use of canned foods in a recent article, the company encouraged the *Journal* to leave out "outworn epigrams slurring upon the use of canned foods."[79] Frederick promptly responded, arguing that she believed in canned foods and encouraged their use, citing her ten years of work on behalf of purity in canned foods.[80] Only a few months later Frederick received a letter from the *Journal* in response to a letter she had written. The writer warned her not to accept an offer from a manufacturer to endorse a product. The *Journal* could no longer employ her if she did so, and the two women who had done this "greatly injured themselves" in the process. "I think the time is coming," continued Theresa Walcott, household editor, "when there will have to be a distinction between the editorial and advertising domestic science and household writers."[81]

The endorsement offer may have come from the California Packing Company in response to Frederick's declaration that she was a supporter rather than a critic of canned foods. The series of letters illustrates that, whatever the source of the offer, the *Journal* deemed the outright endorsement of products incompatible with writing advice columns in the magazine. Mrs. Sarah Tyson Rorer, who wrote fifty-four cookbooks and booklets, may have been one of the women Walcott was referring to. Rorer wrote for the *Ladies' Home Journal*, but after an advertisement appeared in the *Journal* for her coffee, she no longer contributed. Although there is no proof of a causal relationship there, it seems likely that the *Journal* staff preferred a personal endorsement through letters to a printed endorsement in the pages of the magazine. The criteria for the magazine may well have been visible versus invisible rather than ethical versus unethical endorsements. Indirect links between the magazine and its advertisers in the teen years grew more solid and made their way into policy in the twenties, when advertisers offered their wares directly through increased copy and through advice copy rather than indirectly through letters to and from readers.

Contrary to the *Journal*'s advice, however, Christine Frederick decided that she wanted to endorse particular products, and she began to do so as early as the following year, the same year that she stopped writing for the *Journal*. In a 1920 booklet entitled "You and Your Laundry," Frederick wrote of the wonders of the Thor washing machine. Her instructions told women how to use a washer, why a washer was worth buying, and how to iron, using, of course, a Thor iron. Chapter Ten of the booklet, "Let Your Husband Read

This," outlined the pertinent technical information on the product.[82] Frederick's other booklets included "Come Into My Kitchen," which endorsed Vollrath cookware; "Frankfurters as You Like Them," which endorsed Stahl-Meyer; and "Hershey's Favorite Recipes."[83]

At Frederick's Applecroft Home Experiment Station on Long Island, which she founded in 1910, her relationship with manufacturers was even more direct than it was in her employment with the *Ladies' Home Journal.* The station had about five hundred visitors in 1920, and each was given a tour of the modern kitchens and laundries set up to teach scientific housekeeping methods. Manufacturers provided appliances to the station for six months, free of charge; in return Applecroft drew attention to the brand names, distributed the manufacturers' circulars, and wrote articles featuring the specific appliances. In a 1921 letter to McGray refrigerators, Frederick told the company that Applecroft needed a refrigerator of certain specifications, if McGray was interested.[84] Frederick continued this kind of work through the 1920s culminating in a 1929 publication, *Selling Mrs. Consumer.*[85] Dedicated to Herbert Hoover, the book assumed the voice of Mrs. Consumer, who purchased 80 to 90 percent of all retail goods sold, and who supposedly could have brought the great manufacturers to their knees.[86] Frederick encouraged manufacturers to understand this woman, to study her psychology. In a sense, the book brought together all of what had occurred throughout Christine Frederick's career and through these years in the *Ladies' Home Journal* as well. Women took on the consumer role, women's magazines incorporated that role into their very fiber, and the distinctions between advertisers, manufacturers, and magazine writers and publishers became much less clearly defined.[87]

During the teens and twenties women heard promises that their work would become more and more professional, more valued. Yet the emphasis on new methods of housekeeping was always connected, sometimes subtly and sometimes not, with an accompanying emphasis on the consumer role for women. The two went hand in hand, although few promoted women using their consumer power in a political manner. "Encouraged by the combined wisdom of the periodicals which have set up high standards of advertising acceptance," Frederick wrote of the modern woman, "and given ever more benefits through the enlightened efforts of high-class manufacturers, she has developed a 'consumer-acceptance spirit'–a readiness to follow where she is led, that has had an immense bearing upon the American industrial prosperity and standards of living."[88]

Although Christine Frederick moved on from the *Journal,* her followers promoted scientific housekeeping methods in the *Ladies' Home Journal* through the 1920s. Her most skilled followers were not always the advice writers, however; they were often the advertising copywriters, who used scientific housekeeping principles directly to justify and encourage increased consumption. As advertisements became more visually enticing in the 1920s, with the increased use of color, they also became more sophisticated. Copywriters followed a 1920 article on "Selecting the New Floor," for example, with advertisements about linoleum coverings.[89] Proper floor coverings, they argued, were more efficient and could help to lessen women's work in the home. Another copywriter, in a Hotpoint Appliance advertisement, proposed that women read the advertisements rather than the tedious editorial columns to get the real story. This headline read: "For the Woman Who's Too Busy to Listen to the Reams of Advice."[90] Copywriters took this opening, the lack of clarity between editorial material and advertising, and used it to bolster their reputations as advice givers. Sometimes the copywriters told their stories in a more amusing way or more convincing way than did the columnists; when this happened, they began to compete seriously for reader attention.

In January of 1924, for example, Mabel Jewett Crosby wrote an article entitled "The Kitchen Cabinet as a StepSaver."[91] She described the convenience of the cabinet and outlined how women could store their utensils and spices in easy-to-reach places. All the proponents of scientific housekeeping praised this type of cabinet. In theory, the woman who owned such a cabinet had everything she needed to prepare a meal right at hand; she did not waste steps walking from the pantry to the table to the counter. The article was interesting, but the Seller's Cabinet advertisement which appeared the following month was arguably more convincing and undoubtedly more entertaining. The Seller's advertisement told the story of Betty and Jim Hall, the new residents of Ebury Street. Once they had settled in, a buzz of conversation ensued among the neighbors. Betty seemed to arrive home only minutes before Jim every night. This was scandalous. Did they eat canned foods every night? Jim looked healthy, but how could Betty have prepared proper meals in such a short period of time? Mrs. Pullman was given the role of detective, and she arrived at the Hall's house one night just before supper time and asked to borrow a cup of flour. There stood Betty, in front of her kitchen cabinet, beginning the meal. While Mrs. Pullman chatted, Betty prepared biscuits, cherry pie, vegetables, salad, and a thick juicy steak. Mrs. Pullman became convinced of the efficacy of Betty's system and, apparently, so did the other nosy neighbors. Within a few weeks, "an amazing number of Seller's Cabinets were delivered along Ebury Street."[92] Some advertisements even included little maps just like those Christine Frederick included in her articles, outlining how many steps the use of their products would save. These colorful ads featured "real" women and promised not only the reward of less work but the implied rewards of greater autonomy, romance, and lasting youthfulness. In short, steps saved in the ads promised to be steps more worth saving.[93]

Some advertisements also promised something Christine Frederick and her followers in the editorial section of the magazine shied away from: men's involvement in the kitchen. Another Seller's Kitchen Cabinet advertisement promised that things had become so easy in the kitchen with the use of the cabinet that even men would join in. The ad pictured a man wiping dishes in front of the cabinet. A Paramount Pictures advertisement, titled "Everybody steps lively on Paramount night," promised that if women invited their husbands out to a movie after dinner, the men would be so excited that they would help out in the kitchen to be sure to arrive at the cinema on time. A General Electric advertisement, titled "If Fathers did the washing just once!" argued that men would be exhausted if they participated in household chores; they certainly would purchase electric washing machines. In these ads and others like them, women could fantasize about what received only negative attention in the editorial matter: eliminating the strictly gendered nature of housework.[94]

The connection between housekeeping and consumption continued to grow through these years. In a 1929 article, "The New Era in Housework," a writer argued that things had certainly changed; women were more powerful members of society because of, rather than in spite of, the housekeeping component of their work.[95] Statistics support the argument that consumption increased but not the notion that such a development translated into power. Women spent $162 million on canned goods in 1909. By 1919 the amount had reached $575 million, and by 1929, $930 million. They spent $6 million on cleaning and polishing items in 1909. By 1919, that amount reached $27 million, and by 1929, $46 million. Women bought more mechanical appliances and spent ever greater proportions of their total expenditures on household items.[96] Outside the *Journal*, various organizations promoted the political action such spending could generate. The Consumers' League, for example, organized boycotts and mobilized consumer pressure to end child labor. Some home economists urged consumer action, although as historian

How I Made My Country Kitchen Efficient

By Mrs. Christine Frederick

National Secretary, Associated Clubs of Domestic Science

FORTUNATELY it is small, only ten by twelve. I think most country kitchens are too large; they are often a combination sitting-room and kitchen, which is a poor plan, because it entails the presence of too many objects unrelated to the actual work. It is much better to have the sitting-room separate so that the tired cook may sit down in a different room from that she has worked in.

In planning for any kitchen I have found after close study that there are just two sets of processes in all kitchen work; every task can be placed under one group or the other. Group I includes all the processes which *prepare* the meal; Group II includes all the processes which *clear away* the meal. Each of these processes or groups covers *distinct equipment*. The reason for so much inefficiency in kitchen work is almost solely because these two processes are not kept separate and because their equipment is mixed up. Let me state it in this way:

GROUP I

PREPARING MEAL	EQUIPMENT
1. Preparing Foods	Ice-Box, Pantry, Table, Cabinet
2. Cooking Foods	Stove, Utensils
3. Serving Foods	Table, Trays

GROUP II

CLEARING MEAL	EQUIPMENT
1. Removing Foods	Trays, Tables
2. Washing Utensils	Sink
3. Laying Away Utensils, Dishes	Pantry, Closet, Ice-Box

Suppose, for instance, we make an omelet. We take the eggs from the ice-box or from the pantry, beat them at the table or the cabinet, cook them on the stove, lay them on a platter on the serving-table and take them to the dining-room. These steps close Group I. On the return trip (or Group II) we take the empty platter from the dining-room to the sink, wash it and lay it away on the open shelves.

Now if the kitchen tables, pantry (or kitchen cabinet) and stove are placed in the best relation to each other we can make an omelet, or any other dish, without waste motion and waste steps, and in the least possible time. Taking up the separate equipment of Group I we see that they are in order, this way:

Pantry—Table—Stove—Table

Taking up the equipment of Group II, the clearing-away process, we see that they are in order:

Sink Table—Sink—China Closet—Pot Closet

If the equipment is arranged on this plan there will be few lost steps in preparing and cooking meals. Making an omelet with properly arranged equipment our feet would follow a straight path across the kitchen to the dining-room; making an omelet, if the kitchen table and pantry are across from the stove and the ice-box in the farther corner near the sink, would have made our track like the crossing and recrossing of a dog after a hare.

In my small kitchen, therefore, beginning at the south wall, I have an ice-box, then comes a kitchen cabinet, then the stove, then the small table from which I serve, but on which I never prepare foods or lay soiled dishes. On the other side of the room comes, first, a long china closet with simple shelves, then the drainboard of the sink, then the sink, and last, at the right, a small sink table on which to stack soiled dishes. By this simple arrangement of the principal equipment I begin the process of making an omelet with taking an egg from the ice-box, beating it at the board of the cabinet, frying it on the stove directly adjacent, laying it on the platter on the serving-table to the right of the stove, with never a move back or across the room.

IN THE second process I take the soiled dishes straight to the sink table, wash them in the sink, drain them at the left, and place them at once, without carrying, on the shelves at the left of sink.

Each table and sink, the surface of the cabinet and the cook stove are all at the right height for my height. Notice whether or not your stove is just the right height for convenience—it may be too low or too high.

"Down cellar" is the place where most edibles are kept in the country. This necessitates much going up and down steps at the expense of the home-maker's energy. I have installed in my kitchen an elevator ice-box which works on pulleys and which can be raised or lowered in a moment. It also comes in the screened "pie-closet" style, and, either way, it keeps the every-day supplies of milk, butter and meats cool in the cellar and yet allows the housewife to get them to the kitchen in a moment, without any steps.

I store all surplus vegetables and canned fruit in the cellar, in a cool storage place, bringing up only such supplies as are needed at the time. Flour, sugar and excess staple groceries are in closets in the dining-room, although a small pantry, with outside opening, would be better.

Package goods, a moderate supply of flour, sugar, staples and spices, are kept in the kitchen-cabinet top; and bowls and most pots and pans are in the lower part. I consider a kitchen cabinet the best kind of step-saver and superior to loose and unrelated shelves and closets. I have had built in it a little drawer for the filing cook-book I described recently in THE LADIES' HOME JOURNAL. A large calendar, a kitchen memorandum, a notebook and a billhook are hung at the side of the cabinet, and a tested kitchen scale.

The molding-board of my cabinet is my surface for preparing food and making bread. I group small utensils in every case according to the large process or task of which they are a part. By the wall of the kitchen cabinet I have hung those small articles connected with the preparing process—can-opener, cleaver, bread-knife, egg-beater, measuring spoon and cup, and many kinds of knives.

Over the stove hang its related articles—pancake-turner, skimmer, roasting-fork, large spoon. Over the serving-table are its tools—potato-masher, colander and strainers—and they never hang in the wrong places.

Under the serving-table covered with galvanized iron, which stands thirty-two and a half inches high, is my three-compartment fireless cooker, with a four, an eight and triplicate pails. When wanted it is pulled out so that it can be filled with the pot from the stove directly to the left, and when not in use it is rolled under the table.

THE drainboard of my sink is extended at the left by a small board under which I have a boxed shelf, just deep enough to accommodate the garbage-pail. In the board, covered with galvanized iron, is a hole, eight inches in diameter, fitted with a lower ring of iron. When I prepare vegetables I take out the high stool which just fits under the sink, and prepare them at this board; when done I merely push refuse into the hole, when it drops into the pail beneath—an idea adopted from the tables in fish shops. The outside of the shelf supports my dishpan, drainer, dish mops and cloths. The shelf holds the various washing powders and soaps, out of sight but very handy.

There are several other pieces of equipment in the kitchen worthy the attention of the country home-maker. Foremost is a colander which screws to the table and which is excellent for apple sauce, mashing vegetables and jelly-making. A meat-chopper, with gutter to prevent escape of juices, is a necessity. A double portable oven with a glass door does all my baking, and need not be opened to see the progress of baking. Bread and cake makers are excellent. A wheel-tray, with two large trays mounted on a stand and fitted with rubber tires, can be easily moved in any direction and is invaluable in serving. A teakettle with double-boiler inset saves an extra utensil. Muffin-pans of spherical shape are easy to wash, and a large fruit kettle with an upright handle has a hook on which a strainer can be hung for deep-fat frying. A roll of paper toweling near the cabinet enables me to wipe a cutlet or drain potatoes in a sanitary way. A permanent mixing-bowl beats my omelet, which I cook in a new double omelet-pan.

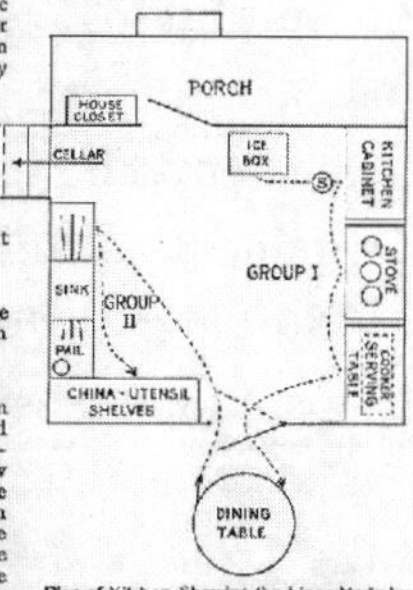

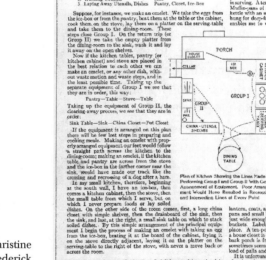

Plan of Kitchen Showing the Lines Made by Performing Group I and Group II With Good Arrangement of Equipment. Poor Arrangement Would Have Resulted in Recrossing and Intersecting Lines at Every Point

IT IS true that in the country there are many "varied industries" of milking, preserving and stock-feeding which are wrongfully brought into the kitchen, so that the country kitchen is often prone to be the scene of confusion and a dumping-ground for all kinds of unrelated utensils and work. It is best to have, as many do, a separate outshed for these distinct tasks, letting the kitchen remain free for its chief purpose—the preparing of foods. Many of my tasks are banished to the cellar, which opens on the garden. I find that vegetables as brought straight from the garden to the kitchen carry too much sand and dirt. City dwellers who know carrots only as they receive them, washed and free from foliage, can hardly believe the amount of earth that a bunch of carrots, "tops and all," will bring to the sink. I wash all vegetables in the cellar before bringing them to the kitchen.

Often, also, the kitchen is made untidy by the presence of unrelated cleaning equipment like mops and brooms. Cleaning tools and mackintoshes do not belong with the bread and the egg-beater. I have built a house closet on the back porch, 5 by 6 by 1, in which I have made a place for all these outside tools. The closet has a shelf across half of it, in which are niches for mops and broom handles. Hooks at the other side hold a lantern, coats, aprons, mackintoshes. The carpet-beater and dust-pans and small brooms are hung on respective nails. The floor is just wide enough to accommodate heavy boots, rubbers, pails and buckets. Labels make it impossible to put anything in the wrong place. A ten-pocket shoe-bag holds dusters, string and rags. Such a house closet is often much needed in the country home, where the back porch is frequently cluttered with a confusion of articles and sometimes seems too burdened and dejected to brace up under its load of pails and pans.

It is unfortunate that the best modern device for the incineration of garbage is operated by gas only, and is thus put out of reach of the very person who needs it most—the country dweller. I have not yet found a satisfactory substitute for the covered garbage-can, but I sterilize often, sprinkle with chloride and with kerosene, that cheapest and best disinfectant. Papers and rubbish are kept in a wire rubbish-burner and are easily reduced to a char.

OFTEN the ceilings of country kitchens are low, but light tones on the walls, particularly pale greens and tans, are cheery and will make the kitchen seem larger, especially if no break is made in the wall surface by a wainscoting. Since the fuels in the country kitchen make unusual soot on walls and ceilings it is best to cover them with washable paint in flat finish, or with washable oilcloth paper, so that frequent cleaning may be possible. My own walls are painted in light cream, the woodwork in white, and the floor is covered with a new kind of thick linoleum which is soft and restful to the feet—a point worthy of consideration to one who stands most of the time.

All the utensils of the kitchen are of aluminum, as these are lighter, of better shape and seamless. Around the kitchen is a small shelf on which I have placed purely decorative utensils, such as a percolator, casseroles and several tea and coffee kettles. It is possible and easy to have the kitchen beautiful and decorative without losing any of its efficiency as a workshop. The country kitchen, set as it is in picturesque surroundings, can be made to have as beautiful an interior as any which the Dutch painters have given us as art treasures.

It is possible for the country kitchen to attain a high degree of beauty and efficiency if the home-maker gives her work thought and care. The whole effect of my kitchen is one of order, cleanliness, light and rest. It is not an expensive kitchen, and the equipment is marked by its simplicity and "fewness" of utensils. It has, too, what all country kitchens should have: a beautiful view from the windows, giving the worker that much-desired "long view" which rests the eyes from close work.

The country home-maker has more duties and problems than her city sister, but, like all hardships, country home-making has its compensations; and I can say stanchly that the health, beauty and independence possible only under conditions of country life more than compensate for the extra work of the country home.

Christine Frederick promised to make housekeeping more of a science and hence more respectable. Here she offered ways to save steps across the kitchen floor. (*Ladies' Home Journal*, July 1913, p. 20)

The hungry husband and the chiffon frock

SHE really didn't need the frock. Even Mrs. Lowe admitted that. But the moment she saw it, she wanted it. The saleswoman promised to hold it until morning. All the way home Mrs. Lowe planned her campaign.

Imagine her dismay then, to discover that she was frightfully late—that Mr. Lowe was already home, and as cross as a husband usually is when neither a smiling wife nor a savory meal awaits him.

At such a moment, action is better than words. A hungry, impatient husband—and the loveliest chiffon frock in the world at stake! No ordinary "pick-up" meal would do.

She flew to the kitchen. From the drawers of her Sellers came her big apron and clean towel. She pulled forward the snowy-white Porceliron Worktable of the cabinet—for with much to do and little time to do it, plenty

Silverware Drawer

of working room was necessary.

Apple pie she must have—Mr. Lowe loved it. And hot biscuits! Down came the Automatic Lowering Flour Bin, level with the table top, while Mrs. Lowe quickly emptied the newly arrived sack of flour into it. A light touch of her hand, and the bin swung back into place. No time lost here.

Swiftly she gathered her work-things together. Mixing bowls, biscuit and pie pans came forward with the shelf, when she opened the lower cupboard door. No stooping or reaching, with the Sellers Automatic Base Shelf Extender. Salt for the biscuits, spices for the pie and sugar in a wide-mouthed tilting glass jar were instantly reached

Extending Drawer Section

when she slid up the Roll Curtain. Coffee, she speedily obtained from the same well-planned compartment.

Steak, thick and juicy, French fried potatoes, peas and a crisp salad of lettuce and tomatoes! None took long—Mr. Lowe liked them all.

Here again the Automatic Base Shelf Extender saved time—bringing the lower shelf forward and needed pans within instant reach. The lids she took from their convenient racks on the lower doors. Every inch of the cabinet space had been utilized to save her time and steps.

The upper cupboard doors contained a rack to hold the cookbook open at eye-level, a flavoring rack, compartments for change and milk tickets, the bill file, egg timer, and printed cards of cooking suggestions.

Nothing had been omitted, it seemed. The bread was just under her hand, in the aluminized metal-lined Bread Drawer. The Ant-proof Casters kept it safe, just as the Dust-proof Base Top protected the lower shelves. The silver was in a special Plush-lined Silverware Drawer.

Never had Mrs. Lowe so fully appreciated the time-saving features of her Sellers. Almost before she knew it, dinner was ready.

Automatic Shelf Extender

That it was a triumph she soon knew, as, with the progress of dinner, she saw a look of blissful contentment effacing the frown on Mr. Lowe's face. Her time had come! "I saw the most adorable chiffon frock today," she casually remarked, "and . . . . . . !"

* * *

Any dealer will show the Sellers Cabinet and its "Fifteen Famous Features" not combined in any other cabinet. Most dealers will gladly arrange convenient terms. Write for nearest dealer's name and our book, "Your Kitchen as It Should Be," showing six Modern Efficiency Kitchens, by the well-known Chicago architects, Schmidt, Garden & Martin.

G. I. SELLERS & SONS COMPANY
Elwood, Indiana

Canadian Branch: Sellers Kitchen Cabinets
Brantford, Canada

THE   BEST   SERVANT   IN   YOUR   HOUSE

The Sellers Mastercraft Cabinet illustrated is 70 in. high, 41 in. wide and 27 in. deep

SELLERS
KITCHEN CABINETS

G. I. SELLERS & SONS COMPANY   155
Elwood, Indiana

Gentlemen: Please send me your booklet, "Your Kitchen as It Should Be."

Name

Street

City   State

Advertisers followed Christine Frederick's lead, connecting professional housekeeping with new appliances and with promises of more free time for the alternative to housework—shopping. (*Ladies' Home Journal*, May 1924, p. 167)

Harvey Levenstein notes, the field of home economics increasingly tended toward a science of consumption rather than a politics of consumption. In 1927, an editorial writer in the *Journal of Home Economics* declared, "[M]ost of us are becoming more and more convinced that a principal function of home economics instruction is to train for the wise selection of and utilization of household goods."[97] The *Ladies' Home Journal* purposefully shied away from the enormous political power such purchasing power suggested, preferring to view women's work as merely domestic, wholly removed from the larger world.

Few women could make of housekeeping the business proposed by Christine Frederick, but all middle-class women helped keep housekeeping-related businesses in business. When they purchased new items, perhaps they found the new technological methods easier, equated consumption with social mobility, or relished the therapeutic role of consuming. Whatever their reasons, middle-class women followed the dictates of the magazine and spent money. But while the *Ladies' Home Journal* reflected women's changing values, it undoubtedly also shaped them, always claiming the apolitical and natural nature of women's work. As housekeeping increasingly became associated with purchasing, and as advertisers increasingly took on the role of advice givers, many women who read these new definitions of women's work in the *Journal* and other women's advertising magazines found their own struggles obscured and their work neither more fulfilling nor less demanding.

Advertisers, understanding women's dissatisfaction with the gendered nature of housework, suggested that given the right incentive even men would help in the kitchen. (*Ladies' Home Journal,* May 1921, p. 30)

three

Women's Paid Work

Setting and Stretching Boundaries

*A*lthough most of the editorial matter and advertising in the *Ladies' Home Journal* in the 1910s and 1920s concerned women's roles as wives, mothers, and homemakers, the topic of single and married women's paid employment also found a voice in the magazine. The *Journal* dealt with the question of women and work by providing a host of arguments on the subject; some favored women's employment, others deplored the very notion of women leaving the household arena, and still others accepted the inevitable and suggested ways of accommodating to women's paid work and the accompanying social changes. While the magazine provided a forum for all sides, however, it consistently favored a particular philosophy: paid employment was an acceptable prelude to marriage for single women but was a detrimental if not disastrous step for married women.[1]

Several developments characterized single and married women's work lives in this period. First, steady streams of people, including many young unmarried women, moved from rural areas to cities, where they found greater opportunities for employment as well as the relative autonomy that accompanied this paid work. In a 1911 article in the *Journal*, a writer offered advice for young women like the one in her title, "Her Sister in the Country Who Wants to Come to the City and Make Her Way." Urban life, she argued, stood out in stark contrast to life in Centerville, "where there seems to be nothing . . . to do."[2] The cities promised young women endless activities, glamour, excitement. As historian Rosalind Rosenberg puts it, the frontier of the nineteenth century appealed more to men than to women; the city of the twentieth century was "women's frontier."[3]

A second change in women's employment opportunities and experiences resulted from the nation's changing business pattern. Between 1870 and 1910, the corporation became the dominant form of business in the United States. As a result, the white-collar workforce, of which women were an important component, grew steadily. Female clerical workers numbered 10,000 in 1870. By 1900 their numbers increased to 400,000, and by 1920 they numbered two million. Women also entered jobs in department stores and in the telephone industry. By 1907, women represented 99 percent of the country's more than 140,000 telephone operators. These changes occurred rapidly, especially in the large cities. Chain stores, which employed large numbers of women and included Woolworth's, A&P, and Rexall Drug, numbered 29,000 in 1918 and 160,000 in 1929.[4]

During the nineteenth century, domestic work had accounted for the majority of women's nonagricultural paid employment–60 percent in 1870. By 1890, however, the percentage had dropped to 40.3, and by 1920 it was down to 18.2. On the other hand, white-collar work accounted for 7.2 percent of women's nonagricultural work in 1870, 13.5 percent in 1890, and 38.9 percent in 1920.[5] These statistics point to obvious and significant changes in women's work lives during these years. Urban, white-collar jobs became far more numerous, and women continued to fill them. The statistics alone, however, obscure the nature of the changes. In the telephone industry a woman could not be "too old, too young, too small, Jewish, or black."[6] Although white-collar work expanded tremendously, most opportunities for employment within this sector were limited to native-born, white women. In the large cities, native-born white women with native-born parents experienced the greatest increases in participation in the workforce from 1900 to 1920–a 35 percent increase.[7] From 1910 to 1930 in Philadelphia, home of the *Ladies' Home Journal,* black women and native-born white women with native-born parents were the ones most likely to be working for wages. By 1930, 78 percent of this group of black women and 48 percent of the white women worked outside the home. But since black women were excluded from white-collar work, native-born white women with native-born parents account for the tremendous increases in female white collar employment.[8] Nationally, between 1890 and 1920, white, American-born women took 90 percent of the clerical jobs available. Conversely, in 1920, 80 percent of all black women wage earners worked as maids, cooks, or washerwomen.[9] The young white women and their mothers, representing the target audience of the *Ladies' Home Journal,* represented the clear beneficiaries of a growing corporate culture and its continued gender-specific but racist and ethnocentric policies in hiring.

A third demographic change in women's employment opportunities concerned the employment of married women, which doubled between 1900 and 1930, increasing six times as fast as single women's wage earning.[10] The numbers remained small, however, and the social stigma attached to married women's paid employment did not disappear, especially among the middle class and especially in the pages of women's homemaking magazines. While the statistics point to a seemingly fixed trend, the cultural battle was fierce, as any measure of economic independence for married women was viewed by traditionalists as a threat to the traditional family, and by feminists as a necessary way to bring respectability to women in general and to women's unpaid work at home in particular. Those holding a middle ground found it acceptable for a married woman to work until her husband attained a certain income, at which point she would quit her job.[11] Even this notion, however, was not entirely acceptable in the *Ladies' Home Journal,* which most often promoted the traditional arrangement.

When married women's wage earning was discussed in the public arena, it was often deliberately linked to feminism and extremism in attempts to discredit the idea of women controlling their own resources after marriage. Since the middle-class marriage contract essentially required women's unpaid work in the home, wage earning could undermine the institution of marriage as it was understood.[12] Many feared that economically independent women might abandon men and marriage. Interestingly enough, then, while the *Journal* and other sources argued the primacy of marriage in women's lives, they also often seemed to suggest that economic dependence was the only thing preventing women from abandoning these relationships. The issue of women's paid work found its way into the public discourse before World War I, but after the war, as Nancy Cott puts it, "It was rare to find a year in the 1920s in which any magazine with a wide middle-class readership, whether high-brow or middle-brow, did not contain an article on this question."[13] College girls wrote about the employment of married women in their student newspapers; economists debated the long-term effects of women's lifelong wage work; vocational bureaus adapted their material to meet the needs of married women and older workers in general.

The *Ladies' Home Journal* joined in this larger debate most often by proclaiming women's allegiances to the home and threatening that the end of the social order would accompany married women's economic independence. However, like many traditionalist arguments, the one put forth most often in the *Journal* contained a host of contradictions. While the editors and writers encouraged married women to value home and hearth above all else, they discovered that married women who were willing to work part time could serve as effective sales agents for the *Journal* and for other Curtis publications. The argument then took a turn to suit the needs of the magazine-as-business: women's primary responsibility, they reasoned, was to home and family, but certain types of work, notably the type the magazine offered, did not threaten the sanctity of the family. A second contradiction was that by continuously offering women promises of better living through purchasing, the magazine helped to make paid work for married women more and more desirable. Sociologist Lorine Pruette observed in 1929 how "the pleasure philosophy," a large part of the *Journal's* agenda, promoted rather than discouraged women's wage earning: "Women need wages, want wages, to keep themselves afloat on the tide. . . . As our pleasure philosophy takes deeper hold, as the demand for luxuries, artificially stimulated by advertising, mounts giddily higher, there is no help for it—the women have to go to work."[14] Although in retrospect the *Journal's* role in this is clear, editors and writers of the day struggled with a concept so essential to the magazine's business but so deeply challenging to traditional definitions of womanhood.

Arguments about women and work proliferated in the *Ladies' Home Journal* through the teens and the twenties. Writers and readers debated the kinds of work single and married women should hold, the effect of paid employment on women's abilities to keep house, and the ways in which women should or could meet both their economic and personal needs. Writers often introduced these questions in the context of discontent, recognizing a general malaise among an increasing number of women who considered how paid work might add a needed component to their lives. The *Journal* addressed the discontent, sometimes by blaming the victim, often by presenting contradictory messages, but always reflecting the problematic nature of women's work and family lives in this time period.

The *Journal* offered a great deal of advice for single women and their parents. Writers generally accepted wage earning among young unmarried women, but they also explored the generational conflicts mothers and daughters experienced over women's changing roles. Mothers feared that their daughters, having tasted the pleasures of working for pay outside the household, would fail to accept their "true" role in the home. Educators concurred, complaining about the failure of modern education to teach women the practical skills they would need to run their domestic businesses. Doctors wrote articles expressing fear that the increasing employment of white women would lead to fewer of these women having children, thus precipitating race suicide. Single women themselves also wrote in to complain, not that they were headed down the wrong path, but that they needed more freedom to choose the directions they would take.[15]

In a "Personal Experiences of Mothers" column in 1914, one mother told the story of her failure with her daughter, a modern girl who represented in every respect a "big" problem. She quickly learned to cook, the mother related, but once she had mastered it she refused to do it any longer. The mother blamed herself for creating a monster, for in trying to give the girl every modern convenience she had raised a daughter with no sense of hard work. The young woman wanted no part of a "woman's responsibilities"; in fact, she refused to marry. "I had allowed her to catch the infection of the modern woman's mental trouble, the dread of the humdrum," lamented the mother.[16] In the minds of this and other writers and editors in the *Journal*, the modern world offered young women ideals which differed sharply from those of their mothers and which encouraged them to escape the humdrum but necessary roles of traditional womanhood. Whether their daughters were responsive or not, one writer argued, women's responsibility was to teach the young to embrace these household roles. Unfortunately, too many young women wanted something more: "They prefer to click typewriters, sell goods, keep books, teach school—do something vocational and remunerative," complained one writer.[17] Readers and writers expressed a great deal of ambivalence about young women's work opportunities. On the one hand, their mothers and their mothers' contemporaries seemed proud of the young women's abilities to make a go of it in the world. At the same time, however, they feared that the resulting independence would lure women away from the home and family. Interestingly enough, few mothers or editorial writers expressed confidence that the domestic life sold itself; they almost uniformly believed that young women had to be pressured to accept a supposedly natural and inherently desirable role.

Women's education in the public schools and colleges often bore the blame for such revolutionary attitudes, and the *Journal* contained several articles that advocated separate and decidedly unequal education for girls. In "The Girls at the Head of the Class," for example, a principal of a large girls' school wrote that when a girl graduated she could perform equations but could not "boil an egg, broil a steak, bake bread, darn a sock. As a wife, as a mother, as a housekeeper," this principal argued, "she would be an absolute failure." A chart accompanying the article outlined on one side what the girl needed to know, and on the other side what she had actually studied. She might have used cooking skills, for example, but she had studied algebra. She might have used a knowledge of household sanitation, but she was taught German. What would become of such a woman? This principal envisioned a dismal future; the young girl could leave high school and go to college, ". . . and for four years more she will be put still further out of touch with the life that God intended a woman should lead, or a practical life. . . . And at the end of four years, if her health survives so long, which I doubt, what then?"[18] Another writer declared that girls needed a "womanly" education, and boys a "manly" one. In educating boys and girls from the same texts, she argued, "we are moving inevitably toward free love." This same writer wanted girls to learn the practical skills: "Teach your girl the plain things first. God loves you if He lets you know that the plain is the great. The dish washed, the skillet or the dinner-pot scoured, the hearth swept, the bed made up, these are the great accomplishments. This is the only education that should be made compulsory."[19]

Some writers, however, namely young women themselves, defended this generation against the legion of criticisms. In a column entitled "Believe *Me*: Some Things are Changing for Us Girls," a young woman complained that parents too often offered girls a twentieth-century education and then expected them to assume nineteenth-century roles. The young women certainly were not to blame. "We may make mistakes," she wrote, enlisting her audience in the struggle, but women were decidedly on the "right track" in assuming their independence.[20] Another woman, writing in the same column a month later argued that the fault did not lie with the young women. This writer saw herself and the women around her caught in a "maelstrom of feminism" in which there were no easy answers. It was a confusing world, she argued, and many women would have liked the "wholesome, unquestioning, rather uneventful domestic life our mothers led as girls, with its simple amusements and its early marriage." The problem, she continued, one which "many of the older generation do not realize, is that most of us cannot."[21] This young woman may have simplified the realities of her mother's contemporaries, but she also articulated very real generational conflicts. And although historians have demonstrated that seemingly radical activities of the emerging youth culture met with fairly strict peer restrictions, less radical generational chasms permeated the middle class.[22]

While many parents expected their daughters to excel in and enjoy their education, some feared that higher education could only lead to disappointment. "If your child has genius you can't beat it out of her short of killing her," lamented one writer, "but you may make her unhappy for a lifetime by hinting to her that she has unusual talents."[23] Parents watched their children being lured by options other than wife, mother, and homemaker. These generational conflicts and the free-spirited nature of women, which many have equated with a post–World War I mind-set, were clearly evident earlier in the century, as the words of a young *Journal* reader in 1911 illustrate: "I am living with a woman friend who loves me and who helps me in every effort I make toward a higher womanhood. We never bore each other. I have congenial employment and a good income. I have my own self-respect. It seems to me that this is better than bringing little children into a home full of discord, or better than enjoying just a taste of domestic happiness and then appealing frantically to the law for relief from an intolerable situation."[24] While few women achieved the level of economic independence necessary to support such a choice, the fact that any woman might choose a female- or career-centered rather than family-centered life was enough to terrify the *Journal*'s writers and editors as well as many readers. Single women's employment was strictly supposed to be something that led up to marriage, never a substitution for it. As a result, when any women made alternative choices, the *Journal* questioned the value—and feared the dangers—of gainful employment for all women.

When it came to work for pay, the *Ladies' Home Journal* focused primarily on these arguments, but it also contained practical advice about careers and job training opportunities for young women, success stories of their accomplishments in the work world, and advice about how women could or did respond to problems they encountered on the job. In "What Shall I Do After High School," Kate E. Turner told women readers what kinds of post-secondary training were required for specific jobs, including nursing, library work, kindergarten teaching, costume design, and secretarial work. She told what salaries women could expect to earn and described the nature of each job. The advice was practical and non-judgmental, removed from any larger debates.[25] The *Journal* contained many such articles, most of which provided thoughtful and reasonable advice. In "How Can I Really Learn a Profession?" for example, Irene Vandyck highlighted the books and government documents available to help women make their career choices.[26] Other writers encouraged women to choose occupations which suited their individual skills and abilities. In "The Girl Behind the Typewriter," Margaret T. Grayson discouraged women who were not good with language from becoming stenographers. The business world was highly competitive, she warned, and women without sharp language skills would unhappily find themselves stuck at the bottom rungs of the employment ladder.[27]

Some of the advice offered in the *Journal* encouraged career-minded women to go to college, but the college route was not deemed the only route to respectable success. Writers described college as the gateway to the professions but also presented secretarial work in a good light. Some of the advice bordered on the ridiculous and illustrates the nature of the just developing field of career guidance in this period. Ruth Neely, in "Where Your Job May Lead," argued that the job of governess could lead to a position as the head of a girls' school; the job of cashier could lead to a position as head of a credit department; the job of stenographer could lead to a position as an attorney. Such cases may have occurred but they were unlikely, especially in the last instance. The notion of vocational guidance revealed its weakest side, though, in a 1921 article by Ethel Spalding Slater. If a woman mailed her a photo, Slater would send back an analysis of the woman's career aptitude. She based her decision on an examination, through the photograph, of the individual's facial features, general health, and digestive power.

The truth outside the pages of the *Journal* revealed that there was little room for advancement within the segregated female job sector, white-collar or otherwise, regardless of what the career books promised. Women's work increasingly became just that—work done solely by women—hence less prestigious and less profitable by definition. Women working in factories earned little more than half of the wages earned by men, and in service jobs women earned even less.[28] Secretarial work often offered the best promise, even to those women with college degrees. Yet the new jobs for women, like the old ones "missed even the bottom rung of the ladder of upward mobility."[29] Fortunately, the usual fare in the *Journal* shied away from promises of wealth and fame and offered instead more practical advice, with writers covering everything from healthy and affordable lunches to the business risks involved in certain job ventures.[30] And in addition to the questionable suggestions about career choices and career suitability, the *Journal* offered its unmarried readers some positive role models. Throughout the teens and twenties the magazine solicited true stories about how women had achieved success, often in the face of adversity. Some of the women wrote their stories on their own; others were provided "as told to" one of the regular *Journal* writers. Many of these articles were fairly straightforward and described how college women managed to earn money while in school. Others, however, recalled the more dramatic, near-death conditions of women who, by strength of character, managed not only to feed themselves but also triumph in the business world. Whether these groups of stories with obvious heroines were true or, as is more likely, written by aspiring women writers, they form one component of the successful young working woman image.

A large number of articles encouraged college students to earn money and to feel good about their abilities to do so. As one writer put it, "no honest work is degrading." She related the story of two college women who did laundry work for the other women in their peer group. Rather than become disgraced by the need to earn money, however, they "kept their own self-respect and the respect of hosts of friends."[31] Although no statistics are available concerning how many college women wrote in requesting this kind of advice, many writers acknowledged reader requests, and articles on the subject continued to be published, growing more numerous during the 1920s. An English professor at Wellesley College, Laura Lockwood, wrote "Can a Girl Work Her Way Through College?" in which she provided a list of suitable and profitable jobs for needy students, including housework, dressmaking, shopping, and shampooing. In "Through College Without Means," Elizabeth Sears recommended typing papers for other students. Some of the suggestions, like the household hints described in the previous chapter, were less than universally applicable and provided no promise of steady income. One article, for example, told the story of a woman who got out of bed half an hour earlier than her dorm mates and went from room to room turning on the heat. Her friends awoke to warm rooms and the enterprising young woman earned fifty cents a week per room.[32] Such suggestions for college women reflect a society in which these women's employment was a novel idea, apt to be treated in a manner more curious than serious.

Women responded to their need for money in a variety of ways, most of which were not highly organized, and few of which were particularly profitable or risk free. Articles encouraged women to try almost anything: baking and decorating cookies, taking photographic portraits, tinting post cards, starting night schools for factory children. It is noteworthy that the list contains so many uncertain and obviously low-paying jobs. It is just as noteworthy, however, that the *Journal* provided so many encouraging articles, however tenuous the suggestions they offered, for women who wanted to attend college but who had to earn money themselves in order to do so.[33] The sheer number of articles attests to both the readers' desires for and their creative attempts towards education and independence and the *Journal* writers' acceptance of women's work as an inevitable outcome of contemporary social changes.

The *Journal* occasionally provided stories of women, usually single, who had assumed male jobs. Interestingly enough, these articles were always laudatory. A 1917 article, entitled "Women Who Have Blazed New Trails: Through the Forest of Men's Work Once Believed Closed to Their Sex," described the careers of a metal worker and an art appraiser. A second article applauded a woman judge and yet another honored a policewoman for blending "the law and the gospel of social service." In another article, entitled "The Real New Woman Who Answers the Question 'What's the Matter With Women?'" the answer, apparently, was that nothing was wrong with the New Women, who included in their ranks Josephine Wright Chapman, one of the first female architects in the United States. In July of 1916 the *Ladies' Home Journal* began to carry advertisements for schools and colleges, a clear sign that women's education and their subsequent participation in the workplace had gained acceptance.[34]

In the 1910s and 1920s, Margaretta Tuttle submitted several success stories that young women supposedly had shared with her. In one such article, entitled "From Hunger to Power: First of Several Stories Told By Women Who Have Succeeded in Business," readers encountered a woman who, apparently through no fault of her own, found herself homeless, without training, and in need of a job. Forced to this low state, she shamefully asked a man on the street to give her some money so she could eat. He directed her to a hotel where he worked as manager and he provided her first with a hot meal and then with a job as a dishwasher. However grateful she felt for the help she received, the woman was not content to remain a dishwasher for long; she observed everything that took place around her and soon knew most of the business of the hotel. Once he discovered this, the manager hired her to work with him and put her natural skills to better use. The woman made a giant leap from dishwasher to assistant manager, bypassing the many other workers in the hotel's hierarchy. The reader is apt to fill in one of two missing pieces as an ending: first, that the woman was originally from a wealthy and cultivated family, which would account for her seemingly effortless success; or second, that the woman and the manager soon fell in love and married.[35]

A second article of this type, "What I Went Through in Trying to Get a Position," provided these kinds of suggestions in an even less subtle manner. In this case, a young woman ventured from her rural home to a large city in search of employment. She went straight to the YWCA and then, when her one-week limit there was up, to a boardinghouse. After five weeks of constant searching for work, she had found nothing. She met girls living on the edge and suspected danger in the guises of friendly men and wily employers. One day, though, she heard herself being described as an "unusual" case, "ladylike and refined." A beneficent woman, apparently noticing the young woman's inherent qualities, decided to help her. Both of these young women succeeded not out of sheer luck or out of a fierce struggle for advancement but, seemingly, because they had some innate qualities which pushed them along and which made them noticeable in the large and often cruel world of the cities. Unlike some of the other success stories, which recalled how women had opened boardinghouses or sold books door to door, these stories provided an escapist approach to the whole notion of women at work. Readers may have felt some relief that their situations, however bad, were better than these. They may also have felt some encouragement that they too would someday be recognized for their special goodness by a loving man or a beneficent woman. Whatever the case, it is significant that the stories' conclusions showed the women achieving success in their businesses rather than escaping to the home, even if that ending is subtly suggested in the first story.[36] For single women, a career could be an appropriate goal in itself.

Women wrote to the *Ladies' Home Journal* to share both their success stories and their failures. While many of the accounts were of women's ascents from sheer poverty to financial success, others stated more simple accomplishments that resulted from women's employment experiences. One of the seemingly simple but obviously rewarding results of work was the ability to generate friendships on the job. In an article entitled "What it Means to Be a Department Store Girl," a woman ranked her friendships above all else: "There are no truer friends and comrades," she wrote, "than those won by working together, shoulder to shoulder, day after day." Work was not, after all, only financial success stories and dreams come true. It meant hard work, day after day, with simple rewards and, often, many problems. In this same article, the writer described the "endless dangers" associated with her department store work. The temptation to steal, she argued, was foremost. Young working women felt pressured, by themselves, their friends, or perhaps by men they met. The specter of men, in the voices of many of these writers, formed an ever present danger in the lives of young working women.[37]

This department store worker faced the unpleasant attentions of men while she was on the job; she and others found it difficult to know how best to respond. In "The Girl Who Works," Martha Keeler acknowledged letters she received on behalf of the *Journal.* "This is a glorious time to live," she wrote. "Never before in the land of self-support were there so many fine opportunities for women as there are today." From this upbeat beginning, however, Keeler turned to more serious matters; women had to be on guard at work. They might find camaraderie and financial independence on the job, but many also encountered the extreme loneliness that left them vulnerable to the pleas of men looking for fun but unwilling to make commitments. In "What Girls Ask," Mrs. Laura Hathaway related the story of a woman who worked at a five-and-ten and who needed helpful advice. A male customer, very friendly and, apparently, fairly wealthy, attempted to initiate a relationship with her outside of the job. Should she accept his offer of a date, the reader wondered. No, Mrs. Hathaway cautioned, steer clear of this man. Wealthy men did not look for wives at five-and-dime stores. The young woman worked hard and deserved to enjoy herself, Hathaway continued, but she had to learn the respectable limits and steer clear of men who obviously fell outside of her class range.[38]

Although the *Journal* avoided discussing sexual relationships in a straightforward manner, the article cited above points to one cultural reality that resulted from the discrepancy between the amounts of women's and men's paychecks. Women workers at the time did accept "treats" from men in exchange for a wide range of attentions. Men like the one described above could provide a working woman with entertainment, including theater tickets, dancing, and drinks. The woman in turn would provide sexual favors that ranged from flirtatious companionship to sexual intercourse. Rosalind Rosenberg argues that these women were not promiscuous, but they did stretch the boundaries of Victorian feminine decorum.[39] In short, as Beth Bailey puts it, dating provided an economic form of exchange, less direct and clear than prostitution, but an economic exchange nevertheless.[40] Single working women had to weigh their values against an increasingly sexually defined work and social world.

90

Women discovered that unknown men paid them attentions; they also discovered, often to their dismay, that known men also requested their friendships, or more. Harriet Brunkhurst discussed this issue in another article, in which she described the situation of a young woman whose boss continually told her stories of his personal life and his problems with his wife. Such a relationship held the potential for grave danger, Brunkhurst warned: listening to the boss was the first step towards engaging in an illicit relationship with him. If the woman could not stop the boss from talking, she had to keep strict confidence and, above all else, remain noncommittal. Women sometimes fell in love with their bosses, or with other men they met on the job, but according to the *Journal*'s advice-givers, these women had to take responsibility for the situation and make the breaks when necessary.[41] In "My Greatest Experience as a Girl," a woman told the story of how she fell in love with her boss and he with her. Her solution: to convince him that she was sentimental and tasteless, then to leave the job. Had she just left he would have tried to stop her; this way, though, she was able to make a clean break. In another episode of "My Greatest Experience as a Girl," a woman told of her business success. "At twenty-four I started a business in a middle-sized Ohio city," she began. On her own, the woman met many people but unluckily fell in love with her friend's husband. Her solution: she told him a tale of a fictional couple in a similar situation. The tale ended happily, as did their dilemma once the man realized the significance of her story. The woman, her friend, and the friend's husband remained close. Many other articles described men as predators and warned women that they alone had to set the limits for all female-male relationships.[42]

Although many single women faced the temptations of noncommittal or married men, others faced an equally difficult problem. Some working women did not receive attentions from men, who felt threatened by their independence and ability to earn their own living. An interesting article on this subject, written by "A.B. Alumna," was entitled "Does the Girls' College Destroy the Wife: A Frank Confession of Why One College Girl Has Not Married." A graduate of Vassar, a teacher, and thirty-five years old, this woman confessed: "I am unmarried, I am a statistic." If the reader expected a further confession in which the woman regretted her education and argued that it prevented her happiness, however, she found something very different. This woman challenged all the conclusions of the statistics that numbered her a failure. Unmarried, yes; without children, yes. But a failure—no. She went to college not to make a fancy career for herself but to be an "abler woman." She had never married because she had never been asked. Men were afraid of her because she earned a higher salary than did many of them. A woman in her position faced the future alone, but she viewed it more as the result of men's problems than her own.[43]

This woman belonged to the generation which was unhappy with the either/or scenario; they wanted both careers and marriage, both public and personal fulfillment. It was no easy task, though, to find men who would support such a notion on more than a theoretical basis.[44] This woman had many counterparts in the world outside the *Ladies' Home Journal.* Freda Kirchway, editor of the *Nation* magazine during the 1920s, initiated a series entitled "These Modern Women." The women wrote of their struggles, successful or not, to integrate work, marriage, and family. Many of the women struggled in isolation, "without glamour or recognition," each woman "alone in her home or office." Their stories depicted the truly interdependent nature of family life for women, many of whom could only entertain their own aspirations if the other members of their families took up the slack of the gendered work women retained responsibility for at home.[45]

A 1927 *Journal* article warned further of the problems women faced competing with men in the work world. Laura H. Carnell, Associate President and Dean of Temple University, counseled women to go out into the business world, but tread lightly around their male coworkers. Allow men to feel superior, she suggested; allow them to think, however incorrectly, that women are illogical. Let men believe they are giving in to the woman as they "gave in to their mother when they were little, just to please her and not to hurt her feelings." The surest road to success in the business world, according to Carnell, was to encourage men to think that women's ideas were their own. She compared women in business to the Virgin Mary helping the Lord in his work. One finds it difficult to imagine how Laura Carnell attained the position of Associate President of Temple University following such advice. Perhaps she viewed the business world differently than she did the academic world; perhaps she knew what the *Journal* wanted and was eager to be paid for her writing; or perhaps she saw her readers as fundamentally different from herself.[46]

In the pages of the *Journal* during the teens and the twenties, then, the topic of single women's paid employment, with all of its ups and downs, found its way into much discussion and occasional debate. While some complained that employment and the training that preceded it made women unfit for their future roles, others accepted the situation and encouraged young women to make the most of their opportunities. The greatest and most consistent fear expressed about these women by *Journal* writers was that they would prefer paid work to household work, and the greatest and most consistent fears expressed by the women workers themselves were poverty and problems with both the wanted and unwanted attentions of men.

While the *Ladies' Home Journal* dealt with the issue of single women's paid employment by providing space for all sides of the discussion, the magazine was less hospitable when it came to married women's wage earning. The *Journal* maintained its position that employment should end when marriage begins during Bok's tenure as editor and through the 1920s as well. The magazine argued, essentially, that married women belonged at home. In a 1911 editorial Bok outlined his basic philosophy: marriage and paid employment were not compatible roles for women. Women wanted choices, he acknowledged, and they had two of them: to marry or not to marry. The woman who chose marriage should also choose domesticity. When a man asked a women to marry him he invited her to create a home, he argued: "She should know precisely what this involves. If she does not, her education is sadly at fault." In this and subsequent editorials on the subject, Bok provided anecdotes to support his stance. One young women admitted to her grandmother that she had one serious reservation about marriage: she did not know how she would be able to handle mere housekeeping after so many years of brain work. The grandmother's mirrored Bok's statements: "'My dear,' replied the old lady. 'I don't know much about mere housekeeping: I never did much of that; but if you succeed at all in *home* keeping you will find that you are just beginning to do your brainwork.'"[47] In another editorial, Bok acknowledged that married women had begun to prove themselves outside the home. While he seemed to accept that he could not reverse this process, the editor complained about the consequences. What happened to the work "that belongs to women" when these women left their houses to go to work? "For when we stop to think," mused Bok, "there is a certain amount of work in this world that can only be women's work and can never be anything else." Like Christine Frederick, Bok predicted inevitable problems in the household when married women held jobs. Neither considered that men could take on some of the household responsibilities, and both correctly envisioned women suffering from exhaustion with their double duties. Bok and Frederick could imagine only one solution: women had to put their household responsibilities first. If they did so, of course, they would admittedly have had little time for anything else.[48] In another editorial, Bok linked women's work to their nervous problems. "Death has a new clutch on us unknown to our mothers," the article began. It continued by describing the nationwide problem of women with nervous conditions. "Every house has its victim," Bok ominously declared. Women should not have suffered from this malady since their ancestors, who worked even harder, never experienced problems with their nerves. "They carried their own loads," argued the editor, "but they were content to be women, wives and mothers, and not voters and reformers besides." Contemporary women had taken on too much, the editor warned, but he had a solution: "Let the girls beginning life read the answer to that question, read it as it is written in the handwriting on the walls of today: that to be a home-maker and mother is a woman's sphere. Her shoulders were made for these burdens and are able to carry them. But let her venture beyond her sphere, and the rebellious nerves instantly and rightly cry out, 'Thus far shalt thou go, but no farther.'"[49]

Bok's superficial treatment of a complex social problem—women's nervous disorders or hysteria—point to his general woman-blaming stance as well as to a general social impatience with women's weaknesses, emotional, physical, or psychological. "Hysteria" was a generic term used in literature, psychology, and popular culture to describe the condition of women who suffered from any of a host of problems, including anxiety, irascibility, and depression. As Carroll Smith-Rosenberg has documented, hysteria resulted when gender roles did not change as readily as demographics, which provided women with longer lives and more years free from child rearing. Hysteria was "one option or tactic offering particular women, otherwise unable to respond to these changes, a chance to redefine or restructure their place within the family."[50] Hysterical women did want it all, but neither their families nor the culture at large were ready to open the gates. The hysteric was both "product and indictment of her culture," argues Smith-Rosenberg, but according to Bok's editorial she was a mere nuisance.[51] It is not difficult to imagine, behind Bok's critical demeanor, a degree of fear of women who would go to such lengths to protest the direction of their own lives.

The discussion of hysteria points to the culture's ambivalence about, among other things, women's paid work, but an article published in 1916 illustrates that many readers of the *Journal* felt less than satisfied with the pat responses they received about the increasingly complicated issue of married women's wage earning. Signed "Secretary of the Wives' League," the article, entitled "Should Married Women Work?" emphatically declared that they should. Ten years ago, the author stated, she would have said they should not, but married women themselves convinced her to change her mind. Married women believed married women should work: "In a year I have met 30,000 who believed it. In the next year I expect to meet 50,000 more!" When a group of women started the Housewives' League in 1906 and discussed the issue of women and work in the *Ladies' Home Journal*, she informed her readers, four thousand letters of inquiry followed within ten days. In the following thirty days, the magazine received ten thousand additional letters. Women clearly wanted outside employment, at least in part because men failed to appreciate or even recognize their efforts or sacrifices. "Contrary to public opinion," wrote the secretary, "it is men, not women, who despise wifehood and motherhood as an occupation. They show it by the ways they are willing to pay for it."[52]

This *Journal* writer, unlike many others, acknowledged both that women had grievances within the household and that paid employment was one solution for some of these problems. Most of the *Journal* writers acknowledged women's grievances but stopped short of suggesting that women choose paid work as a means of bettering their situations. The writers did complain about women's victimization, but they generally advocated change within the family—women or men acting more responsibly or showing more understanding of one another—rather than the more revolutionary change of women leaving the household realm to work for wages. So although the magazine did acknowledge men's shortcomings in marriage, it encouraged women to make up for those shortcomings, to assume the larger share of emotional and household responsibility for the future of the family.

One issue which came up again and again during this period was the problem of money distribution in the household. In a 1911 editorial, Bok spelled it out clearly: "This business of giving the cook so many dollars a week and food and lodging, and getting a housekeeper for nothing because she is a wife, is a transaction in which common fairness has no place; and there are a goodly number of husbands who sadly need to get this truth firmly fixed into their heads."[53] Five years later Bok wrote an editorial on the same subject, and again he argued that a woman was entitled to a fair part of her husband's wages. "So it is that, when a man is paid his wages, those wages have been earned partly by his wife," he wrote. "And as his partner in his earning capacity, she is entitled to her share." Again, the following month, he returned to the topic. "It is not in the interest of this magazine to create discord in any home, or to array wife against husband," he declared, "but it is the duty of the *Ladies' Home Journal* to arouse a wife to a proper standing in the realm in which she rules and is mistress." The ironies of the situation were apparently lost on Edward Bok. The wife would rule a realm in which she yielded no economic power. The culprit husband would change his ways simply because they were not in keeping with "common fairness." Men remained reluctant to share their wages, and women and families suffered when women did not have access to the family funds. In the five years between these two editorials the situation obviously had not improved, yet Bok stopped short of advocating any real action on the part of women, legal, economic, or otherwise.[54]

The *Journal* advocated, for the most part, "her" marriage and "his." "It is a generally accepted fact that while marriage is but an incident in the life of a man, it comprises a woman's whole existence," declared a *Ladies' Home Journal* writer. The author argued that since men became less romantic and attentive after marriage, women had to accept them for what they were. The magazine repeated this message again and again in many contexts: women had to accommodate to the men they married. In what is an especially distressing example to a reader of today, a woman wrote "How I Lost My Attraction to My Husband" in 1917. This woman felt unhappy with her husband, who wanted her to change to suit his tastes. She finally gave in and, as a first step, bought a dress which he liked very much but which she disliked. As a result of her new purchase, he invited her to meet him in the city for lunch, and the process continued from there. She concluded the article by telling the readers what she had told her husband: since she began to cultivate her wardrobe to suit his tastes, things had improved for her in every way.[55]

The *Ladies' Home Journal* consistently advocated the sanctity of the family, and when it seemed that women had to make sacrifices to maintain this sanctity, most writers in the *Journal* supported such a move. In all likelihood, they feared a future in which women would make demands their husbands could not meet. If wives grew less accommodating, they feared, husbands would not grow more so; instead, marriages would fall apart. In fact, this was increasingly the case. While most married women went to work because they needed the money, they often found that work provided them with emotional as well as economic support. The end result for some women was that they chose not to better accommodate to their husbands and family roles but to change those roles, through divorce. The *Journal* writers were not altogether wrong in fearing women's paid employment, since they had no faith in men and little in women.

Divorce rates soared during this period. In 1914, judges granted roughly 100,000 divorces in the United States. By 1929 the number had reached about 200,000 per year. Women requested most divorces, and in the period from 1890 to 1920, about two-thirds of all divorces were granted to women. Wage earning women were the group most likely to request divorces; they also received the social blame. A judge in the Court of Domestic Relations in Dayton, Ohio, argued that women who bought canned goods or who consistently bought dinner at a delicatessen might find that "beans could be breeders of divorce."[56] Writers in the *Ladies' Home Journal* often took a similar approach. Women who reneged on their household responsibilities, rather than men who reneged on their financial or familial responsibilities, forced the breakup of the family. Edward Bok and his successors feared divorce, but never made the connection between stingy or inattentive husbands and this new social phenomenon. Instead, in a series of articles on divorce published in the magazine from the early teens through the twenties, they most often blamed women. In a 1921 article women were warned, even in the title, of the risks they faced. "A Home or a Career?" by Mary Roberts Rinehart, assumed from the outset that the roles of homemaker and career woman were incompatible, and the article specifically stated that when marriage was secondary to a woman's life, divorce often followed.[57]

Other writers in the *Ladies' Home Journal* argued that divorce was bad not for the women themselves but for the children. Again, however, the women and not the men shouldered the responsibility for what happened to the child-victims. A 1916 article stated that women had to be at home for the welfare of their families, especially their sons: "The mother may be doing a much greater thing than she dreams of when she sits by the fire with her knitting. The seemingly careless boy who comes running in from school finds a supreme contentment in seeing her there. You might call this masculine selfishness if you wished to be disagreeable; but again, you might call it, and I prefer this, man's innate and racial feeling for home with a comforting mother in it."[58] The author used the threat of the racialized other as a means of keeping white women at home. At the same time she justified, perhaps unwittingly, black women's employment: their men and children seemed not to share, from this perspective, innate needs for nurturing.

It was bad enough when women negated their responsibilities by holding employment outside the home, but when they broke the family apart through divorce, the consequences worsened considerably. Women received the social blame for juvenile delinquency and for creating children who did not know how to live in the ways which were traditionally acceptable or, as another writer put it, "racially inherent." In an article entitled "Divorce and Child Crime" by Ruth Scott Miller, the author argued that between 80 and 90 percent of all child criminals were the victims of broken homes. She related the story of a child who tramped for six years through the streets—often in the rain—in search of his mother.[59] These arguments attempted to promote, through subtle reference to "the other," values that, although "racially inherent," needed much repeating.

When a woman writer articulated the connection between the money problems mentioned in the *Journal* and divorce, she received a negative reply from the *Journal*'s second in command, Karl Harriman. In "Fifty-fifty Finance," Grace Nies Fletcher cited a 1927 study at the University of Nebraska which had concluded that women's contributions to the family were more valuable, if they were translated into dollar value, than their husbands' contributions. Divorce, she argued, often resulted from money problems at home, and men had to recognize the significant contributions of their wives. While the magazine had earlier supported claims for shared wealth, this claim, that women's contributions were greater than men's, was too much. The editor called the article "ideal divorce fodder" and viewed it as a corrupting rather than empowering addition to that month's offerings.[60]

Aside from Edward Bok, Juliet Virginia Strauss was the most consistent writer in the *Journal* to warn against the evils of women's paid employment. Strauss, whose signature "The Country Contributor" followed each of her submissions, wrote "The Ideas of a Plain Country Woman" for the *Ladies' Home Journal* for more than thirteen years, right up until her death in 1918. She also published an occasional column under her real name, with no indication that Juliet Strauss and the Country Contributor or the Plain Country Woman were all one and the same. A voice of conservatism, Strauss continuously lamented the new ways of women and reminisced about the old. At the same time, however, a reading of her articles reveals the inarticulate longings of her readers and the sometimes articulated and far from satisfied longings of the Country Contributor herself. Strauss's column demonstrates the truly complicated nature of the question of women's work and home lives in the early twentieth century.[61]

"The Ideas of a Plain Country Woman," Strauss's monthly column, often described the country ways that disappeared due to urbanization and women's paid employment. "I love kitchens and backyards and vegetable gardens," she wrote, "and hogs and washings and threshing machines." Strauss argued that city people, tied to large corporations, could not own their own land, be self-sufficient, or retain simple values. As a consequence, city people had less intelligence: "Nobody who hires things done, who buys things ready made, is or can ever be quite as intelligent as the one who does things." For married women, of course, her message rang clear: household work was the only valuable work.[62] Strauss lauded the simple life philosophy promoted by Bok, but she went even further by not advocating consumerism as a positive good. Juliet Strauss admitted that times were changing and acknowledged from time to time that not all of her readers would agree with her. In 1911, she reminisced about forty years earlier when women were the acknowledged wards of men, who were obliged to take care of them. Women in 1911, unfortunately, seemed to want so much more than that. In a 1917 column, Strauss had had enough and plainly equated marriage with housework, each home with a specifically male hero. "Rage if you like when you read this, you modern woman imbued with the thought of the great strides women have been making lately." She argued, in fact, that any woman who did not follow the straight path to marriage and who led men on along the way "is not normal . . . (is) sadly deformed from the image of the perfect woman."[63] Strauss did not feel that women, by performing the roles of wife, mother, and homemaker, missed out on anything. "Motherhood is the largest experience of human life," she argued. Men did have thrilling experiences in the battlefield, in politics, and in the workplace, but women had the opportunity to serve. No mean feat, service ranked "infinitely higher" than achievement. And in Strauss's words, women's accomplishments did sound grand: women "must dignify labor, they must serve, they must produce population, they must handle the raw materials of life."[64] Her descriptions of the specifics, however, sound less convincing. Women had to be practical and reserved in their ambitions, Strauss argued; for them beautifying a plain little yard ranked higher than writing a book.[65]

When the Country Contributor's readers commented on the obvious contradiction between her monthly messages and her ability to earn money by writing this column, Strauss did not back down, but neither did she explain why she needed to earn money when her husband, who outlived her, was better than employed: he owned a small weekly newspaper. In a 1917 column, Strauss acknowledged that she received many letters from readers who envied her ability to work and earn money. "I wish the women who envy me my salary could know how many of the glad fulfillments of a woman's life I miss while I am earning that salary. I have seen home suffer miserably through my own professional work. I have, for years, been a mere boarder in my own house, a mere machine for earning that others might spend."[66] Women's business, she argued again and again, was the home. In another column she praised the "Plain Business Women" of her state, Indiana, who cooked, cleaned, performed chores, did child care, and helped "with life in general." Strauss told her readers that they had to look no further than their own homes for routes to success. "There is no cleverness in woman," she wrote, "equal to the ability to cook a suitable meal and make whatever home she is in restful and comfortable."[67]

Strauss had few kind words for married women who sought paid employment outside the home, and she continuously railed against women whose paid employment caused them to hire other women to care for their children. All children deserved to find their mothers in the kitchen when they returned home; it is "the natural human quest," she wrote, "primitive as hunger itself." Strauss was less subtle than some other writers in appealing to the whiteness and native-born status of her audience as she extolled their supposed racially inherent and shared values. "I make an earnest appeal to mothers to look after their children themselves. I proclaim to you that unspeakable evils due to carelessness, ignorance or wickedness of nursegirls are shockingly common. This is especially true of Negroes in the South. There is no natural servant class in America. . . . The help we get in kitchens, if it be American white help, is bound to be the work of some unfortunate person who has failed to reach the standard of education or efficiency that will enable her to command a better position. It was to this class of help that the American wife and mother turned over her kitchen when she decided to get rid of drudgery and live like a lady. Why she preferred the horrors of the trail of slipshod, untrained, mentally and morally deficient women, who have stalked through practically every kitchen in the land, to doing as her mother did—that is, personally supervising all the household work—I cannot tell."[68]

The Country Contributor was quick to blame women when things did not work out at home, and an undercurrent of fear of women's sexuality pervaded her writing. If women were not home to supervise their children, she argued, "morbid tendencies" and "secretive habits" would result. When their daughters ended up in trouble, she euphemistically wrote, mothers should not send their husbands out with shotguns but should blame themselves for their daughters' transgressions. Women had to keep lascivious men away not just from their daughters but from themselves. The woman who dressed noticeably, Strauss argued, "is contributing merely to the abnormal in men's nature." Women had to dress conservatively or they might find that they have called men back "to the moral degeneracy which is the greatest handicap to the human race in its upward journey from the brute to the ideal."[69] Women had to take full responsibility for themselves and their daughters, Strauss argued, but she simultaneously upheld men's rights to direct the lives of women and children. "The man who is making a living for a woman," wrote Strauss, "who is doing her thinking for her, has a right to direct her conduct." Apparently Strauss did not think through the implications of this contradictory challenge for her women readers—to defer to men and to control them at the same time.[70] Like many conservative writers of the time, Strauss herself believed the contradictory notion that only subservient women could tame men's violent nature.

On the surface it appears that the Country Contributor, this Plain Country Woman, believed that women's true role was that of wife, mother, and house-keeper. She consistently argued that women could be happy in the home. If one reads further into her columns, however, a darker and far more subversive picture of traditional marriage emerges, as Strauss reveals the serious problems women encountered in their household and marital roles. In one column Strauss admitted that few women found happiness in marriage. A full two-thirds of women, she believed, felt less happiness after marriage than before, and their discontent could be attributed to one thing: men's shortcomings. Almost every woman "finds the thing so much harder than she dreamed it could be, and the man so much less appreciative of her sacrifice than any one could imagine." Women with high expectations in marriage faced certain disappointment. Men, Strauss argued, did not understand what women gave up when they married: "Remember, no man ever considers a woman's union with him a sacrifice on her part. When you consent to the close relation of marriage with a man you constitute him your master. This is true were you a Princess and he a coach-man. . . . Equality in station is for this reason especially desirable in marriage."[71] Hers is a fascinating analysis of the need for intra-class marriage. The issue was not the ability of the man to support the woman to her liking; it was instead that it would be more difficult for a woman to bow down as she would have to for a man from a lower class.

Juliet Strauss also revealed certain things about her life that complicate her simple and "plain" agenda for women's happiness. She never fully answered the question of why she herself worked for pay, and she even revealed that she had worked outside the home when her children were young. Strauss shared the story of how she earned her first independent money as a married woman. She was writing for her husband's newspaper, apparently without pay, when a wealthy man came to town for his mother-in-law's funeral. He paid Strauss ten dollars to write an obituary. "Ten dollars! Ten dollars all my own!" she later recalled.[72] Here Strauss perhaps unwittingly revealed the ways in which even a small sum of independently earned money might affirm a woman's existence and promote her self-esteem. In the mid-teens, Strauss revealed that she had a "bad case of nerves" and that the doctor had sent her away for a change of climate and a change of scene. "This was a great surprise to my family," she wrote, "who had always believed that Mother could stand anything." Her illness and the lack of sensitivity to her needs on the part of her family notwith-standing, Strauss continued to write. She revealed her lack of satisfaction with her life on several occasions, as when she revealed that she was discouraged by her "seeming failure to impress those nearest to me."[73] On yet another occasion, Strauss's admonition to her readers seems to be a reflection of her own situation: "If things seem piling up on you, if your children are not doing well, and the helpless ones of your family and acquaintances seem trying to pull you down by unreasonable demands on your time, strength and pocketbook, it is a sign that you are the strong one, and you must buckle down to the burdens or fail of your high calling."[74]

Although Juliet Strauss never revealed the real situation in her immediate family, she did suggest a few things about her life that lead one to question her simple country messages. In one instance she admitted that her daughters felt a great deal of unhappiness with their husbands. She blamed their discontent on herself, but one wonders about the degree to which these men represented, even in Strauss's eyes, husbands in general. She was so determined to find for her daughters "the fields where the white clover grows," she wrote, that she gave them ideals "out of proportion to anything that their husbands, now that they are married, can ever give them."[75] Strauss came back again and again to this theme: women who expect much at all from their husbands are sure to be disappointed. "Possibly I may be wrong," she wrote in 1911, "but it is a theory of mine that few men spend much time and thought on the business of making their wives happy."[76] Although men consistently come across as inferior rather than superior in her admissions, Strauss nevertheless directed her readers to believe in the natural superiority of men: "The young girl is allowed to believe that there is no bar to her possibilities," she wrote, "and she grows up without the proper respect for the natural divisions of society, which, not marked out for us as definitely as they are in England and more stable countries, are still as actual as the isothermal lines that circle the world. I believe there is nothing on the earth so impudent as our American claim of social equality."[77]

In another column several years later, Strauss complained about the seemingly unending sacrifice her family expected of her. This argument is a far cry from the praises she generally offered to women who gave their all to their families. For a long time, she reported, she was bitter about the attitude of her children, who "couldn't see why I wasn't perfectly willing to board and clothe them and take care of their children" while they were "having their fling." And although Strauss opened up one column by stating that the first fifteen years of a woman's married life were her happiest, "if she is the mother of children," Strauss later disclosed that she herself had little natural inclination toward child care, even that of her own grandchildren. During the war Strauss urged women to do volunteer child care so other mothers could do war work. Even she would volunteer, she stated, although she was not very successful with children. "Children do not like me unless they are unusually bright," Strauss wrote.[78]

Two other revelations underscore the level of the Country Contributor's discontent with things as they stood. When she spoke of certain women's desire to be called ladies rather than women, Strauss argued that the term "woman" was good enough for her, ". . . though I make no secret of the fact that I should much rather have been a man—a big man with iron muscles, a fine nervous system and a talent for doing things." Strauss also revealed that part of her disapproval of women who worked outside the home may have been personal. A group of women in her town began, at one point, to form what Strauss called a "distinct feminist movement." "I was not invited to join," she wrote. Strauss reported that this snub hurt a great deal, "for women are naturally 'foolish' about society, and, also, the movement was supposed to be instigated and carried on by the 'brainy' women of the community, and I disliked being set outside the pale of the intellectual people."[79]

Juliet Virginia Strauss, the Plain Country Woman, presented a seemingly simple recipe for women's happiness: women would marry, take care of their homes and families, and find contentment. On closer examination, however, one sees that even Strauss struggled to live the life she promoted on the pages of the *Journal* every month. Several of her writings suggest that she, like many of her counterparts, suffered the pains of marriage to a less than attentive husband. Her words offer contradictory messages about women's true nature and proper sphere, but they make her neither a hypocrite nor a writer who wrote simply to fill the page. Instead, these words reveal the difficulties implicit in living the ideal presented in the *Ladies' Home Journal.* Women's real lives were so much more complicated than any simple formula, either urban and sophisticated or rural and bucolic. In the end, the Country Contributor's mixed offerings suggest that women's decisions—to marry, to work, to maintain or relinquish independence—were, like her own, often complex and painful rather than simple and joyful.

Neither the Plain Country Woman nor the *Ladies' Home Journal* ever fully dealt with the issue of married women's paid employment during this period. The magazine contained an occasional article describing how married business women could arrange their homes so that there was a place for them to rest at the end of the day, or how they could arrange for child care.[80] Several articles highlighted the career successes of individual married or widowed women as they made their ways into the world of work. One article featured the first female investment banker in the United States, a second, a woman who made natural dyes from plants and patented her products, a third, a woman who opened a school. These stories, presented simply as case studies, removed the reader from any larger context or debate about women's proper roles. Several articles illustrated how widows could make do after their husbands died: one sold books door-to-door while another, Mrs. Knox of gelatin fame, took over the whole business after her husband passed away.[81]

Most of the attention given to married women workers documented the stories of women who stayed at home with their families but found ways to supplement their family incomes just the same. In "Starting a Business in Your Home," Ruth Evelyn Dowdell argued that the home was the ideal location for the married business woman. "Work in the home eliminates rent," she explained, "one of the largest items of operating expense. It also keeps the mother in the home, where the home's best interests demand that she stay."[82] This became the accepted argument in the *Journal* as the years went by. If married women had to work, and it seemed that more and more of them needed the money and enjoyed the freedom, they could work at home and thus not disrupt the family life for which they remained responsible. The *Journal* sponsored a contest, in fact, entitled "How I Helped My Husband Make More Money," for which women sent in their ideas.[83] Enterprising wives baked cakes, preserved fruit, and sold snacks and beverages to passing motorists. The magazine never encouraged these women to view themselves as wage earners or breadwinners; instead, it defined their financial roles as supplemental labors of love. They helped their husbands as the husbands supported their families. Were these women questioned by census takers, they might simply have described their roles as homemakers, disregarding their own often important financial contributions to the family.

Even when the *Journal* upon occasion presented married women's work as positive or productive, the work somehow appeared odd or distinct from "regular" wage work. As was the case with college women's paid employment, married women's paid employment was difficult for the society, at least for the middle class, to accept. Women found few options and, as a result, some of the stories appear incredibly risky or one-of-a-kind. A column, "Women in Business," which concluded by declaring, "More power to all women in business!" saluted the "turkey czarina" of Idaho. Another article provided details about a woman who had one hair plucked from her head everyday. This hair was threaded through a machine at a cement factory to test the humidity at the plant. This same article praised a woman who made clothes for elephants and camels at a circus and another who, as a vacuum cleaner artist, made designs in flour using a vacuum cleaner nozzle.[84] And as mentioned earlier, the *Journal* itself advertised for women workers. "Wanted: A Good Housekeeper," one advertisement demanded. The ad told how the *Journal* wanted the woman worker "not to help us but to help herself."[85] If she had a little bit of extra income, perhaps, the housewife could even better serve as the stabilizing factor in the family: she could avoid conflicts with her husband over money, develop more self-esteem, and contribute to the magazine, and hence to the society. As was the case with housekeeping, advice about women's work lives often found a more interesting and perhaps more progressive formula in the advertisements than in the editorial matter; ironically enough, this was true even of the *Journal*'s own advertisements. The magazine-as-business found that it could benefit from changes in women's lives that the magazine as "cultural creator" found terribly difficult to accept.[86]

As readers attempted to make the best decisions about their work and family lives in an era of tremendous change, they occasionally pointed out the seeming contradictions in the magazine and in their own lives. But while women tried to sort out the contradictions, advertisers looked for ways to make those contradictions work to their best advantage. They pointed out discrepancies in women's married lives, the difficulties women experienced in raising a family, the promises they lost when romantic boyfriends turned into staid and somewhat dreary husbands. Their answer, of course, always pointed in the direction of purchasing. Libby's, maker of canned foods, offers perhaps the best example of this kind of cunning applied to marketing products to women. A whole series of Libby's ads exposed the contradictions implicit in women's roles and offered a way out through consuming goods. In one, a boy sits on his back porch with his head in his hands. His mother can be seen in the kitchen, through the porch window, preparing supper. The text alerts readers that this woman had believed the message that in order to be a good mother she had to spend a good deal of time in the kitchen. But what of the child? He clearly suffers rather than benefits from his mother's seeming obsession about housework. The solution: if she buys Libby's prepared meats she can serve a wholesome meal and, at the same time, spend time with her child.[87]

Another Libby's ad pictures a woman surrounded by pots and pans. As she looks longingly out the kitchen window, the woman realizes that she is best defined not as a terrific homemaker but as a drudge. She never goes anywhere or does anything outside of the house. If she had only used Libby's canned foods, however, she could have expanded her role and found more pleasure in her life. A third Libby's advertisement shows a bride and groom standing togeth-

"*I Want Some New Clothes*" "*I Want to Go Away*"

SICK OF HUMDRUM OFFICE—OR HOUSEWORK? HERE'S THE CURE!

The *Ladies' Home Journal* generally argued that married women should not work for pay, but when the magazine needed part-time workers it revised its policy and appealed to women's longings for some measure of financial independence. (*Ladies' Home Journal,* June 1920, p. 67)

er in their new home. This woman vows she will never let her housewifely duties interfere with her role as companion to her husband. Her solution, of course: Libby's prepared foods. In the final installment of this series, the ad asks of the woman reader, "Do Your Guests Find You as Interesting as Your Dinner?" The implication, of course, is that the meals she prepares are important but that the woman, too, is important; she needs something to talk about in a social setting besides recipes and other "women's concerns." Any woman, the argument goes, could accomplish this by using Libby's prepared foods, thereby allowing herself the time to keep up with the affairs of the world.[88]

A few advertisements in the *Journal* addressed the needs of wage-earning women. Kotex advertisements described the busy working woman who needed the security of Kotex to function well in all of her varied environments. Automobile advertisers often addressed women not only in their roles as chauffeurs/mothers but also in their developing roles as professionals. For the most part, though, ads, like most of the editorial material, correctly assumed that married wage-earning women also kept house, and they often promoted consumer goods as the best solutions for women's boredom, exhaustion, or general discontent at home. In this, as in many other things, advertisers struck a nerve. The term "superwoman" was used as early as 1919 to describe women who tried to do it all. From all accounts, even men who considered themselves feminists did not help with the chores that were traditionally female chores, so women's burdens grew.[89] Advertisers saw the benefits in addressing these conflicts and offering their own common denominator: all women, married and single, could find solutions to the problems of the day through consumption. A Pillsbury Health Bran advertisement, for example, promised that bran could help women deal with exhaustion they suffered from stressful work situations. A 1923 Hotpoint advertisement, entitled "To The Business Woman Who Does Her Own Housekeeping," offered sixteen different appliances. The ad tried to encompass it all: "One great American novel that remains to be written is about the modern business woman. It may be written by a man, or by a woman—but one thing it will emphasize. The faculty of the business woman for making her *home-building* instincts a *help* rather than a hindrance to her business career."[90]

According to the advertisements, women could do it all, successfully, if they used the right tools. According to many readers, though, and most of the editorial writers in the *Journal,* the woman could not do it all—she would have to sacrifice somewhere. In retrospect, the readers and writers were correct; women cannot do it all. Many tried, but most, unfortunately, followed the lead of advertising and women's magazines and looked individually to products rather than collectively to new social policies, in order to make their lives easier. The visions of women and work in the *Ladies' Home Journal* of the 1910s and 1920s represent a spectrum of attitudes and a fair degree of ambivalence on the part of all except those who perhaps had the most to gain in the short term—the advertisers. Perhaps women heeded the invitations of the advertisers in part because they offered "it all." With the ads women did not have to choose: they could have efficient homes, companionate marriages, well-adjusted children, and rewarding careers. The uncertainty always brewed just below the surface, however, even in the advertisements, which offered many promises but few lasting solutions.

Advertisers promised women that they could have it all, not by changing social or work patterns but by adding certain products to their household repertoires. (*Ladies' Home Journal,* June 1920, p. 57)

four

Stoves for Women Votes for Men

The Journal and

Women's Political Involvement

"Here is an anagram describing something women
should know how to use," said the puzzle giver.
"It is O-T-S-V-E."
"I know," said the suffragette happily. "It is VOTES."
"No," growled the anti, "it is STOVE."[1]

n February of 1916, the *Ladies' Home Journal*
offered its readers this joke about suffrage. Entitled
"Depends on How You Look at It," the joke named the
terms of the debate as they were generally expressed in
the magazine: votes and stoves were mutually exclusive
categories. The topic of women's suffrage engendered
much debate in and outside of the magazine, but the
most basic question for the *Ladies' Home Journal* was this:
if women took on this additional responsibility—and
additional political independence—would they abandon

their kitchens and turn housekeeping into little more than a hobby? Although the *Journal* proclaimed that the majority of women did not want the franchise and were well satisfied with their household roles, the vehemence with which the magazine campaigned against suffrage suggests that the editors, particularly Edward Bok, may have envisioned voting women literally walking away from their pots and pans and marching to Washington, never to return.

Although the *Journal* approached women's political involvement not only as a menacing but also a recent development, historians have documented the wide variety of reform efforts engaged in by middle-class women during the nineteenth century and through the Progressive era. Nancy Dye argues that women "filled the Progressive landscape," pressing legislators to pass minimum wage and maximum hours statutes, mothers' pensions, juvenile justice codes, prohibition of child labor and industrial homework, and compulsory school attendance. "The body of state and federal legislation for which women progressive reformers worked," she writes, "provided much of the foundation for American welfare legislation for the remainder of the twentieth century."[2] Even in 1910, at the beginning of this study, women formed a significant part of many reform efforts. The *Ladies' Home Journal* could not altogether ignore the efforts of these women, especially since many of them described the natural alliance they discovered between household and family responsibilities and political reform as they attempted, writes Dye, to "protect what they saw as the integrity of the home from the forces of the market."[3]

Editors at the *Ladies' Home Journal* were not averse to many elements of the national Progressive agenda, and even Edward Bok accepted that his readers would become involved in certain reform efforts. Like many people, Bok had his own favorite causes, and those found their way into the pages of the *Journal*. Campaigns against patent medicines, common drinking cups in public places, highway billboards, and the use of aigrette feathers in women's fashions formed the top of Bok's hierarchy of social concerns, and he eagerly enlisted the support of his readers in those struggles. The real conundrum for people like Edward Bok, though, who promoted their own progressive measures but who wanted at the same time to set limits on women's political experiences, was that women often used those small-scale projects as starting points for greater political involvement. Local progressive reform often led to national efforts, and national involvement on one issue often led to an interest in political participation more broadly defined. Helen Woodward, a contemporary of Bok, later described Bok's billboard campaign in just those terms: "Without quite realizing it, he taught them how to organize that power, so that today women are able to get our ungloved hands into everything."[4] Like other aspects of the *Ladies' Home Journal*, the magazine's stance on women's political involvement overtly discouraged but also, perhaps, unwittingly enhanced women's individual and collective political struggles.

In advocating mild social reform efforts but missing the connection between social reform and political consciousness, Bok and others may not have realized the empowering nature of some of the articles they agreed to publish. In a 1914 article, for example, Jane Addams introduced an idea that became a rallying cry of the late twentieth-century feminist movement: women become more radical as they age. "In their girlhood," she wrote, "they knew no exercise more violent than playing croquet, no diet more rigid than preserves and sponge cake for supper, no notion but that all diseases were Heaven-sent ... but they are now agitating for public gymnasiums and municipal baths, for pure-food laws and a clean milk supply; they are quite tigerlike in insisting that all children shall be protected from contagious diseases through school nursing and medical inspection, and they have come to consider a high death rate among infants as a disgrace and a reproach to the community."[5] An escape from household chores, she related, provided continued youth, not premature old age. Her "tigerlike" women, ignoring any mandates for separate spheres, sound very little like the domestic creatures the *Journal* claimed both to reach and represent.

These tigerlike women might have felt even more empowered by exercising the franchise. In and outside of the *Journal*, the granting of suffrage essentially "settled" the question of women as independent citizens, and that in part explains the magazine's decidedly antisuffrage stance. Female reformers could describe themselves as the nation's housekeepers, but the action of voting relegated women's political involvement to a different, more official realm. The definition of womanhood could now begin with political independence rather than in the home. Bok and others drew the line at this seemingly subtle but culturally significant line. When it addressed the issue of woman suffrage through the 1910s decade, the *Ladies' Home Journal* reinforced the most common fears and took a decidedly antisuffrage stand. In the joke provided above, the antisuffrage woman, depicted as "grumbling," is on the defensive, and much of the antisuffrage writing in the *Journal* comes from such a defensive stance, attempting to protect against what was rapidly encroaching. "My idea, you know, is rather to keep women in the home,"

Bok acknowledged in a letter to a *Journal* contributor, "especially as there are enough writers who are trying to take her out of it."[6] Such a development went against not only the financial agenda of the *Ladies' Home Journal*, which included selling a homemaking magazine and promoting women's consumer role for advertisers, but against its cultural agenda as well. The *Journal* relied on an essentialist definition of womanhood that was based in the home. As did increased educational opportunities and married women's paid employment, suffrage fundamentally challenged the notion that the home was women's most important realm of activity.[7]

Fear of woman suffrage ran through the *Journal* for the entire decade preceding its passage, and even after the question was settled, the implications of women's political involvement remained troubling to Bok's successors. As a prosuffrage climate developed in the nation during the 1910s, the *Journal* had no choice but to embrace or reject it. The teens decade saw the most active suffrage support, with African- and European-American, northern and southern, working-class and middle-class women supporting the struggle.[8] As middle-class women joined clubs and charitable and reform organizations, they began to see themselves, as Helen Woodward suggested, as members of a larger community, as people who could and did make choices and changes in the world. It followed that many women, including many readers of the *Ladies' Home Journal*, would come to view the vote both as a tool to enhance this process and as a right and privilege they had earned. Tools and rights, in the hands of women, were potentially dangerous and challenging to the status quo, but one of the many contradictions in the *Ladies' Home Journal* was that the magazine continued to promote women's participation in club and reform activities without appreciating the empowering quality this work could have for their political as well as social lives.

Outside the *Journal*, many feminists enthusiastically envisioned legions of post-suffrage, politicized women joining together as a bloc to use their votes, as Nancy Woloch has put it, "to purify politics and end war, imperialism, disease, crime, vice, and injustice."[9] They believed that men, in control of the nation for so long, had essentially abandoned causes of social justice; women had to take over and do the job right. Fortunately, according to this theory, women were both well-qualified and temperamentally disposed to make the necessary changes. Although most of the suffragists who made such claims met with disappointment once women achieved the vote and demonstrated fairly conservative and non-gender-specific voting tendencies, the idea that women would join together seemed likely to all concerned, pro- and antisuffrage alike.

While suffragists hoped for the best that women's separate political activity promised, antisuffrage women and men feared the worst: women voting as a bloc would destroy society by voting against their husbands, instigating family problems, inviting social anarchy, and creating–or perhaps acknowledging–a world divided by gender.[10]

The *Ladies' Home Journal* of the 1910s fit in squarely with the often overlooked but never silent antisuffrage sentiment in the United States. From the first antisuffrage association founded in Boston in 1882 through to the National Association Opposed to Woman Suffrage, antisuffrage activists–or Antis–testified before legislatures, produced local and national journals, and lobbied the Congress. However, even though they worked for a common goal, the elimination of woman suffrage or at least the prevention of the further extension of suffrage to women, antisuffrage women and men did not speak with one voice. Their objections to woman suffrage were based on fear of women, fear of men, or, simply, fear of change. Interestingly enough, however, the *Journal* printed strands of all the major antisuffrage positions, perhaps in the hopes that one or another of the arguments would reach individual readers.[11]

As Nancy Cott has argued, the nineteenth-century women's movement left middle-class women with a difficult legacy and three possible directions. One direction was to continue to advocate women's service and social action, such as settlement work and social housekeeping; the second was to advocate women's rights, including the right to vote; the third was to fight for women's independence and self-determination. The *Ladies' Home Journal,* for the most part, published articles that supported the first but not the second or third directions. This three-tier paradigm of women's political activity included a corresponding, decreasing commitment to the society as it existed. And although it was true that all feminists were not the same, when antisuffragists looked, they often saw what they considered the worst: women in the third category, those who had little respect for the existing social structure. One antisuffrage activist, equating all groups of women who struggled for change, put it this way: "Pacifism, socialism, feminism, suffrage are all parts of the same movement–a movement which weakens government, corrupts society, and threatens the very existence of our great experiment in democracy."[12]

Just as Antis simplified the suffragists' arguments, suffragists stereotyped the Antis. Activists like Anna Howard Shaw, who equated Antis with "vultures looking for carrion," both underestimated the numbers and significance of this opposing group and belittled their arguments.[13] The truth is that both antisuffrage and prosuffrage activists came from the same middle-class, educated background. In one family, one sister, Annie Nathan Meyer, who helped found Barnard College, was pitted on the Anti side against her sister, Maud, a leading suffragist.[14] Although the antisuffrage movement was complex, with a variety of arguments about the differences between women and men and about women's proper sphere, several arguments predominated. Two of these, which overlap in their concerns, are worth describing here, for they both found their way into the pages of the *Ladies' Home Journal.*

One of the most popular antisuffrage positions, and one fully in keeping with Bok's philosophy for the *Ladies' Home Journal,* argued that woman's sphere was influence, not power. She could influence the men around her and thereby indirectly improve the well being of the nation. Sounding more than a little like nineteenth-century prescriptive literature, Antis cautioned women to stay out of partisan politics but supported their participation in community charitable and reform efforts. They made distinctions between community work and political work, women's public activities and men's public activities. Even before the suffrage amendment passed, however, the government began to be more involved in sanitation, clean food and milk, child welfare, and prison and hospital reform—all elements of what had been appropriate work for women—and the lines between political and nonpolitical work blurred. Nevertheless, both the antisuffragists in general and Edward Bok in particular continued to make a distinction and to draw the line firmly at the exercise of the vote.[15]

Although Antis by no means originated the women's influence argument, they wholeheartedly promoted it, and of all their arguments it is the one that links them most closely with the *Ladies' Home Journal.* While Bok employed many themes to dismiss the importance of the ballot for women, his first mention of suffrage in the teens decade relied on this supposed strength of women. According to Bok, women could easily do as much good using their influence as they could with the vote. In a 1911 editorial he stated his point of view clearly and, as it sets the tone for the *Journal*'s pre-suffrage coverage of the debate, his words are worth quoting at length: "The woman who wields no ballot with her own hands must not suppose that she is thereby ruled out of the business of saving the country. She will have accomplished as much as any voter if by her influence she has held the men of her household true to the highest standards of citizenship and given them a home that they feel is worth protecting with their bullets, or their lives if need be. With her native instinct for right, reinforced by reasonableness and tact, she can outcharm

114

the spellbinder, disable the party boss, expose the wiles of the tempter, and put to rout the fomenter of violence. The woman who ignores her responsibility as the central moral force in the family offends as seriously as the man who abuses the privilege of the ballot."[16]

Recent work on the antisuffragists emphasizes this moral element. "We Anti-Suffragists feel that we not only can be and are citizens without the ballot," wrote one Anti, "but that we shall remain better citizens without it than with it."[17] Women, moral creatures that they were, would only be corrupted by politics in the same way men had been. Many of Bok's readers, however, did not accept this argument. With a "native instinct for right," as he called it, they felt they would clean the political house rather than become corrupted by it. In the case of suffrage, however, Bok refused to give in to his most numerous or most vocal readers. At the beginning of the decade, Bok declared that the *Journal* was neutral on the suffrage question. His approach, however, strayed far from neutral. In 1910, the magazine sent out a letter to prominent women in New York society, soliciting one-line answers to the question, "Do You, as a Woman, Want to Vote?" The page-long list of responses published in 1911 contained only negative responses. Bok's editorial comments asserted that these findings revealed where "the real New York women stand." He further emphasized that his select group was "authoritative" and from "the oldest and foremost families of New York."[18]

The magazine's obvious bias on this topic so irked one group of prosuffrage Colorado women that they took action against the magazine. The women were provoked several times in 1911 when Bok roundly criticized woman suffrage in Colorado, where the vote had been secured in 1893. First he highlighted the comments of a former suffragist who argued that the "best thing" for Colorado women would be if "tomorrow the ballot for women could be abolished."[19] The following month's issue of the *Journal* provided an anecdote which further mocked woman suffrage in Colorado. While a family sat down to supper, the daughter told her mother the story of a thirty-five-year-old man who had married a fifteen-year-old girl. The woman's reaction was that if women could vote, they would prevent such things from happening. The husband then informed the wife that this had happened in Colorado, where women already had the vote. "'Well,' said the wife, and she kept on serving."[20] Finally, two months later the *Journal* provided a series of interviews with nearly twenty prominent women in Colorado, all of whom concluded that suffrage had "produced no good effect."[21] Women in Denver reacted to these slurs by staging a boycott. Although the extent of the boycott is unclear, it drew Bok's comment in the very next issue. The effect of this action, he argued, and he may well have been correct at least in the short term, was to increase sales of the *Journal.* Bok continued, however, with a veiled threat against the women who might further organize such actions. "This magazine could easily and with some very conclusive and picturesque facts, become personal as regards some of the present leaders in the equal-suffrage agitation," he wrote. "But what would be gained by it?"[22]

Bok's response to the boycott continued into the next issue, where he allotted a whole page to antisuffrage women from Colorado whose quotations were said to represent the point of view of women of "undisputed social and civic prominence."[23] The *Journal* dropped the issue after that for some time but raised it again a year later. Apparently the boycott had spread; several women's groups had joined in the crusade against the *Ladies' Home Journal.* Bok chose as the editorial's title, "The Gentle Art of Boycotting this Magazine," but his reaction was hardly gentle. Boycotting was illegal, he wrote, and women's club leaders should know that they could be summoned to court for promoting such behavior: "This is not a personal or veiled warning. These words are printed as information: as a preventer of trouble, particularly to those ladies in the states where women have voted for a number of years, who, one might think, would by this time have learned enough of civics and laws to be careful about how they create a boycott on this or any other magazine or company."[24] The threat of mudslinging and then legal action on the part of Edward Bok was unusual, as he generally tolerated and often joked about differences of opinion he had with readers. He may have remembered the boycotts initiated by the National Consumers' League, a progressive women's organization founded in 1890. Florence Kelley, founder and longtime executive secretary, reported that as a child she watched her aunt refuse to buy cotton and sugar because slave labor had produced them. She encouraged the League to pursue similar tactics on a larger scale. For the most part, though, rather than boycotts, the League favored "white lists," published names of manufacturers that conformed to the League's social agenda.[25] Nevertheless, Edward Bok knew that the women consumers he reached, if they organized the power of their purchasing, could bring any industry to its knees.

Bok's hostile tone in this editorial hints at something more immediate than a memory of small consumer victories; it suggests something of his own personal vulnerability in misreading or misunderstanding his readers. It was not simply the issue of the boycott that so irked Bok; if anything, as he claimed, in the short term it improved his business rather than hurt it, and high circulation figures and fairly conservative readers figured into Bok's editorial plan. Suffrage was such a vexed issue for Bok because, like women's economic independence, it contradicted his opinion of women as a class. Bok had made his mark in the magazine world by assuming that women needed help, his help in particular, and the symbolism of woman suffrage was far from lost on him. "A girl may plan for herself the most dazzling of futures," Bok wrote in 1912, "but marriage and home are her destiny. That is eternal truth, and every woman knows it, no matter what she says."[26] Bok argued that he knew women, sometimes better than they knew themselves, and if pushed, he would use suffrage as his proving ground.

A sufficient number of readers complained about Bok's treatment of suffrage in Colorado to warrant a further response. In March of 1912, in an exasperated tone, Bok formally broke with his supposedly neutral stance on the suffrage question.[27] Women wrote in, he related, asking why the *Journal* went out of its way to offend "a great many estimable women" with antisuffrage articles. Bok then reviewed what he had done so far, including avoiding the subject, presenting both sides, soliciting the views of prominent women, and now, finally choosing a side. Bok revealed that some women had circulated a rumor that he had paid the antisuffrage Colorado women featured in the *Journal* $500 each to state that suffrage was a failure in their state. This suggestion, Bok argued, "has not the first scintilla of truth to it."[28] The *Journal* editor accused Anna Howard Shaw, president of the National American Woman Suffrage Association, of having started the rumor, and stated that he had written to her half a dozen times for proof but received no response.

From a position of veiled subjectivity, Bok moved the magazine toward a harsh and consistent denunciation of women's demands for the ballot—and of the women who demanded the ballot. The next month's issue contained a joke about the effect of woman suffrage in the suffrage states. A man attempted to educate his wife about the issues of the campaign before they voted, but she preferred to gossip to him about why she didn't like the wife of the better candidate. This better candidate lost, "for it seemed that many women didn't like the Colonel's wife."[29] Bok was willing to do what it took to keep women in the home: praise their accomplishments, belittle their intelligence, or threaten that they might lose their husbands if they failed to put their all into their homes.[30] Women, he believed, could change the course of the nation in other ways; they did not need to vote. And more than unnecessary, the ballot threatened to harm women themselves, their marriages and families, and the nation as a whole. Bok's antisuffrage fears multiplied when he considered women obtaining better educations, working outside the home, and abandoning their consumer roles in addition to wielding the ballot. Eventually, he admitted that in the long run he could more profitably run the magazine by giving in on the suffrage issue, by modifying the definitions of "ladies" and of "home" in the magazine's title, but he refused to do so. At an advertising conference in 1913, Bok reversed his earlier argument and estimated that he could gain 100,000 readers by adopting a prosuffrage position. He steadfastly refused. "We find the line that we think is absolutely honest," he told his audience, "and then go ahead on it."[31] Since the corporate records of the *Journal* no longer exist, it is difficult to know whether the "we" Bok speaks of represents his staff or only himself.

Political independence for women threatened the very existence of a women's homemaking magazine, and on some level Bok must have been responding to that. He knew the ballot meant an independence unprecedented for women, with potentially frightening results. Once political, economic, and social issues became part of women's daily lives, their traditional roles in the home could not remain unchanged. Just after women gained the vote in Washington, for example, the city's main union newspaper, the *Seattle Union Record*, transformed the women's department from a page on women's issues—home, food, and fashion—to an entire section on newly defined women's issues—suffrage and international news. The new editor, a woman, even made connections between women who stayed at home and those who worked for wages.[32] The *Ladies' Home Journal* would have experienced great difficulty in making such a transition. One *Journal* writer hinted at what had to be one of the central fears of a women's advertising magazine like the *Journal*; men don't "go shopping," the unnamed author argued. Nor do business or professional women. They buy things when they need them, "which is a very different matter."[33] This would have been terribly frightening to Bok for whom, as Helen Damon-Moore put it, there was "only one important reason for women to leave the homefront regularly, and that was to buy."[34] When he thought about suffrage Bok must have envisioned a changed readership and the potential demise of a magazine such as the *Ladies' Home Journal*.[35] Bok's invective illustrates how harshly he could judge his readers when they even hinted at abandoning their jobs in the home and/or in the marketplace.

A second popular argument posed by antisuffrage activists and promoted in the *Journal* was that if women were to take on the responsibility of the vote, they would ultimately have to neglect a responsibility somewhere else: the home was sure to suffer. Antis sometimes grudgingly allowed that some women might participate in certain affairs of the world but made it clear that few women could handle such complex responsibilities.[36] Young, white, single, educated, civic-minded women could perhaps participate in community reforms, but other women were to remain silent even on those issues. Antisuffragists as well as many suffragists based their arguments on assumptions about class, race, and ethnicity, and openly acknowledged their prejudices. It was wrong for an immigrant, African-American, or working-class white woman to participate in any community reform work; it was even more frightening for the antisuffragists to imagine these women voting. "We have suffered many things at the hand of Patrick," wrote Margaret Deland in 1910. "The New Woman would add Bridget also. And—graver danger—to the vote of that fierce, silly, amiable creature, the uneducated Negro, she would add the vote of his sillier, baser female."[37] Deland's verbal racism against Irish- and African-Americans mirrored actions taken in other, more progressive sectors of the society. Theodore Roosevelt, running for president on the Progressive ticket in 1912, conducted a "Lily White" campaign to attract southern voters. Woodrow Wilson, once elected, passed legislation that mandated widespread segregation in government agencies.[38] Prosuffrage activists revealed their racism when they also used the race issue to woo support. Alice Paul, leader of the militant National Woman's Party, spoke longingly of finding a secluded home where "some American people" still lived.[39]

Mothers, whatever their class, race, or ethnic background, were also deemed incapable of simultaneously voting and performing their necessary home duties. These women were not so much denied the vote, Antis argued, as they were excused from it.[40] The Reverend Lyman Abbott made this argument in the *Journal* when he stated that it would be unfair to burden the American woman, who already had more than enough obligations, with the additional responsibility of governing eighty million people.[41] A Massachusetts woman argued this same position succinctly, and her words echo not only Lyman Abbott on suffrage but also Edward Bok on married women and employment outside the home: "A good mother of three or four children already has more than she can do well. If she takes up this whole new department of life and thought, I am convinced that she will have to let something go, and . . . that 'something else' seems to be her home."[42] Bok promoted this same argument, admonishing women for seeking broader public participation and reminding them that their children's lives rested in their hands.

People gave far too little recognition, he declared, to what women accomplished as mothers and caregivers in the home. He complained about having read a newspaper column entitled "Women Who Count." This article praised famous women who had made contributions to move the world forward. But the real women who count, the heroines of the *Journal*, declared Bok, could not be found in these photographs. Rather than plant beautiful gardens, as one of the featured women had, real women planted boys and girls, the youngsters teachers noticed for their exemplary behavior in school classrooms. Bok concluded by again addressing the question of the ballot and denying its significance for women's lives: "Many would consider it worthy to agitate the question of votes for women," he stated, "but can anybody doubt that it is more worthwhile to make men who are worthy of the ballot?"[43] Here Bok mixed the two predominant antisuffrage arguments: women do best through influence, and women who step outside the home are certain to raise unmannerly children and, by extension, politically irresponsible men.

Bok presented this argument again in a second 1912 editorial, providing an anecdote that made it clear not only that the supposedly neutral period in the *Journal* had ended, but also that women who disagreed with him were at best wrong, but more likely dysfunctional or morally corrupt. A teacher, asked to attend a suffrage meeting, provided the following reply: "No thank you my dear. I know these women as you do not: I have had their children to teach: I have had the task of trying to undo the mess that they made. The mistake you make is this: these women are not there because they are successful women, but because they are failures as mothers. It wasn't that they found their jobs in the home too small: it was too big for them."[44] It seems unlikely that the act of walking to the poll and registering a ballot could in itself cause such corruption; it was the larger significance of women as persons capable of and entitled to making choices about home and family that struck a raw nerve. And wielding the ballot, women might make as much of a mess of the home as men had made of the nation.

Bok rightly wanted to give women more credit for the contributions they made in the household, contributions Bok claimed to view as central to the well being of the society. The woman at home was the *Journal*'s unsung heroine, the moral barometer of the home. Just as importantly, however, this woman reader was the person his potential advertising clients sought to reach. Although the *Journal* could have provided a forum for readers to explore the importance of women's contributions to society, to argue the many sides of the growing suffrage debate, Bok limited the discussion. Siding with good business sense, further editorial control, or basic mistrust of women's likelihood to do on their own the "right thing," he instituted and stuck to a hard line on woman suffrage.

Edward Bok was the prominent voice in the *Ladies' Home Journal* when the issue was suffrage. Although he stated that despite his own opposition to woman suffrage he would allow the magazine to serve as a forum for debate, this rarely occurred.[45] In one of the few articles published in favor of suffrage, Bok solicited the writing of Margaret Deland, who three years earlier had penned the "Patrick and Bridget" piece mentioned previously. Deland had modified her opinion on suffrage, provided, as she suggested in the title of her *Journal* piece, suffragists could find a "third way": race, class, and ethnic exclusion. Deland agreed with Bok on almost every measure, differing only on whether or not women should, in the end, vote. Suffragists also believed, she remarked, that woman's primary responsibility was to her family. Voting, however, would not necessarily hamper the woman's ability to handle the family role. Woman suffrage could help women at home by advancing laws concerning good bread and healthy conditions for workers, both of which directly affected the ability of women to assist their families. However, Deland, a self-described moderate, made it clear that she did not favor universal suffrage. Switching from the Irish- and African-Americans she vilified in the earlier article, Deland lamented the fact that there were Italian men who could not speak English but who could vote while she could not. She argued that the vote for women could help to rectify this unbalance, if accompanied by a test for "intelligence in matters of government."[46]

The *Journal* did include a prosuffrage article by Jane Addams, who countered in her writings several of the antisuffrage arguments. Women had to assert themselves outside their restricted sphere, she argued, so they could effectively raise their children and maintain their homes in an increasingly urban and increasingly technologically advanced society. She argued further that women could not always influence their husbands and sons in positive ways; they needed a voice of their own to make women's and children's concerns known.[47] As Michael Hummell puts it, "it would have been difficult for the *Journal* to find a more conservative rationale to support suffrage. Jane Addams and a few other suffragists in the magazine remained essentially quiet on constitutional, equalitarian, and other arguments."[48] Hummell notes the magazine's exclusion of any of the noted suffragists of the day. Nevertheless, even Jane Addams's argument was a step forward for the conservative

Journal, and the sentiments Addams expressed may have been appropriate for and appealing to the readership of the *Ladies' Home Journal.* The Plain Country Woman echoed Jane Addams in complaining that men had a tendency to treat women as inferior, which had resulted in women engaging in "frivolities." The Country Contributor did not find an answer to this social problem in politics; however, instead, women could try gardening. "See what some digging will do," she suggested.[49] The Country Contributor had earlier expressed a fear about women and men fraternizing at the polls. If women wanted to vote, she argued, they should wait until they were at least fifty years old, when they could readily leave their homes without jeopardizing its existence. One wonders what else she feared might happen at the polls between younger women and men.[50]

By mid-decade Bok gave in to his readers, not by supporting woman suffrage but by adding a new column to explore the workings of local, state, and national government. This column, "My Government and I," took the pressure off Bok in terms of suffrage, but it may have furthered rather than hampered women's identification with the political world.[51] Nevertheless, the suffrage jokes continued, and Bok continued to rail against women's rights advocates. Had women married good men and satisfied their instincts in "the normal and ideal way," he argued in 1916, they would feel no need to "pound lecterns and shout slogans on behalf of the feminist movement."[52] Suffrage threatened not only Bok's vision of the woman at home, living the simple life, but also the very purpose of his magazine, which offered women advice and products for their individual and domestic, rather than collective and political, lives. "You are in danger of creating a new version of the story of creation," an invited editorial writer cautioned, "that will make Adam the side issue, not Eve."[53] If women followed through on the most radical of the suffragist-feminist pursuits by turning to communal housekeeping, egalitarian marriages or women-centered lives, shared child rearing, and/or economic independence, the *Ladies' Home Journal* would hardly serve their needs. Suffrage was the first step along on a slippery slope.

It was not until 1918, in the midst of World War I, that suffrage seemed, apparently even to the *Journal*'s editor, inevitable. When that happened he reluctantly accepted it, resigning himself to having a chance to influence the way some women—his readers—would cast their ballots. In the end, Bok's seemingly personal battle against woman suffrage may have precipitated his resignation from the *Journal,* which occurred at the end of the decade. The *Saturday Evening Post,* Cyrus Curtis's other publication, held a prosuffrage position throughout the 1910s, and Curtis had been pressuring Bok to modernize the *Journal*.[54] Although it may be purely coincidental that Bok's retirement became effective January 1, 1920, just as the suffrage battle wound to a close, it provides a curious farewell for the editor who took pride in failing to understand women.[55] He had much praise, but little faith, in the housekeeping women he so carefully addressed for three decades.

When the *Journal* paid tribute to the retiree in the January 1920 issue, marking the thirty years of his "masculine excursion," Bok gave thanks to those who had helped him. He thanked first Louisa Knapp Curtis, his predecessor, and second, publisher Cyrus Curtis. Following that, Bok thanked the associate editors who, in his words, "in their unerring feminine instinct, again and again guided the necessarily halting male judgment over shoals that he saw not and deep waters that he dreamed not of."[56] Finally, Bok thanked his readers. One wonders about the degree to which he followed the advice of his associate editors and the degree to which he simply dictated policy, but it is not surprising that Bok thanked his readers last, as he generally felt he knew better than they did and that they needed him a great deal more than he needed them.

The United States' brief but intense entry into World War I gave the *Ladies' Home Journal* an opportunity to focus anew on the importance of women's household activities, making connections between the war effort in Europe and housewives' efforts at home. "The time for wasteful housekeeping is over," wrote editor Bok. Article after article summarized women's abilities to save scraps of meat, knit scarves and socks for soldiers, conserve wheat flour, sugar, butter, and lard. Interestingly enough, though, women also faced demands that they relax their standards rather than fill their time with housekeeping. "You are working for the Kaiser," wrote the Plain Country Woman, "if you are still scrubbing and scouring and keeping up style in your household."[57] Inevitably, as women let up on their standards to conserve precious energy and scarce resources, they filled their spare time with war work—and many relished the political educations they received. Women's work and women's war efforts remained visible throughout the war. The National American Woman Suffrage Association knitted socks, raised and canned foods, sold Liberty Bonds, and prepared supplies for the Red Cross. They then enlisted non-political war workers to join their suffrage efforts. As Nancy Cott argues, the suffrage movement benefitted from "the highly visible support of women for this extremely popular war."[58] Membership in the National American Woman Suffrage Association doubled during the war, reaching a peak of two million in 1919.[59] The inevitability of a postwar suffrage victory seemed clear to *Journal* readers and editors alike.

In the first of many wartime articles in the *Journal*, Isaac Marcossen readily acknowledged that the suffrage question had been settled. "The war is not only building the New World," he wrote, "it has already created the New Woman." He predicted greater equality between the sexes by arguing about men that "the mere fact that he is a man will no longer entitle him to special privileges." [60] Edward Bok even commissioned a series of articles by Anna Howard Shaw, his earlier nemesis and now head of the Women's Committee of the Council on National Defense, who outlined the contributions women had made to the war effort as well as the issues women and men alike needed to rally around and vote for.[61] Bok clearly knew the contents of Shaw's and others' articles before publishing them since he paid for articles only after he had read and approved them, never in advance.[62]

On August 26, 1920, seven months after Edward Bok's retirement from the *Ladies' Home Journal*, the Nineteenth Amendment, guaranteeing woman suffrage, became part of the United States Constitution. The magazine now had to negotiate a new way in a changed world. The editors who followed Edward Bok in the 1920s, Barton Currie and Loring Schuler, maintained the focus on women in the home but followed and expanded on Bok's final lead in including more articles about women's broader sphere. As they accepted a more broadly defined civic role for women, however, they used their influence to steer readers in the direction of moderate politics, favoring the League of Women Voters over the National Woman's Party, discrediting the Equal Rights Amendment, and still arguing the primacy of women's influence over their power. The magazine increased its scope but firmly remained a consumer-oriented, politically moderate, homemaker's magazine. When Bok first left and H. O. Davis managed the magazine until Currie took over, he announced a "radical" change in the *Journal*: fashions would become a more important element of the magazine.[63] Fashion rather than politics defined "radical" for the postsuffrage *Journal*. Politics never became a defining element of the magazine; instead, it remained a necessary but sometimes seemingly annoying part of the recipe. Writer Harriet Abbott published a credo about the New Woman during the same month that suffrage became law, and her words effectively sum up the *Journal*'s position for the twenties:

> I believe in woman's rights; but I believe in woman's sacrifices also.
> I believe in woman's freedom; but I believe it should be within the restrictions of the Ten Commandments.

I believe in woman suffrage; but I believe many other things are vastly more important.

I believe in woman's brains; but I believe still more in her emotions.

I believe in woman's assertion of self; but I believe also in her obligation of service to her family, her neighbors, her nation and her God.

Following that faith we have the most modern expression of feminism. The newest new woman deifies not herself, but through her new freedom elects to serve others.[64]

Nevertheless, once the suffrage amendment passed, women's voting preferences, patterns, and practices assumed a role in the *Journal*. Editors now described women's political participation and their domestic happiness as mutually dependent, rather than mutually exclusive. A March 1920 editorial encouraged women to vote: "More power to their brooms," and "Let them drive the rats out of the political pantry," Davis argued, using the domestic language suffragists had by now long employed.[65] Once women had become legal voters, the next task of the *Ladies' Home Journal*, as Bok himself had reluctantly realized, was to assist and perhaps influence its readers in their new role. In 1920, breaking precedent, the *Journal* contained political advertisements. Both the Republican and Democratic National Committees took out ads promoting their presidential candidates; the Republicans bought a full page and the Democrats two full pages. It seems unlikely that Edward Bok would have either solicited or accepted advertisements that so blatantly acknowledged and promoted women's voting participation and suggested their partisanship. Both political parties, interestingly enough, highlighted suffrage as accomplishments they took pride in.

Many of the fears shared by antisuffrage women and men during the early part of the century lingered on once women won the suffrage battle, and several fear-based articles found their way into the *Journal*. The National Woman's Party, formed from a renegade wing of the National American Woman Suffrage Association and led by radical feminist Alice Paul, seemed particularly threatening to the *Journal*'s agenda. In response, several articles were published attempting to steer women towards joining one of the existing parties rather than participating in a sex-based party like the NWP. If women voted as a group, many feared, they would vote only for other women. Political chaos would ensue. Historians have documented that this in fact did not occur, but the *Journal*'s attention to the issue suggests that such fears died hard. Women, as Margaret Woodrow Wilson argued in one such article, should not organize separately, for they had the potential to become the "great unifying force in the United States." Wilson, suffragist and daughter of the president, acknowledged that women as a group had potential power but favored inclusive practices and seriously feared exclusive ones.[66] She realized, as Bok had, that women did share a common status due to their gender, and although it was acceptable to discuss that shared status when one spoke of the home, it was dangerous to discuss it in relation to politics. The *Journal* continued to urge women to view the marital bond as the primary bond, to accept a heterogeneous rather than a homogeneous identity as voters, and to argue for power in the name of the family and not in the name of women.

In keeping with the conservative bent of the *Journal*, then, articles favoring the League of Women Voters predominated, but fears of a gender-based political party like the National Woman's Party were not strictly the domain of the reactionaries; many middle-class women simply favored the more accommodating tactics of the League of Women Voters. One contributor to the *Journal* expressed the split well. She had attended the 9th Congress of International Woman Suffrage Alliance in Italy and offered some revealing information about the discussions or disagreements that took place at the conference: "It was agreed rather generally that women can best work inside existing political parties, although there were remarks made—and very eloquent ones—about the errand-girl principle which men political leaders are so fond of."[67] As Nancy Woloch has argued, the women who favored the League over the National Women's Party were the "reform-minded mainstream of the suffrage movement."[68] It is no surprise that they represented the leading voice of the *Ladies' Home Journal* in the 1920s.

After a series of cautionary or even reactionary articles early in the decade, the emphasis began to change. There is no evidence to suggest that there was another boycott against the *Journal*. Perhaps Barton Currie was more favorably disposed towards women's political participation. He could have downplayed his own disagreements with Bok until he established his own voice as editor. It is also possible that he was less likely to deny the importance of the vote once it was secured, more likely to see that he could play a positive role in how it was used, and no less certain than Bok that there were appropriate and inappropriate ways in which women could use this newfound privilege. Currie commissioned a series of articles on the subject, including, in the same issue as the Margaret Woodrow Wilson article, one by Cora Harris, "Practical Politics for Gentlewomen," which urged antisuffragists to join the ranks of the enfranchised and get involved.[69] Many writers made the connection between women's traditional roles and responsibilities at home and their new roles and responsibilities in the political arena, finally adopting an argument popular among suffragists for decades. Women excelled in their roles as the finance administrators in their families: they knew how much money came into the home, how much money subsequently left, where it went, and why. If they found their grocer unfair, they would search for a better grocer. If they purchased canned goods of an inferior quality, they would find a better brand for the money. Once women had the power of the ballot, they were encouraged to use it to enlarge this financial vision. Now they could make the same kind of demands on the government that they made on the grocer or the butcher or the canned goods manufacturer. Women's views on thrift had saved many a family through difficult times and through the scarcity of the war years; now these views could lead the nation to a more respectable and economically secure future. In an article entitled "$10,000 an Hour: What are you Paying? What are you Getting?" Rose Young argued that women could and should choose political leaders who represented their views on thrift. Mary Roberts Rinehart, in "Waiting for the Stork," came to a similar conclusion. Women were actually more qualified than men to make political decisions, she wrote, for they made them all the time. Rinehart dubbed the leader of the nation a President-housekeeper, who used as many female tools for decision making as he used male ones.[70]

Although many writers encouraged women to use their votes well, others realized that most women remained unprepared to make the transition from the private to the public sphere, regardless of their other qualifications. So many obstacles to women's full participation in government still remained firmly in place. Rose Young's February 1920 article, "The End of a Great Adventure," lamented the lack of preparation of most new voters. Now that the suffrage battle had been won and there were twenty million new voters, were the women ready for the task at hand? No, she declared, they were not, for they had received no preparation, no guidance, no civic training. It was up to women, Young realized, to train themselves and others to use the ballot wisely and well; they could depend on no one else. In the following month's issue, Young took on the task herself. In "Madam, Meet Your Congressmen," she provided introductions to political figures of the day. Young connected the larger political arena to women's concerns again two months later in an article entitled "Congress as a First Aid to Housewives." Women could use the political process to their benefit, Young counseled, but they had to educate themselves about the issues and then make clear and reasoned demands.[71] Interestingly enough, Rose Young had been a suffrage leader, the director of the National American Woman Suffrage Association's press bureau. In the postsuffrage era, she made a living, at least in part, by bringing suffrage and civic education to a wider audience.[72]

The education process continued in the *Ladies' Home Journal* with other writers who discussed a myriad of issues: some pacified fears about the woman's vote, others incited anger over the social problems of the day. A series of articles promoted the hopeful notion that women, because of their dedication to home and family, would prove better voters than men. In a 1921 editorial, Barton Currie argued that equal suffrage could mean equal apathy, but his faith led him to believe that women, with more at stake than men, would accomplish more with their newfound political rights. An article by Elizabeth Jordan, "The Big Little Things for Women in Politics: Employ the Ballot Early and Often for Your Community Benefit," suggested that women's politics differed from, and ranked superior to, men's. Enlist your husbands in your battles, she argued, since women recognized community needs more than men.[73] One of the few prosuffrage male writers in the *Journal*, David Lawrence, argued that women's political choices did differ from men's choices in one significant way: the woman voter, he stated, "frowns upon bossism" and might vote out machine politicians.[74] In another article on the subject of how women voted, Marie Cecile Chomel stated that women voted independently on moral issues but with their husbands on purely political issues. The language of essential difference between women and men continued on in the *Journal* of the twenties, where women faced the additional expectation that their difference from men would make an enormous difference in the nation's political health.[75]

Writer Alice Ames Winter presented the *Ladies' Home Journal* readers with a narrative case study of this argument. She related the fairytale–like success story of a small town in Oregon populated by only 150 voters and a corrupt local government. When the women complained about the corruption, the men laughed. When the women complained again, the men jokingly remarked that they would like to see the women do better. Accepting the challenge, women ran for political office and won seven seats. The new mayor, recorder, treasurer, and four councilors cleaned up the town. Winter, using the popular analogy, described their actions as an extension of their housekeeping duties: the women took on the task as they would have taken on the task of an unkempt house. The town became a model of respectable government, and the women served as a model for all women of the importance and absolute necessity of political participation.[76] Historians today argue that when women first secured the ballot they did not, as feminists hoped and antisuffragists feared, have different voting patterns from the men in their families. Women did not join together to elect women in large numbers, nor did they exhibit a different approach to voting on moral issues. They wiped out neither war and disease nor marriage and the family. Those in favor of and those against woman suffrage had overestimated women's solidarity and ability to overcome their cultural lessons and identities.[77]

In the *Journal* of the 1920s, readers found exhortations to use the vote and use it well to secure better child custody legislation, fight for child labor laws, safeguard the quality of food, and defeat measures that threatened the safety of children or the sanctity of the home. Rallying around children, a theme popular with middle-class women for decades, fit in well with the home-based agenda of the *Journal* and with new ideas about children that resulted from declining birthrates and developments in child and family psychology during the 1920s. The *Journal* offered articles defending voters and politically active women from stereotypes about their inattention to children. Elizabeth Jordan, in "New Women Leaders in Politics," reacquainted readers with the now clearly unreasonable antisuffrage fears. She recalled stories of deserted homes filled with neglected husbands and children. The children in these stories, reduced as they were to the fringes of society, often played with matches. The real picture, according to Jordan, differed significantly. She named several women politicians across the United States and argued that they had clean homes, happy husbands, and healthy children.[78] Several writers illustrated that women had been successful in politics on the local level, having secured living wages for teachers and policies for garbage removal, housing, and water systems. Others urged reader participation in the League of Women Voters or, more rarely, the National Woman's Party. These groups, among which numbered many skilled women politicians, writers instructed, could fight for five or six big laws, insist upon reforms at the state level, and participate in local government all at the same time. The home was the training ground for female politicians, one writer declared, and women could count on those same politicians to bring women's concerns to the forefront of political debates.[79]

In "A Woman Politician and Proud of It," Florence E. S. Knapp, a ten-year veteran of politics, argued that women were needed in politics more than ever. Dean of Home Economics at Cornell University, Knapp did not feel that women should limit their activities to the home. As the heads of the nation's households, women already had the leadership qualities they would need to advance in the political arena; they simply had to direct their energies to that purpose. Knapp did so herself, using World War I as her springboard into politics. During the war she traveled for fourteen months as the Associate Director for Food Conservation for the U.S. government. After the war she became the first woman state official in New York. Another writer, Elizabeth Breuer, described as "the valiant two percent" those women who dedicated themselves to political work. Some currently held seats in state legislatures and others faced good prospects in the Senate and on the Supreme Court as well. The League of Women Voters, she wrote, currently worked in favor of 242 measures concerning child welfare, social hygiene, protective labor legislation, living costs, education, and efficiency in government. The LWV had also helped to defeat thirty-one measures they opposed, Breuer eagerly reported.[80]

Several *Journal* writers acknowledged the difficulties women faced when they tried to broaden their involvement in the public sphere. Men resisted, holding tight to the reigns of power with a mixture of fear and hostility. One woman reported that both the Democratic and Republican parties discouraged women's participation; she claimed that one woman had been offered $10,000 to leave one of the parties.[81] Women also faced ridicule at the polls. "You'll never get the flappers to the polls unless you offer a permanent wave for every vote cast," one man reportedly argued. This comment came from a man who favored woman suffrage! Some men felt that women would only vote if it were fashionable; others believed that women would band together and threaten the very existence of the two-party system. The criticisms varied, and women's defenses often referred to the home, women's most vulnerable spot as well as their strongest defense. If they could prove that political work did not take away from their responsibilities at home, they could justify the vote—and a great deal more.[82]

Writers in the *Ladies' Home Journal* of the 1920s argued again and again that the vote did not take away from women's femininity. They argued that women could legitimately choose to do more than "influence" men by involving themselves more fully in the political process, but they were careful to tread lightly on this issue. Introducing a new column by Mary Roberts Rinehart, Currie argued that her perspective came "not from an exclusively feminine or feminist slant," but from a new, *Journal*-related position that valued all of women's roles equitably.[83] When they defended female politicians, however, *Journal* writers continued to assert that the women managed to be good public and good private servants: their husbands, children, and homes were well tended to. Superwomen, who could do it all, repeatedly sprung up in the pages of the *Journal.* Once suffrage passed, the *Journal* abandoned the view that women could not do it all; now they had to, and few women would risk the admission that something had to give. The assumption, which the *Journal* shared with the larger society, was that the women could either do it all or return to their old roles. Not a single writer mentioned greater participation on the part of men in the household. Rarely did they mention child care or cooperative housekeeping or relaxed standards of cleanliness or of motherly attention in the postsuffrage decade. They established a clear rule: women had to prove that they could take on a new role and still keep the old one in check.

By the end of the decade, the pressing issue for feminists was the Equal Rights Amendment. Editor Loring Schuler, who followed Barton Currie, sounded more than a little like his most famous predecessor when he railed against the amendment, calling it "ineffective, uncertain, destructive, and expensive."[84] The magazine had, in some ways, come full circle and back home again. It promoted women's entrance in what it still saw as men's sphere only in the name of the home. It fostered the notion of essential differences rather than innate similarities between women and men. It fulfilled the role of a woman's advertising magazine and a "home" journal. The *Ladies' Home Journal* struggled with readers and writers and even with large political bodies, but although it finally acknowledged that votes could be for women, it never joked either that stoves might be for men or that stoves might not be for all women.

As with most other subjects covered in the *Ladies' Home Journal,* the topic of suffrage and women's political participation found a voice on the advertising pages as well as on the editorial pages. The vote and women's developing political lives were used, in short, to sell products. Since one of the women readers' inarticulate longings was political freedom, the advertisers promised that their products could deliver that freedom. A 1924 Pond's cold cream and vanishing cream advertisement provides an excellent example of how advertisers capitalized on women's inarticulate—and sometimes clearly articulated—longings for a political voice.[85] With the help of the women copywriters at the J. Walter Thompson advertising agency, Pond's ran a series of endorsement ads in 1924. The women who endorsed the ads, primarily socialites and actresses, included in their ranks Princess Matchabelli and Mrs.

Cordelia Biddle Duke.[86] One advertisement, however, featured Alva Belmont, a socialite who also happened to be an executive member of the National Woman's Party. Belmont, an interesting and controversial woman, raised eyebrows over her personal and political life decisions. "Yes, I am a militant and I glory in it," she told a friend.[87] Belmont married and subsequently divorced William Kissam Vanderbilt, the grandson of Cornelius Vanderbilt. The divorce prompted a great public reaction and Belmont was the subject of much scandal. A year later Alva Belmont married Oliver Hazard Perry Belmont, the son of the wealthy utilities and street-railway magnate August Belmont. Soon after, British suffragist Sylvia Pankhurst introduced her to feminism. As her biographer puts it, the meetings with Pankhurst and the harsh public reaction to her divorce transformed Belmont from "an insular society hostess into an ardent feminist."[88] Belmont donated hundreds of thousands of dollars to feminist causes and affiliated herself with Alice Paul and the more radical wing of the National American Woman Suffrage Association. This group, which eventually formed the National Woman's Party, conducted its initial strategy sessions at Belmont's Newport, Rhode Island, mansion.

Pond's Cold and Vanishing Creams used Alva Belmont—and the National Woman's Party—to sell a product in the pages of the *Journal.* One could argue that it was the personal, scandalous side of Alva Belmont's life that really sold the Pond's creams, promising *Journal* readers a bit of romance, a bit of wealth, perhaps a bit of scandal. The advertising text, however, does highlight Alva Belmont's feminist activities. And, certainly, Belmont made her own intentions clear from the start. She did not receive any payment for the advertisement; her check went directly to the National Woman's Party.[89] In using feminism as a selling device, Pond's seems to have furthered the cause of everyone involved with the advertisement. Belmont's cause received money and publicity, the *Journal* continued to broaden its appeal, and Pond's secured another promoter. The only loser, perhaps, was the "feminist woman," who was now defined as much by Pond's creams as by Belmont. The advertisement operated with the premise that women, even the rich and cultured, had to keep their youthful beauty. Alva Belmont asserted that women's importance rested on this. "A woman who neglects her personal appearance loses half her influence," she stated. "The wise care of one's body constructs the frame encircling our mentality, the ability of which insures the success of one's life. I advise a daily use of Pond's Two Creams."[90]

Pond's managed, in one page, to include all of the definitions of womanhood that struggled to dominate the *Ladies' Home Journal* in the 1910s and 1920s. By including gossip, feminism, and beauty, Pond's sold not one but two creams. It would be wrong, though, to conclude that the advertisers were the big and hence the only winners here; perhaps the feminist message meant as much to the readers as did the consumer message. Nancy Cott argues that the marginal women of the 1920s, namely the feminists, laid a good deal of groundwork. "The growing presence of such women," writes Cott, "was the surest accomplishment if not the best promise of feminism."[91] In the case of the Belmont-Pond's advertisement, Alva Belmont found herself reduced to the mainstream, to the world of cold creams. At the same time, however, a self-described radical feminist met the readers of the *Ladies' Home Journal* on equal terms, as someone who had the same everyday concerns as millions of other women. Were her other ideas then quite so radical? Perhaps she had something to offer besides soap; perhaps her ideas about women also had practical relevance to the *Journal*'s many readers. In the end, although the advertisers surely found a way to draw attention to their product, they also pulled Alva Belmont and her radical ways nearer to the readers of the *Ladies' Home Journal.* In this case at least, feminism came a bit closer to home.

Other advertisements of the period, which on first glance seem merely to coopt women's political longings, may also have presented more of a mixed message to *Journal* readers. A Hoosier kitchen cabinet advertisement featured the headline, "Every Woman Has a Right to a Hoosier." Women may have been debating the limits of women's rights, the ad implies, but "everywoman," the average American woman who was as much a product of magazines and marketing as of reality, knew that her real right was the right to consume the best kitchen cabinet. A Royal Baking Powder advertisement featured a veritable army of women dressed in military-looking dress with banners across their shoulders. The woman in the foreground held a placard, and the left hand side of the placard stated "Women Will Win." The right hand side of the placard, however, revealed that these activists would win not suffrage but "The Fight for Pure Food." The advertisement's text paid tribute to women, who demanded involvement in "all the great issues of our times." The ad repeated several times the brief but compelling message: "Women will win." They would win, of course, not by voting, not by legislating the production of pure food, not by marching and striking, but by purchasing Royal Baking Powder, the gun powder of the middle-class woman.[92]

The American Canners Association used the same theme to promote the general consumption of canned foods. Canners' ads featured women in settings that appeared military but were actually home kitchens. The women themselves looked official, dressed in clothing similar to that used in the Royal Baking Powder advertisement and truly dissimilar to what most women wore while cleaning or cooking. A Canners Association Seal filled a great deal of space for the majority of ads in this series, and the seal implied a government-mandated role for women. That role, in the end, was not to fight for pure food, not to write legislation, not to join the military, but, simply, to purchase canned foods.[93]

One manufacturer used the women's rights theme in naming its product, the Liberty Motor Car. Aimed at women and probably reminiscent of wartime Liberty bonds, Liberty advertisements featured women drivers with full social and personal agendas. The ads implied that women sought freedom from old roles and that the automobile was an important means of achieving that freedom. What better automobile than the Liberty Motor Car? Other automobile manufacturers followed suit. A Ford advertisement showed a woman at a desk, talking on the phone and looking out the window at her automobile. This woman obviously used her car as an escape both to and from her many obligations.[94]

Advertisers of the 1910s and 1920s linked consumption to improved marriages, lighter household responsibilities, and, not incidentally, greater political freedom. They promised that they could meet the needs unmet by the rest of the magazine or by the women's husbands, families, or jobs. Advertisers recognized that politics, for many women, had become an essential rather than a peripheral part of their self-definition, and promised that by consuming particular products women could prove themselves community-minded, politically astute, and sophisticated. They recognized that the average woman addressed by the *Journal* was perhaps not so simple, not so homebound, not so satisfied with traditional roles. In doing so, they may also have unwittingly increased women's interests in real rather than consumer politics. Unfortunately, however, the promises of advertising were both far more numerous and far less sincere than other invitations for women's political autonomy. Advertisements promising women prestige and power had little to back them up. By linking women's freedom to consumption, what advertisers offered was in the end no more liberating and no less politically restrictive than the ambiguous promises offered elsewhere in the magazine.

The Editor's Personal Chat

Here are Some Worth-While Letters

THE advertisements in a magazine are not usually that part of the contents which readers will select to write to an editor about. And in reading thousands of letters recently received from our readers, we were particularly struck with the actual mercantile part that THE JOURNAL advertisements had played in the lives of its readers.

Of course, this man's letter has an amusing side to it which we didn't fail to appreciate. He had something to learn, but the spirit in which he now writes of having learned it is both pleasing and masculine:

When we were married, I confess I was taken aback by my wife's saying to me: "Let's buy our home things through THE LADIES' HOME JOURNAL." I didn't get the idea, so I asked: "How do you mean?" "Why, through its advertisements."

I looked at my young wife, and thought: "Woman, woman!" But I knew, as surely another man knows, that it is no use to argue with a woman when she puts you up as a mentor of all that is right and holy; for my wife is like so many other women that I know: she puts me next to her Bible. So there was nothing for me to do but to say: "All right, dear." But, believe me, I used caution, because I had had experience with answering advertisements; but not, of course, with answering yours. But my wife went blissfully on with that confidence in me that other men envy, and to my surprise the stuff was all right in every case. So I let loose on the strings a little more, and, of course, in the end she had her way. Our home things were bought through you, and, I must say, without a single unpleasant experience or regret. All told, we must have sent orders to twenty-five or thirty firms.

I congratulate you; I really do. That was five years ago. I never read a copy of your magazine before that time. For the last three years I have read every copy, and when my wife suggested raising my baby by your counsel I fell in like a lamb. (And she has done it! So, editorially and advertisingly (is there such a word?) you are all right. Go right ahead.

Here is an interesting letter from another man, who writes:

I wonder if many write to you about what your advertisements really mean to your people. Take my case, for instance. I was figuring it out with my wife and we found that during the past year we had ordered and bought over five hundred dollars' worth of household contrivances and clothes through your advertisements. My wife's wardrobe, for example, last autumn was bought entirely from your magazine: also a complete new set of silverware for the table and a rehabilitation of our kitchen. And, what is more to the point, in not a single instance were we disappointed. The goods bought were always up to the advertisements. This is a distinct service that you render your readers outside of that which you render in your editorial contents.

Another—this time a woman—writes:

I wonder if this will surprise you. To me you are not a magazine, but an actual, wonderful personality, silently guiding, shaping, molding my ideals, clarifying my visions of duty, finally determining my decision for right in moments of supreme test, and entering my practical life as well by being an unerring trade director. How? By your advertisements. I have learned, through several years of experience, to trust them, and I send my money to your advertisers without the slightest hesitation, never yet having received less than was represented, but in several cases more. I know you edit well your literary part; but I know, too, what I don't think all your readers realize—that you edit equally well your advertising part. Thank you, sir, for carefulness in both fields.

Here is a "lefthander" which we can't help printing:

Why don't you make your literary contents as good as your advertising department makes the advertisements?

It is the complete confidence that years of care with our advertising policy has instilled into the minds of our readers that pleases us. As, for instance:

I want to commend you, in particular, on your advertising policy, its cleanliness and its complete reliability. I speak from experience, and I never fail to mention to my patients that an advertisement in THE LADIES' HOME JOURNAL is, so far as I am concerned in ten years of buying through you, as good as a Government bond. I congratulate you that your work to help us to buy wisely and with confidence.

This is very pleasant to know and to feel, and we appreciate it; just as we do this approval from a Canadian subscriber:

Thank you for your evident pains to make your advertising columns as reliable as your editorial expression. I have tried scores of your advertisements and never have I found one wanting. You have made your readers feel that THE LADIES' HOME JOURNAL is a guarantee of the worth of your advertisements.

This, too, is an appreciated word with a new angle:

Of course you make money out of your advertisements, and it is right and proper that you should. But do you realize that your readers save money out of them too? We buy through them, and buy safely and well, and know we are sure to get good value every time. So, the shoe isn't all on one foot!

Here is a suggestion that we gladly pass on, both to the advertisers in the field suggested and to the advertising department:

I wish you could induce the makers of men's clothing to put their advertisements in your magazine. Do the makers of these men's clothes realize the very important influence which women have in the selection of their husbands' clothes? No, I'm not a woman; I'm a man, as you will see from my signature and this testimonial. My wife has absolute faith in your magazine—swears by it and buys everything she can through it. I used to laugh at her about it, and then I began to read you, and I have the same faith that she has. I realize that you are playing the game straight, and I should like, as I think other men would—as I know they would, in fact—to buy my duds through you as my wife buys hers; as many daughters buy theirs, as a matter of fact. You have an enormous merchandising influence whether you know it or not. No doubt you'd like to get these men's clothing advertisements as much as I want you to have them, but I am speaking from the buyer's end. Pass the word on to these fellows, why don't you?

We will, my friend; we are doing it, as you see.

Another instance is interesting on account of its completeness:

Here is what you have done for one family: We found the plan of our home in your magazine. Then, through your prize offers, we earned over one-half the money to buy our lot. Then we decided on the furnishings of our home through your interior decoration hints, and, lastly, we bought two-thirds of all the furniture and fixings in our home through your advertisements. That is serving one family pretty thoroughly, don't you think?

We do think so, and we are pleased and proud of the fact, particularly of the feeling of satisfaction with which you tell of it.

From far-off Arkansas comes this pleasant word:

Just as invaluable to my home-making as is your editorial part, equally invaluable is my housekeeping to your advertising part. In financial pinches I thought I should have to discontinue your magazine; then, through your advertisements, I have bought and saved enough to justify the subscription. So your advertisements are a help in more ways than one.

And so we might go on with other letters. One fact is gratifying: that the publishers of THE LADIES' HOME JOURNAL have so widely succeeded in convincing its readers of the reliability of the advertisements that are printed in the magazine.

Women are enlisting

all over the country in movements affecting the great issues of our times.

In every field that makes for human good they are thinking, planning, acting.

In no field have they done so much as in the battle for cheaper, purer, better food.

The women will win. Women never give up.

Years ago alum was widely used in bleaching flour for bread. Doctors and chemists objected, women protested, and such use was prohibited. Today alum is used in some baking powders. It is necessary for the women to protest again. They will do it, and they will win.

Royal Baking Powder is fighting beside them because it is an enemy to alum and to all food adulteration.

ROYAL
BAKING POWDER
Contains no Alum   No Lime Phosphates

Royal Baking Powder is Chief Aid to pure, healthful and economical food.

Aware of women's desires for greater civic participation, advertisers promised that individual women could reach collective political goals through purchasing.(*Ladies' Home Journal,* April 1915, p. 49)

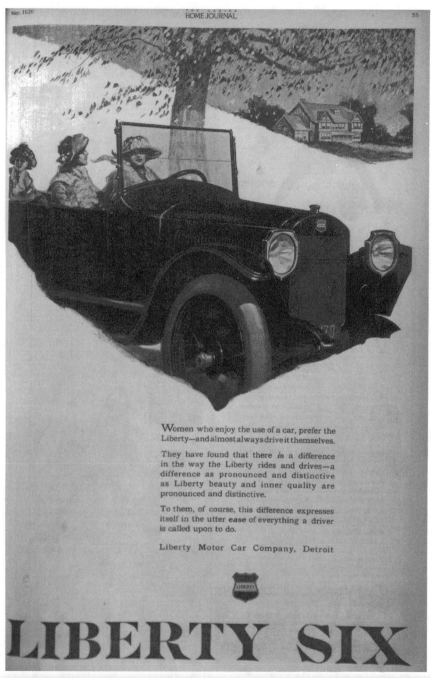

Women who enjoy the use of a car, prefer the Liberty—and almost always drive it themselves.

They have found that there *is* a difference in the way the Liberty rides and drives—a difference as pronounced and distinctive as Liberty beauty and inner quality are pronounced and distinctive.

To them, of course, this difference expresses itself in the utter *ease* of everything a driver is called upon to do.

Liberty Motor Car Company, Detroit

LIBERTY SIX

Automobile advertisers lured women with promises of independence, offering suggestions of female autonomy in advertising drawings, texts, or, as in this case, the very name of the product. (*Ladies' Home Journal,* May 1920, p. 55)

five

The Amateur Rebel

Female Protagonists in
Ladies' Home Journal *Fiction*

his chapter begins with an anecdote, one of my own. During my Ph.D. oral examination in history, I was asked to start things off by discussing my dissertation, an earlier version of this work, which was at that time in its infant stages. I spoke of the value of using artifacts of popular culture to examine cultural definitions of womanhood. As I introduced the aspects of the project and their significance, the one part that struck a sour chord among some of the participants was my discussion of magazine fiction. My examiners agreed that the magazine advice and the advertising would reveal cultural information and thus warranted scholarly study, but the fiction, "cheap" as it was, seemed merely ephemeral and hardly instructive. "Do you mean," one examiner challenged, "that you would use, say, the Harlequin romance to teach a course on twentieth-century womanhood?" Since I came to women's history from literature, steeped in the classics of the British and American canon, I too felt the shaky nature of the ground on which I stood. Daily household chores, inattentive husbands, and unmannerly children figured low on the hierarchy of great literary struggles. I somewhat mildly asserted that I would use romance fiction in the history classroom, hoping to escape without having to offer too much further justification.

My examination committee was not alone in questioning the scholarly value of popular fiction in general or women's magazine fiction in particular. When historians and other scholars of the period have debated the merits of magazine fiction, many have been dismissive. Ruth Schwartz Cowan argued that fiction of the 1920s and 1930s revealed little about women's lives; if one wanted accurate information, she stated, one had to look at the magazine's nonfiction material. Even those who found the fiction worthy of study then found little to recommend it. Kathryn Weibel argued that female protagonists in women's magazine fiction were "dependent, ineffectual, unemployed, or underemployed." Similarly, Helen Franzwa argued that in limiting the roles of female protagonists to mother and housewife, these tales merely told "the same old stories."[1] Perhaps the only complimentary analysis of magazine fiction of the period comes from early advertising copywriter Helen Woodward, who in 1926 described the female protagonists of magazine fiction as having a "wrapper" of goodness which covered characters of tougher and more complicated design. These were "experienced women," wrote Woodward, "who somehow managed to creep into the pure and beautiful bodies of eighteen-year-olds." According to Woodward, women's magazine fiction allowed readers to view the wrapper but also promoted their exploration of its underside, which was contradictory, bold, and feminist.[2]

On the balance, I believe the *Journal*'s fiction is neither simply reactionary nor boldly feminist; instead, it looms uncertainly in the magazine's ambivalent and ambiguous attempts to both shape and please middle-class readers. The scholars cited above are correct in finding in these stories characters who fail to self-actualize and happy endings that fail to satisfy. At the same time, though, the contradictions that Woodward describes can be found in much magazine fiction, and they render the happy endings less than convincing to readers as well as historians. This reading of several pieces of *Journal* fiction will focus on the contradictions, on the ways in which the stories promise happy lives through traditional means, but expose those means—and those ends—as less than satisfying for women.

The fiction in the *Ladies' Home Journal* is as important a component of the magazine as any other and is, for me, the most fun. It is the stage upon which women's lives are acted out, where their possibilities and limitations are played out in a more dramatic fashion than elsewhere in the magazine. While the stories themselves provide fairly predictable plot lines, the themes they address cover a wide range of women's concerns: love, sexuality, marriage, children, careers, homemaking. The fiction explores the mundane nature of women's lives—the duties of meal preparation, for example—but also addresses the mysteries—a discovery of inner feelings, budding sexuality, a yearning both for more broadly defined and more intimate life experiences.

Like the other elements of the magazine, the fiction tries to express women's wrongs and rights, providing a socially acceptable means of both redressing the wrongs and keeping the rights in check. More explicitly than the advice, however, and more thoroughly than the advertising, the fiction also addresses the mysteries of women's lives, those aspects that cannot be easily defined, culturally or otherwise. It is this mystery that I found difficult to articulate in my Ph.D. exam, and which draws me to popular fiction written by and for women. My visual image of the fiction is that it provides readers the opportunity to put the magazine down and dream. This mystery, I believe, points to a site for the truly subversive in women: their ability to dream of another, vastly different world. The fiction's validation of the mysteries and the realities of womanhood makes it immensely valuable to historians and readers alike.

My work has benefitted enormously from recent work in feminist literary criticism, which provides researchers with the support to claim the value of popular fiction, especially popular fiction written by and for women. As Janice Radway, Tania Modleski, and others have illustrated, elements of popular culture consumed primarily by women, including romance fiction and soap operas, reveal what women feel oppressed by and what they long for. In the *Journal,* the fiction validates women's life experiences and their values. It provides identification, escape, and catharsis. And like the other elements of the *Ladies' Home Journal* recipe, the fiction is worth studying because of its popular appeal and mass audience, not in spite of it.[3]

Popularity often sounds a death knell in scholarship in the humanities, both for critics on the right and on the left. In history the enemy has been popular culture, in literature, popular fiction. Since the 1930s critics have argued that mass art, a crippling tool of capitalism, harms the mind. According to their definition, mass art is dominated by ideology while high art offers critiques of that same ideology. Fredric Jameson and others have illustrated, however, that capitalist ideology influences both mass culture and high culture—neither is exempt. At the same time, neither mass art nor high art is made wholly perverse from such invasions. Popular literature and other aspects of popular culture do promote the most pervasive ideology, but while they do so they also mock it, expose its shortcomings, and criticize it. The critique is perhaps less evident, less immediately effective, but it undoubtedly exists.[4] Thanks to recent work in feminist literary criticism and cultural studies, the study of popular fiction has gained a more valued standing in academic scholarship.

Other work in feminist literary criticism provides a more general foundation for this reading. Groups of critics have been rereading the canon, reassessing the great works to determine the ways in which gender has influenced their canonization. Do the great works point to the universal characteristics of people or rather of "man," more specifically white, educated, affluent man? Such studies reveal a great deal about the literary canon apart from questions of style or literary excellence. In her study of "Rip Van Winkle," for example, Judith Fetterley added gender as an element of analysis. How does one read this story of a man escaping civilization and all that civilization entails, embodied in the character of his wife, when one is a woman? In the same manner, as others have argued, how does a woman read the eternal man-against-nature or man-against-himself struggle that takes place on sailing ships or in vast jungles when one has spent the better part of one's life in a kitchen? Perhaps these universal tales, feminist critics argue, are not quite as universally applicable as we have been taught.[5]

Another aspect of reexamining the canon is the process of recovering neglected women writers from the past who have not been included in this list of great works and great authors. From Aphra Behn to Zora Neale Hurston, the process is well underway. For example, American women writers of the nineteenth century wrote the bestsellers that far outsold the works of Nathaniel Hawthorne, Herman Melville, or Ralph Waldo Emerson. This "damned mob of scribbling women," as Hawthorne so bitterly and, thanks to recent feminist critics, now so infamously called them, have traditionally been neglected or renounced by critics. Researchers are now rereading these works and asking why they have been ignored, if the canon can encompass them, and if the idea of the canon itself must be redefined rather than simply expanded. As Jane Tompkins has argued, for example, why is *Uncle Tom's Cabin* not a part of our literary canon?[6] Is it because it is not up to par with the classics of the nineteenth century, because it was written by a woman, because it focuses on the lives of African-Americans, or because it was a popular work?

In the struggle to define value in fiction, literary critic Janet Todd argues, perhaps we can join the canonized with the uncanonized, the high art with the popular art, and create layers of meaning and understanding. She puts it well when she urges literary critics to "aim for some reconstructions of the past that allow its richness, texture, and strangeness to emerge."[7] The methods employed here aim to do just that. I make no claims for the literary excellence of the stories included in the *Ladies' Home Journal* nor for the literary talents of the authors. But while no Zora Neale Hurstons or Aphra Behns hide in the pages of the magazine and these stories will never vie for an exalted rank, canon status and historical value are two different things. The argument for the consideration of this fiction rests on its cultural rather than literary merit, on its link to the social world of women, and on the ways in which, as a form of popular culture, it exposes the wrongs of the world it celebrates.

This social world of women, the world of kitchens, husbands, and children, fills the pages of *Journal* fiction because like the whale, the lone journey, and the long sleep, these elements represent the stages of the *Journal*-reading woman's possibilities, commitments, and growth. As Radway argues about romance fiction, stories in the *Journal*, like myths of oral cultures, relate a story already familiar to the people who choose to read them.[8] These particular tales speak of female self-sacrifice, the gifts of marriage, the rewards of traditional gender roles. The stories, like the *Journal*'s advice columns, praise "woman's" values, those values that, although supposedly inherent, shared, and natural, warrant a great deal of repeating. By reading the fiction employing the practice that Janet Todd and others call reading "against the grain" though, by examining the conflict as closely as its resolution, the stories appear to be as much about resignation as they are about satisfaction. Female protagonists, to arrive at the happy endings, have to struggle with men, with children, with gender roles, with themselves. And although the stories generally deliver those happy endings, readers may be as moved in the end by the women's struggles and the paths not taken as they are by even the happiest of endings. In this way, the fiction invites subversive as well as prescriptive readings.[9]

Reading the fiction in this manner provides us with a look at the "grounds" Nancy Cott writes of in *The Grounding of Modern Feminism*, the building blocks of the modern feminist movement. The *Ladies' Home Journal* never advocated divorce, for example, but neither did it deny in its fiction—or elsewhere—that marriage and childrearing were rife with problems. In exploring the problems, a piece of fiction perhaps inadvertently allowed readers to explore a variety of solutions in addition to the one promoted at the story's conclusion. Readers of the *Journal*'s fiction, who probably did not identify themselves as feminists, followed the struggles of the girlfriend, wife or mother character as she attempted to fit middle-class definitions of womanhood. Continued recognition and examination of these struggles could lead readers to question their roles and eventually to participate directly or indirectly in a renewed feminist movement. Modern feminist strategies and ideologies were, arguably, built in part on the grounds of discontent revealed here in the fiction.[10] Unfortunately, however, so were the very real grounds for modern women's inaction, their feelings of inadequacy, and their reliance on a consumer culture to meet unmet needs.

What I hope to illustrate in this discussion is that while it has been clear that middle-class notions of respectability and definitions of womanhood did not apply to the vast majority of black women, poor and working-class white women, or lesbians, it is also increasingly clear that standard, pat definitions of middle-class womanhood did not even easily apply to those who most nearly fit the bill. The happy endings of the stories often come across as less than happy, even for the women who desire and believe in them. This adds complexity to our notions of middle-class women's lives during this period; it also has broader implications, since entering womanhood culturally in twentieth century history has meant, for various groups of women, agreeing to enter or attempting to enter the apparent reality described here. Janice Radway argues that popular fiction may be addictive to precisely the women who cannot get out of the bind they are in with their own lives.[11] In the case of the *Journal,* the more the developing middle-class reality failed the expectations of recently married women, new mothers, or seasoned wives, the more these readers may have needed the fiction to validate, mystify, and then minimize their complaints. The pattern of addiction would change slowly as women of different ethnic, religious, and class groups entered the dialogue.

The following eight stories reveal the ways in which many personal concerns of contemporary women found a voice in the *Journal* in the 1910s and 1920s. Since the magazine published fifty to sixty stories a year, these few cannot be said to represent the *Journal*'s fiction during this time period, but the purpose here is not to survey a twenty-year collection of short fiction. Instead, the discussion explores the contradictions apparent in a group of stories written by women that advertise, through their titles, drawings, or captions, the theme of personal conflict over gender roles. This discussion leaves out stories of true love, stories of adventure, and stories that focus primarily on men or on children. These pieces of fiction can be said to represent a handful of the most pronounced explorations of gender role conflict in *Journal* fiction from 1910 to 1930. The main character, always a woman, experiences fear, discomfort, or disillusionment with her role in life. She sees herself in relation to others, usually husbands or potential husbands, and attempts to define or redefine an unbalanced relationship to better suit her needs. She chooses a solution that, in keeping with the magazine's mission, maintains marriage and family, but may also modify existing definitions of marriage and family along the way.

The women in these stories express four of the major complaints middle-class, European-American women had in the early twentieth century. They also arrive at solutions that, although diverse, would please the magazine's editors and resonate with the *Journal*'s middle-class readership, who wanted change within certain socially mandated boundaries. The first complaint voiced by these women is their uncertainty about the degree to which they should meet their own needs or the needs of others. Tradition told women to serve their husbands and families, yet the social discourse also spoke to them of individualism and personal autonomy. Women realized that self-sacrifice meant more than helping others: it meant losing some control over their own lives as well. The second conflict was the dispute over women's work, domestic and wage-earning. As women's wage-earning capacities nearly disappeared in the home, they struggled with accepting the new consumer role and the accompanying loss of economic power and status in the family. Middle-class women had to weigh loyalties and examine opportunities. The third conflict expressed in this fiction concerns the marriage contract. When women and men married, they agreed to a shared life with shared responsibilities. Many women found, though, that their contract had been breached: their responsibilities in the marriage were increasing and, seemingly, neverending. Married couples lived "her" marriage and "his," in which her marriage was one of continual self-sacrifice and assistance, and his one of receiving, of returning home and seeking and expecting sustenance there after the long work day had ended.[12] The fourth complaint of the modern woman, expressed clearly in the *Journal*'s fiction, concerned women's sexuality. Because female sexuality was at once recognized and then as quickly limited to heterosexual, monogamous marriage in this period, it was, to some degree, doomed. Companionate marriage promised but did not often deliver the emotional support and companionship women and men both had previously found in same-sex relationships. Instead, companionate marriage meant inequality in domestic and parental responsibilities, and when such responsibilities became overwhelming, as they did for many women, there was little room left for women to affirm and explore their newfound sexuality.[13]

These four conflicts, which are interrelated and which come up again and again in the fiction, mirrored conflicts middle-class women felt in their daily lives. And like the readers, the fictional protagonists arrived at a variety of conclusions about their individual situations. For the purposes of discussion here, the final decisions of the protagonists in these eight stories can be grouped into three categories: flirting with alternatives, then choosing traditional solutions; modifying traditional roles when they are found wanting; or planning life choices to match new and different expectations. Like the female characters Weibel sees in magazine fiction, all of these women err on the side of accommodating rather than abandoning the men in their lives, yet Woodward's contradictions also emerge, since the simple solutions to real problems are in the end no more convincing than are the difficulties that precipitate them.

In "The Amateur Rebel," writer Phyllis Duganne introduces her heroine with the following opening line: "Suzette Pendleton admitted that there was no excuse for her conduct: she must have been born a rebel."[14] Duganne's tale chronicles Suzette's growth from young womanhood to adult womanhood—and the sacrifices she must make along the way. Suzette belongs in the first group of protagonists, those who finally opt for the most traditional roles and traditional lives. Like the other heroines, Suzette is only an amateur rebel. Her story and the two that follow would be familiar to readers of the *Journal*, since they mirror messages found in the editorial material: women can find happiness in traditional marriages, where men ultimately make the important decisions and where women perform the emotional and the family caretaking. Their stories also reveal, however, that women had a lot to lose in these relationships, and one wonders in the end how far one has to scratch the surface of contentment to discover a brooding woman underneath.

Suzette, or Zette as she is called, is the only child of Richard and Elinor Pendleton, the "happiest couple" in Hendon. Zette's father is a successful lawyer, her mother the president of the Hendon Women's Club and secretary of the Literary Society. Photographs of their elegant home have been featured again and again in the pages of the "ultrasmart" *City and Country* magazine. It is the kind of upbringing any young woman should cherish, but Zette is unhappy. She feels stifled in a house where nobody fights; in fact she often wishes she lived instead with the O'Ryans in their dirty, rambling house, with a drunken father and scolding mother. There at least, she feels, she would find energy. When at age seventeen Zette finds her first opportunity to openly defy her parents, she pursues it with determination. After an unhappy birthday and a fight with her best friend, Zette encounters Ada Langley, an actress who has created quite a stir in Hendon. Miss Langley approaches Zette and initiates a heart-to-heart talk with the obviously unhappy girl. Zette pours out her feelings, expressing in particular her outrage that her best friend, Marian, is going to give up a promising singing career when she marries because her husband, a real estate agent, has asked her to do so. Ada Langley understands and appreciates Zette's feelings and encourages her to follow a more independent path in life. Zette's parents, upon hearing of this conversation, issue their first command: Zette is not to see Miss Langley again. The daughter promptly refuses to yield to her parents' demand. A week later, though, Miss Langley moves on, leaving a tearful and confused Zette waving on the train platform.

Zette formulates a plan to escape the mediocrity that defines life in Hendon: she will leave home at age eighteen, the date of her legal emancipation. On the occasion of her birthday, Zette makes the announcement to her parents: "I'm going to New York." When her mother asks why, Zette launches into an indict-ment of the family's very existence: "Why didn't you know? Can't you see that I hate it all? Can't you see that I hate nice, wholesome things? I–I'd rather live in a hotel than a house; I'd rather have a Pomeranian than a baby."[15] Zette's parents' reaction is not what she expected. Rather than express horror, they laugh, urge her to take a later train, and help her pack. Zette moves to New York and into the apartment of her friend Helen Emerson, who works as a secretary. When Zette meets Helen's friends she finds them a group of homesick working girls rather than urban rebels. Finally, Zette visits Ada Langley, who provides her with a bit part in a play and the names of several young actresses and actors. In this group Zette finds the bohemians she eagerly had hoped to befriend. One young man who joins the crowd, however, is quite traditional in dress and manner. Unexpectedly, Zette finds herself drawn most to this young man, Christopher Hewett. She tries to convince herself that he, a Harvard graduate, is too stuffy, but despite her resolve Zette grows to like him more and more.

One day Helen asks Zette if Chris has proposed yet, and Zette answers curtly that she does not believe in marriage. Helen expresses her surprise: she knows that they often speak that way but she thought that once the right man came along, even they would marry. Zette vows to prove that she will remain true to a life of freedom; she will flirt with another man and prove that Chris has no hold on her. When at a party she does just that, Chris approaches her, tells her this other fellow is a "bad sort," and counsels her to avoid him. "I don't know whether I like having you in love with me," snaps Zette, "if you're going to start restricting my friends. It's too much like going home to my parents."[16] The story reaches a climax when this other man, Ernest Blanchard, urges Zette to ride with him to his house on Long Island for breakfast after the night-long party. Zette tells Chris of her plan to go and he, disgusted, tells her to go ahead. At this point, realizing she has gone too far, Zette fears she has lost Chris. She tells him so, confessing that she is really just an "amateur rebel," as he had once called her, who wants him to stop her when she is foolish. To her relief, Chris replies by asking her to marry him.

In "The Amateur Rebel," Duganne's protagonist dabbles in alternative roles for women. She initially despises the idea that a woman would give up any measure of independence for a man but eventually admits that, given the right man, she is equally willing to make the same kind of sacrifice. The reader imagines Zette and Chris marrying, becoming the model of a happy couple in their town. One expects them to take on roles like Zette's parents, unlike Ada Langley, whose reputation is questionable, and unlike the Irish neighbors, who live up—or down—to their ethnic stereotypes. Zette tells Chris that she wants him to restrict her behavior, to set limits for her. Her earlier opposition, like that of her friend Helen, amounts to little more than talk. Zette's growth to womanhood is demonstrated by her willingness to embrace everything she had earlier renounced.

In "All You Need is a Cookbook," Sophie Kerr presents us with another young heroine who dabbles in alternatives before choosing a traditional role.[17] We are introduced first to Robert March, a newlywed who apparently married a woman like the one Zette nearly became. Robert is happy but somewhat bewildered by the turns his life has taken. He never thought he would marry a business woman, reside in a business apartment, live such a business-like life. He had always envisioned a traditional marriage "with all that implies." What he had not envisioned, it seems, is that he would fall in love with Emily, who is "modern to the tips of her long eyelashes." Robert married Emily, "with her feminist ideas," but he hoped that after marriage she would change and accept the traditions they had both grown up with. Emily has other ideas. She chooses an apartment designed for the business couple: it is small and requires little upkeep. She insists on sharing expenses and is determined that when they have children she will quit work but return as soon as the children are old enough. Robert expresses a limited understanding of Emily's struggles, as his words illustrate: "When I look at you, with those big brown eyes and that curly hair and those cutie dimples, and then when I hear you talking like a red-hot feminist, the contrast tickles me to death. You've no right to be so pretty. You're pretty enough to have no brains at all, d'you know that?"[18] For Robert, feminist and feminine form mutually exclusive categories, and he is troubled when Emily crosses the boundary. He loves her, though, and is willing to put up with her eccentricities, mostly because he does not take them seriously.

The biggest problem Emily and Robert encounter in their early marriage concerns her attitude not about children or finances but rather about food. Emily is health conscious to the extreme, and as a consequence they eat only the most nutritionally sound meals, even at the holidays. In this Emily is presented in a most unfavorable light: she fails to see the psychological significance of food as ritual, as comfort, or as part of a sharing relationship. Robert occasionally grows nostalgic thinking of the holiday dinners he had as a child and wishes they could have more than bran and lettuce for Christmas. Emily learns the extent of his discontent one day when she reads a letter from his mother, a letter which she had not realized was private. Mrs. March was upset to learn about Emily's strict attitude about food and horrified to think of her son eating such a meager holiday dinner. Emily feels embarrassed when she reads the letter and decides she must prove herself to Mrs. March. Anyone can cook a meal, she thinks; she simply had chosen not to do so in the past. Emily convinces Robert to invite both families for Christmas dinner and she, Emily, will prepare the entire meal.

The rest of the story outlines Emily's nearly disastrous attempt to prepare the holiday feast. "Any dumb-bell can cook," she grumbles. "All you need is a good cookbook to go by. There's nothing to it at all."[19] Emily quickly learns otherwise. The cookbook instructs her to buy oysters for the soup, but as Emily does not know how many oysters are needed, she orders six quarts. In the same vein she orders ten pounds of chestnuts for the stuffing, ten pounds of butter, and the largest turkey the butcher can find. When the food is delivered, Emily has to tie things to the window sill, for the kitchen overflows with the dinner's ingredients. When she sees the turkey, Emily realizes the extent of her problem. "No use to fool herself," the narrator tells us, "that bird would no more go into the oven of her range than it could take wings and fly to the moon."[20]

Emily drags the turkey and stuffing ingredients down to the street and begins to look for a restaurant with an oven large enough to cook her bird. When she enters her favorite restaurant, the owner immediately turns her away; they refuse to touch "that kind of food." Soon Emily finds herself in front of Robert's favorite restaurant, his clandestine eating place, "that horrid little Copper Kettle tea room." Out of desperation she enters and once inside, exhausted and at the end of her rope, bursts into tears. The owner of the Copper Kettle, Mrs. Parshall, coaxes the whole story out of Emily and then offers to help. First she introduces Emily to Lena the cook, who agrees, after giving Emily a good scolding about silly modern young women, to cook the turkey. Mrs. Parshall and Emily then return home, where Mrs. Parshall puts everything in order. She prepares cranberry jelly, onions, sweet potatoes, white potatoes, pudding, and a chicken pie. Emily, who helps by washing and cutting vegetables, feels quite humbled. When Mrs. Parshall finishes and offers to buy the many leftover ingredients at cost, Emily gives her the food but refuses to accept any money. She does not need the money, she informs Mrs. Parshall, for she has a job. "You've got a job, eh," Mrs. Parshall begins severely. She continues: "Oh, one of those married couples where the wife works and doesn't care anything about housekeeping. I see. And I had been thinking you were just one of the young ones whose folks spoil them by never making them learn anything useful. Well, I'm going to tell you, just as if you were my own daughter, you're on the wrong track. You've got hands, haven't you? Well, train 'em as sensibly as you train your brains, for in any one of life's close pinches they'll be what'll help you out. Now you remember that."[21] After a Christmas dinner that rivals any either family has ever had, Emily resolves to learn cooking from Lena and Mrs. Parshall. She tells Robert the whole story, and he is quite pleased: "And Robert, divining something of what had happened and guessing that he had won the first inning of his war game, had sufficient tact to use his time not to speak approval or pleasure but to give a silent Christmas kiss."[22]

In this story, as in "The Amateur Rebel," the heroine learns a lesson about herself and her relationship to the world. In the spirit of rebellion and of a new age, both Suzette and Emily make demands from their men for independence and equality in their relationships. In Zette's case she initially refuses marriage, viewing it as an outmoded and male-privileged arrangement. She comes to realize, though, that she wants this arrangement more than any other and she also wants her man to set limits and tell her what is best for them. In Emily's case, she feels certain that she and Robert have begun their marriage the right way with a simple home life that can accommodate two careers. Her lesson is also clear. She had denigrated traditional women's work, believing it would stifle her creativity and restrict her freedom. But Emily receives lectures on the education that served her poorly and the attitude that may break up her family. Her answer is neither a few good cooking lessons nor, as she suggested at the beginning of the story, a good cookbook, one that specifies amounts of foods needed. Instead, like Zette, she has changed her path and will eventually renounce everything that made her so modern. In both cases, the women resolve their conflicts not through further experimentation and change but instead through a retreat to the old, supposedly proven ways. Emily and Zette will, in the end, side with their mothers and against the women of their generation who demand new definitions of womanhood. Acceptance of tradition, in these stories, indicates female maturity.

"Tomorrow's Mother," by Josephine Daskam Bacon, offers a similar solution for a woman who had attempted to define herself first as a woman rather than as a wife or mother.[23] This is the story of Phyllis and Bob Fellowes, a young couple with two children. Bob works in a successful law practice, and Phyllis runs a business. Although the exact nature of Phyllis's work is unclear, she performs some type of prison reform work. Their story unwinds through the gathering of a group of four women, old friends and confidants who meet to spend the evening together after the coming-out party of one of their daughters. Sue Turkington, Vivi Winquist, and Betty Girard are incredulous at the news they hear: Phyllis and Bob plan to separate. The three friends await Phyllis's arrival so they can appease their collective wonder. Could this really be happening to the Phyllis they knew: "They had watched her take, one by one, the ditches and hedges of the great steeplechase of married life, and now that they had seen her triumphantly driving that tricky three-in-hand, her husband, her children and her business, now that she, the wonder of her little circle, had proved so much, so well—what had happened?"[24]

Phyllis eventually arrives and, after being assured of their continued loyalty, tells them the whole story. While Phyllis was away on a business trip to Albany, Bob Fellowes received a wire inviting him to become the senior partner at his brother's law firm in Los Angeles. Bob wired back an acceptance without discussing it with Phyllis, who subsequently refused to quit her job and move across the country. Bob replied that she could have a divorce but that he would keep the children. Phyllis tells her friends that she cannot give up everything for her children, even if she should. She and Bob have reached an impasse, and a separation appears to be the only solution: "We went into this with our eyes open, and on the basis of a firm; well, the partnership dissolves, that's all."[25]

Phyllis's friends are quick to give their advice. Yes, they argue, what Bob did was reprehensible. The idea that men can decide where their families will live and when they will move is wrong and, hopefully, a dying principle, sure to be gone by their children's generation. But, Vivi argues, the marriage produced children, and children are enough of a reason for two people to stay together. She uses Phyllis's business jargon to describe marriage, "the only kind of a firm that leaves the partners with two extra human beings as a result of the partnership." Sue thinks further on this, though, and argues that perhaps separation or divorce is better for children than is living in a hostile environment. Ultimately, the women agree that any decision should be based on the children's and not the parents' needs.

What follows next in this story makes the traditional ending both complex and troublesome. One by one the women reveal the marital problems they have had and the ways in which they came to terms with their troubled relationships. Each woman remains married, each has accommodated her needs to the greater needs of the family, and they counsel Phyllis to follow the same road. The women offer a traditional solution, women's accommodation, to a common problem, women's dissatisfaction, but as they do so they reveal the fact that none of them is entirely happy even now; as a rule, it seems, problems permeate marriage. For example, when one of the women suggests that Phyllis go away for a while, we learn that Betty had already tried this solution, with limited success. When the "bottom fell out" in her marriage, Betty took her two children and moved to Europe. She stayed there two years, seeing her husband only occasionally, and then returned and "settled down." When Sue asks her if her return was a good thing, Betty's reply is hardly enthusiastic: "'I don't know.' Betty's eyes grew somber and her rich voice dropped a tone." Betty later revealed that she had fallen in love with another man but gave up both him and a productive life in Europe for her children's happiness.

Vivi, it turns out, has also made sacrifices for her family. They had lived in New York City, where Vivi was quite happy but Victor, her husband, was terribly unhappy. The doctor told Vivi they should move to the country for her husband's sake, so they did. When they moved, however, the marriage was at such a low point that Victor asked her if she would rather get a divorce than go with him. She felt she should work it out for the sake of the children. "There's nothing lasts but that," she counsels her friends.

Finally, the fourth woman, Sue, reveals that she too had a problem, debilitating headaches, but she has now recovered. The telling of this piece suggests that once Sue's expectations of marriage disappeared, the headaches disappeared as well. The women join together to tell Phyllis that she will grow to love her children as they love theirs; she will one day recognize that any and all sacrifices made in the name of family are good and just ones for a woman to make. At that, Phyllis begins to cry, to the surprise of these friends who had never seen her cry before. Her crying was unique, "only those shaking shoulders and the silence of a man."

It is when she cries, it seems, that Phyllis crosses a bridge between making a hard decision and demonstrating a willingness to compromise; she moves from the silence and solitary resolve of a man to the tears and nurturing sensibilities of a woman. Phyllis has undergone a transformation, but, as the writer tells us, the process was one of breaking down rather than changing: "Broken in every bone of her soul, drowsy from exhaustion, Phyllis Fellowes staggered to her feet."[26] There is no happiness in Phyllis' decision at this point; the feeling of resignation and of having been broken reigns. Phyllis has given up the things that define her as a person. Today she is a woman, but tomorrow, as the title suggests, she will instead be a mother. Interestingly, this group of women do not believe that women have no right to expect more from marriage; they simply find it unlikely that any man will compromise further or provide more than what Bob Fellowes has offered.

Phyllis goes straight to bed at Vivi's house, only to be awakened at midnight by a remorseful Bob and her own worried father. Bob reveals to her that he is willing to stay and she reveals to him that she is willing also, to go. In this final scene Bob tells her how she is unfit for marriage, but since they had taken that step they should see it through: "The whole thing was probably a mistake. Women like you should not marry, probably. But I took you on your own terms, and though they were wrong I must not gamble at the results. You could not help your type; you were the result of your training and environment. You have borne children, but I believe you to be fundamentally sexless. You cannot understand the meaning of a wife."[27] These are rather harsh words from a supposedly contrite husband, but Bob goes on. When the broken Phyllis asks him to tell her what a wife is, he replies that he is not sure: "I doubt if any man knows. But we know what it is not: It is not a partner, it is not a 'pal,' it is not a mistress, it is not a friend. It is not even the mother of one's children. It is something different from its parts."[28] The couple reunites in the end, and Phyllis falls asleep with her husband and her father watching guard over her. This woman of yesterday has become "Tomorrow's Mother."

These three stories promote traditional solutions to women's conflicts over appropriate gender roles. The women wonder about the degree to which they should meet the needs of others; they struggle over definitions of women's work inside and outside the home; they reluctantly define marriage as a very different experience for women than for men; and they only temporarily question traditional definitions of marriage and sexuality. Although each of the protagonists and, in the last story, each of the minor characters arrives at a traditional solution, when we read the stories against the grain, questions remain; the happy endings seem difficult to swallow. In the first story, it is true that Zette has opted for the traditional role of subservient wife, but there is no guarantee that, given the rebellious nature of her youth, she will excel in or enjoy that role without modifying it. The young woman who wanted a Pomeranian rather than a baby suddenly wants to emulate her parents as closely as possible. The reader may conclude that Zette has grown up; she may also be reminded of her own youthful dreams and the directions she might have taken with her own life. She might put down the *Journal* and daydream about the risks she did not take, the paths she avoided, the men she shied away from.

Zette's story also clearly recognized and then quickly contained a young woman's sexual yearnings. Ernest Blanchard, the man with the car and the private party on Long Island, represented sexual experimentation, which Zette initially wanted and finally renounced. One wonders which characters the reader is most likely to remember and/or fantasize about, the earnest husband-to-be or the wealthy and romantic suitor. One wonders which parts of the story the reader is most likely to remember, Zette's final choice or the interesting and unorthodox choices she makes along the way. Reading the story against the grain reveals Zette's happiness but hints at what she has given up, and the loss may give as much pause as does the romantic ending.

Reading the second story against the grain, it is difficult to imagine that Emily March, who had despised cooking and had felt so strongly about a modern marriage, would successfully, after one ill-fated cooking adventure, abandon her career, move into a "family" home, rather than a business apartment, and take up cooking and cleaning full time. Readers might suggest she buy a good cookbook and go on with her life as usual. Robert may be pleased with the choices his wife has made at the end of the story, but he may be setting himself up—or at least setting her up—for disappointment by expecting it will either come naturally to her or satisfy her modern yearnings. And readers may be as moved by the degree to which Robert fails to understand his wife as they are by the degree to which he loves her.

In the final story in this group, "Tomorrow's Mother," Phyllis Fellowes is outwardly depicted as having matured. Or, has she, as the narrator suggests, simply been broken? This story leaves the reader with a woman reconciled to her role, but even more than Zette's or Emily's stories, it is hardly a celebration of wifehood or motherhood. Phyllis's work takes a clear second place to her husband's work, even though they are both professionals. Phyllis and her friends share an understanding that marriage lacks something fundamental for them, and that something is more than faintly sexual. Their sexuality is confined to heterosexual, monogamous marriage, and while none makes this claim, subtle signs of discontent and dissatisfaction remain in all their relationships. They all share a dream but none lives it. Nevertheless, the women all agree that their own personal happiness must be secondary to this larger cause, the family. The reader comes away with a double message: on the one hand, a woman can learn to find contentment in marriage; on the other hand, this happiness often comes at tremendous personal cost. Reading the story against the grain, the women's unhappiness weighs most heavily. Actual readers may have put down the magazine and daydreamed about divorces for Phyllis and some of her friends, and, perhaps, for themselves; while marriage remained a cultural mandate for the *Journal*, divorce increased fifteen-fold in the United States between 1870 and 1920.

The next two stories offer quite different solutions to the individual woman's second-class marital status. In both, the protagonist, a married women, sees that her husband and children take advantage of her. She recognizes the importance of her role but feels that the other members of her family increasingly do not. These women come to different conclusions than do the women in the first three stories; they do not find a way, in the end, to accommodate themselves to traditional expectations and family demands. Instead, they assert themselves and force those around them to change. Husbands and children learn that they have to treat their wives and mothers with newfound respect or they may lose them to divorce, in one case, or madness, in the other.

Author Sophie Kerr introduces us to her heroine, Ethel Blaise, in "Little Winged Birds, So Happy," at the beginning of a lovely spring day.[29] Mrs. Blaise's first thoughts upon waking are of the loveliness of nature and of the romance and adventure such a day promises. The real day quickly breaks in and shatters her early morning daydreams, though, and the pace of the story quickens. Has the bread been delivered for breakfast, does she have time to iron her son's pants, will the washerwoman come today? Ethel Blaise's movement takes on a hum as she moves about, getting dressed in the bathroom so she does not wake up her husband, setting out his things for shaving and bathing, opening windows, straightening pillows, emptying ashtrays.

Mrs. Blaise appears to be quite efficient; she even finds time to make muffins for breakfast when she realizes that the bread has not arrived. In the meantime, her husband Gerald performs his one household duty, waking the children, who begin to get ready upstairs. In the middle of mixing the muffins, Ethel

Blaise looks out the window and sees a sky that reminds her of the day her husband had proposed to her. She mentally reviews the whole experience: "His voice had trembled when he told her that he wanted only to devote himself, his life, all his energies to making her happy. And at that memory Mrs. Blaise smiled the smile that many wives have smiled before her and many shall smile after her. It is made up of regret, amusement, and disillusion." Gerald is a good husband, she admits, "as husbands go." There is, however, something missing. When Ethel Blaise turns from the window to the mirror she sees a woman, thirty-eight years old and hardened, who looks like she expects the worst of life. "These were the gifts of her married years," the narrator informs us.[30]

Daily life interferes with Mrs. Blaise's thoughts as the family descends to the kitchen. Gerald senior is grumpy, angry that there is no bread, only muffins. The children have their demands as well. Gerald Junior wants five dollars for his fraternity; Bob wants his mother to bake cookies for when he returns home from school; Jean wants a new evening dress since her friends are outdoing her with their fashions. As quickly as they can voice their various complaints and demands, they finish their meal and leave Ethel alone. And, left alone, Mrs. Blaise begins to feel badly about herself. Her husband thinks of her as a drudge; her children have incessant demands but little appreciation. Depression sets in: "She could feel it, right on the back of her neck, weighing her down. Innumerable other Mrs. Blaises know that feeling."[31]

Ethel Blaise's condition is exacerbated by the sight of a neighbor, Mrs. Thompson, in the yard next door. The blond Mrs. Thompson flirts with all the men and spends most of her time in club activities rather than cleaning and cooking, yet her husband brings her candy and flowers, they attend the theater together twice a week, and her two sons seem both attentive and obedient. Mrs. Blaise wonders at the contrast between her life and that of Mrs. Thompson. Theoretically, Ethel should be the happy one, devoted as she is to her family. It seems, however, that the opposite is true. These reveries are also interrupted, this time by the voice of Mrs. Thompson, who appears on the porch asking if she can come in for a moment. She had recently attended a lecture given by a disciple of Freud and felt the subject was especially relevant to Mrs. Blaise, for the speaker discussed repressed people. These people, who keep everything in and fail to enjoy life, should let their words fly free, like little winged birds. Mrs. Thompson then runs off, leaving Ethel confused and more than a little annoyed. As the moments pass, though, she realizes the accuracy of Mrs. Thompson's diagnosis: Ethel has done much for others, but has repressed her own needs. Ethel Blaise now sees herself as a truly unhappy, repressed person.

As the day progresses Mrs. Blaise formulates a plan for change. She herself needs a new outfit, she decides, more than her daughter needs a gown or her son needs his fraternity. They can learn the value of money by earning it. From now on they will perform chores for her, relieve her of some of her burdens, and in return earn some of the money they clamor for. In addition, they will see their mother in a new dress and, perhaps, in a new light. By the time the family returns home that evening, the new Mrs. Blaise is visible and radiant. Clad in her best dress, Ethel serves the dinner she had prepared with herself in mind: lamb stew, salad with garlic, spinach, and sour-cream peach pie. As dinner commences she makes the following announcement to the spinach-hating group before her: "My dear husband and children, for years I've catered to your tastes and wishes in the way of food and foregone my own. Now I've turned Bolshevik. These are the things I like."[32] When Mrs. Blaise finishes and sits down, she sees everyone at the table diligently eating their spinach. Ethel Blaise realizes this is only the beginning of the revolution, but she is ready to engage in battle with her family. As a final assault for the day, Ethel announces that the children will clean up the supper dishes; she and her husband are going to the movies. As she and Gerald walk to the cinema, he tells her how thrilled and ashamed he is. Ethel has reawakened their love, and he realizes how inattentive he had been for so long. They walk hand in hand, stopping like young lovers to kiss along the way.

Mrs. Ethel Blaise, rather than give in to the pressures of family life, rebelled against them. She recognized that the responsibilities of the wife and mother were not clearly outlined and that she had lost a great deal of ground in the struggle for self-definition. When Ethel Blaise declares herself to be a Bolshevik, she outlines terms for revolution among white, middle-class women. One can carry out a revolution, and in fact at times one has no other choice, but that revolution occurs within the family. Ethel Blaise does not abandon her family, get a divorce, or even get a job. Instead, she asserts her right to define limits, demands respect and assistance, and in the end get what she wants—the best of all worlds.

The story of Ethel Blaise's rebellion includes three of the four conflicts discussed above. She feels that self-sacrifice has been harmful, practiced as she had practiced it. She never considers work as an alternative but clearly feels that her husband does not do his part in the marriage. The fact that his only chore is to wake the children, and the fact that he grumbles about the home-baked muffins are not lost on the reader. Finally, this story is the first to introduce sexuality as a significant factor. When Mrs. Blaise denied her children something and made her own needs a priority, she became radiant and sexy, her husband's date for the evening. The story recognizes female sexuality and also suggests that a traditional marriage sounds a death knoll for the expression of that sexuality.

"The Woman Wins," by Cora Harris, follows the theme of "Little Winged Birds, So Happy."[33] The drawing on the first page pictures a woman standing in the midst of a disheveled room with a golf club raised over her head. The caption reads, "She dealt a blow too deep to be mended with varnish." This in itself is impressive, since women are rarely, if ever, depicted as violent beings in the *Ladies' Home Journal.* The story begins not by explaining the woman's actions but by describing the place where she lives, Altahama, "a young city which, until recently, was an old town." The men had contributed to the growth of this city by building factories, residences, and golf links; the women added flowers, shrubs, a fountain, and a war monument. Such a setting leaves us unprepared for the introduction of a desperate woman who enters her house and begins to destroy everything before her. She tears the curtains down, knocks over furniture, and picks up a golf club and hits tables and chairs with it. Finally, she tears off her clothes, picks up a shirt of her husband's out of the mess she has made, puts it on, and falls to bed. She may have put on the shirt, the narrator revealingly informs us, "because never before in her good and submissive life had she shown the least leanings toward anything pertaining to man's estate or his powers, prerogatives, or clothes."[34]

The story then shifts to the history of this as yet unnamed woman and her family. The Styles family had come to Altahama thirty years earlier when they were a young married couple with a baby, Luella. Mr. Styles was a dedicated worker who wanted to "be somebody in the world," Mrs. Styles a "devoted wife, ambitious and thrifty." Mr. Styles grew in importance as the town grew and eventually became president of a new bank. Luella went to a prestigious college in the east and became a suffragist. In spite of this, or perhaps because of it, nobody wanted to marry her. Mrs. Styles watched her family change while she remained the same, supportive and always present, dedicated more to her family than to outside activities.

How then, does one explain such a change in attitude, such a severe physical action or reaction? For a time, we are told, Mrs. Styles has been helping a neighbor, Mrs. Henderson, who suffers from nervous attacks and who spends a good deal of time in bed. One day, Mrs. Styles experienced a realization about her neighbor's condition: "The net results were obvious. Mrs. Henderson had every care and everything she wanted. She was humored and relieved of every responsibility. Henderson was a hard man, but he was like putty in his wife's hands. It was obvious to Mrs. Styles that this woman led a life of ease and luxury because she was selfish and worthless. She, on the other hand, had a life of service and sacrifice in vain. It had netted her nothing in the way of appreciation or consideration from her family."[35]

Mrs. Henderson's story parallels that of Mrs. Blaise's Freud-studying neighbor, Mrs. Thompson, in the previous story; they represent the women who do not follow traditional roles and still, or perhaps subsequently, get what they want from their lives. Mrs. Styles's rebellion includes imitating the actions of the pampered Mrs. Henderson, just as Mrs. Blaise had rebelled by emulating her attractive blond neighbor. Mrs. Styles's rampage at home follows her moment of clarity, and Mr. Styles and Luella arrive home to find the house destroyed and Mrs. Styles in bed clad in her husband's shirt. Mrs. Styles, quietly watching them rush about, feels that there is something enjoyable in stirring up her husband's feelings, "like receiving payment for a debt long past due." Certain that Mrs. Styles is dying, her husband and daughter send for the doctor, who comes at once and as quickly, it seems, diagnoses the problem. "There was something curiously lucid in his look, a sort of niggling beam in his eye," the narrator relates, "as if he had discovered wit and deceit where he had always supposed only simplicity and dumb dutifulness resided."[36] When Dr. Markham gets a few moments alone with his patient, he draws the real story from her. "What's the game," he asks, and she tells him she has quit, "with a bang." She feels used by her family, who are good, smart, successful—but insensitive. The doctor agrees with her and supports her action, but he also issues a warning: "But go slow. Hysteria is a habit-forming self-addiction of the nerves very difficult to overcome." Dr. Markham fears that Mrs. Styles will grow accustomed to this measure as an only means of escape, as so many others had done before her.

Dr. Markham then tells Mr. Styles and Luella of Mrs. Styles's condition. "This is a new and mysterious disorder. . . . It is peculiar to our time, as skin diseases were to the middle centuries," he explains. "Your wife is suffering from emotional suppression. I doubt if she has spoken her real mind in years."[37] The doctor issues a prescription: they are to defer to Mrs. Styles in everything, take on her responsibilities in the house, and provide her with cheerful surroundings. The distressed husband and daughter eagerly take over, but as the days pass they realize the extent of the wife/mother's burdens. Luella has to cancel several speaking engagements and resign from one of the national committees of the League of Women Voters. Mr. Styles has to give up golf and a trip to the Bankers' Convention. Mrs. Styles, meanwhile, "had risen to a strange prominence" in Altahama. Recognized, really, for the first time, she rests and gradually recovers in a room filled with flowers and visitors.

Mrs. Styles's story contains an interesting description of neurasthenia or hysteria, the nervous condition that afflicted many Americans, female and male, during this period. Tom Lutz's description of neurasthenia as a "nearly universal trope for the individual's relation to cultural modernization," describes in part Mrs. Styles's reaction to changes that seem to outdistance her. Between the Civil War and World War I, hundreds of women and men, many of them prominent figures such as Jane Addams, Theodore Roosevelt, Charlotte Perkins Gilman, and Fannie Farmer, suffered from neurasthenia, experiencing many of the symptoms Mrs. Styles appropriates in her quest for social status and family appreciation.[38] Carroll Smith-Rosenberg argues that women, consciously or not, chose hysteria as a response to isolation, loneliness, depression, and the burdens of frequent pregnancies, the demands of children, and the daily exertions of domestic work. When a woman like Mrs. Styles, who had only one child, found that gender roles did not change as readily as demographics, hysteria was one option open to her.[39] Unlike most victims of hysteria, however, Mrs. Styles received a prescription that challenged rather than promoted traditional gender roles. Most physicians treating the illness offered treatment plans determined strictly on the basis of gender: women were to refrain from activity and rest while men were to engage in challenging physical activity. Mrs. Styles' doctor offered a different prescription; she was to socialize and have her way at home. Rather than expose her fraud, the doctor encouraged her to make the most of his diagnosis, provided she realized the addictive nature of her actions.

Like Ethel Blaise, Mrs. Styles resorts to an extreme action to correct inequalities in family responsibilities. But unlike Ethel Blaise, she sees no means of modifying her responsibilities by talking with her family or by neglecting one or two of her chores and assigning them to others. The only way out is to make a radical statement and then, in a sense, begin again. In both cases the family begins again with new definitions both of the importance of and the demands upon the mother/wife. These two stories, read against the grain, also demonstrate the limited choices women faced as they attempted to make changes in their lives. Mrs. Blaise and Mrs. Styles win out, but the reader might wonder if their gains would be temporary rather than permanent ones and if their families' contrition expresses fleeting empathy rather than lasting solidarity. While the first set of solutions, choosing traditional paths, seems fairly unconvincing, the notion that families will radically change in midstream may have been equally unconvincing. Readers may have sympathized with the protagonists in their struggles; they may also have believed that women need to take even more drastic action to effect any real changes. They may have empathized or sympathized, but either way they participated in a recognition of the limitations of traditional marriage.

The final set of stories suggests that women can find the middle ground they desire if only they plan well from the start—and if they are lucky enough to find men who will support and participate in redefining gender roles. The protagonists in these stories ultimately choose marriage, but they challenge that institution, demanding modified gender roles and ongoing respect for their individuality. They will not be broken by marriage, as is Phyllis Fellowes, nor will they accept the roles played by their mothers and grandmothers, as do Zette and Emily March. These women point to new arrangements and suggest that, even in the *Ladies' Home Journal*, change is possible.

In the June 1914 *Journal*, "The Pretty Suffragette," by Louise Elizabeth Dutton, features three drawings, the largest of which is accompanied by a caption.[40] The two smaller drawings are on the upper left and right hand corners of the page: both feature the same woman, but in one case she is wearing a banner that reads "Votes for Women" and in the other she is wearing an apron and carrying a tray with steaming cups of coffee. The large drawing shows this same woman in the foreground, washing dishes, and a man in the background drying. "Billy followed her into the transformed kitchen," the caption reads, "and meekly wiped dishes." The reader is immediately prepared for a conflict between this "pretty suffragette" and Billy, and the nature of this conflict quickly becomes apparent.

Francesca Foster, vice-president of the Intercollegiate Alumnae Equal Suffrage League, also happens to be "the prettiest girl Billy Waring ever knew." She is so pretty, the narrator relates, that when she lectures people become convinced of the necessity of votes for women whether her argument is sound or not. Billy, who wants to marry Francesca, feels that women are unfit for the franchise; he is looking for a way to convince her to marry him and settle down. Billy decides that perhaps a weekend in the country with some married friends of his will convince Francesca of the joys of domestic life, so he makes arrangements for them to visit Joe and Bella Morton and their two children. Billy and Francesca are the only ones to get off the train at Cremona, the lonely spot where the Mortons live. They walk down the main street to where the sidewalk ends, up a hilly street with no sidewalk, and through a stubby field to the family's bungalow.

The Mortons immediately welcomed Francesca; in fact, Bella Morton's "plump arm was around Francesca's waist" as they toured the small house. Bella has prepared a simple but, Billy thinks, elegant meal. Joe and Bella clearly have little money to spare, but Billy admires Bella's accomplishments with furnishings, food, and clothing. When Francesca speaks nothing of women's rights but instead relaxes and gazes at the fire, Billy muses that she looks "like a sweet, human woman by her own fireside, sheltered and content." Like Robert March in "All You Need is a Cookbook," Billy Waring believes there are two kinds of women: those who are happy at home, and those who know nothing of the joys of home life. He, too, loves his feminist woman but hopes to change her, domesticate her, make her more of a "human" woman.

The evening proceeds well, but the next morning brings problems. The older Morton child was up sick all night, the water tap leaks on the sink, the gas range fails to work, and the maid has not come to clean up the dishes from the previous night's dinner. During breakfast Bella pours the coffee but only brown water comes out; she had forgotten to put in the grinds. Finally, Bella breaks one of their few real tea cups and runs out of the room crying. Billy and Francesca can hear her through the thin walls of the tiny house. She cries to Joe that Billy should take Francesca, "that awful girl," away. Bella senses everything Billy had dreaded but had been blind to: Francesca the feminist has at least some measure of disdain for this commonplace household situation.

Francesca leaves the dining room abruptly and enters the kitchen, but Billy remains at the table, unsure of what steps to take. Eventually he gathers the nerve to enter the kitchen and tell Francesca he is ready to leave on the next train. Before he makes his next move, however, Francesca reemerges, not in tears but clad in an apron, carrying coffee. She disappears up the stairs and into Bella's room. Meanwhile, Joe comes down and apologizes to Billy. Bella has simply had another attack of her nerves, he explains, and to make things worse she has developed a dislike for Francesca. A few moments later, Francesca passes by again, and again disappears into the kitchen. When Billy follows her he finds her hard at work, "her broad brows wrinkled faintly with the born housekeeper's concentration that no man dares interrupt."[41]

As the day progresses, Billy grows more and more impressed with Francesca. He had brought her here hoping that she would learn domestic economy from Bella, but he sees that Francesca knows far more than he had imagined. When he has the opportunity later in the day, Billy reviews the many sides of Francesca he had witnessed that day, as she dusted flour on his burned hand and gave him the most sympathetic look he had seen "in her kind"; as she knelt by the sick boy's head and assured the tearful mother that the doctor was not needed; as she lovingly bathed the infant. Billy saw something else too, however. He saw how tired she was from this work, and he realized the difficulty of women's work. In one fairly ordinary day in the life of a family, Francesca had spent all of her energy.

Billy slowly comes to terms with the situation: he cannot ask Francesca to marry him and take on such a heavy load. But at this point, incapable of imagining any other solutions, Billy feels ready to give up. Francesca, on the other hand, has come to a very different conclusion. After dinner that evening they go for a walk and Francesca rails against Bella's incompetence, with which she is furious. She then brings up her own cause, suffrage. "Billy, the 'Cause' is strong enough to fight its battles without me," she tells him. "There's a bigger fight for any woman—for me—to make, a place that nobody but me can fill, a 'cause.'" Billy interrupts her to tell her of his own realizations, but Francesca will not listen: "The faintest of smiles curved the corners of Francesca's mouth. But her brown eyes were not smiling: they looked at Billy straight and true. 'I've had a long, hard day, but I've got one more hard thing to do,' she said rather breathlessly; and she did it. 'Billy, I love you,' she said. 'Will you marry me?'"[42]

Francesca Foster's story, on the surface, tells of a woman who comes to terms with being a woman, who realizes the true definition of a "cause" as it applies to her life. Billy believes that Francesca's abilities as a suffrage leader preclude any abilities at housekeeping. It seems that they do, in fact, for at the end Francesca gives up one for the other, deciding that the one cause can continue without her because she will now dedicate all of her energy to the other. Beneath the surface, however, lies a more complicated picture. Bella Morton has chosen the traditional role. She apparently has no other ambitions, is at least partly happy with her role as a wife and mother, and resents Francesca because she does have other concerns. Bella Morton, however, is a failure in her role. She cannot fulfill all her obligations, and her difficulties manifest in a nervous condition. In the end Francesca faults Bella, complains of her inability to handle the family, budget money, even dress herself well. Bella, perhaps, is headed down the road of nervous exhaustion and an inability to cope—elements of women's lives Mrs. Styles experimented with in an effort to create change. In Bella's case, however, it is no act.

Francesca has other plans. Unafraid to tackle new tasks, she uses her education to advance her expertise in the household, and, because of rather than in spite of her suffrage activity feels ready to take on this new cause. Interestingly enough, Billy recognizes the limitations of the role he wants Francesca to enter just as she decides she is ready to handle it. One thing is certain, though: Francesca will handle this role very differently than did Bella, and the first proof of this is that she, certain of what she wants, proposes to Billy. The ultimate goal is still marriage in this story, but the reader comes away with a feeling that in this marriage things will be different. Francesca does not go so far as to combine employment and marriage, but she does suggest a more businesslike and woman-friendly household arrangement than that of the Mortons.

Francesca Foster is the type of character who could make the most of what the *Ladies' Home Journal* had to offer. She has welcomed education and the advancement of women, but when she becomes a woman she sees that her true cause is the home. She will not sacrifice the potential domesticity Billy Waring offers; in fact, she will pursue it with determination by asking his hand in marriage. At the same time though, she will use her education and suffrage skills to run her household in a new, modern, efficient manner. One can imagine Francesca Foster reading the *Journal* advice, following scientific housekeeping principles, combining activities outside the home with her household duties, and excelling in everything. Francesca will read the advertisements thoroughly as well, always examining critically her options and making wise consumer choices. She identifies problems with the typical housewife's role but feels that as an individual woman she can make the appropriate changes.

Another story by Sophie Kerr, "Babe Grows Up," explores the theme of single women contemplating marriage, and again suggests that changes are possible.[43] The drawing that accompanies this story shows a group of people dancing in the background and a couple in formal dress on a balcony in the foreground. The caption reads "A woman who wants a great career mustn't ever think of marrying. That was why I made up my mind I wouldn't." We are soon introduced to this young woman, Babe, who has fallen in love with the young doctor who has, in turn, fallen in love with Babe's older sister, Virginia. Unbeknownst to Babe, Virginia and Dr. Ted Warburton have made plans to marry. Babe, meanwhile, has made plans to cut one of the tires on Ted's automobile so that he cannot take Virginia on another evening ride. When she sits near the car deliberating on this admittedly rash action, Dr. Ted calls her name and invites her for an evening ride. Babe, convinced that he has seen the light, experiences a disillusioning automobile outing. Instead of proclaiming his love for her, Ted Warburton tells Babe that he and Virginia are to marry and how happy he is finally to have a younger sister.

The months of preparation for this grand affair are dark ones for Babe, who barely utters a word to either Virginia or Ted. She keeps hoping the doctor will change his mind before that fateful day. When the weekend of the wedding arrives, Babe reluctantly participates in the festivities. On the first night she meets Ted's younger cousin, Ross Abell, her escort in the wedding. The two teenagers find they have a lot in common, particularly as they discuss their feelings about this outmoded custom, marriage. They find a great deal to say to each other about their dreams and then about Virginia and Ted's decision to marry. "But what does it amount to?" asks Babe. "They'll settle down to the dull atmosphere of domesticity. I can tell you, I'm never going to marry." Ross agrees. He doesn't care for poetry, he tells her, for it is part of a marriage plot: "It's all a part of the game to get a man tangled up with some nice girl, and the next thing he knows he's paying rent for an apartment and buying near-Colonial furniture on the installment plan. No, a man who wants to do anything must stay single."[44]

As the wedding weekend continues, Babe and Ross spend a great deal of time together, walking, talking, dancing, eating. They discuss many topics, from their favorite movies to politics, from food to marriage, and agree in everything. When the wedding ceremony itself ends, Ross comments that Virginia and Ted are now tied for life. "Isn't it fearful?" he asks. "Frightful," Babe replies. When it is time for Ross to leave, he is visibly unhappy to be saying goodbye to Babe. He prefaces his departure with a short speech about marriage. He has been thinking it over, he explains, and he thinks that perhaps marriage need not be discarded altogether; perhaps, instead, it can be modified. Two people could marry, he argues, and still have their careers, if the man is willing to support the woman in her cause. Ross asks Babe to write him a letter right away and let him know what she thinks—does she think such an arrangement is possible?

The story ends with Ross running off to catch his train and Babe rushing off to bed. Phrases of the letter she is to write the next day form in her mind. She laughs when she remembers her earlier expectation—that she would spend this night brokenhearted. Instead, she spends it blissfully, envisioning a fulfilling and exciting, if somewhat traditional life. The reader meets an adolescent girl experiencing her first love and is left, at the end, with a somewhat mature young woman realizing the possibilities that await her in life. While Babe and Ross come to realize that some of their discussion together was just the bragging, rebellious talk of young people trying to impress each other, they also realize that they have some options in their own futures. The two young people ultimately yearn for an arrangement that is not altogether different from the arrangements they know and had grown up with. In fact, perhaps they would one day have a marriage that is more similar to, than different from Virginia and Ted's marriage. At the same time, though, they suggest that a modification of the roles is possible as well as desirable, and Ted recognizes that the man shares some measure of responsibility in making this happen. "I've heard of such things," Ted tells Babe. He had heard that people strove for greater equality in marriage, and he was looking forward to that possibility for himself. In the end, then, while this story leaves us with two young people rebelling against but finally looking forward to marriage, it also leaves us with the idea that in some ways, at least, this marriage will be a new institution.

Finally, as in the story of Mrs. Blaise and her new dress, there is a great deal of hinting about female sexuality in this story. Babe is the precursor to Ethel Blaise: in her youth she finds the promise of sex tremendously exciting, so exciting that she can shake off one grand infatuation for another in the course of a weekend. She dreaded the wedding night, expecting to lie awake thinking of the married couple. Instead, when the night ends Babe can hardly settle down and stop thinking of her future prospects with Ross Abell. The story channels Babe toward a companionate marriage, but she will clearly enter with at least the expectation that the mystery will last. Of course, readers might realize, so did the many Mrs. Blaises of the world. Perhaps Babe will be luckier with Ross, the male equivalent of the New Woman.

The final story in this group continues the theme of finding the right man and combining domesticity and personal autonomy. "Connie," by Phyllis Duganne, appears to be the most blatantly anti-feminist story, in the way that it juxtaposes arch-feminists Dorothy and Paula against their more traditional sister Connie.[45] On one level this is a story of two kinds of women, and the more domestic wins out over the radical. A reading against the grain, however, reveals the ways in which the actions of the traditional sister at times stray far from traditional; she achieves her end result, domesticity, by making some fairly nontraditional choices and by taking some risks. Like the two previous protagonists, Francesca and Babe, Connie finds a way to achieve happiness through a modified marriage arrangement.

The narrator first introduces Dorothy and Paula Brett by describing their relationships with men. "Man, as a sex, had little to do with the lives of Paula and Dorothy Brett, Decorators. Although now, after fifteen years of business together, they had several dozen of the species on their payroll. Brett and Brett did not, however, dislike men, either separately or en masse. They were ardent feminists, both of them, and all that they demanded of man was that he approach as closely as possible that human perfection toward which they, as practical, modern women, were striving."[46] These feminist sisters have little patience with their sister Connie, who they thought was their clay to mold as "creators of perfect womanhood." When their father died, Paula and Dorothy took over the job of raising Connie, but when the story opens they feel particularly dissatisfied with the results. Contrary to their expectations, Connie eloped with a redhead named Tommy O'Toole, who sailed a week later to join the war and died in action. Connie is bewildered at her misfortune: a quick marriage, no real opportunity to know her husband well, and a sudden loss. Her sisters, on the other hand, are "relieved," at least in part because she is rid of the Irishman. They expect Connie to get a job and chose a more independent route, but Connie soon discovers she is pregnant; she subsequently gives birth to twins, Timmy and Terry. With her sisters' help, Connie gets a job in a lingerie shop on Fifth Avenue and has a woman care for her children during the day. She feels unhappy with the work, however, for she had envisioned a life of domesticity. When the three sisters each receive an inheritance of one thousand dollars, Connie decides to make a move. One day she enters the office of Brett and Brett, Decorators, and announces that she will quit her job and move to Vermont. Paula and Dorothy are incredulous. She knows one thousand dollars is not a fortune, Connie assures them, but she had heard that Vermont was nice and was certain that people there would help her if she encountered difficulties.

When Connie leaves the office, the sisters do not react immediately. Their first business is to attend to the room, which the twins had nearly destroyed during their visit. Waste baskets had been overturned, cookie crumbs littered the room, and the chairs were arranged like train cars in a row. In this scene we see the two sisters' intolerance–their inability to enjoy children or even accept the business of children, which of course is play. Once the room is in order, Paula and Dorothy can think about Connie and the children and wonder how they will survive. One day they see a "disreputable" truck pull up outside their office. Connie has come to tell them that she bought a house for five hundred dollars and is ready to take her furniture out of storage. Again the sisters are incredulous. If she spent half of her money on the house, and will spend a good bit more on the storage fee, how will she live? Has she found work? Connie calmly informs them that she has no intention of working; she will grow vegetables to survive. In that case, Paula and Dorothy urge, she must find a husband, a source of support. "Thank you. Oh, thank you very much," replies Connie, "but I–I'd like to just be let alone, if you don't mind. I'd like to just manage myself."[47]

At this point, although the sisters are portrayed as judgmental, cold, and intolerant, and the reader is urged to side with Connie, this is no simple task. Connie appears as ambiguous as they are certain. She does not want to be away from her children, and her real drive is to have a house and be at home, but she has already made several unconventional decisions. As a single parent she moved to a place she had never been before simply because someone, and she could not remember who, had said it was nice there. Once there, she found a way to survive without marrying and firmly discounted the possibility when her sisters introduced it. Connie, by definition, wants what her sisters consider a traditional life, but her actions show that she practices some rather unconventional behavior.

As the story continues, the reader meets Brian O'Ramey, who, while at the storage warehouse on an errand, hears an argument between the manager and a woman. He falls fast in love with the voice before he even sees the woman, Connie. When Connie cannot secure her furniture without more money, Brian follows her out of the door and tells her he had overheard the argument. He further tells her that he too is going to Warren, Vermont, and that he will pay her to take his things along with hers in the truck—in that way she will have enough money to pay her bill. When Connie asks him if he is moving to Warren, he tells her he is, and when she asks him if by chance he is buying the house next to hers, he again replies that he is. The clever Connie, we later learn, has realized his game but seen a way to profit from it. On the road to Vermont, she stops to telephone the owner of the vacant house and asks him if he would pay her a commission for any price over five hundred dollars she can get him for the house. She counsels him then to demand one thousand dollars from a Mr. O'Ramey, who is sure to call shortly. Connie receives her five hundred dollar commission, one hundred percent of the cost of the house. She later sells O'Ramey three acres of her land for another five hundred. By the time Brian asks Connie to marry him, which he soon does, she has successfully earned one thousand dollars.

When Brett and Brett, Decorators, receive notice that Connie has remarried, their response is hardly joyful. "Another mick!" Dorothy exclaims. One day, though, when Connie pays them a visit, they are impressed both with her elegant appearance and her extraordinary business acumen, as she relates the story of her earnings. Most incredible of all, however, is that they learn the true identity of Connie's new husband: "The Brian O'Ramey, of New York, Newport, and Castle O'Ramey, the Brian O'Ramey whom everyone who ever looked at a newspaper knew as well as the Prince of Wales."[48] An elegant town car pulls up to the curb and they watch Brian O'Ramey emerge. The sisters have to decide what it is that has pulled Connie through. Is it her luck, her beauty and simplicity, or her business sense, which had proven to be sharp? In any case, she has, seemingly, achieved it all. Even the hard, feminist sisters show some signs of softness here, as they recognize that perhaps Connie has found the balance needed in life. They, Brett and Brett, Decorators, seem defeated in the end.

Connie Brett O'Toole O'Ramey represents, on the one hand, a traditional woman who dreams of domesticity. With two children in tow she acquires the unhurried existence of small-town life and, eventually, a devoted husband. Connie comes across in the story as a far more sympathetic and lovable creature than do her ardently feminist sisters. However, Connie hardly plays the part of the conventional woman. Had she, she would never have taken the brave steps she took, steps which clearly led her to this man and to this marriage. When she met Brian, Connie knew he was bluffing about Vermont but recognized an opportunity to advance her own interests and security. She refused both an ungratifying job and a marriage of protection. In a manner that can only be defined as independent if not feminist, Connie went off on a daring adventure, risking her children's as well as her own survival. In one sense this story is pure fantasy: a poor but innocent young woman meets a wealthy and caring young man. Brian O'Ramey, similar to the hero of romance literature, is intuitive enough to see the innate goodness of the humble Connie.[49] In another sense, though, the story introduces a woman who would have made it on her own had she not met Brian O'Ramey, a woman willing to take some fairly radical steps to get what she wants.

Francesca, Babe, and Connie, amateur rebels like the rest, end their stories not independently, but by dreaming about, planning, or entering a marriage. They do not abandon the life path followed by the other protagonists discussed here. Nevertheless, the marriages they envision or enter remain true to their ideals, which demand independent, resourceful women and progressive, supportive men, each ready to modify their definitions of marriage to accommodate the needs of both partners. Francesca proposes marriage to Billy, setting the stage for a new realm of cooperative decision making in marriage. Babe fantasizes about Ross, fully expecting a life of equality, even in marriage. Connie wants and gets all the trappings of married life, yet she never surrenders her decision making—not to her feminist sisters, nor to her wealthy husband.

But reading these stories against the grain reveals the degree to which even independent women relied on men to foster change. If Billy Waring turns out like Mr. Blaise, Francesca may become a broken woman like Phyllis Fellowes. Readers may have recognized the unlikely nature of such changes in men; recognizing the degree of male privilege, without putting that label on it, they might have believed that such happy endings would be short-lived.[50] Perhaps even when they did, however, and they put their magazines down, their dreams suggested the desire for changes that feminists later in the century would put in words: economic independence, cooperative childrearing, recognition of women's sexuality, shared household responsibility, and shared power and decisionmaking.

These stories exemplify some of the struggles that occurred in and outside of the *Ladies' Home Journal* in the 1910s and 1920s. Women wanted to redefine themselves and push their limits, and the magazine's fiction provided a forum for this activity. Like the advertisements and the advice, the fiction helped to set limits in defining womanhood, but again, like the advertisements and advice, it also contained questions that could lead to further change. It exposed the wrongs of the institutions it promoted as right. As women actively struggled with the roles laid out for them, they questioned the degree to which wifehood and motherhood held the keys to their identity and happiness. They identified career considerations and personal fulfillment as life choices. Female sexuality also found a voice, and women wondered about the degree to which they could expect or demand sexual fulfillment. Women's inarticulate longings found their way into the pages of the fiction, just as they had into the advice and the advertising. Here, however, they worked in more subversive ways, as they became an integral part of women's daydreams and, once voiced, collective political consciousness.

Although the *Ladies' Home Journal* counseled its readers to make fairly traditional choices rather than radical changes, although it warned against careers, divorce, economic and personal independence, and unbridled sexuality, the magazine's fiction acknowledged many of the real problems women encountered, and illustrated that traditional methods did not always suffice. It urged them, for the most part, to follow the life choices of their mothers and grandmothers, yet it also provided them with a forum in which to see changes explored, read several kinds of happy endings, and look ahead as well as behind. This popular fiction reflected the dominant ideology, but it also exposed it. For every satisfied Emily March there would be a broken Phyllis Fellowes. But hopefully, for every Mr. Blaise there would be a Ross Abell. Readers of the *Journal*, who might perhaps have said, "I'm not a feminist but ... ," would certainly have recognized the seeds of complaint, if not revolt, implicit in these simple tales of American womanhood.

six

Advertising Women

The J. Walter Thompson Company Women's Editorial Department

*I*n addition to advice and fiction, the third and final essential ingredient in the *Ladies' Home Journal*'s recipe for success was advertising, and the next two chapters explore some of the ways in which advertising worked in and outside of the pages of the *Journal* to influence women's lives. In the early twentieth century, the magazine and advertising industries developed in conjunction with each other. Magazines depended upon advertisers to support their efforts financially, and advertisers relied on magazines to tap into a growing national audience. The two industries promoted themselves as part of the growth of the nation. Women's magazines played a particularly important role in this growth, recognizing the consumer purchasing power wielded by the nation's homemakers. Magazines and advertising offered readers and, by extension, consumers, a particularly twentieth-century, capitalist version of democracy defined by each citizen's ability to acquire goods–the many wares offered in the pages of the magazines as well as the magazines themselves. Since advertising advanced rapidly in its aesthetic as well as its cultural appeal, the relationship provided the *Ladies' Home Journal* with a winning combination of features, and the *Journal* consistently ranked first both in readership and in advertising revenue.

In women's magazines in general and in the *Journal* in particular, the line between the magazine's internal departments, the editorial material and fiction, and the advertising, which came from external agencies, was often less than clearly drawn. Advertisers accomplished their objective of attracting loyal customers in part by pursuing successful strategies followed in editorial material or in the fiction. For example, they imitated the magazine's advice columns by providing a doctors' signature for a health care product, or a society hostess's testimony for a skin care product. Recognizing the appeal of successful fictional approaches, they provided narratives of women's struggles to live full and rewarding lives in advertisements for home care products or canned goods. Conversely, fictional pieces occasionally imitated advertising when they concluded that the consumption of goods satisfied a heroine's need for autonomy or marital happiness. Editorial columns accommodated advertising by providing articles on healthy eating adjacent to advertisements for food products. Similar tacks were used for articles and advertisements about housekeeping, wage work, and political activity. This complementary relationship, however, was not without tensions. Those tensions, as described in earlier chapters, illustrate both the inventiveness of the advertising industry and the general consumer direction of the magazine as a whole. The following two chapters take a different turn and focus specifically on the producers of and the dissemination of advertising messages. The magazine's winning arrangement of advice, fiction, and advertising came to be dominated more and more by advertising over the course of this twenty-year period. This discussion will examine the nature and complexity of that development, exploring first the work lives of a group of women working at the J. Walter Thompson Advertising Agency, and second, several of the Thompson campaigns launched in the *Ladies' Home Journal.*

For the most part, historians have defined women's role in the cultural environment of consumer activity as that of the passive recipient, the consumer. Women who worked in the advertising business have been overlooked by historians of women, historians of advertising, and historians of consumer culture. Yet women played an active role in the development of the industry. In some fairly paradoxical ways, women helped create what has become a particularly female and, by most accounts, particularly disempowering twentieth-century consumer culture.[1] While they did, they also helped create new tiers of professional employment for educated women, and helped form a growing body of consumers whose needs would ultimately not be met by the *Ladies' Home Journal* or other strictly homemaking magazines.

While few today would deny the exploitation of women in advertisement copy or as consumers by the advertising industry, the early roots of this conflict are complicated rather than simplified by attention to issues of gender. Women did not unwittingly buy products or accept a consumer culture as their own; they sought an improved standard of living and a positive social identity, both of which advertising promised and sometimes delivered. In the same vein, women did not accept jobs in advertising with the intention of exploiting other women and subsequently getting ahead themselves, although on first glance early advertising women might seem to have done just that. Writing copy to persuade other women to consume, advertising women undoubtedly achieved a measure of autonomy, both personal and economic, that many of their readers lacked. However, these women often approached their work with a missionary spirit about the consumer culture, a spirit many of them carried over from the progressive politics of their college educations, suffrage activities, or social work experiences. They saw their work not as exploitation but as a positive good. The paradox of "advertising women" challenges commonly held assumptions about the hegemonic development of the advertising industry in the early twentieth century.

Women were recognized as consumers long before the twentieth century, but advertising agencies were quick to recognize and then exploit this consumer base during this century, especially through the medium of the women's magazine. "The proper study of mankind is man ... but the proper study of market is woman," wrote an ad executive in the 1920s.[2] Women were the purchasing agents in the nation's homes. In the 1920s, researchers estimated, women purchased at least 80 percent of the total goods accumulated in families.[3] They bought food, clothing, electrical appliances, linoleum, and home furnishings. They also purchased items one might expect men to have bought, such as automobiles and automotive accessories. Mary Louise Alexander, a researcher at the Batten, Barton, Durstine and Osborne advertising agency in New York City in the 1920s, believed that women's role in purchasing was an almost omnipotent one: "You might think the family car is under the man's thumb," she argued, "but no, our researchers show that women are a large factor in the buying of gasoline and oil so that it appears as though men determine for themselves little more than their hair cuts."[4] Although Alexander implies that advertising researchers were simply recording what they saw, the notion of women's omnipotence in purchasing goods was as much a social construction of these marketing experts as it was an observable social phenomenon.

Women's magazines were the most important medium for reaching these female consumers, and by 1917, advertising agencies handled 95 percent of the national advertising being promoted in the magazines.[5] The *Ladies' Home Journal* and others kept their subscription rates low and readership high by soliciting the most artistic and compelling advertisements for products from Crisco to Pond's Cold Cream, from Goodyear Tires to Yuban Coffee. While 56 percent of the magazine's revenues came from sales and subscriptions in 1879, the situation had changed dramatically by 1919, when nearly two-thirds of all magazine revenues came from advertising.[6] Due to its financial importance alone, then, advertising would secure a more influential role in the magazine's policy-making than would the advice or the fiction.

Among the many prominent advertising agencies the *Ladies' Home Journal* dealt with, the J. Walter Thompson Company stands out. For one, it was the most successful agency in the United States, pulling ahead of its competition early in the 1920s and retaining that top spot well into the 1970s.[7] In 1925, the Thompson agency broke a world record by placing $230,000 worth of advertising in a single publication, the April volume of the *Ladies' Home Journal.* In October of that same year, the agency broke its own record by placing an additional $25,000 worth of advertising, again in the *Ladies' Home Journal.*[8] In an era in which people's incomes rose and manufactured products grew increasingly more affordable, the middle-class consumer could afford to make purchasing decisions based on considerations other than price.[9] J. Walter Thompson, with its reputation for expert quality and artistic originality, produced advertisements that spoke to existing consumer desires and, increasingly, defined new ones. The second reason the Thompson agency stands out is that it prided itself on providing professional opportunities for women. In an era in which male professions were increasingly defined by the degree to which they were not populated by females, the Thompson position is remarkable. As historian Sharon Hartman Strom has argued, "Discrimination against women was one of the hallmarks of male professionalism after 1910."[10] Men restricted access to professional education, professional training, and professional organizations. What Strom calls the "particularly virile" professional identity in the business world encouraged employers and educational institutions to exclude women. When an adult extension program in business at Columbia University attracted as many women as it did men, the university decided to segregate the women in secretarial training, limiting the business training only to men. The Harvard Graduate School of Business Administration kept its doors closed to women until 1963.[11]

Women made up 35 percent of the professional workforce in 1900 and 45 percent of the professional workforce in 1930, but while their numbers grew quickly, their range of occupations did not. The majority of women educated at liberal arts institutions found work in teaching, social work, or home economics. As Strom has demonstrated, it was opportunity rather than appropriate education they lacked, as the majority of men entering law or medicine had also been trained in the liberal arts.[12] Women looking for professional work generally found it only in what Joan Jacobs Brumberg and Nancy Tomes call "the dirtiest" of professional fields, those requiring the most human contact. Women's greatest opportunities, they argue, resulted from "the massive social dislocation caused by immigration, poverty, economic uncertainty, and labor exploitation—social problems that necessitated the creation of a vast army of social workers, public health nurses, and public school teachers."[13]

At a time when professional opportunities for women outside the helping professions were scarce, the J. Walter Thompson Company established a reputation for taking a more progressive position on the employment of women. In a 1924 publication intended for external use, the Thompson agency outlined the number of women employed in various departments, and then claimed, as one of the thirteen most important attributes of the agency, "The J. Walter Thompson Company employs more women in creative, responsible positions than does any other agency."[14] A female employee similarly argued that although women in other agencies got the "lesser and run of the mill jobs," women at Thompson had ample and unusual opportunities for success in the field.[15]

Further research will indicate the degree to which women also developed successful careers in other agencies. A 1926 study of fifteen agencies found women working in a variety of jobs including research, space buying, and writing copy.[16] The Thompson agency was not unique in hiring women, then, but its success in providing many women with "responsible" positions may have been due to its progressive attitude and to the fact that amongst other agencies, it alone organized its female copywriters into a separate department, the Women's Editorial Department. This department, run by women and, no less directly, primarily for women consumers, provided advertisements for products aimed at women: household and cleaning items, food and beauty products, clothing and accessories. The women copywriters' separate existence makes it difficult to measure their success relative to that of male copywriters; however, it may to a large degree account both for their professional success and their seemingly easy acceptance by male coworkers or male executives. Physical distance, in this case, may have both eased male insecurity and bolstered female opportunities for success. The few other exceptions to women's employment limitations during the period also occurred in "women-only" areas, namely women-supervised "women's departments" in banks, insurance companies, and investment agencies.[17] The women's separate existence does make it easy to measure their enormous economic contribution to the agency: in 1918, the billings for the copy written in the Women's Editorial Department totalled $2,264,759 out of the total of $3,902,601 for the company.[18] The Thompson agency clearly depended upon the work of these advertising women.

In the J. Walter Thompson Women's Editorial Department, a group comprised largely of white, native-born, middle- or upper-middle class, college-educated women was able to carve out for themselves an unmistakably successful professional workplace. Their employment applications and biographical files, as well as Thompson Company newsletters and staff meeting minutes, provide a picture that adds significantly to our knowledge about women's entrance into the professions, female professionals' receptivity to the ethos of consumption, and the ways in which class and race in addition to gender informed cultural definitions of womanhood in the early twentieth century. The remainder of this chapter will focus on a group of 42 women employed in the J. Walter Thompson Women's Editorial Department in the 1910s and 1920s, 16 of whom began their tenure there during the teens decade and 26 of whom were hired in the twenties.[19]

The J. Walter Thompson Company is remembered best not for the legacies of its namesake, James Walter Thompson, but for the legacies of Stanley Resor and Helen Lansdowne Resor, who took over the agency in 1916 and subsequently pushed it past all competition. From 1916 to 1918 they were part of a team of three which administered, in Helen's words, "all policies of the J. Walter Thompson agency, the payroll, and practilly (sic) all personnel."[20] Stanley became the first president of the J. Walter Thompson agency, and although Helen never became vice president and did not even officially become a director for another eight years, she was clearly influential in the firm's policymaking and instrumental in its success from the start. Helen Lansdowne started the Women's Editorial Department, and for this she was praised in an article Harriet Abbott wrote for the *Ladies' Home Journal* in 1920: "She not only put manufacturers' products and her own agency on the map; she made a place in advertising geography for women, a place no advertiser or agency ever before had granted them. She pioneered the way for women in advertising, marking a trail for which successful women today are grateful to her."[21]

In the Women's Editorial Department, Helen Lansdowne Resor assembled, as Stephen Fox has claimed, a "wing of women copywriters whom she hired, trained, and mothered."[22] Under her direction, women in copywriting worked as group heads, writers, and assistant writers. She set high standards for herself and for the women she employed, but she never doubted that either she or they were in any way less than able to produce the necessary results. When Helen Lansdowne Resor started working for J. Walter Thompson, the firm employed fewer than 100 people. When she died in 1964, the Thompson agency had 6,913 employees. She was largely responsible for this growth, because as she correctly saw it, the growth of modern advertising relied on the modern female consumer and hence on the work of the Women's Editorial Department. "The success of the J. Walter Thompson Company has been in large measure due to the fact that we have concentrated and specialized upon products sold to women," Resor argued in one of her few remaining written statements.[23]

Helen Lansdowne Resor, unlike most of her employees, was not college educated. After graduation as valedictorian of her high school class in Kentucky, Lansdowne secured her first job in advertising. She quickly became, as she herself acknowledged, "the first woman to be successful in writing and planning national, as opposed to retail, advertising."[24] Lansdowne first made her mark in the advertising world in 1910, when she worked for her future husband in the Cincinnati office of J. Walter Thompson. She was given responsibility for a new Thompson client, Woodbury's facial soap, manufactured by the Jergen's company. Lansdowne essentially invented the use of sex appeal in advertising with her advertisement, which she titled "A Skin You Love to Touch." Using muted sexuality and what may now appear to be tame physical contact between a man and a woman, Lansdowne created a sensation, and sales of Woodbury's facial soap increased 1000 percent in eight years.[25] Resor and the women she employed succeeded in addressing female consumers not only as women with money to spend but also as sensuous and sensitive women. What has turned into one of the major controversies in advertising—women as sex objects—was developed by a woman who most likely saw the recognition of women's sexuality as a step forward in an advertising world that had primarily portrayed women as asexual wives and mothers.

In January of 1911, Helen Lansdowne moved to Thompson's New York headquarters. In 1916, at age 31, she married Stanley Resor, but her work did not stop at marriage. She continued to direct the Women's Editorial Department, where she left her legacies: decades of encouragement and an example of professional accomplishment for other women to follow. The *Ladies' Home Journal* article mentioned above described Helen Resor's techniques on the job. When she interviewed women for jobs she looked the woman, or "girl," in the eye, hoping to find a flicker of genius. If she caught that, she hired her. After that, she "coaches her and stands back of her and develops her into part of the company's corporate genius." A serious employer, this woman cautioned prospective candidates that the advertising world was not one of glamour and cleverness but of persistent hard work, based on research and statistics and the in-depth study of manufacturing and markets. Many of the women had college degrees, according to the article, but this employer did not believe that a college education alone dictated ability. She sought to determine the value of that education for the individual woman:

> The agency searches back into her interests in college. Was she attracted by economics, psychology, sociology, history? Was she a real student; did she really dig out the causes of things, think for herself, enjoy thinking for herself? Or did she learn texts and lectures by rote, pass "exams" with amazing A-pluses, bury her nose constantly in the alcoves of the college library or keep an eye forever over a 'scope? What was her mother like? Was she a constructively minded woman, seeing a big future dawning for women over the horizon, even though she herself stayed at the grindstone to put her daughter through college? Did she breathe this faith of hers into her daughter, filling her young mind with the vision of a new day for women when they should stand squarely beside men on the platform of achievement?[26]

Helen Lansdowne Resor was protective of her private life, and outside of a stockholder's affidavit and some biographical material on file in the Thompson Archives, few details of her private or work life were recorded. In her stockholder's affidavit she mentioned that various magazines and four large newspaper syndicates had requested that she write or provide interviews about herself. "As publicity of this kind does not appeal to me," she declared flatly in 1924, "I have refused these requests."[27] It is unlikely, then, that she agreed to an interview for the *Ladies' Home Journal* article. Nevertheless, unpublished biographical information about Resor and the personnel files of these 41 other women indicate that Harriet Abbott's remarks were not far off the mark.

Almost every one of these women's personnel files contains an employment application form. The applications changed slightly over time but follow the same basic format, a company format used for both male and female employees. They first solicit personal information, including age, marital status, birthplace, occupation of parents, education, religion, and memberships. A series of questions follows which require slightly more descriptive answers. These questions, not unlike those suggested in Harriet Abbott's article, asked prospective employees to describe their interests, level of energy, judgment, self-confidence, optimism, and imagination. How serious were they in their work? How did they spend their unoccupied time? What ambitions did they have? Following this, the applicants provided information about previous employment, including what they were most proud of, why they left, and why they were now applying at J. Walter Thompson. The last part of the application form asked the women to choose three "effective" advertisements from a recent volume of the *Ladies' Home Journal* or *Saturday Evening Post* and discuss them. A few of the applications still have, attached to them, several-page long autobiographies. Although this is a fairly straightforward and perhaps typical application form, the collection of applications reveals a great deal about these women's personalities and interests, and provides us with a fascinating profile of the professional J. Walter Thompson woman in the 1910s and 1920s. It also further attests to the connection between the *Journal* and the Thompson agency and the relative importance of the *Ladies' Home Journal* at that time.

One must question the accuracy of self-description when a job is at stake, but the candid manner in which the women both praise and deride themselves suggests a sincerity, perhaps surprising to the late twentieth-century reader, that underscores the value of these documents. Florence Dorflinger, for example, when asked what she lacked, answered "Patience, tolerance, experience, genius, money, beauty, and a position."[28] Alice Luiggi, when asked if she had poise, answered "Have my balance in relation to my world pretty well now, particularly since a fairly complete mental analysis made by a psychoanalyst."[29] Frances Maule, replying to a question about previous employment experience, admitted that she had been fired, "Twice–for refusing to do certain

"A Skin You Love to Touch"

PAINTED BY
PAUL STAHR

How to get this beautiful picture for framing

THIS painting by Paul Stahr, the well-known illustrator, is his interpretation of "A Skin You Love to Touch." It has been beautifully reproduced from the original water-color painting. Size 15 x 19 inches. Made expressly for framing. No printed matter on it. Send for your picture today. Read offer below.

You too can have the charm of
"A Skin You Love to Touch"

SOFT, smooth skin, the clear glowing complexion that everyone admires—these you, too, can have.

You can give to your skin the texture, the life, the color that has such matchless charm.

Whatever the condition that is keeping your skin from being as attractive as it should be, it can be changed. In a much shorter time than you would imagine, your skin will respond to the proper care and treatment.

Why your skin can be changed

Your skin changes continually. Every day it is being renewed. Old skin dies—new forms. This is your opportunity, for as this new skin forms, you can keep it fresh, soft and clear as Nature intended.

Is your skin dull, lifeless, colorless? Begin today, as the new skin forms, to make it clear and glowing. If you are troubled by an oily skin—a shiny nose—begin today to correct it.

Disfiguring blackheads, conspicuous nose pores, distressing pimples and blemishes—every one of these troubles you can, with proper care, be rid of.

Learn just what is the proper treatment for your particular trouble, and use it persistently every night before retiring. Let it become a daily habit. In the Woodbury booklet, "A Skin You Love to Touch," you will find simple, definite instructions for your own and many other troublesome conditions of the skin. Within ten days or two weeks of the use of the proper Woodbury treatment, you will notice a decided improvement—a promise of that greater loveliness which your skin will gradually acquire.

How to get these treatments

The Woodbury booklet of skin treatments is wrapped around every cake of Woodbury's Facial Soap. You will find that for a month or six weeks of any one of these Woodbury treatments a 25c cake will be sufficient. Woodbury's Facial Soap

is on sale at drug stores or toilet goods counters throughout the United States and Canada—wherever toilet goods are sold. Get a cake today and begin your treatment.

This picture with sample cake of soap, samples of cream and powder with book of treatments for 15c

For 15c we will send you a cake of Woodbury's Facial Soap—large enough for a week's treatment—with the booklet, "A Skin You Love to Touch," and samples of Woodbury's Facial Cream and Facial Powder. In addition to the samples and booklet, we will send you a reproduction in full colors of the beautiful painting shown above, made expressly for framing. This picture will be very popular; secure your copy at once. Write today to *The Andrew Jergens Co., 103 Spring Grove Ave., Cincinnati, Ohio.*

If you live in Canada, address The Andrew Jergens Co., Ltd., 103 Sherbrooke St., Perth, Ontario.

A special treatment for an oily skin and shiny nose is among the famous treatments given in the Woodbury booklet you get with the soap. Secure a cake today and the booklet that goes with it.

For enlarged pores, try the treatment given in the booklet, "A Skin You Love to Touch." With your Woodbury's Facial Soap you will get one of these interesting booklets.

Although the physical contact in this advertising series may seem tame now, it initially caused a great stir, and it is now widely accepted as the first "sex appeal" series in American advertising. This 1918 example features a World War I soldier. (*Ladies' Home Journal*, March 1918, p. 116) things required by newspapers."[30] At other times the women were as forth-coming with self praise. Elizabeth Devree, for example, responded to the question about initiative in the following way: "Yes; my own decisions have governed my life."[31] Mary Tucker offered proof in response to the same question: "Yes. I changed my profession after four rather successful years of it."[32] Finally, Dorothy Lampe, when asked about self confidence, stated "Goodness yes. But so far it has always been justified."[33]

An interesting set of responses reveals that many of the women took pride in their accomplishments at work. "Have done writing, editing and manuscript reading since my babies came in spite of my domestic preoccupations," Rebecca Hourwich wrote.[34] Janet Wing stated that "though I have been married more than ten years, though I have a small daughter, I have always worked."[35] Another, Eleanor Taylor, argued that her concentration was demonstrated by the fact that she had written "in the midst of large offices and even in the thick of a suffrage campaign in which women were being arrested all around me."[36] Finally, Eleanor McDonnell, who also mentioned suffrage, wrote of it in relation to her newspaper work and as though she felt responsi-bility for it: "I saw the suffrage bill safely through the House of Representatives in Washington."[37] If these women wrote to please their audience, they had specific and unusual expectations of what would please employers in the J. Walter Thompson Women's Editorial Department. Certainly these statements did not reflect the images of womanhood the women saw in the *Journal* and *Saturday Evening Post* advertisements they evaluated.

These job applications reveal a fairly homogeneous group of women seeking employment in the Women's Editorial Department between 1915 and 1930. They ranged in age from 22 to 41 and were well spread out through these years. A slight majority of the women, 17, were in their twenties, 16 were in their thirties, 2 were in their forties, and the ages of 6 are unknown. Thirty of the 41 women hired by Helen Lansdowne Resor were single, 5 were married, 3 were separated from their husbands, and 3 were divorced. They came from many geographic regions, including the South, West, Midwest, and Northeast regions of the United States as well as Colombia and Cuba. Many of their fathers were professionals and numbered among them a judge, three lawyers, two clergy-men, four farmers, several business men, a plantation owner, and a retail grocer. Only one woman mentioned her mother, who was an author.

A highly educated group, 40 of the applicants had attended some college; 29 had four-year degrees and 11 of those had master's or doctoral degrees. They were alumnae of the most prestigious women's colleges and numbered among them graduates of six of the Seven Sisters colleges: Vassar, Smith, Wellesley, Barnard, Mt. Holyoke, and Bryn Mawr. They also attended the fastest growing coeducational institutions, including the University of Michigan, University of Wisconsin, University of California, Cornell, and the University of Chicago. In addition, two of the women were graduates of the Carnegie Institute of Technology. Those who had done graduate work had attended Columbia University, the University of Pennsylvania, and the New York School for Social Research, among others.[38]

These women's educational achievements, for the most part, mirrored those occurring in the culture at large during this time period. By 1910 nearly 40 percent of all college students were women, and by 1920 nearly 47 percent of all students in four-year colleges were women.[39] The J. Walter Thompson Women's Editorial group was, however, overrepresented by graduates of women's colleges. During the academic year 1915-1916, 75 percent of all women college students in the United States attended coeducational institutions.[40] Of the Thompson women hired between 1915 and 1919, 50 percent of those who had attended college had attended women's colleges. Of those hired from 1920-1929, the percentage changed in the same direction as that of the larger population: 40 percent had attended women's colleges and 60 percent had attended coeducational institutions. Of the larger group of 41 women, 57 percent had attended coeducational institutions and 43 percent had attended women's colleges. The higher percentage of women's college graduates among the J. Walter Thompson women may be explained in several ways: women's college graduates may have exercised greater job mobility throughout their careers; there may have been a greater concentration of women's college graduates in New York City; or perhaps these women received the assistance of the women's colleges' vocational bureaus, which were set up specifically to help women find jobs in fields "other than teaching."[41] Several of the women's college graduates listed professors or deans of the women's colleges among their references, which suggests that they maintained close ties to their alma maters.

The applications solicited information about the women's religious affiliations as well. Fifteen of the women did not indicate any religious affiliation. Of those who did, 2 specified only "Christian"; the rest with any affiliation were Protestants: 8 Episcopalians, 5 simply "Protestants," 2 Presbyterians, 1 Methodist, 1 Congregationalist. Six of the women stated that they had no religion, including two who were raised Episcopal and one whose father was a clergyman. Interestingly enough, Helen Lansdowne Resor, their employer, also had no religious affiliation.

The women's group memberships, which included many feminist and suffragist causes, reveal a great deal about their interests and ambitions. They belonged to the YWCA, Suffrage League, Consumers League, National Woman's Party, and League of Women Voters. They also belonged to various college alumni groups, honorary societies, and sororities. Their associations were not unlike those of Helen Resor, who served as committee chairwoman for the babies' ward at New York Postgraduate Hospital, board member of the Museum of Modern Art, president of the Traveler's Aid Society, and supporter of woman suffrage and Planned Parenthood.[42] The women's varied interests included gardening, music, hiking, writing, driving a car, and rhythmic dancing. Several included feminism among their interests: "social betterment and improvement of the position of women," wrote one, and "the war and women and the modern trend of the evolution," wrote another.[43]

Is there a J. Walter Thompson Women's Editorial Department type, then? Clearly she was a well-educated, politically and/or socially active woman looking for job advancement. The majority of these women were not fresh out of school and looking for entry-level jobs. Thirty-nine leave records of their employment histories, but only one of those had applied to J. Walter Thompson for her first position. Twelve women applied after having held one or two previous jobs and 26 applied after having held three or more previous positions. The vast majority of these applicants were unmarried women who had been self-sufficient for at least a few years before they looked to Helen Lansdowne Resor for a job. They were working women who saw the possibility of improved work lives at the Thompson agency, and they were willing to make and often accustomed to making job or even career changes.

Since the world offered women of this generation few occupational choices, they had to create what Carroll Smith-Rosenberg calls "alternative institutions and careers."[44] Helen Resor created that for herself and for this group of women in the J. Walter Thompson Women's Editorial Department. Educated in women's colleges or as under-represented students in coeducational institutions, and trained professionally, the Thompson women may have sought out such a female-centered workplace. And in an era in which college-educated women in business found themselves working, for the most part, in clerical work, opportunities to write advertising copy provided a good match for those women interested in exploring their creativity, maintaining their autonomy, and achieving job or career advancements.[45]

The job applications suggest the importance of work in these women's lives. "It is the most important thing I do and think about," wrote one. "I have to work to support myself, but I know I would work just the same if I did not have to," wrote Ruth Waldo.[46] "I get so absorbed in my work," another revealed, "that I do not lead a full enough life." This woman, Lucy Dunham, also described herself, however, as a "pioneer" in personnel management with an ambition to stand "head and shoulders above the crowd."[47] Others revealed their accomplishments at work as well. Perle Dienst, who had worked with the Juvenile Protection Agency in Illinois, stated that she organized a children's home that "ranks among the best in the state."[48] Florence Dorflinger had worked as a copywriter for a men's magazine, *Machinery*. She was very proud of the fact that "without experience, I held a position that fourteen women out of seventeen failed to hold."[49]

Due to their class and educational backgrounds, these women had the opportunity to view work as something more than simply a means of support. In this light, their desire to work in advertising in general and in the J. Walter Thompson agency in particular is especially interesting. The application forms did not ask why the women wanted to work in advertising, but they did ask why the applicants chose this particular agency. Several wrote that J. Walter Thompson had an excellent reputation in the field: "The JWT agency is the only one to which I would like to belong," wrote Mary Tucker. Eight of the women, however, specifically wrote about the agency's reputation for providing opportunities to women. Perle Dienst chose Thompson "largely because of the opportunities it offers to women employees," while Rebecca Hourwich stated that "your company justly evaluates the service of women." Faith Kelley called the Thompson agency "broadminded" in its attitude toward women employees, and Frances Maule stated that she had heard that it "recognizes the special utility that women have in appealing to women as the chief purchasers of goods." Perhaps these women knew that a compliment to an agency might further their chances of employment, but it is noteworthy that so many applicants specifically referred to the agency's reputation concerning female employees.[50] They were conscious of themselves as workers and as women workers, and perhaps they expected the same of their employers.

When questioned about skills which were stereotypically expected of women, the applicants responded less enthusiastically. Asked if she possessed manual accuracy, the usually eager Esther Eaton replied, "No. I sew but rather badly," and another applicant mentioned her lack of sewing skills as well.[51] Frances Maule, when asked if she could operate an office machine, replied in this way: "While I realize the injudiciousness of doing so, I must confess to being able to operate a typewriter and a multigraph."[52] Apparently Maule hoped not to be relegated to secretarial tasks, even though she had no previous experience in advertising. Many of the respondents replied in the negative when asked if they had the often presumed female quality of poise. "I don't know," stated Mary Tucker, who was adamant about her initiative and who, ironically, had worked at fashion magazines for years. "I haven't cultivated it."[53]

The job applications outline each woman's employment history. Only 14, or 34 percent, of the women had worked in the advertising business before they applied at J. Walter Thompson. Of these, most had worked for department stores or advertising agencies; one had worked in banking. Mary Loomis Cook, for example, had been writing advertising copy for the John Wanamaker department store when she applied at J. Walter Thompson. "I have painted joyous pictures of drab merchandise for four years and a half," she stated in her application.[53] Apparently she believed her work would be more varied and more interesting at the Thompson agency. Most of these experienced women, who applied while they still worked at other jobs, saw the Women's Editorial Department as a step up professionally. Seven of the women had previously worked as teachers. Two mentioned that they left the field because of low pay; three others left because they did not like teaching. Elizabeth Gates complained of teaching stenography to "flighty young girls," while Mary Cook put it simply: "I hated teaching." These women had entered the business world hoping for better pay, more personal satisfaction, and more opportunities for professional advancement than they found in teaching, for as Sharon Strom puts it, "the teaching profession was full of women who could find little else to do with their education."[55]

A much larger group, 16 women, came from employment fields commonly identified as more feminist: paid suffrage work and social work. These women present what appears to be the most glaring paradox of advertising women. Not only did they remain independent by encouraging other women to be dependent consumers, but they also challenge what has been deemed an incompatibility between the worlds of progressive activity and business. Although they present a picture, on first glance, of women who, in their professional lives, changed from doing "for" women to doing "to" them, on closer examination, however, the example of the J. Walter Thompson women suggests the compatibility of social work and/or suffrage work and advertising work: social progressives could and did view advertising as a form of social service. Historians of the period must look more closely at the movement between the fields of social service and business and between the frames of reference that accompany those fields.

The J. Walter Thompson women's contemporaries found employment primarily in nursing, teaching, and social work; by 1930, women made up four out of every five people in or preparing for careers in teaching or social work.[56] They faced tremendous antagonism in the business world. As Dr. Alice Hamilton put it, "The American man gives over to the woman all the things he is profoundly disinterested in, and keeps business and politics to himself."[57] As the early decades of the century wore on, women in social work wanted to earn salaries that would enable them to be consumers as well as workers, but as Daniel Walkowitz has demonstrated, opportunities for advancement were extremely limited.[58] For reasons of salary and advancement alone, it is not surprising that female social workers would begin to look for opportunities outside their field. The seeming contradiction, though, is that they would choose the world of business, in particular the world of advertising. Like many other women and men of the day with progressive, social justice agendas, however, women in social work may have seen the world of business as highly compatible with their goals. Susan Curtis' research on the social gospel progressives, for example, reveals that in the teens and twenties this group did not abandon social justice; instead they saw business strength and the ethos of consumption as delivering "abundance, justice, and meaning to Americans."[59] Like Curtis's social gospel reformers, the Thompson women may have been satisfied with "an ideology of self-realization, a diminution of private anxieties, and an improved standard of living for many Americans," all of which both advertising and advertising work promised.[60]

The J. Walter Thompson Women's Editorial Department employees, although not the religious progressives described by Curtis, might have agreed that the home and family could be improved through institutions and "special-ized agencies," advertising among them.[61] The image of the mother had served an earlier generation of reformers with inspiration, but this generation's motiva-tion and inspiration came from the image of the woman worker, the profes-sional. "Paid labor, not social mothering," argues Ellen Carol DuBois about the final generation of woman suffragists, "represented their route to women's emancipation, as well as the organizational basis for their reform efforts."[62] The J. Walter Thompson applicants may have viewed that agency as uniquely appealing, as meeting their own needs for personal autonomy and progressive social activity. New products could help women have an easier time of things at home, and helping other women indirectly through advertising could have been viewed personally as a better use of these women's talents: it provided less burn out and offered more creativity, higher salaries, increased professional responsibility, and greater prestige than social work. In addition, as the image of the social worker began, in the 1920s, to be equated with a meddling and hypocritical investigator, the image of a business professional grew increasingly more positive and more identified with progress.[63]

Employers in the advertising industry at large and in the J. Walter Thompson Women's Editorial Department in particular encouraged employees to contemplate the social and educational importance of their work. Advertisements educated consumers, namely women, in their new relationships with name-brand products and national manufacturers. According to the Thompson *Blue Book*, a compilation of company policies and achievements, selling a product was easily the equivalent of any social work project: "These advertisements educate the people to a knowledge of the comforts, conveniences, and luxuries of life and create the desire to share in their enjoyment. . . . Their minds are led to a national view of life and living and they reflect their broadened education in influence on the community as well as in the advertised articles which are consumed in the home."[64] Invited speakers reinforced the social service goals of advertising. Gertrude Battles Lane, for example, spoke to the Women's Editorial Department on the value of women's magazines in "speeding up and eliminating the usual daily drudgery." Lane argued further that the magazines for which the women at the Thompson agency provided copy lent stimulus to "better housing, dressing, furnishing, better care of children and raising the standard of living generally."[65] The *Ladies' Home Journal*, the most popular women's magazine of the day, provided a direct link between professional women with a social work spirit and, again, that illusory but ever more fully defined average woman, the woman who spent a great deal of money and needed professional guidance to spend it well.

Many in this group of women did, in fact, approach their work with the missionary spirit suggested by Lane. In her employment application, Eleanor Taylor wrote of the personal growth that accompanied her through college and into paid suffrage work and social work. "College meant to me a new world of ideas," she wrote. "What an interesting, exciting world it, after all, was! Dare I become a suffragist, socialist, atheist? I dared, and became them all." For Taylor, the progression from social work to advertising came naturally. "With a gradual decline of interest in great movements has come a much more satisfying interest in people," she wrote. "To understand the needs and the desires and the experiences of men and women, the things which give pleasure, which hurt, or which stir, has a fascination which far exceeds–poking at the roots to make them grow better."[66] Taylor entered the Women's Editorial Department with an impressive employment history including working as a social worker in the United States Children's Bureau in Washington, in publicity for the National Woman's Party, and as editor of *The Suffragist.*

Others of the women were not as specific about their progression from social work or suffrage work to advertising. Gertrude Coit was a graduate of Smith, Columbia, and the New York School for Social Research. Her previous jobs were at the Co-operative League of America, the People's Institute, and Madison House, a settlement. Her work experience included directing a community center and health center and supervising dances, camping trips, and other activities. Coit had no experience in the advertising or business worlds. She reported simply that she felt a "dissatisfaction with social work" that prompted her to seek work at the Thompson agency.[67] Charline Davenport stated that she had been doing social work at the Association for the Improvement of the Poor when her friends and her doctor advised her to look for "younger work,"[68] perhaps indicating a new push for female college graduates to enter the business world. And Ruth Waldo, who also joined the company with previous experience in social work but not in business, was a J. Walter Thompson success story. A graduate of Adelphi College and Columbia University, Waldo provided an extensive social work employment record. She had worked for the Bureau of Social Research, the Harlem and Jefferson County offices of the New York Charity Organization Society, and the Russell Sage Foundation. Waldo stated on her application that she wanted always to be moving ahead: "that is why I wish to leave social work, as I feel in a rut, and why I wish to go into advertising, as I believe that *moves.*"[69]

Ruth Waldo was head of the copy department at the London office by 1922, the chief woman copywriter for the entire agency by 1930, and the first woman vice president of the firm by 1944. In addition to her work at Thompson, Waldo ran a working farm in Connecticut, received an honorary doctorate from Adelphi College, and served as president of the New York Friends Center and as a trustee of and the namesake of a dormitory at Adelphi College. Waldo retired from the agency in 1960 and died in 1975. She was remembered by former colleagues as "way ahead of her time" and "an inspiration to other women." That she learned to drive a car at age seventy was offered as further proof of her remarkable accomplishments.[70] Rebecca Hourwich, a Barnard graduate, had worked at the Henry Street Settlement, organized for suffrage in Massachusetts and New York, and held several paid positions in the National Woman's Party over a seven-year period. Hourwich, separated from her husband, had traveled to nineteen states giving speeches, lobbying, and raising funds for the party. She had organized the first civic club among women clothing workers in Chicago and met with them regularly at Hull House. Hourwich argued in her application that she would be good at copywriting because of these previous experiences: "I have had many contacts among average men and women," she wrote.[71]

Several of the women had combined careers in writing and suffrage work before they looked to the advertising industry for employment. Therese Olzendam, for example, worked as a typesetter and power press operator as well as a suffrage office worker. Her first career was with the Elm Tree Press in Woodstock, Vermont, where, she claimed "I was the first woman to run a power press in that vicinity and also the fastest woman typesetter." She left Vermont to go to Washington, D.C., where she worked as a circulation manager for the *Suffragist*, and then left Washington to move to New York and work as a secretary at the National Woman's Party headquarters. At the time of her application, the Woman's Party office had closed, and Olzendam was looking for a new career as well as a new job. Therese Olzendam established herself solidly at J. Walter Thompson, where she wrote copy until 1951. She carved a niche for herself in the organization by becoming the resident expert on medical research. The company newsletter described her in the following way: "There must be few other men or women who are so knowledgeable in the medical-scientific field and at the same time so thoroughly grounded and experienced in practical advertising." Olzendam once brought a cage of rats to a creative staff meeting. "They are harmless unless they get out of the cage," she stated dryly. The Thompson agency provided this woman, who did not have a college degree, with real opportunities for responsibility and job advancement.[72]

Frances Maule, who also had experience in paid suffrage work but not in advertising, left perhaps the most intriguing job application of all. She had attended the University of Nebraska for two years, but received no degree. Her previous experience included working in publicity for the Henry Holt company, as a reporter for six different newspapers, and most importantly, at least for Maule herself and apparently for Helen Resor as well, as an organizer and speaker for the New York State Suffrage Party and the National Woman Suffrage Association. It was Maule who wrote that her biggest goal was to improve the position of women. When asked whether or not she was optimistic, Maule replied "Yes–Believed we could put our woman suffrage in New York State (by federal amendment) throughout U.S." Maule was quite candid in her analysis of her newspaper career; she was the one who reported that she had been fired twice. When asked what part of her newspaper work she remembered with the most pride, her answer resonated: "That I got out of it early in life." Maule's application reveals a determined woman who, during the year when woman suffrage was passed, sought out a new career. Asked why she chose the Thompson agency, Maule's initial reply was succinct. "Had an introduction to Mrs. Resor." She went further, however: "Because I have heard that it recognizes the special utility that women must have in appealing to women as the chief purchasers of goods."[73]

A note written by Helen Resor in Frances Maule's personnel file recommended hiring Maule by highlighting her suffrage activities. She noted that Frances Maule's husband, from whom she was separated, was the Swedish scholar and translator, Edwin Bjorkman. "I think she has not been living with him for some time, though there is, I believe, no scandal—simply temperamental incompatibility," wrote Resor.[74] Maule's application and Helen Resor's letter indicate the type of woman both welcome at and successful in the Women's Editorial Department: independent, resourceful, confident, and often, feminist. Helen Resor most likely not only understood these women but also fit in well with them. Her secretary later remembered the day that Helen Resor organized women at the office to take part in a large suffrage parade in New York City: "Mrs. Resor got us all big campaign hats to wear of various colors—green, purple, white. Mine was white." She also remembered that Augusta Nicoll, one of the women included in this profile, rode a white horse.[75]

When Frances Maule wrote that her goal was to improve the position of women, she had a clear idea of what she meant by that. Both Maule and her sister, novelist, and suffrage lecturer Florence Maule Updegraff, were members of Heterodoxy, a "band of willful women" in New York City that met biweekly to discuss questions of personal life and social relationships. The women of Heterodoxy were among the first to use "feminism" in a self-conscious and deliberate way.[76] The group also included women more well known than the Maule sisters: feminist lecturer and writer Charlotte Perkins Gilman, lawyer and social activist Crystal Eastman, and black leader and NAACP member Grace Neil Johnson. Part of the already established Greenwich Village community of artists and intellectuals, the Heterodoxy women pushed the boundaries of middle-class womanhood in the early twentieth century. As contemporary historian and Vassar College professor Caroline Ware noted in 1935, Greenwich Village attracted women and men who lived outside middle-class social conventions.[77]

One of the ways in which many of the Heterodoxy women and, apparently, several of the J. Walter Thompson women also lived outside middle-class conventions was through creating women-centered lives. Like several of the other J. Walter Thompson women, Frances Maule lived in Greenwich Village and shared her apartment with women friends. Several other of the applicants listed women as their housemates as well. Edith Lewis, another member of this group of applicants, lived for forty years with Willa Cather; fellow employees described her as being one of the best women writers and as being "devoted" to Cather.[78] A recent biography of Cather argues that the actions of both Lewis and Cather "make this lifelong companionship as hard to examine as they both would have wished," but also calls Lewis a "devoted, wifely companion" as well as a grieving widow who was buried at Cather's feet.[79] As Lillian Faderman argues, after the turn of the century and for the first time in American history, large numbers of women could make their lives with other women. College educations, careers, and the resulting economic independence fostered both the spirit and the money to make it happen.[80]

It is difficult, of course, to determine the ways in which the many single women of the day defined their relationships with other women. As Leila Rupp has argued, there was a broad category of women at this time period who were women-committed women. Judith Schwarz, who wrote about the "radical feminists of Heterodoxy," called Frances Maule a "probable lesbian" who lived an urban, women-centered life.[81] I would argue that Lewis was a lesbian, regardless of Cather's biographers' hesitations in placing the label and in spite of the fact that she herself may not have used that label. I have not yet determined if any others among this group identified themselves as lesbians, but several at least had primary commitments to other women.[81] Whether lesbian or not, many remained single, part of the group that could not marry, not only because they did not want to sacrifice career for family but also, as Lillian Faderman puts it, because "there were few husbands who could be expected to sacrifice their historically entrenched male prerogatives to revolutionary female notions."[83] If some of the other advertising women in this group were also lesbians or women-committed women, they shared with Maule and Lewis a further degree to which they were removed from their real clients: middle-class, married, heterosexual women.

All of these women lived lives far removed from the composite "woman" increasingly targeted by advertising and described earlier in this work. The advertising writers wrote appeals for the "average" woman, but they themselves, in many ways, were far from average. They were white, they were middle-class, but they were not the woman happily mopping her floor in the Wizard mop advertisement; they could not be defined by the "average woman" they promoted. At a staff meeting in 1936, Wallace Boren described the differences between Thompson writers and the people they wrote for. Only one of five writers went to church, except on rare occasions; half never went to Coney Island or similar resorts, the other half once in one or two years; over half had never lived at or below the average national income, and half couldn't name any relatives or friends who lived that way. While only 5 percent of all homes employed domestics, Boren continued, 66 percent of J. Walter Thompson writers employed domestics. Finally, only one in eight of the writers did her or his own shopping. The men writers, in fact, unanimously felt that shopping was "something to avoid entirely."[84] In 1930, according to former Thompson Company archivist Cynthia Swank, the median salary of women college graduates was $1900 while the average salary of all women at Thompson, including those without college degrees, was $2200.[85] It is unlikely that these women writers of the teens and twenties were less removed in salary and lifestyle from their readers.

The Thompson Company archives reveal some information about what the women writers thought of their consuming constituents, of this "average" woman. They often praised the "woman at home," but they also grew frustrated with her, or at least with her limited and limiting image. These advertising women wrote effective advertisements for that consumer, but they attempted also to broaden the definition of woman consumer and citizen to include themselves. Helen Resor's few written statements suggest that she recognized that female consumers had been looked down upon—and that she saw it as the work of the Women's Editorial Department to change that. She attributed her own success not to having overcome her female nature but rather to having acknowledged it. Most of the clients produced items that women, as opposed to men, would purchase or not purchase. In advertising these products, Resor, as she later put it, "supplied the feminine point of view." She continued, "I watched the advertising to see that the idea, the wording, and the illustrating were effective for women." Resor argued further that effective advertising had to be "made with knowledge of the habits of women, their methods of reasoning, and their prejudices."[86] She assumed, then, that regardless of class or other differences, women writers and women readers shared a common knowledge of and appreciation for women.

However, because they were removed from the life experiences of the largest group of consumers, housewives, the advertising women occasionally revealed a degree of condescension in their views, although they never went as far as did Charles Austin Bates, one of the first men to write advertising copy full time. "Advertisers should never forget they are addressing stupid people," Bates wrote. "It is really astonishing how little a man may know and yet keep out of the way of the trolley cars."[87] The women in the Thompson agency generally felt more of an affinity with their readers than did Bates, even though recognition of class and other differences occasionally were exhibited in their descriptions of their work. Mildred Holmes, a graduate of Wellesley College and a writer and then temporary group head in the Women's Editorial Department, wrote an article entitled "Housewives Write the Copy" for the external news bulletin. She described the housewife who answered the investigator's ring as a woman far removed from the pictures in the advertisements. "Her skirt, grown too small in the waist-band, is anchored half way down the placket with a safety pin," she wrote. "Apron and shirt waist are somewhat soiled and on awry. Last year's high heels run over to the outside. She has discouraged wisps of hair about her ears and she eyes the investigators with disillusionment, faintly inquiring."[88] Holmes further describes the housewife as "inarticulate"; the investigator must listen carefully to discern her "motivating preferences." Holmes's article argues somewhat unconvincingly that these housewives, rather than Holmes and her colleagues, write the copy. Holmes sees little in the way of sisterhood between herself and these inarticulate, overweight, overworked women, and one wonders who Holmes really believed should write the copy, she or they. In addition, one wonders who, considering the young, thin, and beautiful women whose images accompanied her advertisements, Holmes wrote the copy for.[89]

Other women in the Women's Editorial Department occasionally resorted to type as well. Aminta Casseres, a group head, and one of the most successful women of this group, wrote a report in 1926 that urged businessmen to hire women. Her arguments were quite progressive: don't expect women to act just like men; don't be afraid men will resent women, since they will but will eventually learn better; don't set higher standards for women than for men.[90] Perhaps she thought better of business women, though, than she did of female consumers. In an article for the news bulletin, Casseres argued that all women are driven by snobbery. "Snobbery is one of the sweetest, deepest vices of women," she argued. Women liked to pay a lot for things, as that allowed their snobbery to emerge. Casseres warned that advertisers should not brag too much about low prices, as that might turn snobby women off, rather than invite them to make purchases.[91]

In an article "The Woman Appeal," Frances Maule urged advertisers to eliminate their practice of talking down to women. They would do well, she argued, to remember the suffrage slogan, "Women are People." There was no composite female; those who looked for one would end up only with an "angel-idiot" in their minds and in their advertisements. Maule argued that women could not easily be categorized, but then she placed all women in four neat categories: housewife, society woman, club woman, and business woman. Her group, business women, was "an ever-increasing class with an entirely different set of needs from the woman in the house." In trying to broaden the category of "woman" to include herself and her peers, Maule had to create another "average," who, although distinct from the housewife, formed little more than a composite herself.[92]

Interestingly enough, some women at the Thompson agency appear to have been openly critical of the narrow definition of womanhood set by the most popular women's magazines. They felt not that the stay-at-home women were inferior, but that magazines sold even these women short. In the late teens several letters and discussions at Thompson meetings centered on a potential conflict with the *Ladies' Home Journal*, the Women's Editorial Department's largest source for advertising placement. One letter stated that some women had written to the Thompson agency complaining that the *Journal* was somewhat "old maidish."[93] One meeting participant argued that "we have heard so many statements of this kind from so many different women that it seems to us worth asking ourselves whether the *Journal* is keeping abreast of the modern woman's needs." The *Ladies' Home Journal* was criticized as appealing to the "stand pat" woman who was likely to shy away from any broader vision for women. Another complaint centered around the magazine's policy on fiction. The *Journal* opposed what one Thompson employee called a movement toward "stronger" fiction in the women's magazines, and, further, did not allow its heroines to smoke.[94] Apparently the Women's Editorial Department women would have liked to dictate how the women's magazines defined womanhood, and their definitions would have expanded to include independent, strong-minded women.

One Women's Editorial Department campaign described in an earlier chapter secured endorsements by famous women for Pond's Cold Cream. The first they secured featured Alva Belmont, the wealthy suffragist and feminist who provided her endorsement in exchange for a $1000 donation to a feminist cause. When Edith Lewis of the Thompson Company secured the endorsement and appeared in the office to share the good news, the other women hugged her and cheered the occasion. Evidently none of the other endorsements received the same response. On another occasion, the Women's Editorial Department received the contract to produce advertisements for *Pictorial Review*, a magazine with a more progressive reputation than that of the *Ladies' Home Journal.* One employee described the scene in the Women's Editorial Department once the word was out: for the first time women literally fought over the chance to write copy for that particular magazine. A newsletter article related their enthusiasm: "Fortunately, the account was big enough and the campaign was 'rush' enough to permit any one to drop anything she might be doing and to pitch in right away on our youngest 'greatest in the field.'" These advertising women looked forward to the chance to write advertisements for a magazine they described as "the most progressive and truly representative of women of wider interests." When they planned their campaign, one Women's Editorial Department member suggested they retell the story of Mabel Potter Daggett, a feminist who had written already in *Pictorial Review* about women and the war, "diluted" for male consumption, and then say "This is the type of woman that PR reaches." The newsletter article ended by saluting the Women's Editorial Department and by suggesting that they urge *Pictorial Review* to play a greater role in the leadership of women.[95]

Some of the Women's Editorial Department women also appear to have been critical of their own limitations at work. The women's group heads apparently complained about the fact that they were not included in the representatives' meetings. Mr. William Day chastised those who felt discriminated against at a creative organization staff meeting, at which many of the copy writers would have been present. "I am no believer, being myself one of the mature members, in the young man's world; nor am I a believer in an old man's world; nor am I a believer in a man's world, nor in a woman's world," he stated. "Those things are hooey and you know them to be hooey, even those of you who advance them."[96] Day gave this speech but solicited no responses. The company rarely saved the minutes of the creative staff minutes, apparently believing they were less important than the representative meeting minutes. Some of the Women's Editorial Department staff recognized that distinction and protested their second-class status.

These advertising women, in writing ads that provided a narrow definition of women's lives—a definition confining women to home and market—secured their own independence, financial and otherwise. However condescending their views about women who did not work for pay, choose to vote, or broaden

February, 1924   *The Ladies* HOME JOURNAL   65

An Interview with Mrs. O.H.P. Belmont
on the care of the skin

"A woman who neglects her personal appearance loses half her influence. The wise care of one's body constructs the frame encircling our mentality, the ability of which insures the success of one's life. I advise a daily use of Pond's Two Creams."

Alva E. Belmont—

IT was in the beautiful great hall of Beacon Towers on Sand's Point, Port Washington, Long Island, that I first talked with Mrs. O. H. P. Belmont.

I was excited and eager for the interview because I knew that Mrs. Belmont not only has given lavishly to women's causes from her colossal fortune, has been and is a tremendous worker, but also is particularly interested in woman's special problem of how to keep her force and her charm throughout her whole life.

From all this I expected to meet a very commanding woman the day I visited Beacon Towers. But Mrs. Belmont, on the contrary, is quiet and gracious and sweet. She could not have been a more charming hostess.

She herself opened the grilled iron door and I stepped into the big hall with its impressive mural paintings of the life of Joan of Arc and its wide doors opening straight onto Long Island Sound.

Here, I felt instantly, is the spirit of beauty strengthened by sincerity.

After we had admired the glorious view she showed me the pictures of her two sons, and of her grandson, who will some day be one of England's dukes, and—very proudly—the latest snapshot of her very young Ladyship, a small great granddaughter.

"How fine textured and fresh her skin is," I thought. "And she has just acknowledged herself a great grandmother!"

Begs Women not to Neglect Themselves

"NOW," she was saying, smilingly, "I suppose you want me to tell you what I think is the relation between a woman's success and her personal appearance."

"Yes," I admitted. "Just how important do you think personal appearance is?"

"It is vital. That is just as true for the woman at home or in business as for those who are socially prominent.

"A person may have great intelligence and yet make a very bad impression if her appearance is careless. So we do ourselves a great injustice if we do not give our bodies great care. It is very wise in every way to cultivate the knowledge of how to keep ourselves presentable and young.

"Don't you know," she said, "how often the woman with an unattractive face fails in the most reasonable undertaking? Nothing is so distressing. Neglect of one's personal attractions generally comes from ignorance and as I am greatly interested in the success of women in every possible way, I urge them not to neglect themselves.

The library of Mrs. O. H. P. Belmont at Beacon Towers on Long Island Sound, where this interview was signed. Mrs. Belmont, President of the National Women's Party, is known all over America for her active services in securing the suffrage for women. Mrs. Belmont is also interested in better conditions for women, is strong for the abolition of child labor, and for the improvement of Children's Homes.

On the artistic side, she is a trained architect, and her three magnificent residences—Villa Isoletta in France, the famous Marble House at Newport, and the imposing country home Beacon Towers on Long Island are the products of time not devoted to politics and business. After years of the burden of great public and private interests, she has marvelously kept her freshness.

Frenchwomen say, Cleanse and Protect

"YOU spend a part of each year in France," I said. "Are Frenchwomen more beautiful than American women?"

"Certainly not, but American women can learn from them. It comes naturally to them to care for their appearance from youth until they are eighty years old!—and they never lose their influence with society or the individual."

"Do Frenchwomen use creams much?" I asked Mrs. Belmont.

"In France," she said, "they have had this knowledge for generations. They have always used cleansing creams and protecting creams, knowing that water is not enough and that the face cannot stand much strain and exposure."

"Then you think women should use two creams?"

"I know they should. That is why I advise the daily use of Pond's Two Creams, so that women can keep their charm and influence as long as they need them—and that is always," she smiled.

Use this Famous Method

GIVE your skin these two indispensables to lasting skin loveliness—the kind of cleansing that restores each night your skin's essential suppleness, and the freshening that, besides protecting, brings each time the beauty of fresh smooth skin under your powder.

For years the laboratories of Pond's were devoted to the development of two preparations that were to meet these two vital needs. Finally two distinctly different face creams were perfected—Pond's Cold Cream and Pond's Vanishing Cream.

Every night—with the finger tips or a piece of moistened cotton, apply Pond's Cold Cream freely. The very fine oil in it is able to penetrate every pore of your skin. Leave it on a minute. Then remove it with a soft cloth. Dirt and excess oil, the rouge and powder you have used during the day, are taken off your skin and out of the pores. Feel how your face is relaxed. *Do this twice.* Now finish with ice rubbed over your face or a dash of cold water. Your skin looks fresh and is beautifully supple again. If your skin is very dry, pat on more cream, especially where wrinkles come first—around the eyes, the nose, the corners of your mouth—and leave it on over night.

After every cleansing, before you powder, and always before you go out—smooth on Pond's Vanishing Cream *very evenly*—just enough for your skin to absorb. Now if you wish, rouge—powder. How smooth and velvety your face feels to your hand. Nothing can roughen it. When you get up in the morning, after a dash of cold water, this cream will keep your skin fresh and untired for hours. And it will stay evenly powdered.

Use this method regularly. Soon your face will be permanently fresher, smoother and you can count on the charm of a fresh, young skin for years longer than would otherwise be possible. Begin now. Buy both Pond's Creams tonight in jars or tubes at any drug store or department store. The Pond's Extract Company.

GENEROUS TUBES—MAIL THIS COUPON WITH 10c TODAY

The Pond's Extract Co.
108 Hudson St., New York

Ten cents (10c) is enclosed for your special introductory tubes of the two creams every normal skin needs—enough of each cream for two weeks' ordinary toilet uses.

Name
Street
City   State

Pond's Two Creams

used by the women who must keep their charm, their beauty, their influence

EVERY SKIN NEEDS THESE TWO CREAMS

Women copywriters at the J. Walter Thompson Company celebrated when they secured the endorsement of feminist and suffragist Alva Belmont for their Pond's campaign. (*Ladies' Home Journal,* February 1924, p. 65)

their sphere to include the public world, though, these women hoped to expand what they saw as a narrow definition of womanhood. They wanted to see themselves in the pages of the magazines. But simply entering the advertising profession would not guarantee that kind of freedom. Instead, as Susan Curtis argues about women's entrance into other professions during this period, "it meant a new kind of confinement, one in which women and men were bound by the rules of bureaucratic structure, professional standards, and the imperatives of consumer culture."[97] And the link between consumer culture and a prescriptive, consumer role for women defined the advertising and magazine fields and ruled the day.

So although this group of advertising women left to others an impressive example of professional accomplishment and advancement, although they succeeded in putting their educations and talents to use in a highly discriminatory social environment, and although they found creative ways to remain economically independent, the J. Walter Thompson women leave a divided legacy. They represent, in a sense, the women in the fiction who made decisions based on their own needs, the women in the advice who sought the divorce from the ineffectual husbands, the advice-givers who lived lives far different from the advice they freely and profitably gave. They represent what the "average" woman, had she been encouraged to try her hand at that public world, might have accomplished.

As history has it, *Pictorial Review*, with its more progressive attitude towards women, went out of business, and the *Ladies' Home Journal*, with its stand-pat attitude, remains strong today. The ultimate paradox for these advertising women is that the success of their work furthered the likelihood that they and women like them would not be featured on the pages of the most popular women's magazines for decades to come. Successful advertising like the majority of ads these women wrote was successful not only in reaching consumers but also in restricting the culture's definition of womanhood to include only white, middle-class, stay-at-home women. Like the African-American or immigrant women these advertising women ignored, they themselves remained nothing more than a "segment" of the population—and an insignificant one at that—as far as advertisers were concerned. As the emphasis for women moved, as Dorothy Brown argues, from "making a living to buying a living," the women who made a living in advertising remained behind the scenes in the development of their own industry.[97] Ironically, it was in part because they did such good work that these women, and the many others like them, remained invisible to the world of women's magazines and advertising for decades to come. Behind the scenes of the *Ladies' Home Journal* in the 1910s and 1920s, and lost to history until now, the J. Walter Thompson women represent the complexities of women's history, the complex legacies of the consumer culture.

seven

"Every Woman Is Interested in This"

Advertising in the
Ladies' Home Journal

*I*n the early twentieth century, the middle-class woman was the darling of the women's magazines, and the *Ladies' Home Journal* was the darling of the advertisers.[1] Manufacturers and advertising agencies had not yet discovered the benefits of market segmentation, the practice of dividing the female market and targeting various groups differently; instead, they based their appeals, for the most part, on one female consumer, the "average" American woman, the *Journal*-reading woman. Some industries, such as automobile manufacturers, would discover and cultivate market segmentation in the 1920s, addressing groups of people on the basis of age, for example, or social class, but most industries operated on the principal of a national mass market until after World War II. Today, using the market segmentation approach almost exclusively, manufacturers and advertisers use demographics, including age, race, education, gender, and income, and psychographics, such as lifestyle and cultural aspirations, to create divisions in a market and exploit those divisions to the greatest financial advantage.[2] In the 1910s and 1920s, however, most manufacturers and their advertising agencies relied on a unified concept of the market and defined that unity as female, middle class, and white. When the copywriters at the J. Walter Thompson Women's Editorial Department wrote their ads, then, they targeted first the *Journal* reader, the woman who read the magazine's advice and fiction, contemplated the mixed messages and her own divided emotions, and purchased the products that might provide at best an improved standard of living and at least a moment or more of therapeutic release.

The *Ladies' Home Journal*'s use of advertising in defining the American woman developed readily with Edward Bok at the helm and Cyrus Curtis in the background. Both men had experience working in advertising when they were young. At age eighteen, Curtis moved to Boston from Maine and worked as a clerk in a dry goods store. An enterprising youth, he used his lunch hours to sell newspaper advertising space to local merchants. After a year of this, Curtis quit his job at the store to sell advertising space full time.[3] Edward Bok worked as an advertising director at Scribner's before Curtis hired him to fill Louisa Knapp Curtis's editorial position at the *Ladies' Home Journal*.[4] The two men grew into their professional lives during the same years in which advertising became both more important and more respectable, and they welcomed advertising's emergence as a natural, beneficial, and extremely profitable occurrence. Cyrus Curtis recognized from the start that advertising would be crucial to his success; he had to solicit enough advertising to keep publishing costs down, and he had to advertise enough himself to ensure steady, if not increased circulation. When asked in later years what had been the key to his success, Curtis was quick to respond: "Advertising. That's what made me whatever I am."[5]

A few statistics illustrate the seriousness of Curtis's commitment to and the degree of his success in soliciting good advertising for the *Ladies' Home Journal*. National advertising revenues multiplied thirteen-fold from 1900–1930, from $200 million to $2.6 billion, and the *Ladies' Home Journal* claimed its place as an advertising leader among all magazines, in particular among women's magazines.[6] In 1900, the back cover of the *Journal* was the highest priced position for any magazine advertisement. In 1911, Curtis organized a department of marketing research, headed by Charles Coolidge Parlin, to gather information about markets and merchandising. This department was a first in the magazine industry, and its sophistication and effectiveness provided lessons in marketing research not only to other magazines but also to many advertising agencies. By 1914, the *Ladies' Home Journal* had the highest advertising rate of any popular magazine, and by 1929 the *Journal* and the *Saturday Evening Post*, another Curtis publication, together accounted for 40 percent of all national magazine advertising.[7]

The Kellogg Company placed the first national advertisement in the *Ladies' Home Journal* in 1906, and from that point on, the *Journal* played a significant role in the development of advertising at this level.[8] Offering promises of high-quality standardized products, national advertising tapped into a national market and insured the continued success of magazines such as the *Journal*. "How do consumers buy breakfast foods?" a grocer from Lynn, Massachusetts, asked in reply to a 1915 Curtis investigation. "They buy what they see advertised in the *Saturday Evening Post* and the *Ladies' Home Journal*. What is advertised in these journals you can depend upon will sell. We are gradually getting rid of all other breakfast foods except those nationally advertised."[9] According to the J. Walter Thompson company, it became customary not just within Thompson but in the industry as a whole to gauge an agency's business by the volume it gave to the *Saturday Evening Post* on men's accounts and to the *Ladies' Home Journal* on women's accounts.[10]

When Cyrus Curtis selected Edward Bok to direct the production of the *Journal*, he chose a man who could balance the delivery of service and advertising. Bok saw it as his duty to assist women in the management of their homes and lives, to provide a service of advice and instruction. Directions for proper living, as the *Journal* editor saw it, included awareness of and increased mastery over the art of consumption. He truly wanted to reform his readers, to make better women of those who looked to the *Journal* for entertainment, friendship, and instruction. Bok believed his magazine could fashion its readers into more loving wives and mothers, more skillful homemakers, and, not incidentally, more professional consumers. In accordance with these beliefs, although Bok did not view each advertisement as inherently good, he did believe that advertising as a whole could and should be beneficial to *Journal* readers and to the society.[11] Viewing his work as a moral exercise, Bok at times drew a line between what was strictly profitable and what was "good" for his readers, and his actions set the stage for company policy for decades to come. "Bad" advertising had no place in the pages of the *Journal*. Under Bok's direction, the magazine developed an advertising code in 1910 to discourage what he called "unfair, and even unmannerly, competition in our advertising columns." He included the following stipulations: ". . . no mail-order advertisements of general merchandise, no installment buying, no alcohol, no patent medicines, no immodesty in text or illustration, no financial advertisements, no tobacco, no playing cards."[12] These items had no place in the editor's plan for simple living.

Bok may have argued the moral imperative of advertising, but publisher Curtis expressed a different opinion about the place of advertising in the *Journal*. "Do you know why we publish the *Ladies' Home Journal?*" he asked a group of manufacturers. "The editor thinks it is for the benefit of American women. That is an illusion, but a very proper one for him to have. But I will tell you; the real reason, the publisher's reason, is to give you people who manufacture things the American women want and buy a chance to tell them about your products."[13] Curtis may have spoken the words he felt his audience wanted to hear, or he and Bok may actually have disagreed on this issue; in either case, Bok took his moral role seriously and Curtis took Bok seriously. He never attempted to prevent Bok from restricting certain types of advertisements or from warning readers of the perils of the marketplace. Certainly Curtis recognized that Bok restricted far fewer advertisements than he accepted and that his basic impulse concerning advertising was to applaud its use and welcome its inclusion in the pages of the *Journal*.

During the 1910s and 1920s, the *Ladies' Home Journal* and the J. Walter Thompson advertising agency took pride in their mutually beneficial relationship. The Thompson Company was impressive by any standards, not the least of which was its prominence with the *Journal*. By 1916 the Thompson research department could offer clients a 650-volume library containing trade publications, chamber of commerce reports, agency portfolios, samples of work done for clients, and additional files on trades and industries, clients and competitors, and media.[14] The agency also took an active role in more than the design of advertisements; they designed packaging, helped manufacturers choose which products to manufacture and which to advertise, and made suggestions for new products to add to existing lines. From 1910 to 1924, the J. Walter Thompson Company did not launch on the market any product that failed.[15] From 1916, when Stanley Resor became president of J. Walter Thompson, through 1929, the national economy increased 2.1 times, advertising expenditures as a whole increased 4.4 times, and Thompson Company business, in the U.S. alone, increased 10 times.[16]

In 1915, discussing advertising in a *Journal* editorial, Bok acknowledged that he had received a "left-handed compliment" from a reader who asked, "Why don't you make your literary contents as good as your advertising department makes the advertisements?"[17] The fact is that the *Journal*'s advertising department did not create the most successful ads in the magazine; the J. Walter Thompson Women's Editorial Department did. The Thompson Company consistently beat out the competition to place the greatest number of ads in the *Journal*, and the Women's Editorial Department, under the direction of Helen Resor, handled much of this enormous volume.[18] Resor was well qualified to handle the *Journal*'s business even before she started the Women's Editorial Department at J. Walter Thompson. In January of 1911, Helen Lansdowne moved from the Cincinnati office to Thompson's New York headquarters to begin work on Procter & Gamble's new product, Crisco. Crisco is remembered as the first product with extensive testing and refining of the product formula, label, and marketing strategy.[19] For this product the manufacturer, Procter & Gamble, broke a twenty-year precedent and sought advertising assistance from an outside agency. They allocated $3 million for the opening campaign alone. Helen Lansdowne made five trips back to Cincinnati from New York to appear before the board of directors and answer the manufacturer's questions about the new advertisements and about the "feminine point of view." She later recalled with pride that "this was the first time Procter & Gamble had ever opened their board meetings to a woman."[20]

Helen Lansdowne often had to go to sales conventions and explain why she designed her advertisements the way she did. Her approach was to mirror the copy of the magazines, particularly of her flagship, the *Ladies' Home Journal*, so that the advertisements blended in with and often could scarcely be distinguished from the editorial matter. She wrote ads, according to one Thompson Company historian, that looked like "disinterested editorial copy."[21] In the case of Crisco, one of Lansdowne's advertisements contained a great deal of text and eight separate headlines, including "A Scientific Discovery Which will Affect Every Kitchen in America," and "Every Woman is Interested in This." This type of advertisement, an illustrated feature story, was a popular approach among copywriters, so although it is unlikely that Helen Resor invented it, her own work was much copied. A Thompson Company writer, evaluating their past successes in 1936, recalled the effectiveness of

Lansdowne's approach. "It has been developed to such a degree that in looking through one of our national magazines it is frequently difficult to distinguish the text matter from the feature story advertisement."[22] The seemingly natural advancement of a consumer culture in the pages of women's magazines was a major development in the history of advertising which Helen Resor was partly responsible for. Through integration of advertising into the magazine text and hence into the magazine's message, she and others effectively merged women's roles as magazine readers and primary consumers.

The J. Walter Thompson Women's Editorial Department generated many successful campaigns for the *Ladies' Home Journal.* Although the Thompson women occasionally complained about the conservative nature of the *Journal,* they recognized its tremendous appeal and importance and took pride in their own accomplishments. The remainder of this chapter will concentrate on two of their campaigns, Woodbury's Facial Soap and Pond's Cold and Vanishing Creams. These particular campaigns demonstrate the contributions of the Thompson women copywriters and hence the *Journal* in promoting national advertising and a national definition of womanhood, in contributing to the development of the female consumer culture, and in acknowledging, giving voice to, and then selling short women's inarticulate longings.

John H. Woodbury first introduced Woodbury's Facial Soap in 1885. After twelve successful years sales took a serious downward curve, and in 1901, Woodbury sold the soap, name, trademark, and goodwill of the business to the Andrew Jergens Company for $250,000. Jergens, in business since the 1880s, hired an agency to provide the advertising, but sales continued to drop. When Jergens turned the account over to J. Walter Thompson in 1910, Woodbury's was being outsold twenty to one by Cuticura, a similar product sold at the same price, 25 cents. The Thompson agency decided to move away from the tone of the earlier Woodbury's advertisements, which had claimed various impossible skin cures, showing illustrations either of frightening, neckless heads or beautiful, captivating young women. Thompson had to find a way to distinguish Woodbury's from the many other beauty soaps that claimed the same results but cost from 50 to 75 percent less.[23] The agency had a large task and little to work with; Jergens had reduced the previous year's advertising budget of $253,000 to only $25,000. That was all they had left to give on that account, Stanley Resor later recalled. "We have had enough," they told him.[24]

The J. Walter Thompson agency took on the campaign with customary zeal. The Women's Editorial Department spent six months working on the

"Every Woman is Interested in This," this Crisco advertisement promised, helping to connect American female identity with the consumption of household products. The ad also points to deep frying as "radical change" for homemakers. (*Ladies' Home Journal*, January 1912, p. 45)

campaign before they introduced a single advertisement. As they often did with new products, the women used the soap themselves at home. They also read over one hundred books on skin care, ordered lab analyses to discover possible allergic reactions or other difficulties with the product, and worked behind sales counters at department stores to determine customer tastes and observe customer decision making practices. They hired a medical doctor as an advisor solely for this product. Finally, they determined consumers' attitudes toward skin care in general and Woodbury's Facial Soap in particular "as disclosed during intimate, house-to-house investigations."[25]

Helen Resor argued that "copy must be believable," and she followed through on that with the first series of Woodbury's advertisements, which focused on realistic skin treatments.[26] The most famous and longest lasting of those treatments featured the headline, "Conspicuous Nose Pores—How to Reduce Them." The advertisement showed an unadorned drawing of a nose and described in a pseudo-scientific way how the "small muscular fibres" of the nose become weakened, collect dirt, and become enlarged. The copywriters divided the treatment for conspicuous nose pores into several parts. First, the woman at home would wring a cloth with very hot water, lather it with Woodbury's, and hold it to the nose. Once the heat had expanded the pores, she would rub gently. After repeating this process several times, she would rub the nose for a few minutes with a lump of ice. This simple, believable, and effective procedure brought tremendous success. "Some retailers were sold out," Stanley Resor later recalled, "yet since their previous rate of sale had only been a cake a month, being sold out did not mean much."[27] The Thompson agency persevered: entering the national media at once, and with only one-tenth of the previous year's advertising expenditure, they stopped Woodbury's falling sales curve for the first time in fourteen years and achieved results which, according to a company newsletter, "seemed at the time impossible."[28]

The nose pores advertisement appears simple and unsophisticated in contrast to advertisements produced later in the decade or in the 1920s. Its success despite its simplicity demonstrates both the immediate effectiveness of national advertising and the tremendous strides made in the advertising industry in a short period of time. It also provides an example of three techniques the advertising industry would come to depend on. First, an advertisement would repeat the brand name again and again. In this case, the nose pores technique, which could be used with virtually any soap, became associated with Woodbury's soap; by almost constant repetition of the brand name, it became the Woodbury's technique. Second, advertisements would emphasize using more of the product than necessary. The nose pores advertisement recommended that the procedure be carried out several times, "stopping at once when your nose feels sensitive." Following these directions, each consumer would consume greater quantities of the product. Shampoo companies, which urge consumers to "rinse and repeat" after they wash, have long held firmly to this concept. Finally, an advertisement would often emphasize repeated use of the product. In addition to using more of the product each time, the Woodbury's advertisement urged customers to use the product often, because one could "not expect to change in a week a condition resulting from years of neglect." Another conspicuous nose pores advertisement concurred by urging women to "use it regularly, not spasmodically," while a third argued that "Before long your skin will take on the greater loveliness which the persistent use of Woodbury's Facial Soap brings."

The conspicuous nose pores campaign is significant for its selling techniques and for its attempts to develop customer loyalty; it is also significant because it was the first copy to consciously talk about the reader as well as the product.[29] "Complexions otherwise flawless are often ruined by conspicuous nose pores," the advertisement warned.

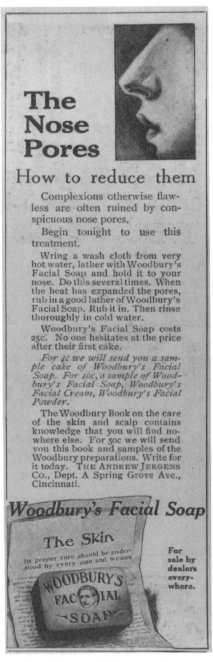

This simple but highly effective advertisement provided women readers with believable copy and the promise of beautiful skin. (*Ladies' Home Journal,* September 1911, p. 69)

This and thousands of ads to follow provided an emotional appeal, promising to those women who took advantage of a certain product's benefits masculine admiration and feminine envy. "The copy is scientific, restrained, conservative, yet also personal and human," the company historian later recalled.[30] This so-called "human" appeal became synonymous with promises that products would meet human needs: household products would ensure social progress, facial soaps would solve loneliness, and breakfast foods would solidify family relationships. As a rule, Edward Bok did not consider these fantastic promises to be misleading advertising, or "unmannerly" and subject to exclusion from the *Ladies' Home Journal*.[31]

The initial Woodbury's campaign focused on specific cleansing treatments for common complexion problems: conspicuous nose pores, blackheads, blemishes, excessively oily skin. Thompson then recommended changing the Woodbury's packaging so that it included a booklet of instructions wrapped around the soap. And from the mid-teens through the twenties, the Women's Editorial Department promoted Woodbury's in the *Ladies' Home Journal* and in other magazines by making of everyday skin care something that required instruction, persistence, and specific products. "No one hesitates at the price after their first cake," the advertisements declared, and statistics bear out this claim. During the first ten years that J. Walter Thompson handled the product, there was only one month during which there was not a sales increase over the corresponding month the year before. By 1920, the advertising appropriation was seven times as great as total sales of the soap had been in 1910.[32] Woodbury's became the best-selling soap in its field, going from $108,286 in sales in 1910 to $1,466,417 in 1929.[33] Woodbury's was a J. Walter Thompson–and Thompson Women's Editorial Department–success story and represents one element of the nation's growing obsession with youth and beauty, for which women spent $17 million on cosmetics in 1914 and $141 million in 1925.[34]

These various skin treatment advertisements provided the backbone for the Woodbury's campaign, but it was "A Skin You Love to Touch," the campaign described briefly in the previous chapter, that brought the most attention to the Woodbury's product. Helen Lansdowne first decided upon this approach as the title for a window display, then after about three years' use in almost every advertisement, the phrase became the official slogan for the facial soap. The ads which featured "A Skin You Love to Touch" did not, in their text, promise anything different than did the treatments offered in other Woodbury's advertisements. The unspoken message–the promise of male attention–really marked these advertisements. The paintings of "A Skin You Love to Touch" changed over time, but the basic message remained the same: the woman Woodbury's user, striking a sensual pose, received the complete attention of an adoring man. Although most historians have located the development of advertisements based on emotional appeal in the twenties, the Woodbury's soap advertisements produced in the J. Walter Thompson Women's Editorial Department in the teens set the stage for emotional appeals to women based on their inarticulate longings for romantic involvement. These advertisements articulated what the *Journal* ignored or perhaps even discouraged in other departments: women's sensuality. The women in the Woodbury's ads did not exhibit wedding rings, they had no children underfoot, and the men at their sides were no "tired business men." These men were dashing romantics, smitten with the Woodbury's women. Women's inarticulate longings for sensuality had found a voice. The advertisements recognized what the culture at large would not, at least for middle-class women, but they also promised two things the product could not deliver: the attentions of men who differed significantly from the "average" man, and the satisfaction of emotional needs through consumption.

Over the course of the late teens, the Woodbury's ads changed little in text or in subtext. The advertisers increasingly used more color, developed new slogans for the same treatments, and devoted more money and hence more space to the advertisements. Thompson advised the Jergens Company to reduce rather than expand the line associated with Woodbury's in order to maintain its reputation for skin care. As a result, Jergens eliminated its Woodbury's tooth powders and tooth pastes. Based on another Thompson recommendation it also doubled the price of the Woodbury's facial powder. "Twenty-five cents for a facial powder is as cheap for a powder as 25 is high for soap," argued Stanley Resor, "so you have an absolute inconsistency."[35] Rather than bring down the price on Woodbury's, of course, they raised the price on the facial powder.

The conspicuous nose pores advertisement was so successful that by 1918 the Thompson agency placed it in all the leading women's magazines and in roughly two hundred newspapers in the United States and in ten in Canada. By 1919, the conspicuous nose pores ads had gone further internationally, including seven publications in Cuba, four in Puerto Rico, and two in Panama. Dubbed "el famoso" in Spanish-language advertisements, Woodbury's Facial Soap provided beauty lessons for women from Trenton to Tulsa and from Halifax to Havana.[36] And whether the women who purchased Woodbury's believed the promises or not, they clearly responded to the suggestion of women's sensual nature.

In the late teens, the Women's Editorial Department changed its approach with the Woodbury's campaign, moving from an encouraging to a somewhat threatening tone in the copy. Earlier ads had promised "A Skin You Love to Touch," but by 1917 some advertisements for Woodbury's suggested that, in the case of too many women, their skin remained untouchable. Negative judgment became an advertisers' rallying cry. As Roland Marchand puts it, "Advertisers, then as now, recognized a much larger stake in reflecting people's needs and anxieties than in depicting their actual circumstances and behavior."[37] Certainly relationships with men constituted one of the anxieties the Thompson women and the *Journal* readers faced as they considered or completed higher education, entered and then competed in the male workforce, and attempted to define themselves in a world that was only beginning openly to recognize female sexuality. One of the first of these negative ads, "Get Your Mirror to Tell You What Your Friends Will Not," threatened consumers with social ostracism if they did not choose the right product. Earlier ads promised that women who used Woodbury's could attract the men they wanted; newer ads threatened that women who did not use Woodbury's risked gaining any male attention at all. In the "Get Your Mirror" advertisement, the judgmental male exists not in person but merely in a photograph on the woman's dressing table. While the woman looks at herself in the mirror, he stares sternly at her from across the room. The message is clear although less obvious than it would rapidly become, as threatening advertisements became both more common and more sophisticated in the course of the following decade.[38]

The Women's Editorial Department's Woodbury's campaign for 1920 featured a mixture of encouraging and threatening advertisements. One advertisement simply instructed women "How to Make Your Skin Noticeably Lovely," while another menacingly asked "Under Searching Eyes–Do You Ever Wince Inwardly?" This advertisement showed a woman talking with three men. She conversed easily because, unlike some of the readers, she did not have a flawed complexion. "You want to shrink into the background," the text reminded readers. "You lose your confidence, your gaiety. Your very personality is dimmed just when you are most anxious to appear at your best."[39] Regular use of Woodbury's, more even than charm school or a relaxation of social codes, seemingly provided the self-confidence women needed to venture out into the world. Other similar ads would follow. "A Man's First

Impression of a Woman" warned readers in 1921 about "that first instinctive summing up of a woman's personality—her charm, daintiness, breeding—no later, more critical judgment takes its place." Advertisements for 1922 included "His Unspoken Thoughts When He Looks Into Your Face—What Are They?" followed by "All Around You People Are Judging You Silently." A 1924 advertisement, "When Failure Hurts the Most," featured a sad-faced woman, obviously returning home alone and early after an evening out. She had "longed to be successful, gay, triumphant," but missed out on the good times other "girls" were having. The copywriters abandoned subtlety almost altogether in this advertising campaign, which dictated that women took care of themselves in order to be pleasing to men who, when not ardent admirers, acted as severe critics. The man in the photograph on the bureau had graduated; he was now full-sized and present, even omnipresent. Since women never knew when they might run into him, they always had to be prepared with rosy clean skin, ready to meet the "stranger's eyes, keen and critical."[40]

In the early twenties, the Women's Editorial Department at Thompson devised yet another approach to the Woodbury's account. They sent out 1200 letters to students and faculty at Vassar College and received 600 replies, the majority from students but 7 percent from faculty. Of the respondents, 54 percent reported that they used Woodbury's. This, the copywriters realized, could form the basis for an endorsement campaign. Edith Lewis reported at a company representatives' meeting that they then decided to approach other groups of women and use the data for a whole series of advertisements. The logistical problem she reported was that they doubted that certain of the groups would return the questionnaires when their only reward was a sample of the Woodbury's product. "We could not send a simple questionnaire to a debutante and expect her to fill it out and return it to us," Lewis reported, revealing her low expectations if not her low opinion of debutantes. The Women's Editorial Department decided to pay two dollars for each response. They argued that since they paid the money whether the woman reported she used Woodbury's or not, they would solicit honest responses.[41]

These investigations resulted in a new series of Woodbury's advertisements, endorsements of sorts. "Four Hundred and Fifteen Girls at Wellesley and Barnard" demonstrated that Woodbury's enjoyed "more than double the popularity" of any other soap among these select and enviable young women. "She is one of the most charming things America has produced—the American college girl," the ad proclaimed. Other ads in the series included "Five Hundred and Twenty Girls at Smith and Bryn Mawr," "Among Philadelphia

"... Watching her from every corner of the crowded room"

Strangers' eyes, keen and critical

can you meet them proudly - confidently - without fear?

STRANGERS' eyes, watching you in crowded restaurants—in theatres and ball rooms—do you shrink and feel apologetic before them? Or can you meet them without awkwardness or dread?

The possession of a beautiful skin gives any woman poise and confidence. It is a charm that any woman can have if she will. For *your* skin changes every day; each day old skin dies and new takes its place.

By giving this new skin the right treatment, you can make it flawlessly clear and soft and smooth—free from the little defects that spoil so many complexions.

Are you using the right treatment for your special type of skin?

Skins differ widely—and each type of skin should have the treatment that suits its special needs.

There is a special Woodbury treatment for each different type of skin.

For instance, you may happen to have the type of skin that is exceptionally sensitive and delicate—so easily irritated by exposure that it is a constant problem to take care of it.

To overcome this extreme sensitiveness and give your skin the power of resistance it should have, you should use each night the following treatment:

DIP a soft washcloth in warm water and hold it to your face. Then make a warm water lather of Woodbury's Facial Soap and dip your cloth up and down in it until the cloth is "fluffy" with the soft white lather. Rub this lathered cloth gently over your skin until the pores are thoroughly cleansed. Rinse well with warm, then with clear, cool water, and dry carefully.

How you can tell that your skin is responding

THE very first time you use this treatment it will leave your skin with a slightly drawn, tight feeling. Do not regard this as a disadvantage—it means that your skin is responding *in the right way* to a more thorough and stimulating kind of cleansing.

After a few nights this drawn sensation will disappear and your skin will emerge from its nightly bath so delightfully soft and smooth that you will never again want to use any other method of caring for your skin.

This is only one of the special treatments for different types of skin given in the booklet of treatments which is wrapped around every cake

of Woodbury's Facial Soap. In this booklet you will find complete treatments for all the different types of skin.

Get a cake of Woodbury's today, at any drug store or toilet goods counter, and begin tonight the treatment your skin needs.

The same qualities that give Woodbury's its beneficial effect on the skin make it ideal for general use—for *keeping* the skin in good condition. A 25 cent cake of Woodbury's lasts a month or six weeks for general toilet use, including any of the special Woodbury treatments.

A complete miniature set of the Woodbury skin preparations

For 25 cents we will send you a complete miniature set of the Woodbury skin preparations containing:

A trial size cake of Woodbury's Facial Soap.
A sample tube of the new Woodbury's Facial Cream.
A sample tube of Woodbury's Cold Cream.
A sample box of Woodbury's Facial Powder.
Together with the treatment booklet, "A Skin You Love to Touch."

Send for this set today. Address The Andrew Jergens Co., 101 Spring Grove Ave., Cincinnati, Ohio. *If you live in Canada, address The Andrew Jergens Co., Limited, 101 Sherbrooke St., Perth, Ontario.*

Copyright, 1921, by The Andrew Jergens Co.

Advertisers alternated promises of beauty with ads like this, which threatened negative social consequences for women who failed to follow proper patterns of consumption. (*Ladies' Home Journal,* January 1922, p. 42)

Debutantes," "At the Ritz Carlton," "At the Lake Placid Club," and "Three Hundred and Fifty-Two Stars at Hollywood." The only advertisement in this series to include African-Americans in the drawing, and one of a very few advertisements prepared by the Women's Editorial Department to do so, was "Among the Debutantes of the South." This ad featured an African-American man serving food and drinks to the debutantes and their male friends. In this case, the Women's Editorial Department relied on all the available stereotypes: African-American servants dressed in white coats and lovely young women put on pedestals and "worshipped" by honorable southern gentlemen.[42] "They have become a legend with us—the beautiful, adored women of the South," the advertisement claimed. "From childhood their beauty is prized, worshipped by the men of their families."

The Women's Editorial Department chose interesting categories for these endorsement ads: debutantes, college women, actresses. In choosing these groups, they further set cultural types and defined cultural roles for women in the United States. They continued a process of defining which women had opinions that mattered, which women's consumer choices warranted imitation. In short, they determined who it was that "counted." While it is true that these groups of women expanded the standard advertising definition of wife and mother, they also defined women along lines clearly delineated by class, race, and ethnicity. The copywriters took this approach a great deal further in a 1928-1929 campaign, again for Woodbury's, during which they essentially mapped out archetypes of American womanhood.

Edith Lewis, Smith College graduate and lifetime partner of Willa Cather, designed this campaign, the Woodbury's contest. She originally planned it as a national beauty contest for which women themselves would send in photographs, but decided that a project of that scope was not sophisticated enough and would probably prove unmanageable. Under her direction the Women's Editorial Department planned instead a fairly private contest. They enlisted Junior League branches all over the United States to help them find beautiful Woodbury's users. Junior League members mailed in hundreds of photographs under the twelve established categories: debutante, wife, co-ed, mother, woman in the arts, sub-deb, sportswoman, high school girl, woman in the professions, bride, grandmother, and business girl. The impressive list of judges included F. Scott Fitzgerald, Cornelius Vanderbilt, Jr., and John Barrymore. Each month for a year one of the winners appeared in all the leading magazines. Each winner won the same prize: an all-expense paid trip to New York City and a visit to Bergdorf Goodman for a costume to fit the winning image.[43]

With this contest, Edith Lewis and her colleagues sold Woodbury's Facial Soap, but they also sold another, equally important product: the composite women. Through Lewis' efforts, the American woman became defined by a brand name, much as she would later be defined as Miss Rheingold, the Clairol women, the St. Pauli girl, or the woman who chooses Jif. Winning women would be defined, ultimately, not by their accomplishments but by a brand name, in this case Woodbury's. They became standardized, as standardized and packaged by the efforts of national advertising as any product had become. Female identity, like soap, had enormous trading potential in the marketplace. The Woodbury's winners represented several possible life paths for women, none of which radically challenged the paths offered in the *Journal*'s advice or in its fiction. On one path, a sub-debutante, like winner Lolita Gladys Gelpi of New Orleans, "nursed by a colored mammy, educated by French convent nuns, speaking French as readily as English," could grow up to become a debutante like winner Natica de Costa, allied with the oldest families in New York and Boston and who, incidentally, used Woodbury's since she was a sub-deb at fourteen. The debutante could become the most beautiful woman in the arts, like drama student winner Julia Evans, or she could become the loveliest of wives like Mrs. George Franklin Hester, who claimed she was not an old-fashioned or a young-fashioned wife, "just a wife!" Those who took another path through life could be the lovely high school girl who graduated to sportswoman and then co-ed, like the twin co-ed Woodbury's winners, Helen and Lois Dodd of Chicago. The co-ed could graduate and become the business girl, the bride, and perhaps even the woman in the professions. All paths would meet at the most beautiful young mother, however, who, like Woodbury's winner Mrs. Richard O'Connor, belonged to a mothers' club and was mature in both thought and outlook. All paths would also end at the grandmother stage, where Woodbury's winners could look back on their accomplishments in making the hurdles from category to category and instruct those who followed them. Of course, while the women had several paths to choose from, one thing remained constant: their choice in soap. Woodbury's Facial Soap transcended all individual differences and helped women form the composite, the winning American woman.

Interestingly enough, these categories also helped advertisers dodge questions of race and class, since working class white women and women of color would find themselves included in the women's magazines when they broke into, not beyond or through, these stereotypical categories. The ads presented a clear message to women; if they did not already belong to one of the categories, they should aspire to belonging to them. Social status and approval, in the world of advertising, supposedly rested not on class or race or European standards of beauty but on one's choice of facial soap. Of course, Edith Lewis and her contemporaries also helped define the American woman, wittingly or unwittingly, as much by what they left out as by what they included in the definition. The American beauty was not only white and young and middle-class; she was also not of African descent, did not speak with an accent, did not worry about the price of a beauty soap. At least some of these categories developed in the Woodbury's advertisements continue to define—and restrict—women in the United States today.[44]

A second *Ladies' Home Journal* advertiser for which the J. Walter Thompson Women's Editorial Department provided advertisements was the Pond's Extract Company. Founded in 1846, Pond's placed its very first ad, in 1886, with the Thompson Company. For the next fifteen years Pond's advertised only its extract, "the old family doctor," a witch hazel-based product primarily used for cuts, bruises, prickly heat, and sore muscles. In 1891, after the Thompson Company completed a survey on face creams, Pond's followed their recommendations and changed its line to focus more on this product. In 1907 they developed Pond's Vanishing Cream and Pond's Cold Cream, two products with which the Thompson Company would have a long and profitable association.[45]

Many creams at that time required a great deal of massaging, but the Pond's vanishing cream, requiring little rubbing, would "vanish" into the skin. Thompson started advertising the Vanishing Cream from the product's inauguration in 1910, and by 1916 Pond's held the lead on vanishing cream sales in the United States.[46] With $42,000 in advertising expenditures for all Pond's creams in 1910, Pond's net sales reached $112,000. In 1915, with less outlay, $31,000 in advertising expenditures, the company's creams earned $209,000 in net sales.[47] According to the Thompson company historian, the Women's Editorial Department handled the Pond's account the way they handled other successful accounts: by keying the ads to women, assuming the reader had intelligence and wanted facts, presenting those facts with "reasoned assurance," recognizing the reader's need to decide for herself, providing sufficient copy to tell the story, and finally, making the copy both educational and emotional.[48]

Helen Resor has been credited with creating the 1912 Vanishing Cream copy that produced record sales. Lansdowne's informational focus explained, as the headline read, "*Why* your skin chaps and *how* to prevent it," with an

Advertisers categorized women as debutantes, coeds, beautiful young wives, and women in the arts, then argued that the thread connecting these representative American women was the brand names they chose. (*Ladies' Home Journal,* December 1929, p. 29)

answer provided by a professor of dermatology at the University of Illinois.[10] In many of the Vanishing Cream advertisements, the Cold Cream and Extract were also listed at the bottom of the page, although mention of the Extract was dropped in 1914, as consumers had already begun to follow the directions of advertisers and buy specialized rather than general use products. A 1916 ad, featuring a woman surrounded by five adoring men, comes close in form and content to the Woodbury's advertising. "What a man looks for in a girl," the headline read, and the opening sentence told all: "The one thing men have expected of women, from time immemorial, is a fresh, clear complexion." Ten smaller headlines, four small drawings of beautiful women and beautiful hands, and a great deal of copy completed this full-page and rather lengthy advertisement.[50]

In 1916, Pond's made a decision to begin an advertising campaign for the Cold Cream as well. Feeling skeptical about advertising both creams and doubling advertising expenses, Pond's followed the Thompson agency's suggestion that they advertise the two creams together. The Women's Editorial Department then developed an enormously successful campaign based on the idea that "every normal skin needs *two* creams." The copy explained the different functions of the two creams and the ways in which they complemented each other. "Read why one cream cannot do both," the advertisements instructed.[51] Thompson launched the series with full-page advertisements; the most expensive cost $8000, or almost twice as much as the next most expensive, and was placed in the *Ladies' Home Journal.*[52] The result, as the Thompson company account histories claim, was that "women now buy two creams where they formerly bought one, and Pond's creams have become one of the most successful examples on record of two products sold together."[53] During the first six months of the campaign, Cold Cream sales increased by 27 percent and Vanishing Cream sales increased by 60 percent. The copywriters continued the same basic campaign for the next eight years until sales began to fall off, with decreases during 1921, 1922, and 1923.[54] The Thompson Company then launched an investigation, including 500 personal interviews, 1800 mail questionnaires, a canvass of a rural community, and two weeks of Women's Editorial Department employees selling behind the counters of department stores. Results showed that the competition, which numbered over 320 products of the same price and "more or less the same merit," had grown more fierce.[55]

The investigations also revealed a paradox for the advertising agency. Women had become so convinced of the importance of taking care of their skin—and of the importance of social status through consumption—that they began to purchase the more expensive brands rather than Pond's. Pond's suddenly lacked exclusiveness. In effect, Pond's success had led to its potential demise. The Women's Editorial Department had to restore the prominence of the Pond's name in order to revive business. Their next campaign is cited in the company's account history as "one of the most brilliant advertising stratagems ever executed."[56] Endorsements of leading society women, including many prominent women from the United States, three reigning queens of Europe, and six princesses, accompanied the Cold Cream and Vanishing Cream advertising. Running during 1924 and 1925, these endorsements accomplished exactly what Pond's needed: they restored the prestige of the product. During the middle of the Pond's endorsement campaign, in January of 1925, the company experienced its greatest monthly sales in company history.[57] In a typical advertisement from this campaign, the Duchess of Marlborough, formerly Miss Gladys Deacon of Boston, intimated that other American women could have her look, and perhaps her luck, if they only used Pond's. For her, nobility and independence went hand in hand: "The woman of social prominence today," she argued, "guards her complexion too, but not with veils and parasols. Instead she strides through wind and rain and sun and frosty air, her skin exquisitely cared for with Pond's Two Creams."[58] The duchess provided a curious mix of the silk-stocking and the New Woman.

The use of testimonials was nothing new in the advertising world. The Thompson agency had traced their use back to 1893, but they were used even earlier. In 1889, for example, *Godey's Lady's Book* featured an endorsement for Pears Soap provided by abolitionist minister Henry Ward Beecher. "Cleanliness is next to godliness," the ad began.[59] By 1927, the Thompson agency used testimonial campaigns for 9 out of 45 accounts, most of which were held by the Women's Editorial Department.[60] The Pond's endorsements continued for more than 30 years, extending by the early 1950s to 46 countries and 18 languages.[61] From the start, the *Ladies' Home Journal* figured first on the list of magazines in which the advertisements would be placed.[62] In the case of the Pond's campaign, the Women's Editorial Department was most enthusiastic about feminist and suffragist Alva Belmont's endorsement, as described in the previous chapter. "There were wild scenes at headquarters," one disapproving onlooker remembered, when the women saw Belmont's coveted autograph. "Work stopped," she recalled, "everybody gathered round and cheered the wangler; three executives kissed her." Belmont endorsed her $1000 check to the National Woman's Party, the onlooker commented further, "to be used in the movement to abolish the Republican and Democratic Parties and divide the country politically into Men and Women."[63] Most of the women endorsers who followed Belmont in the series, though, were strictly society women, not feminists. Perhaps the women copywriters would have preferred more women like Belmont, or more women like themselves, but apparently they felt some pressure to remain conservative with their choices; at one point they reported that they felt compelled to restrict any divorced women from the Pond's endorsements.[64]

The Women's Editorial Department developed the argument that the Pond's endorsers, who included Queen Marie of Romania, Mrs. Reginald Vanderbilt, and Mrs. Condé Nast, led such active lives that their skin needed special care, care that only Pond's creams could provide. "What American woman would dare challenge the authority of Queen Marie of Romania, the most beautiful queen of Europe?" the account history asks.[65] Readers might not have challenged her authority, but they might have questioned whether royalty really would have purchased Pond's creams when they could afford any cream they wanted. Advertisers always had to deal with the credibility issue in using testimonials. "I would absolutely not be a party to having a person say that he used a thing if he did not," Stanley Resor declared at a company meeting. He continued, however, by arguing that "if you can bring about a situation where you can get the product used quickly instead of gradually over a long period of years, I think it is legitimate to use it."[66] To ensure credibility—or at least cover their tracks—the Women's Editorial Department had these women sign an agreement stating they would use the product. Pond's then sent each woman supplies of the creams every three months, "with a letter reminding her she promised to use this."[67]

One Thompson company survey revealed that many consumers had doubts about the veracity of the endorsements. A 1927 investigation in Columbus, Ohio, provided responses from a group of 164 women, 119 housewives and 45 business women. Their comments about the endorsements ranged from approval to amusement to disbelief. One imagined that the women must have provided the endorsements in order to receive "vast sums for pet charities"; another claimed that the women didn't really use the product; a third argued that the women must have believed in the product or they would not have endorsed it. One respondent stated that she could understand an actress needing and accepting money for an endorsement, but a queen?[68]

In the world outside the Thompson agency and the *Ladies' Home Journal,* some critics tried to draw consumers' attention to the flaws in the advertisements and in the products. M.C. Phillips, who wrote *Skin Deep: The Truth About Beauty Aids* in 1934, took the *Journal* and the Thompson agency to task. Phillips argued that J. Walter Thompson products, while relatively harmless, unlike many other terribly unsafe beauty aids, were far too expensive. The *Journal,*

Her Grace in the priceless gown of ivory lace she wore at her wedding, which took place in the historic gardens of Blenheim Palace

The Duchess of Marlborough
formerly MISS GLADYS DEACON *of* BOSTON

Tells how to keep the Tradition of Beauty

"Down to the modern woman," she says, "the social leaders of every age thought that beauty, like a delicate hothouse flower, must be sheltered. The woman of social prominence today guards her complexion, too, but not with veils and parasols. Instead she strides through wind and sun and frosty air, her skin exquisitely cared for with Pond's Two Creams."

And the Duchess adds, "For my own part I never have to think of windburn and chapping. These two Creams keep my complexion so vigorous and healthy."

Blenheim House—the palace of the Dukes of Marlborough near Oxford—was erected in 1705

These Two Creams are chosen by women of high rank to cleanse and protect their delicate skins

HER GRACE, the Duchess of Marlborough, is one of the first peeresses of England. An American by birth, noted for her great beauty, she is the charming mistress of historic Blenheim Palace, manor of the Dukes of Marlborough for over two hundred years.

Among the women of her exalted station traditions play a large part, and the beauty of exquisite grooming is a matter of daily etiquette which none would dream of neglecting. The Duchess herself particularly stresses the need of a clear, fresh skin and points out how much more easily one can preserve this youthfulness today.

Soothing, Refreshing, Cleansing

For cleansing your skin and keeping it fresh and supple use Pond's Cold Cream. Upon retiring and often during the day pat it generously over face, throat and hands. Let it remain a few moments. Its oils, fine and pure, penetrate the pores, removing all dust and powder. Wipe off. Repeat and finish with a dash of cold water. If your skin is dry leave some of the Cream on after the bedtime cleansing.

A Soft Tone, A Delicate Protection

For that exquisite last touch of loveliness for evening and when you go out, apply Pond's Vanishing Cream lightly over face, throat, hands. It not only adds a smooth and glowing finish and takes your powder naturally, but it gives you, no matter how delicate your skin may be, unfailing protection from the irritation caused by dry winds, dust and soot.

Free Offer: *Mail this coupon for free sample tubes of Pond's Two Creams with instructions.*

THE POND'S EXTRACT COMPANY, DEPT. W
107 HUDSON STREET, NEW YORK.

Please send me free tubes of Pond's Two Creams.

Name _____

Street _____

City _____ State _____

Through the use of testimonials, advertisers promised to meet women's longings for social status, beauty, and wealth through consumption. (*Ladies' Home Journal,* September 1927, p. 49) she argued further, had no concern that the product had worth or accomplished what it promised; the magazine rested its faith with the manufacturers and their promises. In fact, according to Phillips, the *Ladies' Home Journal* protested in the 1920s against changes in the Food and Drug Act, changes which would have provided further consumer protection against the fraudulent claims of advertisers.[69]

Whether women's magazine readers believed all the claims of the advertisements, they did respond positively to the campaign. Sales of the Vanishing Cream increased by 45 percent in the first year of the campaign; sales of the Cold Cream increased by 17 percent.[70] The advertisers kept track of which endorsements brought in the most coupon replies. Alva Belmont was not on the list. Gloria Gould, described as "the leader of the smart younger set in New York," ranked high in the fiction magazines and the more "youthful woman's circulations." Lady Diana Manners, described as "the most beautiful woman of English aristocracy," ranked highest in motion picture magazines and in younger circulations. The Duchesse de Richelieu ranked higher in what was called the "conservative" *Ladies' Home Journal.* The Princesse Marie de Bourbon, on the other hand, "was excellent in every type of circulation."[71]

According to these advertisements, Pond's, like Woodbury's, existed for every woman, queen or commoner, society matron or housewife. All women share something in the world of advertising, but again it is not social class, political caste, patriarchal oppression, or life experience; instead, it is soap or perhaps vanishing cream. Products become women's common denominator, and women of wealth become the most respected authority figures. This shift in the advertising premise, from concentrating on the product to concentrating on the user, created not only artificial needs for new products but also artificial relationships among women and artificial definitions of womanhood. It tapped into deep insecurities women felt about their attractiveness, their appeal, their social worth. It promoted consumption as a cure-all for women's inarticulate longings and furthered the cultural prescription that men find pleasure in doing, women in being. The Women's Editorial Department staff may initially have responded to rather than created this aspect of the middle-class culture, the idea that women acted only with the object of then being acted upon, but by creating seemingly educational national advertisements with national power, these copywriters also helped make national the concept that consumption and subsequent male attention, rather than work, political action, or self-awareness, defined woman's true realm.

"To sell a product," argued an advertiser surveying the field from 1920-

1940, "one must sell more than the product; one must sell its use and service, indeed an entire pattern of consumption."[72] This pattern included a composite woman as much marked by social class, race, and interests as by her desire to shop. A shopper, she had to fit into one of the archetypes of the Woodbury's contest winners or emulate the Pond's society women endorsers. Although a 1923 Thompson consumer investigation provided the results of one-hour or longer interviews with 143 women "in all walks of life," including "homemakers, business women, flappers, grandmas, wealthy and poor, educated and uneducated," for example, the opinions of the poor and of the uneducated did not become part of any advertising campaign. The middle-class woman reigned. *True Story*, a working-class women's magazine that generically referred to its common readers as "Judy O'Gradys," could not generate much advertising revenue until the late 1920s, even though it had a circulation near two million in 1926.[73] In 1929, the Thompson agency finally decided to advertise in *True Story*, recognizing that if the readers did not fit their ideal of women, they did fit their ideal of potential purchasing agents. "*True Story Magazine* circulates the information, or the mis-information pretty widely that we are placing a million dollars worth of business with them," a Thompson company executive reported.[74]

When it came to race and ethnicity, advertisers could and generally did ignore potential consumers in spite of information that these women were in fact purchasing products, even their products. Elizabeth Hoyt, in *The Consumption of Wealth*, a 1928 publication, stated that most of the hostilities toward various ethnic groups could be traced to their "violation of the norms of consumption."[75] The double bind, of course, was that advertisers avoided rather than targeted these groups. The only African-American presence in the *Ladies' Home Journal* during the 1910s and 1920s was an occasional servant and, more frequently, characters in advertisements for Aunt Jemima Pancake Syrup and Cream of Wheat, both of which featured prevalent cultural stereotypes. Aunt Jemima, who sold a cooking product, was an authority on the only thing African-American women could be an authority on in that culture: the food she served to white people. The food industry made the most use of African-Americans, using them as "natural" servants. These advertising personalities were "always clean, ready to serve with a crisp smile, intuitively knowledgeable, and distinctively southern in their spoken words," as Joseph Boskin argues. "They epitomized servility with exceptionally natural cheerfulness."[76] In one advertisement, Aunt Jemima talked about how she left the plantation not to improve her life but instead to make the women readers' lives easier. A second advertisement reminisced about the 1893 World's Fair, where Aunt Jemima served as an exhibit from an alien and undeveloped culture, as a clear counterpoint to the growing white middle class.

A 1913 *Journal* advertisement for the George T. Brodnax Company featured a 25 cent pocket knife with a design on the front of "Nigger Eating Watermelon."[77] The *Journal,* of course, did not act alone in providing racist cultural stereotypes during this period. A 1927 Sears catalogue offered for 45 cents a "Chicken Snatcher," describing it as "one of our most novel toys." This "scared looking negro shuffles along with a chicken dangling in his hand and a dog hanging on the seat of his pants. Very funny action which will delight the kiddies."[78] African-Americans and other ethnic or racial groups had a double task: first to escape the stereotypes of the culture and then to enter the limited archetypes offered in their place, archetypes not incidentally dependent upon economic opportunity and disposable income. Black women had to escape the stereotypes of Aunt Jemima, since physically she represented the antithesis of American womanhood. Obese Aunt Jemima had a dark complexion, wore "Negro clothes" and a head rag, and had large breasts. Next, they had to secure employment that would provide them with the income to buy magazines and their advertised products. Only then would they be included in the definition of womanhood. Unlike white, middle-class women, who received daily invitations to enter the consumer culture, women in underrepresented groups had to get the advertising world to acknowledge that their dollars counted; that was no mean feat.

Advertisers and women's magazines continued to avoid African-Americans as consumers even when their own research indicated that this group did have and exercise purchasing power. In 1919, the J. Walter Thompson agency divided consumers into several classes: "wealthy, upper middle, lower middle, poor, illiterate (negroes or foreigners)," including all African-Americans and all foreign-born residents or citizens in the category of illiterates.[79] A 1925 study, "How Many Homes Does Magazine Advertising Reach?" provided graphs for literacy rates in the U.S. population. The literacy rate for African-Americans over ten years of age, according to the study, had reached 77 percent. Although the study posited that literacy provided the deciding factor, however, they went on to disregard their own statistics. "In order to be conservative," they argued, "we have deducted generous parts from the total of foreign-born whites over ten years of age who can read and write and even larger percentages of the Negro population and all of the Indians and Orientals." They subtracted nine out of ten African-Americans, even though

What memories clustered 'round that little cabin!

Aunt Jemima
Bids Goodbye to the Old Plantation

"I's in town, Honey!"

SOME twenty years after the Civil War, Aunt Jemima bade goodbye to her little cabin home down in Louisiana and went to St. Joseph, Missouri.

There, in a big flour mill, under her supervision, was accomplished the mixing by machinery of all the ingredients in her famous pancake recipe.

So today, by simply adding water to Aunt Jemima Pancake Flour, *everybody* can have *Aunt Jemima pancakes*—the real, old-time Southern pancakes. So rich, so tender and so fine-flavored.

Are *you* having them? Aunt Jemima left the old plantation so that you might.

Your grocer has Aunt Jemima Pancake Flour—also Aunt Jemima Buckwheat Flour for delicious buckwheat cakes.

How to get the funny Rag Dolls
Look on the top of any package of Aunt Jemima Pancake or Aunt Jemima Buckwheat Flour to find out how to get the funny Aunt Jemima Rag Dolls.

Copyright, 1921, Aunt Jemima Mills Company, St. Joseph, Missouri

AUNT JEMIMA PANCAKE FLOUR

Advertisers helped define a gendered identity of consumption that relied on race as a counterpoint. African-American women provided products to make the lives of white women

---

"many of the more advanced negroes are regular readers of magazines as well as buyers of modern products."[80]

The ability to consume did not form the bottom line for advertisers or for women's magazines, which reflected the racism and ethnocentrism of the

easier, and the consuming woman was not black as much as she was white. (*Ladies' Home Journal,* January 1921, back cover; March 1921, p. 86)

---

culture as much as they promoted it. Over the course of the 1910s and 1920s, advertisers lightened up on stereotypes about certain groups—or perhaps latched onto others—and selected various ethnic groups to target for their ads. Jewish newspapers in large cities, for example, solicited advertisements from the large advertisers, including the Thompson agency. Prejudice against African Americans was the longest lasting. In the teens, the Thompson agency kept track of demographics by listing people according to the following categories: Native white, foreign born, and Negro. By 1920, they had changed to two incongruous but telling categories: families and negroes.[81] In another instance, during a Thompson Women's Editorial Department store investigation, an employee working behind the counter noted that African Americans in particular purchased Woodbury's Violet Soap. "Well, the colored people come in, and just one whiff of it and they cannot resist," she reported.[82] African-Americans, however, did not become a target group for Woodbury's Soap. When the Thompson Company did finally complete a study on African-American consumption patterns, they reported, perhaps to their own surprise, that the women in their study were "distinctly American" in their buying and cooking patterns, "completely removed from southern and slave origins or from the status of the sharecropper."[83]

Not only was the composite consuming woman limited by race, ethnicity, and class status; she was limited as well in her range of interests. According to the advertising copywriters, this woman had few interests aside from home, family, and shopping–and satisfactory home and family lives were intimately connected to proper shopping habits. "Mrs. Wilkins Read the Journal," an article written by a J. Walter Thompson Women's Editorial Department employee, describes the habits of a supposedly typical reader.[84] Mrs. Wilkins goes about her evening chores, cleaning up the dishes and kitchen, unaware that a copy of the *Ladies' Home Journal* had arrived that afternoon. Had she known, she would have hurried through those chores to increase her leisure time with the magazine. Slightly annoyed that her son has leafed through it first, bending the corners and tainting her aesthetic and sensory experience, Mrs. Wilkins finally does sit with her treasured companion and go through it page by page. The advertisements form a central, not a secondary role in her magazine-reading routine. For Mrs. Wilkins, reading the *Journal* advertisements is rather like the late twentieth-century experiences of purchasing through catalogs or home shopping networks on television. She can be a voyeur, staring again and again at the product and the drawings or photographs of lovely women that accompany the products. "Here was a shopping trip through new and endless department stores but with no tired feet and no embarrassment when you looked too long in the cases and the saleslady said, "Can I help you?"[85] Mrs. Wilkins reads the ads, line by line and, certainly, again and again.

The article describes Mrs. Wilkins' day-to-day life. A woman of narrow interests, she went earlier in the week to the women's club to hear a talk on Europe since the war, but really preferred to talk with her neighbor about her preserves. "Europe was far away and her family's stomachs very near," the narrator explains. Mrs. Wilkins apparently has two forms of self-expression: food and clothes. "Without these to think of," the article states, "her mind would have wandered in an unfriendly world."[86] The unfriendly world, for Mrs. Wilkins's or for many other *Journal* readers, would have differed in many ways from their own. It might have been a world where, for example, Mrs. Wilkins's husband did look up as she entered the room, where he gave her something other than an electric grill for Christmas, where he offered her more of a response than "Hmm" when she commented to him about her reading. It might have been a world which valued women's work, answered women's inarticulate longings for sensuality, self-worth, personal and economic autonomy, and provided all women with social recognition. The advertisements and the consumer culture made many promises to women like Mrs. Wilkins, promises to meet their longings, provide those missing pieces. As it turned out, purchasing could provide women with short-term satisfaction in a world indifferent to their needs and desires: a new dress, for example, might temporarily replace the attentions of a distant husband. Of course, it provided no long-term solutions. The advertising culture, more than the culture at large, acknowledged that one of the things that linked women was a pervasive discontent, but it offered no effective means for addressing that discontent other than in a fleeting, ultimately disempowering way. Mrs. Wilkins and others, facing few better prospects, and none more beautifully and seductively packaged, took what was available.

Women found their inarticulate longings for sensuality, financial independence, and emotional fulfillment channeled through what Jackson Lears calls an "unconscious collaboration," rather than a conspiracy.[87] Advertisers, magazine editors, and publishers in the early twentieth century bought as well as sold; they bought the dream, and then they sold it. They believed that advertising was a positive social good, a means of improving the nation's standard of living, a form of education for the masses. "In your hand at this moment you hold one of the finest textbooks of our school—a magazine for women," Stanley Resor informed his employees. "In it, no doubt, you have been reading some of the school's current lessons—the advertisements."[88] Resor argued that advertising had many lessons but one important subject, "the wise spending of money."[89] Spending money, however, is a political as well as a social act, and Resor, Bok, and others knew as well the role that advertising played in creating their fortunes.

In their roles as promoters of the consumer culture, advertisers and magazine writers continually recognized and stressed that women spent the nation's dollars. However, they left out the issue of whose money women spent or who really benefitted from women's consumption patterns. "Perhaps the best way to measure the value which advertising has for an average women," Stanley Resor argued, "is to point out the economic differences between industries established long before advertising became great and those which have grown up within its regime."[90] Resor apparently saw no inconsistency in his statement; women's interests could most readily be gauged by the success of people outside themselves, sometimes their husbands, sometimes their children, sometimes even the growing corporate culture.

According to the *Ladies' Home Journal* and its advertising, women citizens did well to spend men's money and confine their actions largely to those that were not, as Mrs. Wilkins's case showed, "unfriendly." And "unfriendly" increasingly came to be defined as any action that did not aim to please either men or the consumer culture. Appeals for smart dressing, not women's involvement in politics, became cultural imperatives. In a 1916 *Journal* editorial, Edward Bok recounted the divorce case of a man whose wife did not dress appropriately. "My wife does not seem to be able to get it into her head that she shall appear before her husband and children fresh and neat and clean in the morning," the husband complained. "Every morning it is the same thing: a slouchy kimono slipped on over almost nothing, feet in untidy slippers, and her head in one of those detestable boudoir caps, and that none too fresh." The court granted this man a separation rather than a divorce, but Bok's final message provided a warning to all women: "Women be wise!"[91] Another *Journal* writer provided a similar warning: "Make yourself as attractive as possible; keep your house in perfect order; serve his meals as daintily as you can."[92] The cultural imperative was clear: although women did housework, they could not dress the part, for that part had no worth. Their beauty did not come from within; it came through the eyes of others, namely men. And although the products gave women ways to create the facade, beauty remained elusive, always belonging to someone a bit thinner, a bit younger, a bit more refined. As Stephen Fox puts it, advertising in this time projected "a WASP vision of a tasteless, colorless, odorless, sweatless world"; few real women could fit the bill.[93]

Larger social and political issues, even those women readers expressed an interest in, rarely found their way into the *Ladies' Home Journal.* Readers did want more, as they made clear over the suffrage issue and as they let the investigators know in a Thompson Company survey. The highest number of complaints in the survey, interestingly enough, concerned the *Journal*'s lack of coverage of current news.[94] But news was part of that "unfriendly" territory that might interrupt Mrs. Wilkins's domestic life, and the *Journal*, the advertisements it offered, and the larger culture of consumption would tread very gingerly around news. After all, as the Thompson Company put it, "Modern advertising is news."[95] For the *Ladies' Home Journal*, that was as close as it got.

The women in the J. Walter Thompson Women's Editorial Department, providing many of the advertisements in the *Ladies' Home Journal*, lived paradoxical lives. They worked to create advertisements that would encourage other women to consume and to define their lives by consumption. They did so wittingly and well, taking pride in the fact that they wrote educational copy. However, along with the many other copywriters in the industry, they discovered that advertising was part education and part manipulation, and they succeeded best when they explored both avenues. Here the paradoxes emerged. Many promoted ideals of home and family that had not worked or did not exist in their own lives. They expanded the definition of womanhood to include college women and even, upon occasion, working women, but they still relied for the most part on traditional definitions of womanhood, especially in terms of race, social class, and employment status. Through their endorsement campaigns and their beauty advertisements, they acknowledged that, like themselves, other women had inarticulate longings. In linking those longings strictly to consumption, however, they sold their readers short. Women's inarticulate longings for sensuality, independence, and social worth found a voice in these advertising campaigns, forming, like the magazine's advice and fiction, an undercurrent of revolt in a finely packaged and tremendously successful message of accommodation.

Conclusion

God bless our wives, they fill our hives,
with little bees and honey,
They smooth life's shocks, they mend our socks,
But don't they spend the money!

Walter Thompson *Blue Book*, 1909–1910

*F*or roughly a century of corporate capitalist growth in the United States, women have mended socks and smoothed life's shocks—and spent billions of dollars along the way. But the humorous approach generally applied to women's spending obscures its real significance. One of the most remarkable aspects of twentieth-century consumer culture, in fact, is the degree to which women's spending, tremendously important to the national economy, remains depoliticized. When men spend money they commit a political act; when women spend money they commit a social or cultural act. Clever entrepreneurs of the 1980s coopted the feminist slogan "A Woman's Place is in the House–and the Senate," and manufactured t-shirts, refrigerator magnets, and bumper stickers that read, "A Woman's Place is in the Mall." Attempts to politicize or recognize the political nature of women's activities get tied to consumption again and again, and rather than gain additional significance from the power of money, women's economic activity seems, aside from a lasting value in popular humor, to lose cultural significance altogether. The _Ladies' Home Journal_ and its followers succeeded on many counts, but their efforts in this development certainly resulted in one of their most fascinating accomplishments.

By tying middle-class women's inarticulate longings to consumption, the _Journal_, the J. Walter Thompson advertising agency, and the larger consumer culture of the early twentieth century succeeded both in bolstering capitalism and in nurturing patriarchy. _Journal_ editor Barton Currie complained in 1923 of a "world grown gray with materialism," but the _Journal_, as much as any other cultural medium, fostered that development by actively harnessing all social complaints, especially women's complaints, to consumerism. The magazine offered women readers what Fredric Jameson calls mass culture's "compensatory exchange," gratification in exchange for passivity.[1] Women found a voice for many of their interests, longings, and complaints, but in exchange they accepted a definition of womanhood tied to the home and divorced from politics, a definition in which their potential power, including spending power, would be defined as "influence" and their needs would remain subordinate to those of the men and children in their lives. The consumer culture presented a unified and powerful vision of satisfaction not through social change but through consumption.

As female consumers purchased women's magazines and the products advertised in the magazines, they also purchased an enormously important and pervasive underlying message: since men would not change, women could consume, or as the 1990s would have it, "Shop till you drop." The illustration for a 1934 _New Yorker_ cartoon shows a man in a suit knocking on the door of what appears to be a suburban home. A somewhat disheveled housewife answers with one hand on the door and the other hanging on to an unruly child who has left her toys strewn across the walk. "Good morning, Madam," the cartoon reads, "the J. Walter Thompson Company would like to know if you are happily married."[2] Actually, tho J. Walter Thompson agency–and the readers who laughed at the cartoon–assumed that the woman, overwhelmed by her unappreciated household activities, felt less than satisfied with her life. The Thompson investigator really wanted to identify the specific ways in which the woman felt unhappy with her husband or her domestic role. He wanted to explore the difficulties she faced in living with what Jane Addams called the "family claim."[3] Armed with this information, the agency and the *Ladies' Home Journal* could offer the housewife salvation through consumption—and make a great deal of money themselves as she attempted to better her life on their terms.

The Thompson agency and the *Ladies' Home Journal* promised women that soap, rather than attentive or cooperative husbands, would enhance marital happiness; vacuum cleaners, rather than economic analyses of women's and men's work, would improve women's social status. In making such offers, and in couching these offers in the language of choice and social progress, advertisers and women's magazines helped set the limits both on women's demands for change and on cultural expectations of men. For the most part, other than through consumption, these cultural messengers urged women to refrain from attempting to change their own situations, confront men, or alter social relations. And men, who faced few demands to take responsibility for any unhappiness they generated or benefitted from, remained free to pursue their individual and collective privileges. Maud Waddock expressed this sentiment well in a poem published in the *Journal* in 1922.

> If now and then I seem to tire of wedded bliss, I do not seek a divorce nor yet a soul mate's kiss; Ah no, my cure for ennui is safer than that; I find a nifty little shop and buy a hat![4]

At the same time that magazines and advertisers propped up both capitalism and patriarchy by urging "safe" consumer rebellions, they also had to please women readers. In doing so, as this work has demonstrated, they gave voice to what remained, in much of the larger culture, unvoiced. They recognized women's complaints, desires, and dreams. They recognized the value of women's work—or at least claimed to. And once voiced, those complaints and desires may have succumbed to the broad promises of the consumer culture, but that culture would not and could not satiate women's needs. A new hat may have provided a woman with a degree of distance from the things that made her unhappy, but the dissatisfactions arguably lasted far longer than the hat. The consumer culture, always ready, produced another hat or perhaps a whole outfit to offer up the following week or the following month. It did little to satisfy women's real longings, however, which would remain just at or below the surface.

In appealing to these women readers, magazines and advertisers also created something easily identifiable as belonging exclusively to women. A great deal more research needs to be conducted on the power of reading, but women used these magazines to claim some personal space for their own pleasure.[5] Such an act has political significance, especially within the family. Mrs. Wilkins, a character in a story described in Chapter Six, eagerly anticipated her time alone with the *Ladies' Home Journal*; she resented the fact that her son had fingered the magazine first, disturbing her aesthetic experience in touching the pages. As the *Journal* and its advertisers hoped, Mrs. Wilkins used her magazine to plan purchases, choose brand names, and learn household and decorating tips. However, she also found that the *Journal* offered her more than advice on domestic responsibilities. First, it provided her each month with a means of escaping home and family to a dreamworld in which loved ones valued her contributions and catered to her many needs. In her *Journal*-generated daydreams, Mrs. Wilkins could imagine a world populated by men and children who appreciated women's work and women's sacrifices. Second, the magazine served as an ally by validating for her the work she undertook, the choices she made. It did this consciously and well, connecting Mrs. Wilkins to millions of other women, providing for her a gendered identity grounded in an awareness of what women actually accomplished in their homes and for their families.

As it attempted to reach and please those readers, the *Ladies' Home Journal* invested in middle-class white women the most positive values of the culture. As the nation moved away from a rural, community identity and towards an urban, individual identity, it took on the values of the capitalist culture, favoring increased rather than narrowed limits of free enterprise and the unlimited accumulation of individual wealth. But rather than acknowledge that it had lost values, the culture named women their custodians. The *Journal*, for its part, continually reminded its readers that their values, different from those of men, held the family, community, and nation together. And by continually using race, class, and ethnicity as barometers, the magazine reminded these women of what they did not, as well as what they did represent. As Judith Williamson argues about women in contemporary advertising, the *Journal*'s women became a "kind of dumping ground for all the values society wants off its back but must be perceived to cherish."[6]

As it praised these so-called women's values, the *Ladies' Home Journal* revealed a deep cultural fear of men. "It is useless to say that men should not produce what is not honest. They will," wrote Nellie Nearing and Scott Nearing in a 1912 article.[7] Rather than do something about the many excesses men exhibited, however, the magazine urged women to keep men in check largely by remaining subordinate to them. Men made mistakes, large and costly mistakes, but women's influence rather than their power would minimize the effects of those errors. The Nearings concluded that women "are the final arbiters," yet they did not specify how these powerless women could wield such power.[8] Men's values paled in comparison to women's, the *Journal* argued, but in order to maintain their own better values women had to remain subordinate to men. This contradictory task must have proved confusing to a great number of women.

The *Ladies' Home Journal* and the early twentieth-century culture it reflected not only feared men but feared women as well. Magazine writers and editors worried about what women might do with their leisure time if housework became less burdensome. They feared the choices women might make if they thought of themselves rather than others first.[9] While the magazine argued repeatedly that marriage and family life formed the limits of women's natural world, it also revealed a constant preoccupation that if women were not coerced they would make other choices. Family life and marriage, according to many readers and writers in the *Journal*, did not come readily; women needed to be convinced that these institutions, although difficult, provided their own rewards. The Country Contributor entreated to women about their husbands, "Of course you love the poor fellow, though he spoke unkindly to you, though he seemed selfish with his money and unreasonable in his demands upon your strength."[10] She reminded them of what she feared they might, in their emotional meanderings, have forgotten.

The *Ladies' Home Journal* also revealed, try as it might not to, that Mrs. Wilkins and the millions of other magazine readers like her had the potential to look outside the confines of the traditional family and the consumer culture for solutions to their problems. The manner in which it repeatedly mentioned women's supposedly natural values points to an attempt to convince rather than remind women of these values. If women truly shared all the values attributed to them in the *Journal*, they would not need to be reminded of them every month. Like a zoo or nature preserve, women precariously remained the guardians of past values as the culture rapidly moved on.[11]

In trying to maintain the status quo and please women at the same time, the *Ladies' Home Journal* maintained what Antonio Gramsci called popular culture's "unstable equilibrium."[12] The magazine cautioned married women not to seek work outside the home, but revealed their difficulties in securing money from their husbands and making ends meet. It urged women not to seek personal independence, yet revealed that its women writers made their way in the world by pursuing their own paths and by achieving public success. It denied the importance of paid work, while it provided a growing number of women opportunities for employment and economic autonomy. It attempted to curb sexuality at the same time that it revealed that many women experimented with new definitions of appropriate sexual behavior. It simultaneously promoted companionate marriage and exposed the less-than-companionate nature of most marital unions. Finally, the magazine praised women's work while it demonstrated that the culture at large failed to hold that work in high esteem.

The *Ladies' Home Journal* provided that mix in a fairly convincing, aesthetically appealing, and enormously successful way. And while the magazine can be faulted for offering what it could not deliver, few other elements of the culture made better offers: the magazine encompassed gender, class, racial, and national identity, packaged to include solitary leisure and an opportunity to dream of something more. Of course, consumerism was and is a social and cultural choice. Between 1910 and 1930 in the United States, the middle class made the choice to follow the lead of magazines and advertisers and pursue consumer possibilities wholeheartedly. By 1929, consumers in the United States had six billion dollars tied up in installment payments for automobiles, radios, furniture, and other goods now deemed essential.[13] In October of 1929, just after the stock market crash that precipitated the Great Depression, the *Ladies' Home Journal* published its largest issue to date, 272 pages. This issue broke all previous magazine records by generating the greatest advertising revenue of any single magazine in history, offering the greatest number of four-color advertisements, and devoting the greatest amount of magazine space to advertising.[14] As far as the *Journal* was concerned, the Depression would not pose a great threat to women's roles in the household and in the consumer culture. And ideals of middle-class suburban life, increasingly promoted in the *Journal* of the 1910s and 1920s, found what Margaret Marsh calls "literal and figurative" support in New Deal policies and post-depression cultural notions of American life.[15] Women's role as consumers, once established, would ironically become both more pervasive and less conspicuous as the decades wore on.

The *Ladies' Home Journal*, the J. Walter Thompson advertising agency, and the culture at large promoted a definition of womanhood that excluded at least as many women as it included, set the limits as well as the possibilities of women's lives, and made scores of untenable promises. Those who see only the negative in the *Journal* or in the consumer culture, however, might learn something from their successes, however disturbing those successes might seem. To challenge the consumer path American women have followed, the culture must make a better offer—one that also recognizes the nature of women's domestic responsibilities, acknowledges their rights and their wrongs, and appreciates the mysteries of their daydreams.

Notes

Introduction

1. The *Journal* passed the one million circulation mark in 1904. *A Short History of the Ladies' Home Journal* (Philadelphia: Curtis Publications, 1953), 19, from Curtis Publishing Company Papers, Department of Special Collections, Van Pelt-Dietrich Library, University of Pennsylvania. Although women have been and continue to be the primary consumers, historians and economists have too often regarded consumption as an activity of the generic economic man or of the passive female. Early advertisers, however, recognized women as consumers, addressing them in a variety of ways. For discussions about the assumed gender of the mass of consumers, see Joseph Appel, *Growing Up With Advertising* (New York: The Business Bourse, 1940), 128; Roland Marchand, *Advertising the American Dream: Making Way for Modernity, 1920-1940* (Berkeley: University of California Press, 1985), 64–69. For contemporary evaluations of the consumer culture, see Thorstein Veblen, *The Theory of the Leisure Class* (New York: New American Library, 1912), and Robert and Helen Lynd, *Middletown in Transition* (New York: Harcourt, Brace, and Company, 1937). The magazine industry employed an estimated 40,000 professionals in the early twentieth century, according to Mary Ellen Waller-Zuckerman, "'Old Homes in a City of Perpetual Change': Women's Magazines 1890-1916," *Harvard Business Review*, 63 (Winter 1989), 730.

2. Nancy Woloch, "Sarah Hale and the *Ladies Magazine*," in *Women and the American Experience* (New York: Alfred A. Knopf, 1984), 98. On Sarah Josepha Hale, see Woloch generally, 97–112. Barbara Welter's pivotal article, "The Cult of True Womanhood," in *Dimity Convictions: The American Woman in the Nineteenth Century* (Athens: Ohio University Press,

1976), 21–41, made popular the notion of women's separate spheres. On the movement beyond the separate spheres discussion, see Michelle Rosaldo, "The Use and Abuse of Anthropology: Reflections on Feminism and Cross-Cultural Understanding," *Signs*, Vol. 5 (Spring 1980), 389–417; Linda Kerber, "Separate Spheres, Female Worlds, Woman's Place: The Rhetoric of Women's History," *Journal of American History*, 75 (June 1988), 9–39; Ellen Carol DuBois and Vicki L. Ruiz, "Introduction," in DuBois and Ruiz, eds. *Unequal Sisters: A Multicultural Reader in U.S. Women's History* (New York: Routledge, 1990), xi–xvi. The most recent work in this area focuses on the ways in which a separate spheres notion contradicts the experiences of women of color. Aida Hurtado, in "Relating to Privilege: Seduction and Rejection in the Subordination of White Women and Women of Color," *Signs*, Vol. 14 (Summer 1989), 849, argues that there is "no such thing as a private sphere for people of color except that which they manage to create and protect in an otherwise hostile environment."

3. Woloch, 97–112.

4. Carroll Smith-Rosenberg, in *Disorderly Conduct: Visions of Gender in Victorian America* (New York: Alfred A. Knopf, 1985), argues that during the Progressive era, "new generations of managers and professionals arose as problem solvers" (172). While business professionals have been most frequently discussed as the purveyors of new ideals, advertisers were clearly involved in dispensing information and advice to a populace overwhelmed with social and demographic changes. See also Susan Curtis, *A Consuming Faith: The Social Gospel and Modern American Culture* (Baltimore: Johns Hopkins University Press, 1991).

5. Helen Woodward, *The Lady Persuaders* (New York: Ivan Oblensky, 1960), 63.

6. Edward Bok, *A Man From Maine* (New York: Scribner's Sons, 1923), 92.

7. *A Short History of the Ladies' Home Journal*, 1.

8. Bok's column, targeted to women, was subscribed to by 137 newspapers. See David Shi, "Edward Bok and the Simple Life," *American Heritage*, Vol. 36, No. 1 (December 1984), 100.

9. *A Short History of the Ladies' Home Journal*, 15–17. Bok relates that he married Mary Louise Curtis in 1896 in *A Man From Maine* (277). James P. Wood, *Magazines in the United States: Their Social and Economic Influence* (New York: The Ronald Press, 1949), 106.

10. James D. Norris, *Advertising and the Transformation of American Society, 1865–1920* (New York: Greenwood Press, 1990), 9.

11. Classified Advertisement, *Printer's Ink* (January 25, 1917), 111. On *Negro Digest* see John H. Johnson, *Succeeding Against the Odds* (New York: Warner Books, 1989). Johnson, founder of *Negro Digest*, *Ebony*, and *Jet*, borrowed five hundred dollars, using his mother's furniture as collateral, to start *Negro Digest*. Following its enormous popularity, he founded *Ebony* in 1942 to give returning black veterans something to distract them from "the day-to-day combat with racism," 153. On *Essence*, see Ellen McCracken, *Decoding Women's Magazines: From Mademoiselle to Ms.*(New York: St. Martin's Press, 1993), 224–26. *Essence* became viable when publisher Jonathan Blount could demonstrate that the readership had disposable income and represented the "young, inquisitive, acquisitive black women" (Blount, quoted in McCracken, 224). At the time that *Essence* was founded, the *Ladies' Home Journal*, *Good Housekeeping*, and *McCall's* each had over one million readers categorized as minority; *Essence* went after that substantial population (McCracken, 224). *Latina*, targeted toward Latina American women, was founded in 1982 and is described in McCracken as targeting a monied but neglected group (230). Interestingly, according to Bryan Holme, ed. *The Journal of the Century* (New York: Viking Penguin, 1976), 10, John Mack Carter, editor of the *Ladies' Home Journal* from 1965 to 1973, was the first editor to feature a black model on the cover of a mass magazine. Carter was also editor when a group of feminists staged a sit-in at the *Journal* offices in 1970, protesting the traditional approach of the magazine, particularly its

"Can This Marriage Be Saved?" column. See Jean Hunter, "A Daring New Concept: The *Ladies' Home Journal* and Modern Feminism," *NWSA Journal,* Vol. 2, No. 4 (Autumn 1990), 583–602.

12. Richard Ohmann, "Where Did Mass Culture Come From? The Case of Magazines," *Berkshire Review,* 16 (1981), 99; Todd Gitlin, "Prime Time Ideology: The Hegemonic Process in Television Entertainment," *Social Problems,* 26 (Feb. 1979), 251. On the notion of cultural hegemony, see also Raymond Williams, *Marxism and Literature* (New York: Oxford Univ. Press, 1977), and Antonio Gramsci, *Selections from the Prison Notebooks,* ed. Quintin Hoare and Geoffrey Nowell Smith (New York: International Publishers, 1971). A debate among historians about the value of or methods of studying popular culture can be found in "AHR Forum," Lawrence W. Levine, Robin D. G. Kelley, Natalie Zemon Davis, and T. J. Jackson Lears, *American Historical Review,* Vol. 97, No. 5 (Dec. 1992), 1369–1430. Levine argues that the seeming differences within and among modes of popular culture warrant rather than discount their study: "Indeed, it is the very asymmetry and diversity in popular culture that should convince us that it can be used as an indispensable guide to the thought and attitudes of an asymmetrical and diverse people," (1399).

13. Raymond Williams argues that consumers do judge each other based on the purchases they have made; consumption becomes an important form of communication. Raymond Williams, "Advertising: The Magic System," in his *Problems in Materialism and Culture* (London: Verso Editions and New Left Books, 1980), 185. For a review of theories about the nature of consumption, see Gary Cross, *Time and Money: The Making of a Consumer Culture* (London: Routledge, 1993), 155–164.

14. Nancy Cott, *The Grounds of Modern Feminism* (New Haven: Yale University Press, 1987), 1.

15. On the accomplishments of women in homogeneous organizations and the struggles for cross-race or cross-class cooperation during the Progressive era, see Noralee Frankel and Nancy S. Dye, eds., *Gender, Class, Race, and Reform in the Progressive Era* (Lexington: University Press of Kentucky), 1991. Dye, in the introduction, concludes that "Progressive women's sense of female difference, then, often could not overcome the boundaries of race and class," (7).

16. Stuart Hall, "Culture, the Media and the 'Ideological Effect,'" in *Mass Communication and Society,* ed. James Curran, Michael Gurevitch, and Janet Woollacott (Beverly Hills, CA: Sage Publications, 1979), 33–339.

17. Ellen McCracken argues that the reading pattern, due to the structure of the magazines, offers women control over what they read and when they interrupt their reading. It also, however, furthers the likelihood that advertisements will get as much of the reader's attentions as do other parts of the editorial/advertising formula (McCracken, 8).

18. *Good Housekeeping,* imitator of the *Ladies' Home Journal* since its founding in 1885, pulled out ahead of the *Journal* and of *McCall's,* another *Journal* imitator, in the 1960s (Woodward, 183). Confessional magazines, targeted at working-class women, were founded in the 1920s, and by 1927 *True Story* provided a challenge to both the *Journal* and to *McCall's* for first place in national circulation. On confessional magazines, see Eung-Sook Kim, "Confession, Control, and Consumption: The Working-Class Market of *True Story* Magazine," Dissertation, University of Iowa, 1992. Roland Marchand, in *Advertising the American Dream: Making Way for Modernity, 1920–1940* (Berkeley: University of California Press, 1985), 56, points out that the *Journal* offered seminars for copywriters on the *True Story* approach in the late 1920s.

19. On reading against the grain, see Janet Todd, *Feminist Literary History* (New York: Routledge, 1988), 86.

20. Lois Ardery, "Inarticulate Longings," *J. Walter Thompson News Bulletin,* 1924, J. Walter Thompson Company Archives, Duke University Library, Durham, North Carolina.

one *A Profile of the* Ladies' Home Journal

1. David Shi, "Edward Bok and the Simple Life," *American Heritage*, Vol. 36, No. 1 (December 1984), 100.

2. Gary Cross, *Time and Money: The Making of Consumer Culture* (London: Routledge, 1993), 7.

3. On the spread of electricity during this period, see Rayna Rapp and Ellen Ross, "The 1920s: Feminism, Consumerism, and Political Backlash in the United States," in *Women in Culture and Politics: A Century of Change*, ed. Judith Friedlander, Blanche Weisen-Cook, Alice Kessler-Harris, and Carroll Smith-Rosenberg (Bloomington: Univ. of Indiana Press, 1986), 55. Mary Ellen Waller-Zuckerman identifies the literacy rate for the total population at 94 percent in 1920, in "'Old Homes, in a City of Perpetual Change': Women's Magazines, 1890–1916," *Harvard Business Review*, 63 (Winter 1989), 747. Rural free delivery started in 1898, according to Thomas Schlereth, "Country Stores, County Fairs, and Mail Order Catalogues: Consumption in Rural America," in Simon Bronner, ed., *Consuming Visions: Accumulation and Display of Goods in America, 1880–1920* (New York: W.W. Norton, 1989), 369.

4. Sally Stein, "The Graphic Ordering of Design: Modernization of a Middle-Class Women's Magazine, 1914–1939," *Heresies*, 18 (1985), 8–14. Mary Ellen Waller-Zuckerman notes that the *Ladies' Home Journal* was the first magazine to use color printing and was an innovator in the use of two-, three-, and four-color printing. See Waller-Zuckerman, "'Old Homes, in a City of Perpetual Change': Women's Magazines, 1890–1916," 726.

5. On the home as a natural unit of consumption, see Gary Cross, 41. He also discusses the emergence of the field of home economics, linking it to considerations of leisure time activity of both men and women in the early twentieth century.

6. William Leach, "Strategies of Display and the Production of Desire," in Simon Bronner, ed., *Consuming Visions: Accumulation and Display of Goods in America, 1880–1920* (New York: W.W. Norton, 1989), 100, 107.

7. Roland Marchand, *Advertising the American Dream: Making Way for Modernity* (Berkeley: University of California Press, 1985), 156.

8. T. J. Jackson Lears, "From Salvation to Self-Realization," in Richard Wightman Fox and T. J. Jackson Lears, eds., *The Culture of Consumption: Critical Essays in American History, 1880–1980* (New York: Pantheon Books, 1983), 1–38.

9. Salme Steinberg, *Reformer in the Marketplace: Edward W. Bok and the Ladies' Home Journal* (Baton Rouge: Louisiana University Press, 1979), 3.

10. Steinberg, 4.

11. Steinberg, 5.

12. Steinberg, 4. Ellery Sedgwick, *The Happy Professor* (Boston: Little Brown, 1946), 294, quoted in Steinberg, 4.

13. *A Short History of the Ladies' Home Journal* (Philadelphia: Curtis Publications, 1953), 18, Curtis Publishing Company Papers, Department of Special Collections, Van Pelt-Dietrich Library, University of Pennsylvania. Curtis purchased the *Saturday Evening Post* for $1000. On the origins and early development of the *Journal* and the *Post*, see Helen Damon-Moore, *Magazines for the Millions: Gender and Commerce in the Ladies' Home Journal and the Saturday Evening Post, 1880–1910* (Albany, NY: SUNY Press, 1994).

14. Steinberg, xv.

15. *A Condensed Report of the Advertising Conference* (Philadelphia: Curtis Publications, 1915), 8, Curtis Publishing Company Papers, Department of Special Collections, Van Pelt-Dietrich Library, University of Pennsylvania, Philadelphia.

16. *A Condensed Report of the Advertising Conference*, 7.

17. *A Condensed Report of the Advertising Conference*, 10.

18. *A Condensed Report of the Advertising Conference*, 28.

19. Roland Wolesley, *Understanding Magazines* (Ames: The Iowa State University Press, 1977), 26. The average life span of these early magazines was only fourteen months.

20. *A Short History of the Ladies' Home Journal*, 22–23. The magazine featured a beautiful color painting of the Curtis building's dining room, *Ladies' Home Journal* (May 1912), 20.

21. On department stores, see Susan Porter Benson, *Counter Culture: Saleswomen, Managers, and Customers in American Department Stores, 1890–1940* (Urbana: University of Illinois Press, 1986). On African-American women and popular culture, see Sue K. Jewell, *From Mammy to Miss America and Beyond* (London: Routledge, 1993).

22. On the manipulation of consumers, and on the response of department store customers to manipulation, see Benson, 75. Since the records of the *Ladies' Home Journal* no longer exist, it is possible to "read" reader response only through the magazine and through the records of those who worked, directly or indirectly, for the *Journal*. Even contemporary critics of the *Journal* remarked on its reputation among readers. See M. C. Phillips, *Skin Deep: The Truth About Beauty Aids. Safe and Harmful* (New York: The Vanguard Press, 1934), 187.

23. The cover painting is by Harrison Fisher, *Ladies' Home Journal* (March 1914). Ellen McCracken looks at a group of women's magazines from 1981 to 1983, but many of her insights apply to a reading of the early *Journal*. Ellen McCracken, *Decoding Women's Magazines: From Mademoiselle to Ms.* (New York: St. Martin's Press, 1993), 3.

24. "Editor's Personal Page," *Ladies' Home Journal* (March 1914), 1.

25. Rosalind Rosenberg, *Divided Lives: American Women in the Twentieth Century* (New York: Hill and Wang, 1992), 18.

26. On the eugenics movement during this time period, see Dorothy M. Brown, *Setting a Course: American Women in the 1920s* (Boston: Twayne Publishers, 1987), 115–116. On World's Fairs and the development of national ideas about U.S. imperialism in business, see Robert Rydell, "The Culture of Imperial Abundance: World's Fairs in the Making of American Culture," in Simon Bronner, ed., *Consuming Visions: Accumulation and Display of Goods in America, 1880–1920* (New York: W.W. Norton, 1989), 191–216. On the racist attacks against Sears and Montgomery Ward, see Thomas J. Schlereth, "Country Stores, County Fairs, and Mail Order Catalogues: Consumption in Rural America," in Bronner, 372. On Sears and Ward, see also Richard S. Tedlow, *New and Improved: The Story of Mass Marketing in America* (New York: Basic Books, 1990), 259–261.

27. Dorothy Schneider and Carl J. Schneider, *American Women in the Progressive Era, 1900–1920* (New York: Anchor Books, 1993), 98.

28. Nancy S. Dye, "Introduction," in Noralee Frankel and Nancy S. Dye, eds., *Gender, Class, Race, and Reform in the Progressive Era* (Lexington: The University Press of Kentucky, 1991), 3.

29. "Editorial Page," *Ladies' Home Journal* (March 1914), 5–6.

30. "Editorial Page," *Ladies' Home Journal* (March 1914), 5–6.

31. All of the following are from the March 1914 *Ladies' Home Journal*: "Flossie Fisher's Funnies," 43; C. Durand Chapman, "Self-Made Pictures for the Children's Rooms," 42; Emelyn Coolidge, M.D., "Traveling With a Baby in Winter," 72; W. W. Klein, M.D., "Do Warts and Moles Result in Cancer?" 70; Emelyn Coolidge, M.D., "Young Mother's Guide," 60; Marion Harris Neil, "My Best Recipe," 71; Harriet Whitaker, "The Housewife Who Wants to Economize," 40; "Unique School Parties Where Eats are the Thing," 46.

32. All of the following are from the March 1914 *Ladies' Home Journal:*Frances Duncan, "The Old Back-Yard Fence," 44; Ekin Wallick, "How You Can Furnish a Five-Room Apartment for $300," 41; "What Other Women Have Found Out About Economy in the Kitchen," 50.

33. All of the following are from the March 1914 *Ladies' Home Journal:* Alice Long, "What I See on Fifth Avenue," 28; Ida Cleve Van Auken, "May I Trim Your Hat?" 64; "The New Spanish Dresses," 29; "And the Little Things of Dress," 31. For special patterns see *Ladies' Home Journal* (March 1914), 64–68, 93–104. Edward Bok complains about French fashions, Edward Bok, "Editorial," *Ladies' Home Journal* (April 1914), 5.

34. "What Can I Do? How Can I Make Money and Stay at Home?" *Ladies' Home Journal* (March 1914), 34.

35. "What 35,000 Girls Have Told Me," *Ladies' Home Journal* (March 1914), 54.

36. Una Nixson Hopkins, "The New Girls' Camp," *Ladies' Home Journal,* (March 1914), 11.

37. On the youth culture, see Paula Fass, *The Damned and the Beautiful: American Youth in the 1920s* (New York: Oxford University Press, 1977); Peter Filene, *Him/Her Self* (Baltimore: Johns Hopkins University Press, 1986).

38. "The Ideas of a Plain Country Woman," *Ladies' Home Journal* (March 1914), 36; "How I Won My Two Daughters-In-Law, By the Woman Herself," 69.

39. William Leuchtenburg, *The Perils of Prosperity, 1914–1932* (Chicago: Univ. of Chicago Press, 1958), 162.

40. Courtney Ryley Cooper, "A Man Who is Casting Out Divorce: How Kansas City Has Tried to Solve the Problem," *Ladies' Home Journal* (March 1914), 20.

41. Elaine Tyler May, *Great Expectations: Marriage and Divorce in Post-Victorian America* (Chicago: University of Chicago Press, 1980), 118–19.

42. Annie Russell, "The Tired Business Man at the Theater," *Ladies' Home Journal* (March 1914), 56.

43. On popular amusements and racial discourse, see David Nasaw, *Going Out: The Rise and Fall of Public Amusements* (New York: Basic Books, 1993). According to Nasaw, "To the extent that racial distinctions were exaggerated on stage, social distinctions among 'whites' in the audience could be muted," (2). Nasaw places these popular amusements in a continuum of defining American culture as "white." Whiteness, for the audience, became an important reference point for inclusion–and for exclusion. Not incidentally, the Ku Klux Klan reemerged at this same time, boasting 100,000 followers by 1921 (Brown, 21).

44. The amount of money Americans spent on amusements and recreation increased by 300 percent during the 1920s, according to Dorothy Brown, 10. See also Kathy Peiss, *Cheap Amusements: Working Women and Leisure in Turn-of-the-Century New York* (Philadelphia: Temple University Press, 1986).

45. The column on religion in this issue also focused on divorce. Preacher Lyman Abbott concluded that divorce was too easily attained, "an approach to the paganism of ancient Rome" Lyman Abbott, "How Do You Explain These Things?" *Ladies' Home Journal* (March 1914), 23.

46. "That Reminds Me: Bright Things of All Times That People Have Laughed Over," *Ladies' Home Journal* (March 1914), 2.

47. Dorothea Pearson Greene, "My Experiences With My Servants," *Ladies' Home Journal* (March 1914), 38.

48. Zona Gale, "You and Me: A Story of Love that Moves Mountains," *Ladies' Home Journal* (March 1914), 21, 84–87.

49. Gale, 86.

50. Gale, 86.

51. On the realities of women workers' lives during this period, see Alice Kessler-Harris, *Out to Work: A History of Wage-Earning Women in the United States* (New York: Oxford University Press, 1982). Paula Giddings, in *When and Where I Enter: The Impact of Black Women on Race and Sex in America* (New York: Bantam, 1984), explores the race and class issues faced by black women struggling to improve their lives.

52. "My Pretty Young Daughter: A Young Girl's Dreams at 19 and How I Met Them: By Her Mother: Her First Experience With a Bestseller," *Ladies' Home Journal* (March 1914), 14.

53. *Ladies' Home Journal* (March 1914), front cover.

54. Brown, 19.

55. Frederick Lewis Allen, *Only Yesterday* (New York: Harper & Row, 1952), 73, quoted in Brown, 102.

56. Brown, 153. On undergraduate life for women, see Paula Fass.

57. Lillian Faderman, in her *Odd Girls and Twilight Lovers: A History of Lesbian Life in Twentieth-Century America* (New York: Penguin, 1991), discusses how the focus on Freudian notions of sexual expression allowed some experimentation not only with heterosexuality but with bisexuality as well. See Chapter Three, "Lesbian Chic: Experimentation and Repression in the Twenties," 62–92.

58. Mary Ellen Waller-Zuckerman, "'Old Homes in a City of Perpetual Change': Women's Magazines, 1890–1916," *Harvard Business Review* (Winter 1989), 736. According to Ellen McCracken, the process of "tailing" fiction into the advertising became common as early as the 1890s (65).

59. Post-Toasties advertisement, *Ladies' Home Journal* (March 1914), 35.

60. Susan Strasser, *Satisfaction Guaranteed: The Making of the American Mass Market* (New York: Pantheon, 1989), 52.

61. Wizard advertisement, *Ladies' Home Journal* (March 1914), 59. See also, in same issue, Quaker Oats advertisement, 71; Welch's advertisement, 51.

62. Campbell's Soup advertisement, *Ladies' Home Journal* (March 1914), 69; Pompeiaan Massage Cream advertisement, 52.

63. Woodbury's Soap advertisement, *Ladies' Home Journal* (March 1914), 63.

64. Nestle advertisement, *Ladies' Home Journal* (March 1914), 54.

65. Wizard advertisement, *Ladies' Home Journal* (March 1914), 59.

66. Gold Dust Twins advertisement, *Ladies' Home Journal* (March 1914), 56.

67. On minstrel shows and vaudeville, see Dorothy and Carl Schneider, *American Women in the Progressive Era, 1900–1920* (New York: Anchor Books, 1993), 7; E. W. Kemble, "The Snowmen and the Pickaninnies," *Ladies' Home Journal* (December 1911), 21; "What Eugenics is Revealing," *Ladies' Home Journal* (October 1918), 94.

68. Cream of Wheat advertisement, *Ladies' Home Journal* (September 1921), inside cover.

69. "General Platform on Johnson and Johnson Baby Powder," Account Histories, 1926, 16, from J. Walter Thompson Company Archives, Duke University Library, Durham, North Carolina.

70. See Carroll Smith-Rosenberg, "Captured Subjects/Savage Others: Violently Engendering the New American," *Gender & History*, Vol. 5, No. 2 (Summer 1993), 177–195; and David R. Roediger, *The Wages of Whiteness: Race and the Making of the American Working Class* (New

York: Routledge, 1991). Anthropologists are also looking at the ways in which race informs the lives of white women. See Ruth Frankenberg, *White Women, Race Matters: The Social Construction of Whiteness* (Minneapolis: University of Minnesota Press, 1993). And from a literary/historical perspective, see Toni Morrison, *Playing in the Dark: Whiteness and the Literary Imagination* (Cambridge, MA: Harvard University Press, 1992), and Dana D. Nelson, *The Word in Black and White: Reading "Race" in American Literature, 1638–1867* (New York: Oxford University Press, 1992).

71. Schneider and Schneider, 116.

72. Marchand, 202.

73. "12 Presents for Stout Colored Women," *Ladies' Home Journal* (May 1927), 26; Cartoon (January 1918), 4. On the Mammy image in American culture, see Jewell, Chapter Three.

74. Schneider and Schneider, 26.

75. Ruth Schwartz Cowan, *More Work for Mother: The Ironies of Household Technology from the Open Hearth to the Microwave* (New York: Basic Books, 1983), 124.

76. On changes in the use of color in the 1920s, see Neil Harris, *Cultural Excursions: Marketing Appetites and Cultural Tastes in Modern America* (Chicago: Univ. of Chicago Press, 1990), 185; Stuart Ewen, *Captains of Consciousness: Advertising and the Social Roots of the Consumer Culture* (New York: McGraw Hill, 1976). The cover is from a painted created for the *Ladies' Home Journal* by Gertrude A. Kay. The title page lists ten new Latin American countries specifically and mentions "the rest" of Latin America as well.

77. Little work has been done on the internationalization of advertising, particularly concerning gender. On the J. Walter Thompson Agency's entry into Argentina, see Russell Pierce, *Gringo Gaucho: An Advertising Odyssey* (Ashland, OR: Southern Cross Publishers, 1991).

78. Barton W. Currie, "Editorial: The Filth Uplifters," *Ladies' Home Journal* (August 1924), 20; Elizabeth Frazer, "The Rising Tide of Voters," ibid, 21.

79. Alice Ames Winter, "The Technic of Being a Club Woman," *Ladies' Home Journal* (August 1924), 6, 111. On women's essential nature, see Rosalind Rosenberg, *Divided Lives: American Women in the Twentieth Century* (New York: Hill and Wang, 1992), 63–101.

80. This issue of the *Journal* also contained an article outlining the work of the League of Women Voters Elizabeth Frazer, "The Rising Tide of Voters," 21. "I have no patience with those of you who think you are too good to soil your hands with the dirt of politics," she argues. The *Journal* favored the LWV rather than the National Woman's Party.

81. Barbara M. Solomon, *In the Company of Educated Women: A History of Women and Higher Education in America* (New Haven, CT: Yale University Press, 1985), 63–64.

82. McCracken notes that decades later, when publishers marketed whole publications to high school and college women, they remarked on the young women's brand loyalty and purchasing power (43). *Seventeen*, founded in 1944, told advertisers that its readers, "branded for life," spent their "scholar dollars" at the beginning of each school year.

83. All of the following are from the August 1924 *Ladies' Home Journal*. "A Hat from Paris for Every College Girl," 122; Clothes Necessities and Treats for School and College Girls," 24–25; "Lingerie for the College Girl and Her Admiring Younger Sister," 53; "The College Girl's Everyday Clothes," 54; "A Clothes Budget for the College Girl," 63, 65–66. In "The Rising Tide of Voters," 21, Elizabeth Frazer also emphasizes the need for women to get college girls involved in political work at a young age.

84. Carroll Smith-Rosenberg, *Disorderly Conduct: Visions of Gender in Victorian America* (New York: Alfred A. Knopf, 1985), 177, 282.

85. Dorothy Bromley, "Feminist–New Style," *Harper's* (October 1927), cited in Brown, 24.

86. Quoted in Brown, 138.

87. "Wouldn't You Like to Join Us in Making Extra Money? The Ladies' Home Journal Girls' Club," *Ladies' Home Journal* (August 1924), 131.

88. Helpful Books column, *Ladies' Home Journal* (August 1924), 134.

89. On the standardization of department store layouts, see Benson, 44. On the ways in which advertising messages predominate in women's magazines of the later twentieth century, see McCracken, *Decoding Women's Magazines*, and Gloria Steinem, "Sex, Lies & Advertising," *Ms.*, Vol. 1 (July/August 1990), 18–28.

90. Lever Brothers advertisement, *Ladies' Home Journal* (August 1924), 62.

91. All of the following advertisements are from the August 1924 *Ladies' Home Journal*: Cavalier Furniture, 141; Armstrong Linoleum, 28; Sunkist Lemons, 71; Swan's Down Cake Flour, 68; Odorono, 94; Cutex, 31; Beech Nut, 77; Hoover, 145; Post Bran Flakes, 97; Johnson & Johnson Baby Powder, 110. The process described here occurred, as Roland Marchand puts it, when advertisers evolved from salesman to confidantes, providing advice and offering themselves as working on the same side as the consumers. See Marchand, 13.

92. Harry Tipper, Harry L. Hollingworth, George Burton Hotchkiss, and Frank A. Parsons, *Advertising: Its Principles and Practice* (New York: The Ronald Press, 1915), 505.

93. Loring A. Schuler, Speech to J. Walter Thompson Company, 8–9, from J. Walter Thompson Company Archives, Duke University Library, Durham, North Carolina.

94. All of the following are from the August 1924 *Ladies' Home Journal* "Let a Salad Make the Meal," *Ladies' Home Journal* (August 1924), 102; Kraft advertisement, 112; McCracken, 38. According to McCracken, the "tripartite system" of the magazine cover, the purchased advertisements, and the covert advertisements mean that over 95 percent of contemporary women's magazine content is advertising (4).

95. See, for example, Armstrong Linoleum advertisement, *Ladies' Home Journal* (August 1924), 28; Wallpaper Manufacturers Association advertisement, 109; Sanitas Modern Wallcovering advertisement, 120; Congoleum advertisement, inside front cover.

96. Beech Nut canned spaghetti advertisement, *Ladies' Home Journal* (August 1924), 77; Campbell's Soup advertisement, 27; Hawaiian Pineapple advertisement, 47; Lux Soap advertisement, 98–99; Paramount Pictures advertisement, 37.

97. Schneider and Schneider, 5.

98. On the history of automobile marketing, see Tedlow, particularly Chapter One, "The All-Consuming Century: The Making of the American Emporium," 3–21. On automobiles and women, see Virginia Scharff, *Taking the Wheel: Women and the Coming of the Motor Age* (New York: The Free Press, 1991).

99. Scharff, 82, 84, 85.

100. For automobile ads, see for example Ford Motor Company advertisement and Overland Auto ad, *Ladies' Home Journal* (August 1924), 49, 45; Odorono Deodorant advertisement, 94; Gainsborough Hairnet advertisement, 46.

101. Linit advertisement, *Ladies' Home Journal* (August 1924), 107; Beech Nut Canned Spaghetti advertisement, 77.

102. The following stories are all from the August 1924 *Ladies' Home Journal*: Elinore Cowan Stone, "The Phantom Wagon Train," 18–19, 84, 87; Christine Jade-Slope, "Miss Miggs of Monte Carlo," 26, 119; Royal Brown, "Priscilla is Put in Her Place," 12–13, 93.

two *Housekeeping*

1. Although the readers' letters no longer exist, and the magazine did not regularly document the numbers of letters received, Bok acknowledged in 1915 that readers sent in almost half a million letters in 1914. See Edward Bok, "Editorial," *Ladies Home Journal* (1915), 1. Bok and subsequent editors may have been relieved when advertisers took over some of the letter-answering promised to *Journal* readers. The changing structure of the magazine in the 1920s suggests that the *Journal* provided fewer direct responses to readers through letters and more indirect responses through the text of the magazine.

2. The word "Home" was part of a cover drawing rather than the intended title, which was *The Ladies' Journal and Practical Home Housekeeper*. Reader responses to the first issue, however, in December of 1883, all spoke of the *Ladies' Home Journal*, so Curtis kept that as the name of the magazine. *A Short History of the Ladies' Home Journal* (Philadelphia: Curtis Publications, 1953), 15, Curtis Publishing Company Papers, Department of Special Collections, Van Pelt-Dietrich Library, University of Pennsylvania.

3. Theodore Peterson, *Magazines in the Twentieth Century* (Urbana: Univ. of Illinois Press, 1964), 11. When Bok was feeling particularly uncomfortable with his role as a woman, he went to ask a friend, New York writer Isabel Mallon, to take over. When she asked who Isabel Mallon was, Bok replied, "You are." Mallon then conducted the column for sixteen years. Her last act, according to legend, was to dictate an answer to a reader's letter. *A Short History of the Ladies' Home Journal* (Philadelphia: Curtis Publications, 1953), Curtis Publishing Company Papers, Department of Special Collections, Van Pelt-Dietrich Library, University of Pennsylvania.

4. Salme Harju Steinberg, "Reformer in the Marketplace: Edward W. Bok and the *Ladies' Home Journal*, 1889–1919," Ph.D. Dissertation, Johns Hopkins University, 1971, 170. See also her book, *Reformer in the Marketplace: Edward W. Bok and the Ladies' Home Journal* (Baton Rouge: Louisiana State University Press, 1979).

5. Steinberg, "Reformer in the Marketplace," 169. According to Peterson, three stenographers worked full-time to answer the letters to Ruth Ashmore (Peterson, 11).

6. Edward Bok, editorial, *Ladies' Home Journal* (Sept. 1906), 1.

7. Edward Bok, letter to Christine Frederick, January 13, 1914, Christine Frederick Papers, Schlesinger Library, Radcliffe College. Bok also sent letters to other magazines and reportedly found their responses inferior to those of his staff. Steinberg, "Reformer in the Marketplace," 169. In a letter from Edward Bok to Christine Frederick, he offers to pay her for her letters to readers and to supply the stationery, March 18, 1912 (Christine Frederick Papers).

8. In 1892, the *Journal's* circulation was 700,000. By 1910, the rate had risen to 1,950,000. David Shi, *The Simple Life: Plain Living and High Thinking in American Culture* (New York: Oxford Univ. Press, 1985), 183.

9. Christopher Wilson, "The Rhetoric of Consumption: Mass-Market Magazines and the Demise of the Gentle Reader," in Lears and Fox, eds., *The Culture of Consumption: Critical Essays in American History, 1880–1980* (New York: Pantheon Books, 1983), 54.

10. Steinberg, "Reformer in the Marketplace," 169.

11. On Bok and civic education, see Steinberg, "Reformer," 190–91. Steinberg discusses Bok's resistance to suffrage in "Reformer," 190.

12. Edward Bok, quoted in Shi, *The Simple Life*, 183. Historians have concluded that advice literature tells us more about the people writing the advice than it does about the people reading it. On advice literature, see David Mechling, "Advice to Historians on Advice to Mothers,"

Journal of Social History, 9 (Fall 1975), 44–63; R. Gordon Kelly, "Literature and the Historian," *American Quarterly*, 26 (May 1974), 141–59. On the need for advice from outside the family, see Robert S. Lynd and Helen Lynd, *Middletown: A Study in American Culture* (New York: Harcourt, Brace, and Co., 1929), 150–63. Incidentally, in March of 1923, 355 of 9200 homes in Muncie subscribed to the *Journal*, and 1152 others bought it at the newsstand (*Middletown*, 163).

13. For a description of the simple life philosophy, see David Shi's book, and for another version of his discussion of Bok and the *Ladies' Home Journal*, see David Shi, "Edward Bok and the Simple Life," *American Heritage*, 36 (Dec. 1984), 100–109.

14. Edward Bok, "What is the Simple Life?" *Ladies' Home Journal* (Sept. 1911), 6. Edward Bok, "The Simple Life Amid Plenty," *Ladies' Home Journal* (Nov. 1905), 18.

15. Katherine Fishburn, *Women in Popular Culture: A Research Guide* (Westport, CT: Greenwood Press, 1982), 18, 19, 222.

16. Blanche Merritt, "What I See in New York," *Ladies' Home Journal* (Jan. 1912), 33.

17. Edward Bok quoted in Shi, *The Simple Life*, 184.

18. Edward Bok, "The Simple Life Amid Plenty," *Ladies' Home Journal* (Nov. 1905), 18.

19. Robert S. Lynd and Helen Lynd, *Middletown: A Study in American Culture* (New York: Harcourt, Brace, and Co., 1929), 175. See also footnote to this discussion, in which the Lynds explore the question of home washer versus laundry service.

20. David Shi, "Edward Bok and the Simple Life," 102.

21. On how Bok's simple life philosophy is related to a larger social philosophy, see David Shi, "Edward Bok and the Simple Life," 100–109. Teddy Roosevelt, in a 1907 *Journal* article, argued that excessive materialism was the greatest threat to the nation. He may truly have believed this; he may at the same time have believed that manufacturing and consumerism were the mainstays of the nation and the keys to future success. The simple life philosophy, as Shi argues, sanctioned capitalism with reassurances that many things would stay the same over time. (Shi, 103).

22. Zona Gale quoted in Dolores Hayden, *The Grand Domestic Revolution: A History of Feminist Designs for American Homes, Neighborhoods, and Cities* (Cambridge: MIT Press, 1981), 70. On working women's cooperative housing efforts in Chicago, see Joanne Meyerowitz, *Women Adrift: Independent Wage Earners in Chicago, 1890–1930* (Chicago: University of Chicago Press, 1988).

23. Gilman discussed in Dorothy Schneider and Carl Schneider, *American Women in the Progressive Era, 1900–1920* (New York: Anchor Books, 1993), 30.

24. Charlotte Perkins Gilman, "Why Cooperative Housekeeping Fails," *Harper's Bazaar*, 41 (July 1907), 629, quoted in Cowan, 107.

25. Bellamy Clubs and Gilman's novel described in Harvey Levenstein, *Revolution at the Table: The Transformation of the American Diet* (New York: Oxford University Press, 1988), 65, 70. See "What Diantha Did," in Ann J. Lane, ed., *The Charlotte Perkins Gilman Reader* (New York: Pantheon Books, 1980).

26. Levenstein, 31.

27. Ruth Schwartz Cowan, *More Work for Mother: The Ironies of Household Technology from the Open Hearth to the Microwave* (New York: Basic Books, 1983), 107; see generally Cowan, 73–79.

28. On women's work leaving the household, see Cowan, Levenstein, and Juliet Schor, *The Overworked American: The Unexpected Decline of Leisure* (New York: Basic Books, 1992). Quote from Schor, 102. Cowan on separate spheres, 69.

29. To see how the *Journal* handled the issue of cooperative housekeeping, see the following *Ladies' Home Journal* articles: "One Kitchen Fire for 200 People," (September, 1918), 97; Charles Harris Whitaker, "How Are We Going to Live: Will the Kitchen Be Outside the Home?" (January 1919), 66; Carey Edmunds, "The New Home Without a Dining Room: A Bit Startling at First Until You Begin to Get Used to It," (February 1919), 3; Zona Gale, "Shall the Kitchen in Our Home Go?" (March 1919), 35, 50; Elizabeth Farnwell and Charles E. White, "Communal Homes for Business Women," (June 1919), 3, 74.

30. Nancy Cott, *The Grounding of Modern Feminism* (New Haven, CT: Yale Univ. Press, 1987), 162, 174. On developments in food production and the resulting demands on women, see Schneider, 28, and Levenstein. Levenstein argues that only with the development of one-course meals, such as pizza, could the home delivery of food find a viable market (70).

31. Susan Strasser, *Never Done: A History of American Housework* (New York: Pantheon Books, 1984), 81. Her fourth chapter, "At the Flick of a Switch," describes this process in detail. Although the use doubled, however, electric consumption was not extremely high. Strasser points out that consumers in 1970 bought thirteen times the electricity that customers in 1930 bought.

32. Strasser, 80–81. Most families, according to Strasser, did not buy these luxury items but limited themselves to lights, irons, vacuum cleaners, and curling irons.

33. See Joann Vanek, "Time Spent in Housework: Market Work, Homework and the Family," *Scientific American* (November 1974) 82–89.

34. Mae McGuire Telford, "For the Girl Who Lives Alone," *Ladies' Home Journal* (Nov. 1918), 76.

35. See "The Girl Who Lives in a Flat," *Ladies' Home Journal* (March 15, 1911), 38; this article included recipes for a month's meals. See also "To Board or Not to Board: By One of the Girls," *Ladies' Home Journal* (Nov. 1916), 56, in which a young woman told how she turned her iron upside down and cooked on it—evidence that one could keep house "even in a two by four."

36. "When Girls Live in Groups," *Ladies' Home Journal* (Nov. 1918), 26.

37. See Mrs. Stickney Parks, "Girls' Affairs: Should This Engagement Be Broken?" *Ladies' Home Journal* (March 1912), 29; Mrs. Laura Hathaway, "What Girls Ask," *Ladies' Home Journal* (March 15, 1911), 51.

38. "Little House Problems," *Ladies' Home Journal*, (July 1911), 40. See also Kelly Snead McDonald, "What's New in the Shops for the Little House," *Ladies' Home Journal*, (Oct. 1911), 56; Ethel Peyser, "Housekeeping in the Little House," *Ladies' Home Journal*, (May 1923), 36, 44.

39. "Little House Problems," *Ladies' Home Journal* (Jan. 1, 1911), 47. See also Alice Van Leer Carrick, "Housekeeping in the Little House," *Ladies' Home Journal* (March 1923), 41, 211.

40. "The Best Heating for a Little House," *Ladies' Home Journal* (March 1, 1911), 80.

41. The April 1914 issue of the *Journal* includes the following articles. "A Home To Build in the Country," 97; "Three Houses You Would Like to Live In," 99; "The Six-Room Bungalow," 100; "A Country Home With Three Sleeping Porches," 103.

42. The new column is entitled "Practical Home Economics," *Ladies' Home Journal* (Sept. 1911), 83. The first month's topic, the servant problem, suggests that the intended audience is neither the young working woman nor the woman living in the bungalow.

43. "I'm Glad My Servant Left," *Ladies' Home Journal* (Nov. 1918), 28.

44. "The Ideas of a Plain Country Woman," *Ladies' Home Journal* (April 1914), 28.

45. Christine Frederick, "Will the Eight-Hour Home Assistant Work Out?" *Ladies' Home Journal* (Sept. 1919), 47. See also Zona Gale's articles during the same year: "The Eight-Hour Home Assistant," (April 1919), 35; "Is Housework Pushing the Birth Rate Down?" (May 1919), 41.

46. "What Other Women Have Found Out," *Ladies' Home Journal* (March 1, 1911), 52.

47. "Pretty Girl Questions," *Ladies' Home Journal* (Jan. 1, 1911), 36.

48. Mrs. Julian Heath, "How Housewives Waste Money," *Ladies' Home Journal* (Feb. 1913), 73, 82. Quote, 73.

49. The Chautauqua Circuit, named after two small lakes in Michigan and the community surrounding them, became a travelling lecture show with afternoon and evening programs. Biographical information from Christine Frederick, "Autobiography," from Christine McGaffey Frederick Papers, Schlesinger Library, Radcliffe College. On Christine Frederick's life and work, see Susan Strasser, *Never Done*, 214–19; Glenna Matthews, *Just a Housewife: The Rise and Fall of Domesticity in America* (New York: Oxford University Press, 1987), 18–71, 187, 188; Delores Hayden, *The Grand Domestic Revolution* (Cambridge, MA: MIT Press, 1985), 285, 286; Martha Banta, *Taylored Lives: Narrative Productions in the Age of Taylor, Veblen, and Ford* (Chicago: University of Chicago Press, 1993), 335–340; Mary Ellen Zuckerman and Mary Carsky, "Contributions of Women to U.S. Marketing Thought: The Consumers' Perspective, 1900–1940," *Journal of the Academy of Marketing Science* (Fall 1990), 313–18.

50. Christine Frederick, autobiographical data, Christine Frederick Papers, Schlesinger Library, Radcliffe College. The Advertising Women of New York, still in existence, houses its papers at the Schlesinger Library, Radcliffe College.

51. Christine Frederick obituary, *Los Angeles Times*, April 8, 1970, from Christine Frederick Papers, Schlesinger Library, Radcliffe College.

52. Christine Frederick obituary, *Ad Libber*, Advertising Women of New York, Spring 1970, from Christine Frederick Papers, Schlesinger Library, Radcliffe College.

53. Christine Frederick, *Household Engineering: Scientific Management in the Home* (Chicago: American School of Home Economics, 1915).

54. Frederick, *Household Engineering*, 7–9. See also Frank Gilbreth and Ernestine Gilbreth Carey, *Cheaper By the Dozen* (New York: Thomas Y. Crowell Co., 1948). The father in this story, an industrial engineer and scientific management expert, filmed some of the family activities, including washing dishes and having tonsils pulled, to study and evaluate their efficiency.

55. Banta, 4.

56. Banta, 13–14.

57. The series of articles in the *Journal* all bear the heading, "The New Housekeeping."

58. Christine Frederick, *The New Housekeeping* (Garden City, NY: Doubleday, Page & Co., 1913); *Household Engineering*, n.p. In a letter to Christine Frederick, Edward Bok thanked her for the two inscribed copies she sent him. One, he related, would be kept in the office, the other would stay home with Mrs. Bok (Christine Frederick Papers, Schlesinger Library, Radcliffe College).

59. Frederick, *Household Engineering*, 16.

60. "Tenth Annual Conference of the Advertising Department," Oct. 29–31, 1913, Curtis Publishing Company Papers, Department of Special Collections, Van Pelt-Dietrich Library, University of Pennsylvania.

61. Edward Bok, editorial, *Ladies' Home Journal* (Sept. 1916), 34.

62. "How the New Housekeeping Works Out," *Ladies' Home Journal* (Oct. 1916), 52.

63. Mary Waterstone Stuart, "What's the Value of Your Time?" *Ladies' Home Journal* (Feb. 1920), 208.

64. Christine Frederick was, notes Mary Ellen Zuckerman, "an enthusiastic proponent of consumption," Zuckerman, "Creating Mrs. Consumer: The Career of Mrs. Christine Frederick," paper presented at the Organization of American Historians Conference, April 1994, 7. Frederick called consumption ". . . the greatest idea that America has to give to the world; the idea that workmen and the masses be looked upon not simply as workers or producers, but as consumers," (Frederick, *Selling Mrs. Consumer*, quoted in Zuckerman, 7).

65. "A Talk I Had With My Husband," *Ladies' Home Journal* (March 1918), 42. Ida M. Tarbell, in *The Business of Being a Woman*, 1912, presented a similar argument: "The theory that the man who raises corn does a more important piece of work than the woman who makes it into bread is absurd. The inference is that the men alone render useful service. But neither man nor woman eats these things until the woman has prepared it."

66. Christine Frederick, "The Business Side of Canning," *Ladies' Home Journal* (June 1920), 159.

67. Barbara Ehrenreich and Deirdre English, *For Her Own Good: 150 Years of the Experts' Advice to Women* (Garden City, NY: Anchor Press, 1978), 146–148; Sharon Hartman Strom, *Beyond the Typewriter: Gender, Class, and the Origins of Modern American Office Work, 1900–1930* (Urbana: University of Illinois Press, 1992), 7–63; Strasser, 213–222. Sue Ainslie Clark and Edith Wyatt, in *Making Both Ends Meet: The Income and Outlay of New York Working Girls* (New York: Macmillan, 1911), discussed the benefits of scientific management for women's paid work (223–270). Scientific management, they wrote, "makes an art of all work" (230).

68. Frederick, *The New Housekeeping*, viii.

69. According to Salme Steinberg, readers were receptive to reforms which "could smooth consciences but [which] would not fundamentally disrupt the pattern of their lives" (2). On the hidden violence against women in this time period see *Heroes of Their Own Lives*.

70. Frederick, "The New Housekeeping," *Ladies' Home Journal* (Sept. 1912), 13, 70–71.

71. Frederick, "The New Housekeeping," *Ladies' Home Journal* (Oct. 1912), 20.

72. Frederick, "The New Housekeeping," *Ladies' Home Journal* (Nov. 1912), 19–20.

73. See, for example, "How I Made My Country Kitchen More Efficient," *Ladies' Home Journal* (July 1913), 20.

74. Frederick, *The New Housekeeping*, 101, quoted in Zuckerman, "Selling Mrs. Consumer," 6.

75. Christine Frederick, *Household Engineering*, 384–386. Another frequent argument was that women had to be careful not to be too obsessive with their cleaning: "Nothing drives men, especially boys, from a home more quickly, and the secret of the loss of influence of home and mother with growing boys lies frequently in such conditions." (Bertha M. Terrill, *Household Management* [Chicago: American School of Home Economics, 1907] 198. See also Christopher Lasch, *Haven in a Heartless World: The Family Besieged* [New York, 1977]).

76. Adriana Santa Cruz and Viviana Erazo, *Compropolitan: El orden transnacional y su modelo femenino* (Mexico City: Editorial Nueva Imagen, 1980), 22, quoted in McCracken, 4.

77. McCracken discusses what she calls the tripartite system of women's magazines, which includes the cover, the most important advertisement of all; the covert ads, which are disguised as editorial matter or hidden in some way; and the purchased advertisements, which occupy the majority of pages in most women's magazines. "Understood as this tripartite system, advertising occupies up to 95% of the space in some women's magazines" (McCracken, 4).

78. Karl Harriman, letter to Christine Frederick, Sept. 22, 1915, Christine Frederick Papers, Schlesinger Library, Radcliffe College.

79. Theresa Walcott, letter to Christine Frederick, Feb. 27, 1919, Christine Frederick Papers, Schlesinger Library, Radcliffe College.

80. Christine Frederick, letter to W. E. Loucks, California Packing Company, April 3, 1919, Christine Frederick Papers, Schlesinger Library, Radcliffe College.

81. Theresa Walcott, letter to Christine Frederick, Aug. 27, 1919, Christine Frederick Papers, Schlesinger Library, Radcliffe College.

82. Christine Frederick, "You and Your Laundry," 1920, Christine Frederick Papers, Schlesinger Library, Radcliffe College.

83. Christine Frederick, "Come Into My Kitchen," 1922; "Frankfurters as You Like Them," 1931; "Hershey's Favorite Recipes," 1937. Christine Frederick Papers, Schlesinger Library, Radcliffe College.

84. Frederick set up the Applecroft Home Experiment Station in 1915. Christine Frederick, letter to McGray Refrigerators, July 7, 1921, Christine Frederick Papers, Schlesinger Library, Radcliffe College.

85. Christine Frederick, *Selling Mrs. Consumer* (New York: The Business Bourse, 1929).

86. Frederick, *Selling Mrs. Consumer*, 17.

87. Frederick claimed she started the Applecroft Home Experiment Station at Edward Bok's urging. Christine Frederick, *Selling Mrs. Consumer* (New York: The Business Bourse, 1929), 167.

88. Frederick, *Selling Mrs. Consumer*, 334.

89. Sullivan W. James, "Selecting the New Floor," *Ladies' Home Journal* (Feb. 1920), 195–96, 198.

90. "For the Woman Who's Too Busy to Listen to the Reams of Advice," *Ladies' Home Journal* (May 1922), 164.

91. Mabel Jewett Crosby, "The Kitchen Cabinet as a Step Saver," *Ladies' Home Journal* (Jan. 1924), 80.

92. Sellers advertisement: "No Wonder the Neighbors Were Curious," *Ladies' Home Journal* (Feb. 1924), 177.

93. See Christine Frederick, "The New Housekeeping," *Ladies' Home Journal* (July 1913), 20, and Hoosier Kitchen Cabinet advertisements (December 1911), 54; February 1920, 157; Napanee Dutch Kitchen advertisement (December 1921), 149. Other ads promised women that if they used particular products they would have more free time for shopping or other leisure activities. See Libby's advertisement (March 1920), 57; P & G Soap, (October 1916), 75; Hoosier (November 1916), 97; Paramount Pictures advertisement (August 1925), 39.

94. Seller's advertisement, *Ladies' Home Journal* (June 1921), 94; Paramount Pictures advertisement (May 1921), 30; General Electric advertisement (June 1924), 204.

95. "The New Era in Housework," *Ladies' Home Journal* (June 1929), 24–25, 152.

96. James McGovern, "The American Woman's Pre–World War I Freedom in Manners and Morals," in *Our American Sisters: Women in American Life and Thought*, ed. Jean Friedman and William G. Slade (Boston: Allyn and Bacon, 1973), fn., 254.

97. Editorial, *Journal of Home Economics*, Vol. 19, No. 4 (April 1927), 46, quoted in Levenstein, 156. On the development of home economics, see Glenna Matthews, *Just a Housewife* Laura Shapiro, *Perfection Salad: Women and Cooking at the Turn of the Century* (New York: Henry Holt and Co., 1986) and Susan Strasser, *Never Done*.

three *Women's Paid Work*

1. See, for example, Edward W. Bok, Editorial, *Ladies' Home Journal* (Sept. 1911), 5.

2. Clara E. Laughlin, "Her Sister in the Country Who Wants to Come to the City and Make Her Way," *Ladies' Home Journal* (Aug. 1911), 16.

3. Rosalind Rosenberg, *Divided Lives: American Women in the Twentieth Century* (New York: Hill and Wang, 1992), 18.

4. On the rise of the corporation, see Maurine W. Greenwald, *Women, War, and Work: The Impact of World War I on Women Workers in the United States* (Westport, CT: Greenwood Press, 1980), xiv. On women clerical workers see Margaret Gibbons Wilson, *The American Woman in Transition: The Urban Influence, 1870–1920* (Westport, CT: Greenwood Press, 1979), 115. On women in department stores and in the telephone industry see Greenwald, 11. On chain stores see William Leuchtenberg, *The Perils of Prosperity, 1914–1932* (Chicago: Univ. of Chicago Press, 1958), 192.

5. Greenwald, 121.

6. Greenwald, 197.

7. Wilson, 114.

8. Barbara Klaczynska, "Why Women Work: A Comparison of Various Groups, Philadelphia, 1910–1930," *Labor History*, 17 (Winter 1976), 73–87. On composition of female clerical labor force, see Wilson, 121.

9. Nancy Cott, *The Grounding of Modern Feminism* (New Haven, CT: Yale Univ. Press, 1987), 132.

10. Cott, 129.

11. On increases in the number of married women workers, see Dorothy Brown, *Setting a Course: American Women in the 1920s* (Boston: Twayne Publishers, 1987), 97–98; Klaczynska, 82; Wilson, 121; Frank Stricker, "Cookbooks and Law Books: The Hidden History of Career Women in Twentieth-Century America," *Journal of Social History*, 10 (Fall 1976), 8–13; Lois Scharf, *To Work and to Wed: Female Employment, Feminism, and the Great Depression* (Westport, CT: Greenwood Press, 1980), 12.

12. Brown, 185.

13. Cott, 181.

14. Lorine Pruette, "The Married Woman and the Part-Time Job," *Annals of the Academy of Political and Social Science*, 143 (May 1929), 301, in Cott, 184.

15. "Personal Experiences of Mothers," *Ladies' Home Journal* (Feb. 1914), 28. "The Girl at the Head of Her Class," *Ladies' Home Journal* (Jan. 1912), 24. William Sadler, M.D., "College Women and Race Suicide," *Ladies' Home Journal* (April 1922), 29, 58. "Believe *Me*: Some Things Are Changing For Us Girls," *Ladies' Home Journal* (Oct. 1914), 54.

16. "Personal Experiences of Mothers," *Ladies' Home Journal* (Feb. 1914), 28.

17. The Country Contributor, "The Ideas of a Plain Country Woman," *Ladies' Home Journal* (March 1911), 32; (November 1918), 44.

18. William S. Sadler, M.D., "The Girl at the Head of Her Class," *Ladies' Home Journal* (Jan. 1912), 24.

19. The Country Contributor, "The Ideas of a Plain Country Woman," *Ladies' Home Journal* (February, 1911), 38.

20. "Believe *Me*: Some Things Are Changing For Us Girls," *Ladies' Home Journal* (Sept. 1914), 42.

21. "Believe *Me*: Some Things Are Changing For Us Girls," *Ladies' Home Journal* (Oct. 1914), 54.

22. On the youth culture, see Paula Fass, *The Damned and the Beautiful: American Youth in the 1920s* (New York: Oxford University Press, 1977).

23. The Country Contributor, "The Ideas of a Plain Country Woman," *Ladies' Home Journal* (February 1911), 38.

24. "Why I Did Not Marry," *Ladies' Home Journal* (Aug. 1911), 12, 41.

25. Kate E. Turner, "What Shall I Do After High School?" *Ladies' Home Journal* (April 1912), 10.

26. Irene Vandyck, "How Can I Really Learn a Profession?" *Ladies' Home Journal* (Aug. 1919), 39–49, 42.

27. Margaret T. Grayson, "The Girl Behind the Typewriter: What She Should Do to Earn the Highest Rewards in Her Work," *Ladies' Home Journal* (May 1915), 16.

28. Cott, 130.

29. According to Dorothy Brown, the feminization of clerical work occurred quickly from 1910 through to 1930, when women filled over 52 percent of the clerical positions in the United States (Brown, 95). Quote from Dorothy Schneider and Carl J. Schneider, *American Women in the Progressive Era, 1900–1920* (New York: Anchor Books, 1993), 15.

30. Cott, 132–33. See Kate E. Turner, "What Shall I Do After High School?" *Ladies' Home Journal* (April 1912), 20. Ruth Neely, "Where Your Job May Lead," *Ladies' Home Journal* (Sept. 1916), 29. Ethel Spalding Slater, "Vocational Guidance," *Ladies' Home Journal* (July 1921), 21.

31. "Money-Making Ways: New Ways That Girls and Women Have Found to Make Money," *Ladies' Home Journal* (Jan. 1912), 3.

32. Laura Lockwood, "Can a Girl Work Her Way Through College?" *Ladies' Home Journal* (Sept. 1912), 36. Elizabeth Sears, "Through College Without Means," *Ladies' Home Journal* (Aug. 1919), 45.

33. On women's part-time work, see also Christine Terhune Herrick, "The Way a College Girl Found to Make Money," *Ladies' Home Journal* (March 15, 1911), 20.

34. Mary Hamilton Talbott, "Women Who Have Blazed New Trails: Through the Forest of Men's Work Once Believed Closed to Their Sex," *Ladies' Home Journal* (Feb. 1917), 5. Alice Ames Winter, "The Policewoman of Policewomen," *Ladies' Home Journal* (July 1921), 27, 62. "The Real New Woman Who Answers the Question 'What's the Matter With Women?'" *Ladies' Home Journal* (Sept. 1914), 3.

35. Margaretta Tuttle, "Serving in Other Women's Homes," *Ladies' Home Journal* (Jan. 1917), 20, 58. Margaretta Tuttle, "From Hunger to Power: First of Several Stories Told By Women Who Have Succeeded in Business," *Ladies' Home Journal* (Oct. 1923), 12, 166, 169–172, 175.

36. "What I Went Through in Trying to Get a Position," *Ladies' Home Journal* (March 15, 1911), 15–16. On women who succeeded without meeting fairy godmother types, see Ann Bradley, "The World of Busy Women," *Ladies' Home Journal* (Feb. 1916), 33; "Going Girls and Winning Women," *Ladies' Home Journal* (June 1918), 106; Theresa Hunt Walcott, "What One Woman Has Done," *Ladies' Home Journal* (March 1, 1911), 2–3; "Is the Lady of the House In?" *Ladies' Home Journal* (Sept. 1916), 24.

37. "What it Means to Be a Department Store Girl," *Ladies' Home Journal* (June 1913), 8.

38. Martha Keeler, "The Girl Who Works," *Ladies' Home Journal* (April 1913), 66–67. Mrs. Laura Hathaway, "What Girls Ask," *Ladies' Home Journal* (March 15, 1911), 51.

39. Rosenberg, 23.

40. Beth Bailey, *From Front Porch to Back Seat: Courtship in Twentieth-Century America* (Baltimore: Johns Hopkins University Press, 1988), 22–23.

41. Harriet Brunkhurst, "The Business Girl and the Confidence Man," *Ladies' Home Journal* (March 15, 1911), 26. See also Mrs. Laura Hathaway, "What Girls Ask," *Ladies' Home Journal* (July 1911), 55.

42. "My Greatest Experience as a Girl," *Ladies' Home Journal* (Jan. 1913), 43–44. "My Greatest Experience as a Girl," *Ladies' Home Journal* (April 1913), 20, 90.

43. A. B. Alumna, "Does the Girls' College Destroy the Wife: A Frank Confession of Why One College Girl Has Not Married," *Ladies' Home Journal* (June 1916), 26.

44. See Carroll Smith-Rosenberg, "The New Woman as Androgyny," in her *Disorderly Conduct: Visions of Gender in Victorian America* (New York: Alfred A. Knopf, 1985), 245–296.

45. The series "These Modern Women," edited by Freda Kirchway, started on December 1, 1926. Quote from Brown, 41. The series was reprinted by the Feminist Press: Elaine Showalter, ed., *These Modern Women: Autobiographical Essays From the Twenties* (Old Westbury, NY: Feminist Press, 1978).

46. Laura H. Carnell, "Women Must Understand Their Job," *Ladies' Home Journal* (April 1927), 39, 70.

47. Edward W. Bok, Editorial, *Ladies' Home Journal* (Sept. 1911), 5.

48. Edward W. Bok, Editorial, *Ladies' Home Journal* (Jan. 1917), 7.

49. Edward W. Bok, "Death's New Clutch on Women," *Ladies' Home Journal*, 24 (Oct. 1907), 8.

50. Carroll Smith-Rosenberg, "The Hysterical Woman: Sex Roles and Role Conflict in Nineteenth-Century America," in her *Disorderly Conduct: Visions of Gender in Victorian America*, 200.

51. Smith-Rosenberg, "The Hysterical Woman," 215.

52. "Should Married Women Work?" *Ladies' Home Journal* (April 1916), 66.

53. Edward W. Bok, Editorial, *Ladies' Home Journal* (Jan. 1, 1911), 6.

54. Edward W. Bok, Editorial, *Ladies' Home Journal* (Dec. 1916), 36; (Jan. 1917), 28.

55. "Things Women Keep Quiet About," *Ladies' Home Journal* (Oct. 1913), 21, 86; (Dec. 1913), 22. "How I Lost My Attraction to My Husband," *Ladies' Home Journal* (March 1, 1911), 18.

56. Jean Friedman and William G. Slade eds., *Our American Sisters: Women in American Life and Thought* (Boston: Allyn and Bacon, 1979), 233–34. Nancy Woloch, *Women and the American Experience* (New York: Alfred A. Knopf, 1984), 274. Brown, 122.

57. Rinehart, "A Home or a Career?" *Ladies' Home Journal* (April 1922), 25, 53.

58. "The Ideas of a Plain Country Woman," *Ladies' Home Journal* (Sept. 1916), 36.

59. Ruth Scott Miller, "Divorce and Child Crime," *Ladies' Home Journal* (March 1927), 26, 67, 168. For two opposing viewpoints, see Frederick F. Van de Water, "A Divorce for Every Marriage," *Ladies' Home Journal* (February 1927), 20, 160, and Albertine R. Valentine, "The Married College Woman and Divorce," *Ladies' Home Journal* (March 1911), 20.

60. Grace Nies Fletcher, "Fifty-Fifty Finance," *Ladies' Home Journal* (June 1927), 42, 184, 187. Edward W. Bok, Editorial, *Ladies' Home Journal* (June 1927), 38.

61. The Plain Country Woman's identity was revealed in December of 1918, several months after her death, when Edward Bok and other editors paid her a tribute. "She lived amid the most simple surroundings, and she kept her life as simple and sweet as were her writings. She was intensely a home woman and her dominating passion was the glorification of the simplest home task. It is this message that she preached so consistently and so effectively in

her writings, and the good that she did cannot be estimated in words." *Ladies' Home Journal* (December 1918), 20.

62. Juliet Virginia Strauss, "The Ideas of a Plain Country Woman," *Ladies' Home Journal* (April 1918), 30; (January 1911), 30; (March 1918), 30.

63. Strauss, "The Ideas of a Plain Country Woman," *Ladies' Home Journal* (January 1911), 31; (February 1917), 40; (March 1911), 34.

64. Strauss, "The Ideas of a Plain Country Woman," *Ladies' Home Journal* (May 1911), 28; (January 1911), 31; (April 1918), 30.

65. Strauss, "Why Women Become Morbid and How They Can Get Over It," *Ladies' Home Journal* (November 1911), 18.

66. Strauss, "The Ideas of a Plain Country Woman," *Ladies' Home Journal* (March 1917), 38.

67. Strauss, "The Ideas of a Plain Country Woman," *Ladies' Home Journal* (June 1914), 34; (April 1911), 32.

68. Strauss, "The Ideas of a Plain Country Woman," *Ladies' Home Journal* (April 1914), 42; (January 1911), 31; (April 1914), 42.

69. Strauss, "When a Man Thinks of a Woman as a Pretty Fool," *Ladies' Home Journal* (January 1912), p. 16.

70. Strauss, "The Ideas of a Plain Country Woman," *Ladies' Home Journal* (January 1911), 31; (March 1911), 34; (February 1914), 30.

71. Strauss, "The Ideas of a Plain Country Woman," *Ladies' Home Journal* (April 1911), 32.

72. Strauss, "The Ideas of a Plain Country Woman," *Ladies' Home Journal* (September 1918), 40.

73. Strauss, "The Ideas of a Plain Country Woman," *Ladies' Home Journal* (May 1914), 40.

74. Strauss, "The Ideas of a Plain Country Woman," *Ladies' Home Journal* (May 1911), 28.

75. Strauss, "The Ideas of a Plain Country Woman," *Ladies' Home Journal* (June 1911), 30.

76. Strauss, "The Woman Who Frets Over Things: The Men We Love and the Men We Marry," *Ladies' Home Journal* (October 1911), 8.

77. Strauss, "Why Women Become Morbid and How They Can Get Over It," *Ladies' Home Journal* (November 1911), 18.

78. Strauss, "The Ideas of a Plain Country Woman," *Ladies' Home Journal* (April 1918), 30; (June 1911), 30; (June 1918), 34.

79. Strauss, "The Ideas of a Plain Country Woman," *Ladies' Home Journal* (November 1918), 44.

80. N. Margaret Campbell, "Restful Rooms for Business or Professional Men and Women," *Ladies' Home Journal* (Feb. 1920), 204, 206. "A Community Children's Place," *Ladies' Home Journal* (Feb. 1919), 97.

81. All of the following are from the November 1916 *Ladies' Home Journal:* "Women Who Have Blazed New Trails: Through the Forest of Men's Work Once Believed Closed to Their Sex," 5; "Going Girls and Winning Women," 106; "The Real New Woman Who Answers the Question 'What's the Matter With Women,'" 3; "Is the Lady of the House In?" 24; "Going Girls," 106. Another article in this issue described how a woman began an insurance business and wrote policies for women after she had been widowed and left without insurance, "How I Saved Other Wives From Trouble," *Ladies' Home Journal*, 31.

82. Ruth Evelyn Dowdell, "Starting a Business in Your Home," *Ladies' Home Journal* (Aug. 1920), 87.

83. "How I Helped My Husband Make More Money," *Ladies' Home Journal* (July 1914), 1.

84. "Women in Business," *Ladies' Home Journal* (Aug. 1928), 22, 38. "Jill of All Trades," *Ladies' Home Journal* (Feb. 1929), 10, 172.

85. "Wanted: A Good Housekeeper," *Ladies' Home Journal* (Aug. 1918), 47.

86. Lawrence W. Levine, in "The Folklore of Industrial Society: Popular Culture and Its Audiences," *American Historical Review*, Vol. 97, No. 5 (December 1992), 1369–1399, prefers the terms "cultural creation" and "cultural reception" to "cultural production" and "cultural consumption," 1399. The asymmetry and diversity he sees in various forms of popular culture can, as in this instance, be found in a single source, the *Ladies' Home Journal.*

87. Libby's advertisement, *Ladies' Home Journal* (April 1920), 57.

88. Libby's advertisement, *Ladies' Home Journal* (May 1920), 57; (June 1920), 57.

89. Anne Warnick, "You Went to France: Now What Did it Do to You?" *Ladies' Home Journal* (Sept. 1919), 43, 108. On feminist men and housework, see Stricker, 11.

90. Hotpoint advertisement, *Ladies' Home Journal* (March 1923), 217.

four *Stoves for Women, Votes for Men*

1. "Depends on How You Look at It," *Ladies' Home Journal* (February 1916), 8.

2. Nancy S. Dye, introduction to Dye and Noralee Frankel, eds., *Gender, Class, Race, and Reform in the Progressive Era* (Lexington: University Press of Kentucky, 1991), 1–9; quotes from 1, 2. See also Seth Koven and Sonya Michel, eds., *Mothers of a New World: Maternalist Politics and the Origins of Welfare States* (New York: Routledge, 1993).

3. Dye, 4.

4. On Bok's progressive causes, see Walter Davenport and James C. Derieux, *Ladies, Gentlemen, and Editors* (Garden City, NY: Doubleday and Co., 1960), 174–185. Helen Woodward, *The Lady Persuaders* (New York: Ivan Oblensky, 1960), 75.

5. Jane Addams, "Need a Woman Over Fifty Feel Old?" *Ladies' Home Journal* (October 1914), 7.

6. Edward Bok, Letter to Maurice Hewlett, Jan. 1, 1908, Bok Letterbooks, Philadelphia.

7. On fears about women choosing self-development over self-sacrifice, see Nancy Cott, *The Grounding of Modern Feminism* (New Haven, CT: Yale Univ. Press, 1987), 39.

8. Cott, 30.

9. Nancy Woloch, *Women and the American Experience* (New York: Alfred A. Knopf, 1984), 355.

10. On women's voting patterns, see Woloch, 355, and Cott, 101–102.

11. On woman suffrage, see Aileen Kraditor, *Ideas of the Woman Suffrage Movement, 1890–1920* (New York: Columbia Univ. Press, 1965); William O'Neill, *Everyone Was Brave: A History of Feminism in America* (Chicago: Univ. of Chicago Press, 1971); Nancy Cott, *The Grounding of Modern Feminism* (New Haven: Yale, 1987); Leila J. Rupp and Verta Taylor, *Survival in the Doldrums: The American Women's Rights Movement, 1945 to the 1960s* (New York: Oxford, 1987), 4–6, 38–39. On the antisuffrage movement, see R. Susan Goldberg, "The Women Who Opposed Suffrage: Female Anti-Feminism in the Early Twentieth Century United States," presented at the 7th annual New England Women's Studies Association Conference, 1988; Manuela Thurner, "'Better Citizens Without the Ballot': American Antisuffrage Women and Their Rationale During the Progressive Era," *Journal of Women's History*, Vol. 5, No. 1 (Spring 1993), 33–60. The National Association Opposed to Woman Suffrage journal was called *The Woman's Protest* and was published from 1911 to 1918.

12. *The Woman's Protest* (April 1917), 15, quoted in Cott, 61.

13. Anna Howard Shaw, quoted in Thurner, 34.

14. Rosalind Rosenberg, *Divided Lives: American Women in the Twentieth Century* (New York: Hill and Wang, 1992), 57.

15. Goldstein, 8.

16. Edward Bok, Editorial, *Ladies' Home Journal*, 38 (May 1, 1911), 6.

17. Elizabeth McCracken, "Woman's Civic Work better Done Without Suffrage," *The Woman's Protest* (January 1916), 16, quoted in Thurner, 47.

18. "Do You, as a Woman, Want to Vote?" *Ladies' Home Journal* (Jan. 1, 1911), 17.

19. "Do You, As a Woman, Want to Vote?" 17.

20. Edward Bok, Editorial, *Ladies' Home Journal* (Feb. 1, 1911), 5.

21. Is Mrs. Goddard Alone in her Position That Woman Suffrage in Colorado is a Failure?" *Ladies' Home Journal* (April 1, 1911), 6.

22. Edward Bok, Editorial, *Ladies' Home Journal* (March 1, 1911), 44. During the following year, Bok reported that in 1911, despite and perhaps because of the boycott, the *Journal* experienced the largest increase in its history, 350,000 additional subscribers. Edward Bok, "Editor's Personal Page," (March 1912), 1.

23. "Is Mrs. Goddard Alone in Her Position that Equal Suffrage in Colorado Has Been a Failure?" *Ladies' Home Journal* (April 1, 1911), 6.

24. Edward Bok, "The Gentle Art of Boycotting This Magazine," *Ladies' Home Journal* (March 1912), 1.

25. On the National Consumers' League, see Dorothy Schneider and Carl J. Schneider, *American Women in the Progressive Era, 1900–1920* (New York: Anchor Books, 1993), 72–73; Alice Kessler-Harris, *Out to Work: Wage-Earning Women in America* (New York: Oxford University Press, 1982), 167, 171; Lynn Y. Weiner, *From Working Girl to Working Mother* (Chapel Hill: University of North Carolina Press, 1985), 68.

26. Edward Bok, Editorial, *Ladies' Home Journal* (April 1912), 6.

27. Edward Bok acknowledged taking on an antisuffrage stand, Editorial, *Ladies' Home Journal* (March 1912), 1.

28. Bok, Editorial (March 1912), 1.

29. "That Reminds Me," (April 1912), 2.

30. Bok praised the stay-at-home woman, Editorial, *Ladies' Home Journal* (July 1912), 3; the joke mentioned above belittled women's intelligence; Bok threatened women that "it is the hearthstone woman who holds a man," Editorial, *Ladies' Home Journal* (March 1913), 6.

31. Salme Harju Steinberg, "Reformer in the Marketplace: Edward W. Bok and the *Ladies' Home Journal*, 1889–1919," Ph.D. Dissertation, Johns Hopkins University, 1971, 204.

32. Actions of the *Seattle Union Record* in expanding its coverage to include women's activities, more broadly defined, described in Cott, 31.

33. "My Ideas of a Foreseeing Woman," *Ladies' Home Journal* (June 1919), 51.

34. Helen M. Damon-Moore, "Gender and the Rise of Mass-Circulation Magazines: The *Ladies' Home Journal* and the *Saturday Evening Post,* 1883–1910," Ph.D. Dissertation, University of Wisconsin, Madison, 1987, 151. See also the expanded version of her dissertation, *Magazines for the Millions: Gender and Commerce in the "Ladies' Home Journal" and the "Saturday Evening Post," 1880–1910* (Albany, NY: SUNY Press, 1994).

35. Kathy Oberdeck, "From Wives, Sweethearts and Female Relatives to Sisterhood: The Seattle

Women's Label League and *Seattle Union Record* Women's Pages," 1905–1919, unpubl. paper, Yale University, 1984, in Cott, 31.

36. Goldstein, 6.

37. Margaret Deland, "The Change in the Feminine Ideal," *Atlantic Monthly*, Vol. 105 (March 1910), 299, quoted in Schneider and Schneider, 7.

38. Arthur S. Link, "Theodore Roosevelt and the South in 1912," *North Carolina Historical Review*, XXIII (July 1946), 313–324. See also "Correspondence Relating to the Progressive Party's 'Lily White' Policy in 1912," *Journal of Southern History*, X (November 1944), 480–490; Nancy J. Weiss, "The Negro and the New Freedom: Fighting Wilsonian Segregation," *Political Science Quarterly*, LXXXIV (March 1969), 61–79; Christine A. Lunardini, "Standing Firm: William Monroe Trotter's Meetings with Woodrow Wilson, 1913–1914," *Journal of Negro History*, LXVI (Summer 1979), 244–264. All cited in Christine A. Lunardini, *From Equal Suffrage to Equal Rights: Alice Paul and the National Woman's Party, 1910–1928* (New York: New York University Press, 1986), 27.

39. Christine A. Lunardini, *From Equal Suffrage to Equal Rights*, 27.

40. Nancy Woloch explores the issue of antisuffrage arguments in general, and the argument of women's "excused" status in particular, in *Women and the American Experience* (New York: Alfred A. Knopf, 1984), 337–339.

41. Lyman Abbott, "Why the Vote Would Be Injurious to Women," *Ladies' Home Journal* (February 1910), 21–22.

42. Anne Hallowell Davis, "The Function of the Normal Woman," *Antisuffrage Essays by Massachusetts Women* (Boston: The Forum Publications, 1916), 125, quoted in Goldberg, 6.

43. Edward Bok, Editorial, *Ladies' Home Journal* (April 1912), 5.

44. Edward Bok, Editorial, *Ladies' Home Journal* (July 1912), 3.

45. Hummell studied the amount of space allotted to pro- and antisuffrage articles and argued that although Bok eased up on suffrage through the decade, the amount of space still favored the antisuffrage position. Michael D. Hummell, "The Attitudes of Edward Bok and the *Ladies' Home Journal* Toward Women's Role in Society, 1889–1919," Dissertation, North Texas State University, 1982, 268.

46. Margaret Deland, "A Third Way in Woman Suffrage," *Ladies' Home Journal* (January 1913), 12.

47. Jane Addams, "Why Women Should Vote," *Ladies' Home Journal* (January 1910), 21–22.

48. Hummell, 275.

49. Jane Addams, "Miss Addams," *Ladies' Home Journal* (June 1913), 21; Country Contributor, "The Ideas of a Plain Country Woman," *Ladies' Home Journal* (March 1916), 36.

50. Country Contributor, "The Ideas of a Plain Country Woman," *Ladies' Home Journal* (September 1908), 38.

51. The Washington bureau of the *Ladies' Home Journal* opened in February of 1916. Managed by Dudley Harmon, a reporter for the New York *Sun* newspaper, "My Government and I" explored the relationship between women and civic issues.

52. Edward Bok, "Editorial," *Ladies' Home Journal* (April 1916), 12.

53. Dorothy Mills, "The New Girls "Goblin". She Doesn't See it But the Man Does; Who is Right?" Guest Editorial, *Ladies' Home Journal* (May 1915), 3.

54. Steinberg, *Reformer in the Marketplace*, 143.

55. Bok, writing in the third person in his autobiography, *The Americanization of Edward Bok*, praised his own distance from women: "Bok's instinctive attitude toward women was that of avoidance. They never interested him. Nor had he the slightest desire even as an editor to know them better or seek to understand them," quoted in Davenport and Derieux, 175.

56. "Thirty Years," *Ladies' Home Journal* (January 1920), 1.

57. Country Contributor, "The Ideas of a Plain Country Woman," *Ladies' Home Journal* (July 1918), 34.

58. Cott, 171.

59. Rosenberg, 72.

60. Isaac F. Marcossen, "The After-the-War Woman," *Ladies' Home Journal* (September 1918), 87, 28.

61. Anna Howard Shaw, "2 New Cabinet Members and an Assistant Secretary of Labor: A Woman," *Ladies' Home Journal* (April 1919), 47. Anna Howard Shaw was President of the NAWSA from 1904 to 1915. For the Council of National Defense Shaw coordinated women's voluntary activities. Sara Evans, in *Born for Liberty: A History of Women in America* (New York: The Free Press, 1989), 172, argues concerning Shaw and Carrie Chapman Catt, who also worked for the Council, "Though they had little power or influence, they succeeded in claiming the mantle of patriotic citizenship for women's efforts."

62. Salme Harju Steinberg, *Reformer in the Marketplace: Edward Bok and the Ladies' Home Journal* (Baton Rouge: University of Louisiana Press, 1979), 58.

63. H. O. Davis, Editorial, *Ladies' Home Journal* (January 1920), 122. See also Barton Currie, Editorial, *Ladies' Home Journal* (January 1921), 28–29, and Editorial (February 1921), 26; Loring Schuler, Editorial, *Ladies' Home Journal* (August 1929), 22.

64. Harriet Abbott, "What the Newest New Woman Wants," *Ladies' Home Journal* (August 1920), 154.

65. H. O. Davis, Editorial, *Ladies' Home Journal* (March 1920), 1.

66. Margaret Woodrow Wilson, "Where Women in Politics Fail," *Ladies' Home Journal* (Sept. 1921), 10, 70. On women's voting patterns, see Woloch, 355. On Margaret Wilson, see Lunardini, 81.

67. "Women's Congress Against Women's Parties," 25.

68. Woloch, 383.

69. Cora Harris, "Practical Politics for Gentlewomen," *Ladies' Home Journal* (Sept. 1921), 16, 155.

70. Rose Young, "$10,000 an Hour: What Are You Paying? What Are You Getting?" *Ladies' Home Journal* (June 1920), 43, 178. Mary Roberts Rinehart, "Waiting for the Stork," *Ladies' Home Journal* (Aug. 1920), 26–27, 113.

71. Rose Young, "The End of a Great Adventure," *Ladies' Home Journal* (Feb. 1920), 37, 60; Young, "Madam, Meet Your Congressmen," (March 1920), 37, 190; Young, "Congress as a First Aid to Housewives," (May 1920), 43, 100, 102.

72. Rose Young was also a member of Heterodoxy, a club for "radical women" in New York City. For further discussion of women in Heterodoxy, see Chapter Seven on the J. Walter Thompson advertising women, Frances Maule in particular. See also Judith Schwarz, *Radical Feminists of Heterodoxy: Greenwich Village, 1912–1940* (Norwich, VT: New Victoria Publishers, 1986), 25, 128.

73. Elizabeth Jordan, "New Women Leaders in Politics," *Ladies' Home Journal* (Dec. 1920, 6–7, 192–93.

74. David Lawrence, "Mrs. New Citizen," *Ladies' Home Journal* (March 1919), 33, 103.

75. Marie Cecile Chomel, "Does the Wife Vote Like Her Husband?" *Ladies' Home Journal* (May 1919), 33, 88, 92.

76. Alice Ames Winter, "To Vote or Not to Vote," *Ladies' Home Journal* (Oct. 1924), 155, 157.

77. On women's voting patterns see Woloch, 335; Susan D. Becker, *The Origins of the Equal Rights Amendment: American Feminism Between the Wars* (Westport, CT: Greenwood Press, 1981). Anna Howard Shaw issued a less optimistic assessment of women's abilities to work together through their differences once the suffrage battle had been won, believing that underlying divisions of race, ethnicity, class and religion would be too powerful to overcome. "I am sorry for you young women who have to carry on the work in the next ten years," she remarked. "[S]uffrage was a symbol, and now you have lost your symbol. There is nothing for the women to rally round" (quoted in Rosalind Rosenberg, *Divided Lives*, 75).

78. Elizabeth Jordan, "New Women Leaders in Politics," *Ladies' Home Journal* (Dec. 1920), 6–7, 192–93.

79. On women and local politics, see "What do the Women Want Now," *Ladies' Home Journal* (Jan. 1921), 29, and Jordan, "The Big Little Things for Women in Politics," (Jan. 1921), 20, 78, 81. On the League of Women Voters, see Jordan, "Women in the Presidential Campaign," (Oct. 1920), 3–4, 138; Mrs. John King Van Rensselaer, "Our Social Ladder to Newport–The Town of Paradoxes, Vanities, and Extravagances," (June 1923), 8–9, 75; Elizabeth Frazer, "The Rising Tide of Voters," (Aug. 1924), 21, 132. On the National Woman's Party, see "What Do the Women Want Now," (Jan. 1921), 29, and "Women's Congress Against Women's Parties," (Aug. 1923), 25, 32.

80. Florence E. S. Knapp, "A Woman Politician and Proud of It," *Ladies' Home Journal* (May 1927), 37, 194–95; Elizabeth Breuer, "The Valiant Two Percent," (July 1923), 25, 132.

81. "Fooling the Woman in Politics," *Ladies' Home Journal* (Sept. 1923), 29, 159–60.

82. "That Negligible Woman Vote," *Ladies' Home Journal* (Nov. 1925), 38.

83. Barton Currie, "Editorial," *Ladies' Home Journal* (February 1921), 26.

84. Loring Schuler, "Editorial," *Ladies' Home Journal* (August 1929), 22.

85. "An Interview with Mrs. O. H. P. Belmont on the care of the skin," *Ladies' Home Journal* (Feb. 1924), 65.

86. The Pond's endorsements ran in 1924. The subjects of the interviews were as follows: April, Mrs. Cordelia Biddle Duke; May, Mrs. Julia Hoyt; July, Mrs. Marshall Gould; October, Gloria Gould; November, Princess Matchabelli.

87. Lunardini, 8.

88. Lunardini, 7–8.

89. Lunardini, 40, 50, 60, 112.

90. "An Interview with Mrs. O. H. P. Belmont," 65.

91. Cott, 278.

92. Hoosier advertisement, *Ladies' Home Journal* (April 1916), 78; Royal Baking Powder advertisement (April 1915), 49.

93. American Canners Association advertisement, *Ladies' Home Journal* (April 1921), 76.

94. Liberty Motor Car advertisement (May 1920), 55. Ford advertisement (May 1924), 62. On

the relationship between women and automobiles during this time period, see Virginia Scharff, *Taking the Wheel: Women and the Coming of the Motor Age* (New York: The Free Press, 1991).

five *The Amateur Rebel*

1. Ruth Schwartz Cowan, "Two Washes in the Morning and a Bridge Party at Night: The American Housewife Between the Wars," *Women's Studies* (1976), 147–172; Kathryn Weibel, *Mirror Mirror: Images of Women Reflected in Popular Culture* (Garden City, NY: Anchor Press, 1977); 168.Helen Franzwa, "Working Women in Fact and Fiction," *Journal of Communication* (Spring 1974), 105.

2. Helen Woodward, *Through Many Windows* (New York: Harper and Brothers, 1926), 116.

3. Janice Radway, *Reading the Romance: Women, Patriarchy, and Popular Literature* (Chapel Hill: Univ. of North Carolina Press, 1984); Tania Modleski, *Loving With a Vengeance* (New York: Methuen, 1982); Madonne Miner, *Insatiable Appetites: Twentieth-Century American Women's Bestsellers* (Westport, CT: Greenwood Press, 1984). For another view of women and romance fiction, see Kay Mussell, *Fantasy and Reconciliation: Contemporary Formulas of Women's Romance Fiction* (Westport, CT: Greenwood Press, 1984). See also Susan J. Douglas, *Where the Girls Are: Growing Up Female with the Mass Media* (New York: Random House, 1994).

4. Janet Todd discusses Q. D. Leavis in her *Feminist Literary History* (New York: Routledge, 1988), 94. See Fredric Jameson, "Reification and Utopia in Mass Culture," *Social Text*, 1 1979, and his "Postmodernism, or the Cultural Logic of Late Capitalism," *New Left Review* (July/Aug. 1984).

5. Judith Fetterley, *The Resisting Reader: A Feminist Approach to American Fiction* (Bloomington: Univ. of Indiana Press, 1978). Women read these male tales but do not benefit from them. "Intellectually male, sexually female, one is in effect no one, nowhere, immasculated," argues Fetterley (xxii). One must become, as the title suggests, a resisting reader, who is able to name and resist the realities she encounters in her reading. See also Nina Baym, "Melodramas of Beset Manhood: How Theories of American Fiction Exclude Women Authors," in *The New Feminist Criticism: Essays on Women, Literature and Theory*, ed. Elaine Showalter (New York: Pantheon Books, 1985), 63–80. Baym argues in part that the most highly praised literature of the United States provides a "consensus critique of the consensus" (69). In other words, the members of the dominant society illustrate through literature their feelings of partial alienation from that same society.

6. On nineteenth-century women writers, see Sandra Gilbert and Susan Gubar, *The Madwoman in the Attic: The Woman Writer and the Nineteenth-Century Literary Imagination* (New Haven: Yale Univ. Press, 1979) and Sandra M. Gilbert, "What Do Feminist Critics Want? A Postcard from the Volcano," *The New Feminist Criticism*, 29–45. On challenges to the canon, see Gayle Green and Coppelia Kahn, *Making a Difference: Feminist Literary Criticism* (New York: Methuen, 1985); Fetterley; Lillian Robinson, "Treason Our Text: Feminist Challenges to the Literary Canon," *The New Feminist Criticism*, 105–121. In fact, most of the readings in this collection, *The New Feminist Criticism*, are helpful in this context. Hawthorne quoted in Jane Tompkins, "Sentimental Power: *Uncle Tom's Cabin* and the Politics of Literary History," *The New Feminist Criticism*, 83. Tompkins, 83–104.

7. Todd, 96.

8. Radway, 198.

9. Radway, 11, 16, 54, 81, 213.

10. Nancy Cott, *The Grounding of Modern Feminism* (New Haven: Yale Univ. Press, 1987).

11. See Radway, especially Chapter Two.

12. Margaret Marsh, in *Suburban Lives* (New Brunswick, NJ: Rutgers University Press, 1990), 74–83, argues that middle-class men did become more involved in domestic life during the early twentieth century. She locates a shift away from that participation after World War I. In the *Ladies' Home Journal*, however, men's participation in "female" affairs was suspect throughout the 1910s and 1920s.

13. On women and sexuality during this period, see Elaine Tyler May, *Great Expectations: Marriage and Divorce in Post-Victorian America* (Chicago: University of Chicago Press, 1980); Carroll Smith-Rosenberg, *Disorderly Conduct: Visions of Gender in Victorian America* (New York: Alfred A. Knopf, 1985).

14. Phyllis Duganne, "The Amateur Rebel," *Ladies' Home Journal* (Feb. 1922), 6–7, 149–50, 152, 155.

15. Duganne, "The Amateur Rebel," 150.

16. Duganne, "The Amateur Rebel," 155.

17. Sophie Kerr, "All You Need is a Cookbook," *Ladies' Home Journal* (Dec. 1928), 3–5, 76, 79, 80, 82.

18. Kerr, "All You Need is a Cookbook," 4.

19. Kerr, "All You Need is a Cookbook," 79.

20. Kerr, "All You Need is a Cookbook," 80.

21. Kerr, "All You Need is a Cookbook," 82.

22. Kerr, "All You Need is a Cookbook," 82.

23. Josephine Daskam Bacon, "Tomorrow's Mother," *Ladies' Home Journal* (Sept. 1914), 7–8, 156.

24. Bacon, 7.

25. Bacon, 7.

26. Bacon, 156.

27. Bacon, 156.

28. Bacon, 156.

29. Sophie Kerr, "Little Winged Birds, So Happy," *Ladies' Home Journal* (March 1923), 26, 189–90, 193–94.

30. Kerr, "Little Winged Birds," 26.

31. Kerr, "Little Winged Birds," 190.

32. Kerr, "Little Winged Birds," 194.

33. Cora Harris, "The Woman Wins," *Ladies' Home Journal* (June 1926), 6–7, 59, 61.

34. Harris, 6.

35. Harris, 7.

36. Harris, 59.

37. Harris, 61.

38. Tom Lutz, *American Nervousness, 1903; An Anecdotal History* (Ithaca, NY: Cornell University Press, 1991), 20. On neurasthenia and gender, see Carroll Smith-Rosenberg, "The Hysterical Woman: Sex Roles and Role Conflict in Nineteenth-Century America," in her *Disorderly Conduct*, 197–216, and Charlotte Perkins Gilman, *The Yellow Wallpaper* ([1892] New York: The Feminist Press, 1973).

39. Smith-Rosenberg, 200.

40. Louise Elizabeth Dutton, "The Pretty Suffragette," *Ladies' Home Journal* (June 1914), 4–5.

41. Dutton, 5.

42. Dutton, 5.

43. Sophie Kerr, "Babe Grows Up," *Ladies' Home Journal* (March 1922), 12–13, 44, 47.

44. Kerr, 44.

45. Phyllis Duganne, "Connie," *Ladies' Home Journal* (Feb. 1925), 8–9, 106–111.

46. Duganne, "Connie," 8.

47. Duganne, "Connie," 106.

48. Duganne, "Connie," 111.

49. For a profile of the romance hero, see Radway, 106, 215.

50. On feminist women's relationships with their husbands, see Elaine Showalter, ed., *These Modern Women: Autobiographical Essays From the Twenties* (Old Westbury, NY: Feminist Press, 1978).

six *Advertising Women*

1. Although the ratio of men to women working in advertising in these years was approximately ten to one, Roland Marchand argues that women played a more influential role in advertising than in any other industry except publishing, movies, and department store retailing. Roland Marchand, *Advertising the American Dream: Making Way for Modernity, 1920-1940* (Berkeley: University of California Press, 1985), 33. Because their numbers are so small, women have been mentioned but not discussed in much detail in any of the significant histories of advertising. Even Marchand makes clear in the first sentence of his book that he will use the term "advertising man" throughout, 1.

2. *Printer's Ink*, 7 (Nov. 1929), 133, quoted in Marchand, 66.

3. *News Bulletin*, 191 (Dec. 1, 1927), 497, in J. Walter Thompson Company Archives, Duke University Library, Durham, North Carolina.

4. Marjorie Schuler, "Women's Role in Advertising Eased by Buyer's Point of View," *Christian Science Monitor*, 25 Nov. 1931.

5. Daniel Pope, *The Making of Modern Advertising* (New York, 1983), 144.

6. Pope, 137.

7. Stephen Fox, *The Mirror Makers: A History of American Advertising and Its Creators* (New York: William Morrow and Company 1984), 79.

8. "J. W. T. Establishes Another World's Record," J. Walter Thompson Company *News Bulletin*, 100 (Oct. 1, 1925), J. Walter Thompson Company Archives, Duke University Library, Durham, North Carolina.

9. For a discussion of changing patterns of manufacturing, packaging, and distribution of goods, see Susan Strasser, *Satisfaction Guaranteed: The Making of the American Mass Market* (New York: Pantheon Books, 1989).

10. Sharon Hartman Strom, *Beyond the Typewriter: Gender, Class, and the Origins of Modern American Office Work, 1900-1930* (Urbana: University of Illinois Press, 1992), 327.

11. Strom, 65, 79.

12. Strom, 65.

13. Joan Jacobs Brumberg and Nancy Tomes, "Women in the Professions: A Research Agenda for American Historians," *Reviews in American History*, Vol. 10 (June 1982), 287-88.

14. The J. Walter Thompson Company Portfolio Comprising of Facts and Figures," 1924, 9, 37, J. Walter Thompson Company Archives, Duke University Library, Durham, North Carolina.

15. Ruth Waldo, quoted in Marchand, 35.

16. Marchand, 33.

17. Strom, 93. On women's separatist political strategies in public life, see Estelle Freedman, "Separatism as Strategy: Female Institution Building and American Feminism, 1870-1930," *Feminist Studies*, No. 3 (Fall 1979), 512–529.

18. Helen Resor, Stockholder's Affidavit, March 1924, 70, J. Walter Thompson Company Archives, Duke University Library, Durham, North Carolina.

19. The women included here are those whose personnel files are open or those for whom I could gather sufficient information through other sources. The personnel files of women who left J. Walter Thompson at least 40 years ago or who died at least 25 years ago are available to researchers. The full list of women included in this sample is as follows: Ann Carter, Aminta Casseres, Ruth Cochran, Alice Coester, Gertrude Coit, Mary Cook, Charline Davenport, Elizabeth Devree, Perle Dienst, Florence Dorflinger, Lucy Dunham, Esther Eaton, Elizabeth Gates, Mildred Holmes, Rebecca Hourwich, Lucia Houpt, Faith Kelley, Peggy King, Eve Kittleson, Ruth Lamb, Dorothy Lampe, Alice Lee, Edith Lewis, Alice Luiggi, Frances Maule, Eleanor McDonnell, Ella Myers, Augusta Nicoll, Therese Olzendam, Ruth Oviatt, Blanche Perrin, Gladys Phelan, Lucille Platt, Agnes Rogers, Eleanor Taylor, Helen Thompson, Mary Tucker, Alice Wakefield, Ruth Waldo, Lelia Welles, Janet Wing.

20. Helen Resor, Stockholder's Affidavit, 69, J. Walter Thompson Company Archives, Duke University Library, Durham, North Carolina.

21. Harriet Abbott, "Doctor? Lawyer? Merchant? Chief? Which Shall She Be? Women's New Leadership in Business," *Ladies' Home Journal*, (July 1920), 45, 164. Although Helen Resor is not mentioned by name in the article, an article published after Resor's death argues that "the reader familiar with the J. Walter Thompson Company and its history will have little trouble in linking up Harriet Abbott's words with Helen Lansdowne Resor" ("Mrs. Resor Lauded in 1920 Magazine Article," J. Walter Thompson Company *News*, January 10, 1964, 10, J. Walter Thompson Company Archives, Duke University Library, Durham, North Carolina.)

22. Fox, 91.

23. Helen Lansdowne Resor, Stockholder's Affidavit, 69, J. Walter Thompson Company Archives, Duke University Library, Durham, North Carolina.

24. Helen Lansdowne Resor, Stockholder's Affidavit, 69, J. Walter Thompson Company Archives, Duke University Library, Durham, North Carolina.

25. Fox, 81. In 1948, the son and daughter of two followers of the famed efficiency expert Frederick Taylor wrote the story of their family life, *Cheaper By the Dozen*. The tale related the adventures of the Gilbreth family, twelve children and their two efficiency expert parents. The book was quite popular and followed later by a movie version. In one instance in the book the father described their car, "Foolish Carriage," with a take off on Helen Lansdowne Resor's advertisement: "Four Wheels, No Brakes. The Tin You Love to Touch." Frank Gilbreth and Ernestine Gilbreth Carey, *Cheaper By The Dozen* (New York, 1948), 222.

26. Abbott, 45.

27. Helen Resor, Stockholder's Affidavit, 70, J. Walter Thompson Company Archives, Duke University Library, Durham, North Carolina.

28. Florence I. Dorflinger, Personnel File, J. Walter Thompson Archives, Duke University Library, Durham, North Carolina.

29. Alice Luiggi, Personnel File, J. Walter Thompson Company Archives, Duke University Library, Durham, North Carolina.

30. Frances Maule, Personnel File, J. Walter Thompson Company Archives, Duke University Library, Durham, North Carolina.

31. Elizabeth Devree, Personnel File, J. Walter Thompson Company Archives, Duke University Library, Durham, North Carolina.

32. Mary Tucker, Personnel File, J. Walter Thompson Company Archives, Duke University Library, Durham, North Carolina.

33. Dorothy L. Lampe, Personnel File, J. Walter Thompson Company Archives, Duke University Library, Durham, North Carolina.

34. Rebecca Hourwich, Personnel File, J. Walter Thompson Company Archives, Duke University Library, Durham, North Carolina.

35. Janet Wing, Personnel File, J. Walter Thompson Company Archives, Duke University Library, Durham, North Carolina.

36. Eleanor Taylor, Personnel File, J. Walter Thompson Company Archives, Duke University Library, Durham, North Carolina.

37. Eleanor K. McDonnell, Personnel File, J. Walter Thompson Company Archives, Duke University Library, Durham, North Carolina.

38. Although the applicants mention the New York School for Social Research, they may have been referring to the New School for Social Research, which was founded in 1919. None of the J. Walter Thompson women are listed in the Alumni Records of the New School, but they claimed to have taken graduate courses there, not to have earned degrees.

39. Strom, 73.

40. Strom, 73.

41. Strom found that between 1910 and 1923 women's college administrators and alumnae established 15 college placement bureaus. The most effective of these, the Intercollegiate Bureau of Occupations (IBO), founded in 1911 by alumnae of nine leading eastern women's colleges, registered nearly 4200 applicants by 1917 and placed more than half of those in jobs. The more prestigious of the women's colleges made arrangements for their graduates to study on the graduate level at "genteel" institutions like the Katherine Gibbs school (328–29). On the first women faculty at coeducational institutions, see Geraldine Joncich Clifford, *Lone Voyagers: Academic Women in Coeducational Universities, 1870-1937* (New York: Feminist Press, 1989).

42. Gar Schmidt, obituary of Helen Lansdowne Resor, Resor biography file, 3, J. Walter Thompson Company Archives, Duke University Library, Durham, North Carolina.

43. Frances Maule and Eleanor K. McDonnell, Personnel Files, J. Walter Thompson Company Archives, Duke University Library, Durham, North Carolina.

44. Carroll Smith-Rosenberg, "The New Woman as Androgyne: Social Disorder and Gender Crisis, 1870-1936," in her *Disorderly Conduct: Visions of Gender in Victorian America* (New York: Alfred A. Knopf, 1985), 245–296, quote from 257.

45. College vocational bureaus often promised that clerical work could lead to managerial or

executive positions; this rarely happened. See Strom, 331. On college women in office work, see Strom, 336.

46. Ruth Waldo, Job Application Form, J. Walter Thompson Company Archives, Duke University Library, Durham, North Carolina.

47. Lucy H. Dunham, Personnel File, J. Walter Thompson Archives, Duke University Library, Durham, North Carolina.

48. Perle Dienst, Personnel File, J. Walter Thompson Company Archives, Duke University Library, Durham, North Carolina.

49. Florence I. Dorflinger, Personnel File, J. Walter Thompson Company Archives, Duke University Library, Durham, North Carolina.

50. Mary Tucker, Perle Dienst, Rebecca Hourwich, Faith Kelley, Frances Maule, Personnel Files, J. Walter Thompson Company Archives, Duke University Library, Durham, North Carolina.

51. Esther Eaton, Personnel File, J. Walter Thompson Company Archives, Duke University Library, Durham, North Carolina.

52. Frances Maule, Personnel File, J. Walter Thompson Company Archives, Duke University Library, Durham, North Carolina.

53. Mary Tucker, Personnel File, J. Walter Thompson Company Archives, Duke University Library, Durham, North Carolina.

54. Mary Cook, Personnel File, J. Walter Thompson Company Archives, Duke University Library, Durham, North Carolina.

55. Elizabeth Gates, Mary Cook, Personnel Files, J. Walter Thompson Company Archives, Duke University Library, Durham, North Carolina; Strom, 327.

56. Daniel Walkowitz, "The Making of a Feminine Professional Identity: Social Workers in the 1920s," *American Historical Review*, Vol. 95, No. 4 (October 1990), 1055. See also Brumberg and Tomes.

57. Dr. Alice Hamilton quoted in Rosalind Rosenberg, *Divided Lives: American Women in the Twentieth Century* (New York: Hill and Wang, 1992), 29.

58. Walkowitz, 1062; 1060.

59. Susan Curtis, *A Consuming Faith: The Social Gospel and Modern American Culture* (Baltimore: Johns Hopkins Univ. Press, 1991), xiii.

60. Curtis, 14.

61. Curtis, 33.

62. Ellen Carol DuBois, "Harriot Stanton Blatch and the Transformation of Class Relations Among Woman Suffragists," in Noralee Frankel and Nancy S. Dye, eds., *Gender, Class, Race, and Reform in the Progressive Era* (Lexington: The University Press of Kentucky, 1991), 162–179, quote from 163.

63. Walkowitz, 1062.

64. *J. Walter Thompson Company Blue Book*, 1910, 23, J. Walter Thompson Company Archives, Duke University Library, Durham, North Carolina.

65. *News Bulletin*, March 25, 1922, 14–15, J. Walter Thompson Company Archives, Duke University Library, Durham, North Carolina.

66. Eleanor Taylor, Personnel File, J. Walter Thompson Company Archives, Duke University Library, Durham, North Carolina.

67. Gertrude Coit, Personnel File, J. Walter Thompson Company Archives, Duke University Library, Durham, North Carolina.

68. Charline Davenport, Personnel File, J. Walter Thompson Company Archives, Duke University Library, Durham, North Carolina.

69. Ruth Waldo, Personnel File, J. Walter Thompson Company Archives, Duke University Library, Durham, North Carolina.

70. "Ruth Waldo Dies: Early Advertising Woman," *New York Times* (Sept. 5, 1975), J. Walter Thompson Company Archives, Duke University Library, Durham, North Carolina.

71. Rebecca Hourwich, Personnel File, J. Walter Thompson Archives, Duke University Library, Durham, North Carolina.

72. Therese Olzendam, Personnel File, J. Walter Thompson Archives; "Therese Olzendam–Thumbnail Sketch," Sept. 20, 1948, J. Walter Thompson Company Archives, Duke University Library, Durham, North Carolina.

73. Frances Maule, Personnel File, J. Walter Thompson Company Archives, Duke University Library, Durham, North Carolina.

74. Helen Resor, letter in Frances Maule's personnel file, J. Walter Thompson Company Archives, Duke University Library, Durham, North Carolina.

75. Helen Lansdowne Resor, Biographical File, J. Walter Thompson Company Archives, Duke University Library, Durham, North Carolina.

76. Judith Schwarz, Kathy Peiss, and Christina Simmons, "We Were a Band of Willful Women,'" in *Passion and Power*, ed. Kathy Peiss and Christina Simmons (Philadelphia: Temple University Press, 1989), 118.

77. Caroline F. Ware, *Greenwich Village, 1920-1930: A Comment on American Civilization in the Post-War Years* (Berkeley: University of California Press, 1994; 1935).

78. "Early Important Women," Bernstein Client Files: Chesebrough-Ponds, J. Walter Thompson Company Archives, Duke University Library, Durham, North Carolina.

79. Hermione Lee, *Willa Cather: Double Lives* (New York: Pantheon Books, 1989), 70, 71. Lillian Faderman, in *Odd Girls and Twilight Lovers: A History of Lesbian Life in Twentieth-Century America* (New York: Penguin, 1991), describes Willa Cather's practice of calling herself Dr. William and dressing in male drag while a student at the University of Nebraska. According to Faderman, Cather became more quiet about her relationships with women after the turn of the century "because she was aware of the fall from grace that love between women was beginning to suffer," 53.

80. Faderman, 12.

81. Judith Schwarz, *Radical Feminists of Heterodoxy* (Norwich, VT: New Victoria Publishers, 1986), 36.

82. Leila Rupp, "'Imagine My Surprise': Women's Relationships in Historical Perspective," *Frontiers*, Vol. 5, No. 3 (1981), 61-70.

83. Faderman, 16.

84. Wallace Boren, Staff Meeting Minutes, January 7, 1936, J. Walter Thompson Company Archives, Duke University Library, Durham, North Carolina.

85. Cynthia Swank, "Not Just Another Pretty Face: Advertising Women in the 1920s," Slide Lecture to the Philadelphia Club of Advertising Women, March 9, 1982, 5-6.

86. Helen Lansdowne Resor, Stockholder's Affidavit, 69, J. Walter Thompson Company Archives, Duke University Library, Durham, North Carolina.

87. Charles Austin Bates quoted in Fox, 37.

88. Mildred Holmes, "Housewives Write the Copy," *News Bulletin*, No. 97, April, 1923, 7, J. Walter Thompson Company Archives, Duke University Library, Durham, North Carolina.

89. Walkowitz, 1062, provides an interesting parallel to the advertising woman's description of her clients in a contemporary drawing showing a young, thin, professionally dressed social worker talking with an older, heavier, toothless client.

90. "Early Important Women," Bernstein Client Files: Chesebrough-Ponds, J. Walter Thompson Company Archives, Duke University Library, Durham, North Carolina. Interestingly, Aminta Casseres, in a company publication, was referred to as "a swell advertising man," "Minutes of a Representatives' Meeting," October 21, 1930, 5, cited in Marchand, 34.

91. Aminta Casseres, "How Important is the Style of the Copy?" *News Bulletin*, No. 100, July 1923, 3, J. Walter Thompson Company Archives, Duke University Library, Durham, North Carolina.

92. Frances Maule, "The Woman Appeal," *News Bulletin*, No. 105, January 1925, 2, 5, J. Walter Thompson Company Archives, Duke University Library, Durham, North Carolina.

93. *News Bulletin*, July 11, 1916, 1, J. Walter Thompson Company Archives, Duke University Library, Durham, North Carolina.

94. *News Bulletin*, July 11, 1916, 2.

95. *News Bulletin*, No. 61, August 12, 1918, 1–5, J. Walter Thompson Company Archives, Duke University Library, Durham, North Carolina. *Pictorial Review* offered a $5000 annual award to the American woman who made, in the last ten years, the greatest contribution to national life in letters, arts, science, philanthropy, or social welfare. See "Win Pictorial Review Award," *The Independent Woman*, Vol. 7, No. 12 (December 1928), 561.

96. Minutes, Creative Organization Staff Meeting, March 5, 1932, 8, J. Walter Thompson Company Archives, Duke University Library, Durham, North Carolina.

97. Curtis, 71.

98. Dorothy Brown, *Setting a Course: American Women in the 1920s* (Boston: Twayne Pubs., 1987), 106.

seven *"Every Woman Is Interested in This"*

1. Advertisers used the term "darling" in relation to middle-class women, according to Kathryn Weibel, *Mirror, Mirror: Images of Women Reflected in Popular Culture* (Garden City, N.Y.: Anchor Books, 1977), 158.

2. On the phases of development from a small domestic market through the national market to almost universal market segmentation, see Richard S. Tedlow, *New and Improved: The Story of Mass Marketing in America* (New York: Basic Books, 1990). Ellen McCracken, in *Decoding Women's Magazines: From Mademoiselle to Ms.* (New York: St. Martin's Press, 1993), discusses the market segmentation applied to selling contemporary women's magazines (1981-1983) to groups based on age (*Seventeen*), race (*Essence*), and special interest (*Modern Bride*), among others. Not surprisingly, the one thing all the readers share is the desire to consume. *Seventeen* readers, argues the publisher, are "Born to Shop" and "branded for life"; the reader of *Modern Bride* is "determined to *spend* the rest of her life" (5, 143).

3. Stephen Fox, *The Mirror Makers: A History of American Advertising and its Creators* (New York: William Morrow and Co., 1984), 32.

4. Salme Steinberg, "Reformer in the Marketplace: Edward W. Bok and the *Ladies' Home Journal*, 1889-1919," Dissertation, Johns Hopkins, 1971, 129.

5. Cyrus Curtis, quoted in Fox, 32. In an article in *Printer's Ink* (Oct. 28, 1896) quoted in Fox, 33, Curtis explained his philosophy: "I want businessmen to advertise in the *Journal*, and to show them that I believe in the principles which I advance, I advertise largely myself. . . . A man can never advertise too much."

6. Stuart Ewen, *Captains of Consciousness: Advertising and the Social Roots of the Consumer Culture* (New York: McGraw Hill, 1976), 62.

7. Steinberg, footnote, 18, 102, 89, 184. In 1924, the *Ladies' Home Journal* carried more than $13,500,000 in advertising revenue, more than any other magazine except the *Saturday Evening Post*, according to "Advertising Charts, 1919-1924," Curtis Publications, 1925, 3, Curtis Publishing Company Papers, Department of Special Collections, Van Pelt-Dietrich Library, University of Pennsylvania. In 1926, the *Journal* reported that it had contained more advertising revenue in the past six years than any other women's magazine had in its entire history, according to "Advertising in Women's Publications," Curtis Publications, 1926, Curtis Publishing Company Papers, Department of Special Collections, Van Pelt-Dietrich Library, University of Pennsylvania.

8. Susan Strasser, *Satisfaction Guaranteed: The Making of the American Mass Market* (New York: Pantheon Books, 1989), 52.

9. W.S. Hixon Co. Grocer, quoted in "Food Products and Household Supplies." Interviews by C. C. Parlin and H.S. Yonder, Curtis Publishing Co., 1915, Curtis Publishing Company Papers, Department of Special Collections, Van Pelt-Dietrich Library, University of Pennsylvania.

10. *News Bulletin*, No. 76, April 1921, 2, J. Walter Thompson Company Archives, Duke University Library, Durham, North Carolina.

11. "To be sure," Steinberg argues, "Bok did not regard advertising as the primary purpose of his magazine. Nor did he view it as a necessary evil. His attitude was founded in his fundamental faith in the American business system" (6).

12. Steinberg, 86. Bok became more comfortable with one of these issues, installment buying, as time wore on. In a *Journal* editorial (February 1917, 30), Bok argued that installment buying could meet a consumer's cultural, even spiritual needs. With the help of the *Ladies' Home Journal* and other popular magazines, Americans purchased over 60 percent of their automobiles, radios, and furniture on installment plans by the end of the 1920s (Roland Marchand, *Advertising the American Dream: Making Way for Modernity, 1920-1940*, [Berkeley: University of California Press, 1985], 4).

13. Cyrus Curtis quoted in James D. Norris, *Advertising and the Transformation of American Society, 1865-1920* (New York: Greenwood Press, 1990), 36–37.

14. Strasser, 32.

15. Howard Henderson, *Some Basic Roots of the J. Walter Thompson Company: A Starting Point for Future Growth, Officers and Staff, Speeches and Writings* (November 1959), 8, J. Walter Thompson Company Archives, Duke University Library, Durham, North Carolina.

16. Henderson, 35.

17. Edward Bok, "The Editor's Personal Chat," *Ladies' Home Journal* (April 1915), 49.

18. *News Bulletin*, No. 76, April 1921, 2, J. Walter Thompson Company Archives, Duke University Library, Durham, North Carolina.

19. Strasser, 14.

20. Marchand, 5; Helen Resor, Stockholder's Affidavit, 68, from J. Walter Thompson Company Archives, Duke University Library, Durham, North Carolina.

Notes

21. Henderson, 13.

22. Notes in Helen Resor biography file, Jan. 24, 1936, J. Walter Thompson Company Archives, Duke University, Durham, North Carolina.

23. Jergens, Clients, Howard Henderson Papers, J. Walter Thompson Company Archives, Duke University Library, Durham, North Carolina.

24. Stanley Resor, "Woodbury's Facial Soap," Account Files, Jergens, J. Walter Thompson Company Archives, Duke University Library, Durham, North Carolina.

25. Account History, Andrew Jergens Company, Woodbury's Facial Soap, April 1926, 2, J. Walter Thompson Company Archives, Duke University Library, Durham, North Carolina.

26. "Helen Lansdowne Resor, 1886–1964," *J. Walter Thompson Company News,* January 10, 1964, 9, J. Walter Thompson Company Archives, Duke University Library, Durham, North Carolina.

27. Stanley Resor, "Woodbury's Facial Soap," 3.

28. Account History, Andrew Jergens Company, Woodbury's Facial Soap, April 1926, J. Walter Thompson Company Archives, 7; *News Bulletin*, No. 78, May 14, 1921, 3; Frank Comrey, "Fundamental Appeals in Advertising," speech delivered Dec. 18, 1930, at the School of Commerce, Northwestern University, quoted in *J. Walter Thompson Company News* (January 10, 1964), 9, J. Walter Thompson Company Archives, Duke University Library, Durham, North Carolina.

29. John C. Sterling, "General and Women's Magazines, Space Selling," in *Careers in Advertising and the Jobs Behind Them*, ed. Alden James (New York: Macmillan, 1932), 363–374.

30. Henderson, 25.

31. Roland Marchand, 10, argues that by 1914 it was common for advertisers to sell the benefit of the product to the consumer rather than the product itself. Nevertheless, he argues, the majority of ads in the 1910s remained product-centered.

32. Resor, "Woodbury's Facial Soap," 3.

33. By 1924, Woodbury's was the largest selling soap in its field, Account History, Andrew Jergens Company, Woodbury's Facial Soap, April 1926, J. Walter Thompson Company Archives; Clients, Jergens, Howard Henderson Papers, J. Walter Thompson Company Archives, Duke University Library, Durham, North Carolina.

34. On the cult of youth and beauty, see Elaine Tyler May, *Great Expectations: Marriage and Divorce in Post-Victorian America* (Chicago: University of Chicago Press, 1980); the statistic on cosmetics comes from John D'Emilio and Estelle B. Freedman, *Intimate Matters: A History of Sexuality in America* (New York: Perennial, 1989), 279. See also Kathy Peiss, "Making Faces: The Cosmetics Industry and the Cultural Construction of Gender, 1890–1930," in *Unequal Sisters: A Multicultural Reader in U.S. Women's History,* ed. Vicki L. Ruiz and Ellen Carol Dubois, 2nd. edition (New York: Routledge, 1994), 372–394.

35. Stanley Resor, "Woodbury's Facial Soap," 6.

36. Andrew Jergens Company, Woodbury's Facial Soap, Microfilm Research Reports, J. Walter Thompson Company Archives, Duke University Library, Durham, North Carolina.

37. Marchand, xxi.

38. "Get Your Mirror to Tell You What Your Friends Will Not," Woodbury's Facial Soap Advertisement, *Ladies' Home Journal* (April 1917), 112.

39. "Under Searching Eyes," Woodbury's Facial Soap Advertisement, *Ladies' Home Journal* (May 1920), 69.

40. "A Man's First Impression of a Woman," *Ladies' Home Journal* (June 1921), 45; "All Around You People are Judging You Silently," *Ladies' Home Journal* (December 1922), 45; "His Unspoken Thoughts When He Looks Into Your Face," *Ladies' Home Journal* (September 1922), 51; "When Failure Hurts the Most," *Ladies' Home Journal* (August 1924), 37; "Stranger's Eyes, Keen and Critical," *Ladies' Home Journal* (January 1922), 42.

41. "Investigation Among College Women," Woodbury's, Andrew Jergens Company Research Report, December 1922, J. Walter Thompson Company Archives; Meeting Notes, Production and Representatives Meeting, April 9, 1928, p. 16, J. Walter Thompson Company Archives, Duke University Library, Durham, North Carolina.

42. Woodbury's Ads, *Ladies' Home Journal* (September 1925; June 1925; January 1926; July 1925; August 1925; October 1925; February 1926). A Woodbury's Shampoo advertisement in the April 1918 *Ladies' Home Journal* featured an African-American woman. Although both Aunt Jemima and Cream of Wheat were Thompson clients, ads for both were produced outside the New York office.

43. Edith Lewis, Personnel File, J. Walter Thompson Company Archives, Duke University Library, Durham, North Carolina.

44. In addition to the monthly winners, the *Ladies' Home Journal* ads profiled the judges in February of 1929 and urged readers to follow each monthly announcement in August of 1929. Advertisers continue to restrict by race in women's magazines and, of course, by sexual preference; lesbians are only now beginning to be recognized as a monied, perhaps desirable, market by mainstream advertising agencies.

45. "The Story of Pond's, 1846–1909" (1937), 1, Account Files, J. Walter Thompson Company Archives, Duke University Library, Durham, North Carolina.

46. *News Bulletin* (internal), Sept. 12, 1916, 4, J. Walter Thompson Company Archives, Duke University Library, Durham, North Carolina.

47. Client Files, Pond's Extract Company, Howard Henderson Papers, J. Walter Thompson Company Archives, Duke University Library, Durham, North Carolina.

48. Henderson, 20–21.

49. William Allen Pusey, A.M., M.D., Professor of Dermatology, University of Illinois, named in "Brief Pictorial History of Chesebrough-Pond's, A JWT Account Since 1886," Bernstein client files. p. 1, J. Walter Thompson Company Archives, Duke University Library, Durham, North Carolina.

50. "What a man looks for in a girl," Pond's Vanishing Cream Advertisement, *Ladies' Home Journal* (March 1916), 79.

51. "Why your skin needs two creams," Pond's Vanishing Cream and Cold Cream Advertisement, *Ladies' Home Journal* (March 1918), 89.

52. *News Bulletin* (internal), August 1, 1916, J. Walter Thompson Company Archives, Duke University Library, Durham, North Carolina.

53. Pond's Extract Company, Account Files, January 1926, 2, J. Walter Thompson Company Archives, Duke University Library, Durham, North Carolina.

54. Pond's Extract Company, Account Files, 8, J. Walter Thompson Company Archives, Duke University Library, Durham, North Carolina.

55. Pond's Extract Company, Account Files, 2.

56. Pond's Extract Company, Account Files, 3.

57. *News Letter*, No. 76, April 16, 1925, 3, J. Walter Thompson Company Archives, Duke University Library, Durham, North Carolina.

58. Pond's Extract Company advertisement, *Ladies' Home Journal* (September 1927), 49.

59. Pears Soap Advertisement, *Godey's Lady's Book* (February 1889), n.p.

60. Minutes, Representatives Meeting, September 1927, 5, J. Walter Thompson Company Archives, Duke University Library, Durham, North Carolina.

61. Henderson, 29.

62. Pond's Extract Company, Account History, 7.

63. Alva Johnson, "Testimonials, C.O.D.," n.p., Bernstein Testimonial Advertising File, J. Walter Thompson Company Archives, Duke University Library, Durham, North Carolina.

64. Alva Johnson, n.p.

65. Pond's Extract Company, Account History, 3.

66. Minutes, Special Production and Representatives Meeting, April 9, 1928, 18, J. Walter Thompson Company Archives, Duke University Library, Durham, North Carolina.

67. Aminta Casseres, quoted from Minutes, Special Representatives Meeting, April 9, 1928, J. Walter Thompson Company Archives, Duke University Library, Durham, North Carolina.

68. "Consumer Investigation, Columbus, Ohio, November 1927, Pond's Extract Company Microfilm Research Reports, J. Walter Thompson Company Archives, Duke University Library, Durham, North Carolina.

69. M.C. Phillips, *Skin Deep: The Truth About Beauty Aids. Safe and Harmful* (New York: The Vanguard Press, 1934), 39, 162, 187, 197.

70. Pond's Extract Company, Account History, 8.

71. *News Letter*, No. 132, May 13, 1926, 119–120, J. Walter Thompson Company Archives, Duke University, Durham, North Carolina.

72. Otis Pease, *The Responsibilities of American Advertising: Private Control and Public Influence, 1920–1940* (New Haven: Yale University Press, 1958), 34.

73. Marchand, 56.

74. Minutes, Representatives Meeting, May 28, 1929, 4, J. Walter Thompson Company Archives, Duke University Library, Durham, North Carolina.

75. Elizabeth Hoyt, *The Consumption of Wealth* (New York, 1928), quoted in Ewen, 95.

76. Joseph Boskin, *Sambo: The Rise and Demise of an American Jester* (New York: Oxford University Press, 1986), 136, 139. William M. O'Barr, in *Culture and the Ad: Exploring Otherness in the World of Advertising* (Boulder, CO: Westview Press, 1994), 107–156, presents a "visitor's guide" to African-Americans in twentieth-century advertising.

77. George T. Brodnax Company Advertisement, *Ladies' Home Journal* (November 1913), 65.

78. Boskin, 141.

79. "Outline of Data Concerning a Product or Line of Products to be Obtained Through Field Investigation," 2, in "Report of the Committee on Standardization," 1919, J. Walter Thompson Company Archives, Duke University Library, Durham, North Carolina.

80. "How Many Homes Does Magazine Advertising Reach?" *News Bulletin*, No. 111, January 1925, 20, J. Walter Thompson Company Archives, Duke University Library, Durham, North Carolina. James Norris, 9, argues that from 1870–1920 literacy increased tremendously, with the most gains in the black population, where figures went from close to 80

percent illiteracy in 1870 to close to 80 percent literacy in 1920; literacy in the whole population in 1920 was at 94 percent.

81. *Population and Its Distribution* (New York: J. Walter Thompson Company, 1920), J. Walter Thompson Company Archives, Duke University Library, Durham, North Carolina.

82. Stanley Resor, "Woodbury's Facial Soap," 10.

83. Officers and Staff Files, Bernstein History, n.d., J. Walter Thompson Company Archives, Duke University Library, Durham, North Carolina.

84. Dorothy Dwight Townsend, "Mrs. Wilkins reads the Ladies' Home Journal," *News Bulletin*, No. 99, June 1923, 1–5, J. Walter Thompson Company Archives, Duke University Library, Durham, North Carolina.

85. Townsend, 3.

86. Townsend, 4.

87. T. J. Jackson Lears, "From Salvation to Self-Realization: Advertising and the Therapeutic Roots of the Consumer Culture, 1880-1930," in *The Culture of Consumption: Critical Essays in American History, 1880–1980*, ed. Richard Wightman Fox and T. J. Jackson Lears (New York: Pantheon Books, 1983), 17.

88. Stanley Resor, "The Dollar-a-Year Graduate School," *News Bulletin*, No. 139, August 1929, 6, J. Walter Thompson Company Archives, Duke University Library, Durham, North Carolina.

89. Resor, "The Dollar-a-Year Graduate School," 6.

90. Resor, "The Dollar-a-Year Graduate School," 7.

91. Edward Bok, Editorial, *Ladies' Home Journal* (October 1916), 42.

92. Mrs. Stickney Parks, "Girls' Affairs," *Ladies' Home Journal* (October 1912), 104.

93. Fox, 101.

94. "The Market for the *Ladies' Home Journal*," J. Walter Thompson Research Department Microfilm, December 1933, 6, J. Walter Thompson Company Archives, Duke University Library, Durham, North Carolina.

95. *The Thompson Blue Book on Advertising, 1909–1910* (New York: J. Walter Thompson Company, 1910), 22, J. Walter Thompson Company Archives, Duke University Library, Durham, North Carolina.

Conclusion

1. Fredric Jameson, quoted in Ellen McCracken, *Decoding Women's Magazines: From Mademoiselle to Ms.* (New York: St. Martin's Press, 1993), 5.

2. Cartoon, *The New Yorker* (June 9, 1934), 19.

3. Jane Addams quoted in Rosalind Rosenberg, *Divided Lives: American Women in the Twentieth Century* (New York: Hill and Wang, 1992), 3.

4. Maud Kennon Waddock, "One Woman's Way," *Ladies' Home Journal* (January 1922), 132.

5. On women and reading, see Barbara Sicherman, "Sense and Sensibility: A Case Study of Women's Reading in Late Victorian America," in Dorothy O. Helly and Susan M. Reverby, eds., *Gendered Domains: Rethinking Public and Private in Women's History* (Ithaca, NY: Cornell University Press, 1992), 71–89.

6. Judith Williamson, "Woman is an Island: Femininity and Colonization," in Tania Modleski, ed., *Studies in Entertainment: Critical Approaches to Mass Culture* (Bloomington: Indiana University Press, 1986), 106.

7. Nellie M. S. Nearing and Scott Nearing, "Four Great Things a Woman Does at Home," *Ladies' Home Journal* (May 1912), 12.

8. Nearing and Nearing, 12.

9. Gary Cross, in *Time and Money: The Making of Consumer Culture* (London: Routledge, 1993), 6, makes the argument that the culture feared men's use of leisure time. The case can certainly be made about fears of women's use of time as well.

10. Juliet Virginia Strauss, "The Woman Who Frets Over Things: The Men We Love and the Men We Marry," *Ladies' Home Journal* (October 1911), 8.

11. Williamson, 106.

12. Antonio Gramsci, *Selections From the Prison Notebooks*, ed. Quintin Hoare and Geoffrey Nowell Smith (New York: International Publishers, 1971), 245. See also, Todd Gitlin, "The Hegemonic Process in Television Entertainment," *Social Problems*, 26 (February 1979), 151-153.

13. Dorothy M. Brown, *Setting a Course: American Women in the 1920s* (Boston: Twayne Publishers, 1987), 23.

14. *Ladies' Home Journal* (October 1929), 1.

15. Margaret Marsh, *Suburban Lives* (New Brunswick, NJ: Rutgers University Press, 1990), 183.

Index

Abbott, Harriet 124, 175-177

Abbott, Reverend Lyman 119

Addams, Jane 17-18, 20, 55, 111, 121-122, 158, 231

advertising: 9, 169-228; images of womanhood 30-37; increasing importance to the *Journal* 43, 47-48; and housekeeping 72-77; national 31, 199, 202, 204, 212, 219; and suffrage 131, 132-134; and business women 192; and sex appeal 176, 178, 206-208; African-American women in ads 34-35, 211-213, 220-224; immigrant women and ads 212-213; threatening ads 32, 208-210; contests sponsored by agencies 211; and divorce 217; as cultural program of magazines 40; see also testimonials

Advertising Women of New York 62

African-American women 5, 16, 18, 20, 26-29, 34-38, 59, 97, 100, 112, 141-142 119, 121, 195, 211, 213, 220; in jokes 26-27; and work 80; in advertising 34-35, 211-213, 220-224

Allen, Frederick Lewis 30

Alexander, Mary Louise 172

antisuffrage movement 113-122

Applecroft Home Experiment Station 61, 71

Ardery, Lois 10

Armstrong Linoleum 43-44

Ashmore, Ruth 50

Aunt Jemina 220-223

automobile advertising 46, 48, 106, 134, 172, 198

"average" American woman, creation of 5-7, 190-191, 195, 197-198; African-American women and the "average" woman 5-7

Bacon, Josephine Daskam 149-153

Bailey, Beth 90

Bates, Charles Austin 191

Behn, Aphra 140-141

Bellamy, Edward 55

Belmont, Alva 132-133, 193-194, 216-217, 219

Belmont, Oliver Hazard Perry, 132

beauty 32, 34, 226

Beecher, Henry Ward 216

Beech Nut 45, 47

Benson, Susan Porter 15-16

Bjorkman, Edwin 188

Bok, Edward 3-4, 12, 14, 17-22, 30, 39, 50-53, 63-64, 93-96, 98, 110-112, 114-126, 198-201, 206, 226

Bok, Mary Louise Curtis 4

Boren, Wallace 190

Boskin, Joseph 220-221

Breuer, Elizabeth 130

Brodnax, George T. 221

Brown, Dorothy 30, 195

Brumberg, Joan Jacobs 173

Brunkhurst, Harriet 91

California Packing Company 69-70

Campbell's Soup 31, 45

Carnell, Laura H. 92

Casseres, Aminta 191-192

Cather, Willa 189, 211

Catholics 17-18

Cavalier Furniture 43

Chapman, Josephine Wright 88

Chomel, Marie Cecile 128

circulation rates of the *Journal* 4, 8

class of *Journal* readers 5-10, 12-15, 52

class differences, explored in *Journal* 23-24, 27-29

Coit, Gertrude 186

college women addressed in *Journal* 41-42; college education and women's happiness 91-92; and work 82, 86-87; college education of J. Walter Thompson Agency women employees 180; 227; and advertising 44, 209-212

consumer choices: of men 118; of professional women 118

consumption as political act 229-230

Cook, Mary Loomis 100

Cott, Nancy 82, 113, 123, 133, 141

Country Contributor, see Plain Country Woman

Cowan, Ruth Schwartz 38, 55-56, 138

Cream of Wheat 220

Crisco 172, 201, 203

Crosby, Mabel Jewett 72

Currie, Barton 40, 51, 124, 126, 128, 130, 131, 230

Curtis, Cyrus 3-4, 12-15, 122-123, 198-200

Curtis, Louisa Knapp 3-4, 123, 198

Curtis, Susan 184

Cutex 45

Cuticura 202

Daggett, Mabel Potter 193

Damon-Moore, Helen 118

Davenport, Charline 186

Davis, H.O. 124-125

Day, William 193

Deland, Margaret 119, 121

department stores 15-16, 89

Depression, the Great 234

Devree, Elizabeth 179

Dienst, Perle 182

divorce 24-25, 96-98, 141, 149-150, 153, 155, 168, 179; and advertising 217, 226

Dorflinger, Florence 177, 182

Dowdell, Ruth Evelyn 104

DuBois, Ellen Carol 184

Duganne, Phyllis 144, 146, 164

Dunham, Lucy 182

Dutton, Louise Elizabeth 159

Dye, Nancy 20, 110

Eastman, Crystal 46, 188

Eaton, Esther 182

Emerson, Ralph Waldo 53, 140

Equal Rights Amendment 124, 131

Essence 5

Faderman, Lillian 189

Fairy Soap 17

Farmer, Fannie 158

fashion 21-23, 49, 52, 124

feminism 85, 122, 125, 130, 132-133, 138, 142, 147, 160, 164-168, 188, 192-194, 216-217; of J. Walter Thompson women employees 181; as selling device 132-134

Fetterley, Judith 140

fiction 137-168; reading against the grain 141, 167; sexuality 143-144, 152, 155, 163-164, 168; women adapt to marital conditions 144, 148-149, 151, 153, 161-162, 167; feminism 146, 164, 167-168; suffrage 156-157, 159; divorce 149-150, 153, 155; men's views of women 151, 154, 157, 160, 163

flappers 45, 46, 130; see also youth culture

Fletcher, Grace Nies 98

food articles in *Journal* 21, 43-45, 65; food and politics 127, 133-134

Food and Drug Act 219

Ford Motor Company 46

Fox, Stephen 175, 226

Franzwa, Helen 138

Frederick, Christine McGaffey 50, 61-76, 93

Frederick, Justus George 62-63

Freud, Sigmund 30, 154, 157

Gale, Zona 54

Gates, Elizabeth 183

Gilman, Charlotte Perkins 54, 158, 188

Girls' Club, *Journal*-sponsored 23, 105-106

Godey's Lady's Book 2-3, 11, 216

Gold Dust Twins 34

Goodyear Tires 172

Gramsci, Antonio 233

Grape Nuts 31

Grayson, Margaret 86

Greene, Dorothea Pearson 27

Hale, Sarah Josepha 2-3; see also *Godey's Lady's Book*

Hamilton, Alice 184

Harper's 42

Harriman, Karl 69, 98

Harris, Cora 126, 156

Hawthorne, Nathaniel 140

Heath, Mrs. Julian 61

Hershey 71

Heterodoxy 188-189

Holmes, Mildred 191

Hoosier Kitchen Cabinets 45, 133

Hoover, Herbert 71

Hormell 34

Hotpoint Appliances 72, 107

Hourwich, Rebecca 179, 182, 187

housekeeping 8, 21, 49-77; cooperative housekeeping 55-56, 131

Housewives' League 94

Hoyt, Elizabeth 220

Hummell, Michael 121

Hurston, Zora Neale 140-141

hysteria see nervous conditions

immigrant Women 16, 18, 20, 26-29, 119, 195; left out of ads 212-213

international scope of *Journal* 46

Irish women 27, 35, 119, 121, 144, 146; Irish stereotypes and fiction 165-166

Ivory Soap 31

Jameson, Fredric 140, 230

Jello 31

Jergens Company, see Woodbury's Facial Soap

Jews 17-18, 20, 26; in advertising 224; and work 80

Johnson, Grace Neis 188

Johnson & Johnson Baby Powder 45

Jordan, Elizabeth, 128-129

Keeler, Martha 90

Kelley, Faith 182

Kelley, Florence 116

Kellogg's 31, 199

Kerr, Sophie 146, 153, 162

Kodak 31

Knapp, Florence E.S. 129-130

Knox Gelatin 104

Kirchway, Freda 92

Kotex 52, 106

Kraft 45

Ladies Magazine see *Godey's Lady's Book*

Lampe, Dorothy 179

Lane, Gertrude Battles 185

Lawrence, David 128

Leach, William 13

League of Advertising Women 62

League of Women Voters 40, 157181

Lears, Jackson 13, 225

lesbians and identity of *Journal* readers 142; among J. Walter Thompson employees 189

Levenstein, Harvey 76

Lever Brothers, Lux 43, 46

Lewis, Edith 189, 193, 209, 211-213

Lewis, Margaret 43

Liberty Motor Car 134, 136

Libby's 105-106, 108

literacy rates in general population 5, 12; among African Americans 5, 221

Lockwood, Laura 87

Luiggi, Alice 177

Lynd, Robert S. and Helen 53

magazines, golden age of 12; characteristics of middle-class magazines 12, 18

Marchand, Roland 13, 35, 208

Marcossen, Isaac 124

marriage in *Journal* fiction 143; as imperative 20; and work 23; and poverty 25; and female sacrifice 96, 102; companionate 143

Marsh, Margaret 234

Maule, Florence Updegraff 188

Maule, Frances 179, 182-183, 187-189, 192

May, Elaine Tyler 25

McCracken, Ellen 45

McCray Refrigerators 71

McDonnell, Eleanor 179

Melville, Herman 140

men limitations and prejudices of 26, 102; and housework 73, 77, 107, 131; African-American men 26-27, 220; as predators 90; and shopping 118; their handling of politics 112, 127; resisting women's participation in politics 130; women's responsibility for 120, 230-231; Italian men 121; cultural fear of men 232-233; men's attitudes toward women 91, 184, 208; conflicts with women in J. Walter Thompson Company 193

Moyer, Annie Nathan 114

Meyer, Maud 114

Middletown 53

Miller, Ruth Scott 97

Modleski, Tania 139

money distribution in households 95-96, 98-99; and divorce 98

mothers: standards and presentation in advertising 31-33; and suffrage 119-120, 129

Nation 92

National American Woman Suffrage Association 117, 123, 125, 128, 132

National Consumers' League 76, 116, 181

National Home Economics Association 55

National Woman Suffrage Association 187-188

National Woman's Party 119, 124-126, 129, 132, 181, 186-187, 216

nativist sentiment 17-18, 20, 34-35

Nearing, Nellie and Scott 232-233

Neely, Ruth 86

Negro Digest 5

nervous conditions 93-94, 157, 160-161

Nestle 31-32

new housekeeping, see scientific housekeeping

New Woman 88, 124-125, 164, 216

New Yorker 230

Nicoll, Augusta 188

Odorono 45

Old Dutch Cleanser 31

Olzendam, Therese 187

Pankhurst, Sylvia 132

Paramount Pictures 73, 77

Parlin, Charless Coolidge 199

patent medicines 200

Paul, Alice 119, 125, 132

Phillips, M.C. 219

Pictorial Review 193, 195

Pillsbury Health Bran 107

Plain Country Woman 24, 52, 59, 98-103, 122-123, 233

Planned Parenthood 181

politics: political participation of women 40-41, 109-136; politicization of women 20; of the *Journal* 6; partisan politics 125

Index

Pompeiaan 31-32

Pond's 172, 192-193; Extract Creams 202, 213-219

Post Bran Flakes 45; Post Toasties 31

Printer's Ink 5, 13, 62

Procter & Gamble 201

Pruett, Lorine 82

Quaker Oats 31

racism 17-18, 20, 34-35, 97, 100, 119, 121, 165-166; in advertising 220-224; in popular culture 18, 34-35; and domestic service 100; and political campaigns 119, 121; on part of J. Walter Thompson Company 221-224

Radway, Janice 139, 141-142

readers interaction with *Journal* 50; relationship with Bok 123;

reading as act 231-232

Religion: of J.Walter Thompson women employees 180-181; religious intolerance 16-18

Resor, Helen Lansdowne 174-177, 181, 187-188, 190, 201, 204, 214

Resor, Stanley 174-176, 200, 202, 204, 207, 217, 225-226

Rinehart, Mary Roberts 97, 127, 130

romance as problematic subject 29-30

Roosevelt, Theodore 119, 158

Rorer, Sarah Tyson 70

Rosenberg, Rosalind 90

Royal Baking Powder 133-135

Rupp, Leila 189

Russell Sage Foundation 186

Russey, Wilma 46

Saturday Evening Post 14, 122, 179, 199

Schneider, Dorothy and Carl 38

Schor, Juliet 56

Schuler, Loring 45, 51, 124, 131

Schultz, Olive 46

Schwarz, Judith 189

scientific housekeeping 62, 76

scientific management see scientific housekeeping

Sears, Elizabeth 87

Sedgewick, Ellery 14

Seller's Kitchen Cabinets 72-73, 75

sexuality and *Journal* advice 24; mixed messages 29-30; women's sexual behavior outside the *Journal* 30, 90-91; in *Journal* fiction 47; 90, 91, 93, 100, 143-144, 155, 164, 233-234; in advertising 176, 178, 206-208; fear of female sexuality 100

Shaw, Anna Howard 113, 117, 124

Shi, David 53

simple life 51-54, 59, 68, 98, 122

Slater, Ethel Spalding 86

Smith-Rosenberg, Carroll 42, 158, 181

social change: desires of middle class 12, 65-66, 143; through consumption 230

social work background of J. Walter Thompson employees 183-186

Stahl-Meyer 71

Strasser, Susan 31

Strauss, Juliet Virginia see Plain Country Woman

Strom, Sharon Hartmann 173, 183

suffrage, women's 17, 40, 51, 55, 62, 183, 185; boycott of *Journal* 115-116, 126; and J. Walter Thompson women employees 183-188

Suffrage League 181

Sunkist 44

Swan's Down Cake Flour 44

Swank, Cynthia 190

Swanson, Gloria 46

Taylor, Eleanor 179, 185-186

Taylor, Frederick Winslow 63

Telford, Mae McGuire 57

testimonials in advertising 131; Pond's Creams 216-220 Woodbury's Facial Soap, 209-214; credibility 217

Thompson, J. Walter Company 10, 45, 131, 170, 198-227, 230, 234; theory and practice of employing women 172-174, 182; 230; Women's Editorial Department 174-196; relationship to *Journal* 172, 192-193

Thor Washing Machine 71

Thoreau, Henry David 53

Todd, Janet 141

Tomes, Nancy 173
Tompkins, Jane 140
Tribune and Farmer 3
True Story 220
Tucker, Mary 179, 182-183
Tuttle, Margaretta 88

Uncle Tom's Cabin 140

Valentino, Rudolph 46
Vandyck, Irene 86

Vollrath Cookware 71

Waddock, Maud 231
Wagner, Charles 53
Walcott, Theresa 70
Waldo, Ruth 182, 186
Walkowitz, Daniel 184
Ware, Caroline 189
Weibel, Kathryn 138, 144
Welch's 32
white racial identity and construction 34-38, 47, 97-98, 232, 213, 221
Williamson, Judith 232
Wilson, Margaret Woodrow 125-126
Wilson, Woodrow 119
Wing, Janet 179
Winter, Alice Ames 41, 128
Wizard Mops 31, 33
Woloch, Nancy 112, 126
women's clubs 41
Woodbury's Facial Soap 31-32; 175, 202, 204-243; and sex appeal in advertising 206-207; advertising in Latin America 207-208
Woodward, Helen 1, 10, 110, 112, 138, 144
women, as "natural" consumers 13, 171; and money 23, 42; influence on men 120, 233; accomodating to men 226, 227, 231-232; women's rights 6-7
work women's paid 8, 79-108; and marriage 80, 93-108; of unmarried women 83-93; of college women 190; of professional women 173; in advertising 173-174, 181-182; tied to consumption 82; as viewed

by Thompson Company women employees 191-192
working-class women and the *Journal* 23-24; and suffrage 112, 119, 121; and middle-class womanhood 142; and advertising 213, 220
World War I and women's work 123; and women's political participation 120, 123-124, 131
World's Fair 18; 1893 Fair 221
Wright, Mrs. 43

YWCA 89, 181
Young, Rose 127-128
youth culture 24, 29-30, 41-42, 46, 83-85; young women as target of *Journal* 57-58; see also college women
Yuban Coffee 172